The UK Economy

CONTRIBUTORS

H. W. Armstrong
University of Sheffield
M. J. Artis
European University Institute, Florence
R. C. Bladen-Hovell
University of Keele
C. J. Green
University of Loughborough
R. L. Harrington
University of Manchester
Geraint Johnes
University of Lancaster
M. C. Kennedy
Manchester
Malcolm Sawyer
Leeds Business School
Jim Taylor
University of Lancaster

The UK Economy

A MANUAL OF APPLIED ECONOMICS

Edited by

M. J. Artis

OXFORD
UNIVERSITY PRESS

OXFORD
UNIVERSITY PRESS

Great Clarendon Street, Oxford OX2 6DP

Oxford University Press is a department of the University of Oxford.
It furthers the University's objective of excellence in research, scholarship,
and education by publishing worldwide in

Oxford New York

Athens Auckland Bangkok Bogotá Buenos Aires Calcutta
Cape Town Chennai Dar es Salaam Delhi Florence Hong Kong Istanbul
Karachi Kuala Lumpur Madrid Melbourne Mexico City Mumbai
Nairobi Paris São Paulo Singapore Taipei Tokyo Toronto Warsaw

with associated companies in Berlin Ibadan

Oxford is a registered trade mark of Oxford University Press
in the UK and in certain other countries

Published in the United States
by Oxford University Press Inc., New York

© the several contributors 1996

First published 1996

British Library Cataloguing in Publication Data

Data available

Library of Congress Cataloging in Publication Data

The UK economy: a manual of applied economics/edited by
Michael J. Artis.—14th ed.
p. cm.
Includes bibliographical references.
1. Great Britain—Economic conditions—1945-1993. 2. Great
Britain—Economic conditions—1993- . 3. Great Britain—Economic
policy—1945- . 4. Finance—Great Britain. 5. Economic
history—1945- . I. Artis, Michael J.
HC256.6.U38 1996 330.941'0858—dc20 96-18539

ISBN 0-19-877512-1
ISBN 0-19-877511-3 (pbk)

10 9 8 7 6 5 4

Printed in Great Britain
on acid-free paper by
Bookcraft (Bath) Ltd, Midsomer Norton, Somerset

FOREWORD TO THE
FOURTEENTH EDITION

This volume represents the fourteenth edition of Prest and Coppock's *UK Economy*. With it we have instituted a number of changes which, we hope, will make the volume easier to use, whilst preserving the basic objectives of the original editors. Individual chapters are shorter (though there are more of them) than before and their content has been redefined. There is greater use of graphical displays and authors have been encouraged to provide suggestions for further reading so that the interested reader can follow up the themes to which he or she has been introduced.

The book is directed principally at those who have already acquired an initial training in economics—say to the level of a typical first-year undergraduate course—though most of the text should be intelligible to readers who lack this level of expertise. The book aims to combine theory with practice: thus part of the authors' purpose is to show how the principles of economic analysis can be put to use. This is, of course, done in the specific framework established by the need to provide an account of the modern British economy.

To provide such an account it is first necessary to set the British economy in perspective—specifically, in the perspective provided by its position in the world economy and by its recent history of development. Moreover it is more than apparent that no account of British economic affairs today can miss the fact that Britain's membership of the European Union provides the immediate context in which British economic policy is made and supplies many of the key economic issues which have to be addressed. For these reasons the book begins by supplying chapters that deal with these issues.

The subsequent chapters begin with an analysis of the UK macroeconomy, which provides the setting for an account of the policy framework. There follow chapters which provide detailed analyses of the UK's financial structure and monetary policy; of the structure of taxation and government spending together with fiscal policy; of the structure of its industrial sector and industrial policies; of its labour markets and the outcomes for social and regional inequalities; and of its foreign trade and trade policy. The book attempts to be as up-to-date as possible. The organization of the book allows the reader to find, for example, a treatment of the UK's position on European Monetary Union, an account of the new issues in regulation raised by the privatization of public utilities, and a discussion of the Bank of England's new-found freedom to target inflation. There is a great deal of meat in these and other topics discussed in the book. There are a few areas of overlap between the chapters and the assiduous reader will detect some occasional disagreement between the authors: there has been no attempt to impose a monolithic view. The essential core of the book is more a mode of working—of showing how economic principles can illuminate the working of the British economy—than it is a set of agreed conclusions about economic policy. This is as it should be: this is a book which is subtitled 'A Manual of Applied Economics'.

M. A.
Florence, February 1996

CONTENTS

6. MONEY AND FINANCE   155
R. L. HARRINGTON

7. FISCAL POLICY AND THE BUDGET   194
R. C. BLADEN-HOVELL

---

8. INDUSTRY: ITS STRUCTURES AND POLICIES TOWARDS IT

MALCOLM SAWYER

LIST OF FIGURES

LIST OF TABLES

ABBREVIATIONS

Economic terms and organizations

APC	average propensity to consume
APS	average propensity to save
CAP	Common Agricultural Policy
CDs	Certificates of deposit
CEC	Commission of the European Communities
CGT	Capital Gains Tax
CI	Community Initiatives
EAGGF	European Agricultural Guidance and Guarantee Fund
ECB	European Central Bank
ECSC	European Steel and Coal Community
ECU	European Currency Unit
EIB	European Investment Bank
EMS	European Monetary System
EMU	European Monetary Union
ERDF	European Regional Development Fund
ESF	European Social Fund
EU	European Union
FIFG	Financial Instrument for Fisheries Guidance
FSBR	*Financial Statement and Budget Report*
GATT	General Agreement on Tariffs and Trade
GDP	gross domestic product
GNP	gross national product
IMF	International Monetary Fund
LIFFE	London International Financial Futures Exchange
MCA	Monetary Compensation Amounts
MMC	Monopolies and Mergers Commission
MNE	multi-national enterprise
MPC	marginal propensity to consume
MTFS	Medium Term Financial Strategy
NIBB	*(Blue Book) of National Income and Expenditure*

OECD	Organization for Economic Co-operation and Development
OFT	Office of Fair Trading
OPEC	Organization of Petroleum Exporting Countries
PFI	Private Finance Initiative
PPS	Purchasing Power
PSBR	Public Sector Borrowing Requirement
R&D	Research and Development
SDRs	Special Drawing Rights
SEA	Single European Act
TFE	Total Final Expenditure at Market Prices
TSS	Total Standard Spending
VAT	Value Added Tax

Journals

AER	*American Economic Review*
BEQB	*Bank of England Quarterly Bulletin*
CJE	*Cambridge Journal of Economics*
DEG	*Department of Employment Gazette*
EJ	*Economic Journal*
ET	*Economic Trends*
EP	*Economic Policy*
ETAS	*Economic Trends Annual Supplement*
FSt	*Fiscal Studies*
LBR	*Lloyds Bank Review*
NIER	*National Institute Economic Review*
NWBQR	*National Westminster Bank Quarterly Review*
OEP	*Oxford Economic Papers*
OREP	*Oxford Review of Economic Policy*

THE UK ECONOMY IN CONTEXT

R. L. HARRINGTON

1.1. Introduction

To begin to understand the UK economy one has to see it in context. There is the historical context: all economic activity takes place in historical time and how an economy has developed in the past will influence its structure and its productive capacity today. Then there is the international context: the UK is dependent on other countries; it trades extensively with them, its companies invest in other countries, and foreign companies invest in it. The UK is a part of the European Union and a member of many international bodies such as the World Trade Organization and the International Monetary Fund. And, of course, there is a constant movement of people, money, and ideas across frontiers.

In what follows, we look first at the main features of the present-day UK economy and at how these have evolved over time. We then look at some of the main groups of countries and geographical regions that compose the world economy and consider their recent evolution. Finally we discuss briefly some of the more important of the international economic organizations.

1.2. The UK Economy: An Overview

Population

The population of the United Kingdom in 1993 was estimated to be 58.2 million. Of this total, 48.5 million were resident in England, 5.1 million in Scotland, 2.9 million in Wales, and 1.8 million in Northern Ireland. The total population has been growing slowly over time: since 1960 growth has averaged about 0.3% per annum with the result that the population has grown by approximately 10% over the period.

This slow increase in population has been the result of two trends which have been evident throughout the twentieth century. First, the birth rate has shown a tendency to fall. There have been considerable short-run fluctuations in the number of live births and there were sharp rises in the 1940s and the 1960s, but the long-run trend has clearly been downward. But counterbalancing this has been the fact that people have been living longer and so the death rate has been falling. Net immigration has, in recent years, had only a small impact on the growth of population.

The combination of a declining birth rate and increasing longevity has meant a slow but steady ageing of the population. In 1961 under 12% of the population was aged 65 or over, by 1993 this figure had risen to nearly 16% and it is predicted to continue to rise. In 1961 less than 2% of the population was aged 80 or over, by 1993 nearly 4% were, and this figure is also expected to rise. These trends, which are common to all developed countries, have clear implications for the cost of providing pensions and health care.

The population of the UK constitutes roughly 1% of the population of the world, which, in 1994, was estimated by the United Nations to be over 5.5 billion. Table 1.4, below, gives a breakdown of world population by region.

Income

The best single indicator of the standard of living of the citizens of a country is national income per capita. This concept is discussed in more detail in Chapter 4. National income can be measured in a number of ways, but we shall confine ourselves in this chapter to looking at one: gross domestic product. This measures the gross value (i.e. before providing for the depreciation of buildings, machinery etc.) of all that is produced in a country; and since all that is produced must be owned by someone, this figure will, apart from a relatively small amount of property income paid fo or received from foreign countries, be equal to (gross) national income. When this figure is divided by the population of the country, we derive income per capita.

But the limitations of the measure need to be stressed. National income cannot be measured with precision and it should only be viewed as giving a general indication of a national standard of living. For the most part, it measures only the value of output that is sold and takes no account of the production that is consumed by those who produce it. All household 'production', do-it-yourself activities, gardening etc., are ignored. As these activities are often of greater importance in developing countries, crude comparisons of national income between developed and developing countries frequently overstate the difference in standard of living. Furthermore, measures of national income do not satisfactorily account for the quality of life as far as things such as pollution, traffic congestion, and crime are concerned.

This having been said, gross domestic product (GDP) per capita remains a useful general indicator of a country's standard of living. If we were to find that in any given year French GDP per capita was 5% greater than that of Britain, it would be safest just to conclude that the two countries had a similar standard of living and that no more precise judgement could be made. If, on the other hand, we found that French GDP per capita was 50% greater than that of Britain, it would be safe to conclude that there was a real difference in the standard of living.

The provisional estimate of GDP for the United Kingdom in 1994 was £669 billion.[1] As we have seen the population was 58.2 million, so it can be calculated that income per capita was just under £11,500. This, of course, does not mean that everyone did receive or should have received an income such as this; in practice the distribution of income is unequal. What it does mean is that the total gross value of all that was produced in the UK during 1994 was equivalent to an income of almost £11,500 for every person in the country.

This figure gives some general idea of the British standard of living to anyone who is aware of the current purchasing power of the pound, but it only provides a single piece of information relevant to one year. It would be more interesting if put into the context of (*a*) how British national income has grown over time and (*b*) how British national income compares with that of other countries.

To make comparisons over time, we have to allow for inflation. We are interested in the growth of real income, not just a growth in money income caused by a rise in prices. Over the period from 1948 to 1994, national income, measured by GDP, grew at an average rate of 2.4% per annum. Allowing for population growth, this means that average income per capita rose by approximately 2% per annum, a rate of growth sufficient to raise average incomes over the period to 2½ times their original level and to transform living standards. It was during this period that the British became a nation of home-owners; they furnished their homes with TV sets, washing machines, hi-fi equipment and, more recently, with personal computers; car ownership grew greatly; and foreign holidays became common. Material life changed at a rate as fast as at any time in British history.

Yet for the most part there has been little sense of achievement or pride in this economic transformation. Instead journalists, politicians and economic commentators have focused on the fact that most other developed countries have achieved faster increases in income than the UK. In consequence the UK standard of living while rising over time has become lower relative to that of other western nations. Fig. 1.1 illustrates this: it shows the expansion of GDP over the period 1960–1994 for the USA, for Western Europe as a whole, and for the UK. It is clear that the rate of growth of income in Britain has lagged behind that of both its European neighbours and the USA.

Growth of income and output has not been consistent, neither in the UK nor elsewhere. Not only have all countries faced continual economic cycles but there have also been some changes of trend. Prior to the mid-1970s, the developed

[1] Gross Domestic Product at market prices: source *NIBB* 1995.

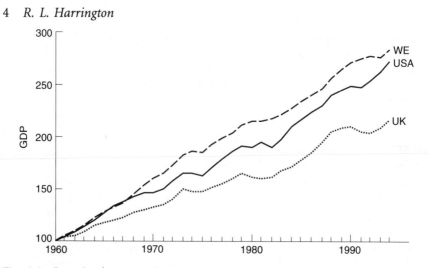

Fig. 1.1. Growth of output 1960–1994 (1960 = 100)

Note: Western Europe comprises the 15 current member states of the EU plus Scotland, Norway, Switzerland, and Turkey.
Source: Data from OECD National Accounts 1960–94, Volume 1, 1996.

countries experienced the long post-war boom: a period characterized by rapid growth of output, near full employment, and, for the most part, low inflation. This came to an end after 1973, when the developed world entered a period marked by OPEC oil-price rises, high and volatile inflation, rising unemployment, and much slower growth of output. After the early 1980s conditions improved somewhat and economic growth was generally higher, although it did not get back to what had been achieved in the earlier post-war years.

Table 1.1 shows the average rates of growth of income achieved by a number of developed countries and by western Europe as a whole during three periods. The first period, 1960–1973, shows the high growth rates of the post-war decades, a period now looked upon as the golden age. Japan was still enjoying

Table 1.1. National income: average growth rates

	1960–73	1974–83	1984–94
USA	4.0	1.8	2.9
Japan	9.6	3.5	3.4
Germany	4.3	1.6	2.8
France	5.4	2.2	2.0
Italy	5.2	3.2	2.1
United Kingdom	3.2	1.1	2.4
All Western Europe	4.8	1.9	2.4

Notes: Growth rates for Germany apply to the former West Germany up to 1991 and to all Germany thereafter.
All Western Europe covers the 15 member states of the European Union plus Iceland, Norway, Switzerland, and Turkey.
Source: OECD, *Historical Statistics 1960–1990* and OECD, *Economic Outlook*, June 1995.

its economic miracle, with output growing by nearly 10% per annum, while both America and Europe were experiencing what, by all historical standards, were high rates of growth. The British growth rate was relatively low.

In the second period shown, 1974–1983, rates of growth of output were everywhere much lower and were, in most cases, less than half of what they had been earlier. Finally in the 11 years to 1994, there was a partial recovery in growth in most countries, although not in all. One notable feature of this last period is that the trend rate of growth of output in the UK appeared to be more in line with that of its neighbours.

The Structure of the Economy

The structure of the British economy has been changing steadily over time. Some of the broad changes can be seen from Table 1.2 which shows the percentage share of national income accounted for by different sectors of the economy at ten yearly intervals over the period 1954–1994. Agriculture, which already accounted for less than 5% of the value of national output in 1954, has continued its relative decline; whilst agricultural output has not fallen in absolute terms, it has grown at a slower rate than the rest of the economy and hence its share has fallen: it now accounts for only 2% of national production. This reflects an on-going trend and is not usually seen as a cause for concern; but a change which was new and which has been the subject of much discussion is the decline in the share of manufacturing industry. This subject is covered in greater detail in Chapter 2. Here, we confine ourselves to

Table 1.2. The structure of the British economy 1954–1994 (Percentage shares in GDP).

	1954	1964	1974	1984	1994
Agriculture, forestry, and fishing	4.9	3.4	2.8	2.4	2.0
Manufacturing industry	35.4	33.8	30.1	24.5	20.9
Energy and water supply	5.9	5.7	4.5	10.3	5.1
Transport and communications	7.9	8.4	7.7	7.9	8.5
Construction	5.7	6.9	7.1	6.2	5.4
Wholesale and retail trade, hotels and restaurants	12.7	11.4	13.3	13.1	14.4
Financial and business services including real estate	2.9	6.5	11.1	13.2	19.2
Public administration and defence	6.2	5.8	6.9	7.2	6.7
Education, health, and social work	3.3	4.4	8.9	10.3	11.9
Other	15.1	13.7	7.6	4.9	5.9

Notes: There are many firms whose activities are difficult to classify. Furthermore, classifications may change over time, e.g. a computer service bureau which is part of an engineering company would be classified under manufacturing industry; if it were the subject of a management buy-out and became a separate company, it would be classified under business services. For these and other reasons, the above figures should be viewed as orders of magnitude rather than as precise indicators of easily demarcated economic activities.
Source: NIBB, various issues.

some summary observations. 'Manufacturing' is a broad category of output covering the production of foodstuffs, textiles, wood and metal products, paper, plastics, rubber, electricals, vehicles, machinery and equipment, and a host of other produced goods. It was the mechanized production of such goods which created industrial societies and enabled the great rises in living standards that occurred in the nineteenth and twentieth centuries. It is perhaps unsurprising that 'de-industrialization' should be seen by many as a sign of economic weakness.

But it is important to be clear about the facts. First, the value of manufacturing output in Britain continues to rise, albeit slowly; it is the share of manufacturing in total output which is declining, not the absolute amount. Secondly, this phenomenon is common to virtually all developed countries. It is evident in the USA, in Western Europe, and in Japan. Thirdly, the present, roughly 20% share of manufacturing in the UK economy is not dissimilar to what exists in most other developed countries.

If this trend is general, how should one account for it? The dominant reason would seem to be that people have a high income-elasticity of demand for services; consequently, as they get richer the pattern of demand shifts in favour of financial services, education, health care, and leisure activities. In Table 1.2 one may note the steady rise in the share of national output accounted for by financial and other business services and by the category of education, health, and social work. The figure for the first sector is very large and reflects the position of London as an important centre for financial, legal, and other professional services, as well as perhaps a certain over-provision in the area of retail financial services. But the general tendency for a rise in the importance of financial services and business services and of education and health is common to all developed economies.

One reason often cited for the relatively slow growth of manufacturing output is competition from the newly industrialized countries of South-East Asia. There is probably some truth in this, but its importance should not be exaggerated. Output in countries such as Singapore, Hong Kong, Taiwan, Korea, Malaysia, and Thailand has risen greatly but so also has their domestic demand for goods and services. These countries do export manufactured goods but they also import manufactured goods. And as yet the share of their produce in the imports of developed countries remains low. Most of the trade of developed countries is conducted with other developed countries. In 1994 less than 20% of imports of goods into Britain came from developing countries, including the rapidly developing ones of South-East Asia.

Before we leave this topic it is worth noting that the manufacturing sector is not the only industrial sector of the economy. The category 'energy and water supply' covers the important industries supplying oil, gas, coal, and water. Over the years the importance of oil and gas has grown and the importance of coal has shrunk.

It is clear that the British economy is, in common with other developed economies, now largely a service economy. These changes in output have been reflected in changes in both the volume and the pattern of employment.

Employment

Table 1.3 shows the growth of the workforce in the UK during the twentieth century. The figures cover all those who were working or were actively seeking work. Given the size and heterogeneity of the workforce the compilation of accurate statistics is difficult and, in addition, there have been changes over time in how the statistics are presented; the numbers should therefore be treated as approximations rather than precise figures. None the less the trend is clear: the total workforce has risen from below 18 million at the turn of the century to around 28 million by the mid-1990s. The latter figure can be broken down into employees (nearly 22 million), the self-employed (somewhat over 3 million), and the unemployed (around 2.5 million).

In the first half of the twentieth century, the growth in the working population largely reflected the growth in the total population; in the second half, it has caused principally by the increase in the number of women working or seeking work. This has more than offset a decline in male activity rates, i.e. the percentage of the male population that is economically active.

Until the 1960s, virtually all males between the ages of 16 and 65 were economically active, either working or seeking work. But by the mid-1990s, only about 85% were in the labour force, with many staying on longer in education and many taking early retirement. In 1993 only one in every two men over the age of 60 was still in work. Meanwhile more and more women have joined the labour force. In 1950 about one in five married women worked and less than half of all women did. By 1993 well over half of married women

Table 1.3. Total workforce in the UK (millions)

1900	17.74
1910	20.08
1920	20.76
1930	20.30
1940	21.91
1950	23.55
1960	24.51
1970	25.31
1980	26.84
1990	28.75
1994	28.00

Notes: The figures for the years 1900–39 exclude those employed in the armed services. All figures cover the employed, the self-employed, and those seeking employment.
Source:
1900–39: *The British Economy: Key Statistics 1900–1966,* Times Newspapers Ltd.
1950–90: *ET* annual supplement 1994
1994: *DEG,* Sept. 1995.

were working and about two-thirds of all women between the ages of 16 and 65 were.

These trends are discussed in greater detail in Chapter 2. We should note, however, that these trends are common to all developed economies. For the European Union as a whole, the activity rate for men aged from 15–64 fell from over 95% in 1960 to approximately 80% in 1990. For women the corresponding figure rose from around 40% to somewhat over 50%.

While the trends are common to all developed countries there remain significant differences among European countries concerning retirement dates and also concerning female participation in the labour force. Fig. 1.2 shows the activity rates for men and women for selected European countries in 1992. It can be seen that the activity rates in Britain are high relative to those in other countries.

Not only has the size and composition of the workforce changed, so has the pattern of activity. In 1950, in Britain, around $1\frac{1}{4}$ million people still worked in agriculture and over 8 million people worked in manufacturing industry. By the mid-1990s these figures had shrunk to less than $\frac{1}{4}$ million and around $4\frac{1}{4}$ million respectively. The structure of employment is discussed further in Chapter 2; however we should note that again the trends observed in the UK have been common to all developed countries. The decline in numbers working in agriculture and in industry and the sharp rise in the numbers working in services is a general phenomenon. Fig. 1.3 shows changes in the composition of the labour-force over the years 1960–1990 for the developed OECD-member countries as a group.

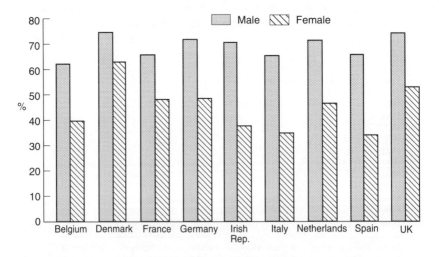

Fig. 1.2. Economic activity rates: selected European countries 1992

Note: Economic activity rates are measured as the civilian labour force aged 16 and over as a percentage of the population aged 16 and over.
Source: Eurostat.

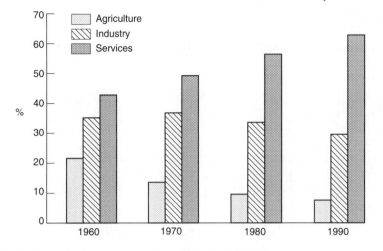

Fig. 1.3. The changing pattern of employment 1960–1990

Note: The figure shows proportions employed in the three sectors in all the OECD member countries.
Source: OECD: Historical Statistics 1960–1990

Trade

Britain, like most other European nations, has always been a trading nation. In the years prior to the First World War, exports and imports each amounted to some 25–33% of national income. That war interrupted established trading patterns and the years that followed were marked by political and economic instability and then by the growth of tariffs and other barriers to trade. There was no growth in the real value of British exports between 1920 and 1938 and the share of exports in national income fell to around 16%. But after the Second World War, successive agreements negotiated under the auspices of the GATT dramatically reduced tariffs. World trade rose rapidly, and with it, British exports and imports. By the mid-1970s exports once again accounted for around one-quarter of national income and they have since remained broadly at this level. In 1994 exports of goods and services amounted to 26% of GDP and imports of goods and services 27%. It is clear that trade is very important for the British economy, but the UK is, in this respect, not out of line with other developed countries. In the USA, foreign trade accounts for somewhat less than 10% of GDP but the USA is a far larger economy, and, other things being equal, the larger the economy the greater proportionally will be internal trade and the less will be external trade. Within Europe, Germany is more dependent on trade than is the UK and France, and Italy not much less so. Among smaller European countries the share of foreign trade in national income is often well over 40%. Fig. 1.4 shows the average share of exports in GDP over the years 1980–1990 for the fifteen existing member countries of the

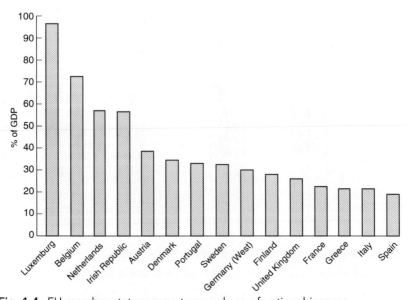

Fig. 1.4. EU member states: exports as a share of national income

Note: The figure shows averages over the years 1980–1990 for each country.
Source: OECD: Historical Statistics

EU. It is apparent that foreign trade is important for all of these countries. Much of this trade is, of course, intra-European trade; see Chapter 11 for further details.

The composition of British trade both in terms of the type of goods and services involved and in terms of the main trading partners has changed greatly during the last century. In the early years of the twentieth century the pattern of trade that had been created during the Industrial Revolution was still apparent: Britain imported mainly foodstuffs and raw materials and exported manufactured goods, of which textiles were the most important single component. The most important providers of imports were, first, Western Europe, and then the USA and the British Empire; exports went in roughly equal proportions to Western Europe, the British Empire, and the rest of the world.

By the early 1990s there was no longer any difference in the broad categories of commodities which were imported and exported. Manufactured goods accounted for the bulk of all commodity trade in both directions and foodstuffs and raw materials (including oil) accounted for approximately one-sixth of all imports and nearly one-sixth of exports. Services account for around 20% of total trade, slightly more for exports, slightly less for imports. There is nothing new in this: in 1938 services accounted for over one-quarter of all exports of goods and services. Britain tends to have a deficit on tourism and to earn a surplus on financial and other business services. A detailed account of recent developments in the UK's foreign trade is given in Chapter 11.

1.3. The World Economy: An Overview

Introduction

The World Economy has changed greatly during the last half-century. Nor has change been confined to the developed nations; there have been profound changes in the economies and societies of countries at all stages of development. Life expectancy in the developing countries has increased dramatically and average incomes have doubled. But progress has been uneven: some parts of the world are developing rapidly while others remain trapped in poverty. The World Bank estimates that in 1995 around one billion people—nearly one-fifth of the population of the world—still live in poverty.

But beyond broad generalizations, it is not easy to comprehend something as complex and diverse as the world economy. In 1994 there were more than 180 independent countries in the world as well as a number of states or territories such as Hong Kong or Puerto Rico which had a distinct economy without having political independence. Thus one can see the world economy as being composed of more than 200 distinct economies each of which has its own history and its own characteristics. There are differences of size, language, and culture and wide disparities in wealth. The richest countries have annual per capita incomes of over $30,000 while the poorest have per capita incomes of less than $300.

Populations vary even more widely. China has an estimated population of more than 1200 million while there are over 30 independent states in the world with a population of less than one million. Total world population in 1994 was estimated to be around 5.5 billion and a breakdown of this total by region is given in Table 1.4. The annual increase in world population is currently around 90–100 million a year, a rate of increase which, if sustained, will lead to a total

Table 1.4. World population by region (millions)

Europe	510
European Union	369
Eastern Europe	129
Other	12
USSR (former)	285
USA and Canada	283
Latin America	458
Africa	682
Asia	3,233
China	1,205
India	897
Japan	125
Oceania	28

Notes: Eastern Europe comprises the former communist states of E. Europe including Latvia, Lithuania, Estonia, and the former Yugoslavia. Other Europe comprises Iceland, Norway, and Switzerland.
Source: Social Trends 1995 and *World Bank Atlas* 1995.

population of 8.5 billion by the year 2023. Current annual growth rates of population are highest in Africa (2.9%), followed by Asia and Latin America (1.1%). The growth rate of population in Europe is low, at 0.3% per annum.

To begin to understand world economic development it is necessary to divide the world economy into a number of separate parts according to type of country, e.g. developed nations and underdeveloped nations, or on the basis of geography, or by some mixture of the two. As with all classifications, there is no one correct way; how one groups countries depends upon what seems relevant for the subject under discussion.

The most basic distinction is between developed and developing nations and this is one frequently used by journalists. It reflects the important historical reality that a small group of countries, either European or settled by Europeans, developed new technologies and achieved high levels of output and income long before most of the rest of the world had commenced its modern economic development. This group of countries was joined in the early twentieth century by Japan and for a time at least they did stand apart from other countries. But beyond these simple facts, simply dividing the world into two parts was always crude and largely unhelpful and it has become less helpful as time has passed.

Between the developed nations themselves there are big differences. Countries such as the USA, Switzerland, and the Scandinavian countries have for a long time enjoyed high standards of living the benefits of which were spread widely. Other countries such as Greece, Portugal, or the Republic of Ireland have had a more uneven development, with the affluence of modern sectors of the economy contrasting with the poverty of those in traditional and largely underdeveloped sectors of the economy.

Among the so-called developing countries there have always been vast differences both between nations and between different sectors or areas within individual nations. Countries such as Argentina and Mexico did experience some early economic development and have always been best classified as middle-income countries. Others such as Hong Kong and Singapore have experienced rapid and sustained economic development in recent years and now enjoy levels of per capita income greater than those of many European nations. At the other end of the scale there remain many countries where there has been little change in the material conditions of life and where the inhabitants earn little and enjoy few of the benefits of modern life.

There are other groups of nations which do not fit easily into any simple classification of countries into the haves and the have-nots. Oil-exporting countries are often distinguished from others because it is assumed they were able to become much wealthier as a result of the high oil prices of the 1970s and 1980s. Where the supply of oil was large and the population was small this was true and some oil-exporting have become rich nations, but for others the income from oil has had only a modest effect on living standards.

Russia and the Eastern European countries provide another example of countries which fail to conform to any simple classification. They have for many years experienced a partial and lopsided economic development under regimes which stressed traditional industries but which provided few incentives for innovation. All are now attempting with varying degrees of success to move toward a mixed economy on the western model.

In what follows we provide a sketch of some of the main features of the world economy. It is inevitably no more than a sketch and, whilst we distinguish several groups of nations, one must never lose sight of the huge diversity of economic conditions between and within nations. In the wealthiest of nations there are usually persistent areas of poverty and in the poorest of nations there are always pockets of affluence.

The Developed Nations

We consider here those nations traditionally seen as developed countries. They comprise eighteen nations of Western Europe,[2] the US and Canada, Japan, Australia, and New Zealand. They are no longer the only wealthy nations and a number of other countries now enjoy similar levels of income, but they have traditionally been seen as a group of countries with certain common economic features and interests.

According to World Bank statistics, in 1992 these 23 countries produced nearly three-quarters of total measured world output; the USA alone accounted for nearly one-quarter of world output and Japan for a further 14%. The United Kingdom produced just over 4% of world output. It should be stressed that all this refers mainly to marketed output and for the reasons given above these percentages overstate what would be the developed nations' share of total global production, were one able to measure such a thing.

It was in these countries that modern economic development began. In Europe there had been a development of new ideas and new technologies over several centuries and in the eighteenth century this was to lead first to dramatic improvements in agricultural output and then to the start of the industrial era. These ideas were quickly taken up in North America, in Australasia, and subsequently in Japan. By the start of the twentieth century much of northern Europe and of North America was already urbanized and economically developed. But two world wars in the space of thirty years were to cost Europe dearly in both human and material terms, and in 1945 much of European industry lay in ruin.

The settlement of the Second World War left Europe divided between a Soviet- (Russian-) controlled East under oppressive and ultimately inefficient regimes and a democratic West which, with the assistance of Marshall Aid from America, began the process of reconstruction. This was to be rapid, and most of Western Europe had regained its pre-war living standards within a decade. West Germany

[2] Austria, Belgium, Denmark, Finland, France, Germany, Greece, Iceland, Irish Republic, Italy, Luxembourg, Netherlands, Norway, Portugal, Spain, Sweden, Switzerland, United Kingdom.

experienced its 'economic miracle' with an average annual growth rate during the 1950s of over 7%. Many other states had growth rates of some 4.5% to 6%.

In the 1960s growth slowed somewhat in West Germany but remained very high for Western Europe as a whole as can be seen from Table 1.1 above. Meanwhile Japan continued its dramatic post-war transformation into a great industrial power with annual growth rates of 9%–10%.[3] In the post-war years the USA saw only modest growth rates of around 2%, but, following the adoption of expansionist Keynesian policies in the 1960s, managed to raise its rate of economic growth significantly, although this still remained below European levels. In 1950 America had accounted for around 70% of the output of all the developed nations, but as the economies of Western Europe and Japan grew rapidly this share fell and it is now, in the mid 1990s, around 40%.[4]

The era of rapid growth throughout virtually all of the traditional developed nations came to an end in the mid-1970s. For much of the period inflation had been a serious problem only in a minority of the developed countries; but inflation rates everywhere began to rise in the late 1960s and the problem was exacerbated in the early 1970s by a world-wide boom which caused the prices of raw materials to rise sharply. In 1973 the Organization of Petroleum Exporting Countries (OPEC), which then included twelve of the leading oil-producing nations, took the opportunity to act as a cartel and to raise the price of crude oil by some 200%. This had the seemingly paradoxical result of giving an added twist to price inflation while at the same time having a deflationary impact on demand. The developed countries, like many developing nations, had to devote a larger share of their resources to pay for a given volume of imports, while many of the oil exporters were unable to increase quickly their demand for the exports of the developed countries.

The need to deal with large balance-of-payments problems and with high rates of inflation led the authorities in virtually all the developed countries to take deflationary measures. Unemployment, which had previously been low in most countries, began to rise rapidly. The long post-war boom was at an end and so, for a time at least, was the era of full employment.

Inflation rose to over 10% per annum in most developed countries and even exceeded 20% in a few, of which Britain was one (see Fig. 1.5). Efforts were made to curb this and there was a shift away from broadly Keynesian policies to more monetarist inspired ones. Targets for the growth of the money supply were introduced in many countries. Inflation declined somewhat but remained high. One consequence was that the real cost of oil fell continually as its price was fixed in terms of the dollar. OPEC responded by new price rises in 1979 and 1980, which further doubled the dollar price of oil.

---

[3] It is worth recalling that an annual growth rate of 5% will double material living standards in just over 14 years; an annual growth rate of 10% will achieve this result in little more than 7.

[4] A comprehensive account of the growth of the world economy after World War II can be found in H. Van der Wee, *Prosperity and Upheaval: The World Economy 1945–1980* (Harmondsworth: Penguin Books 1987).

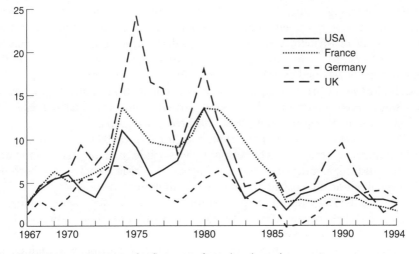

Fig. 1.5. The experience of inflation in four developed countries
Consumer prices in the USA, France, Germany, and the UK 1967–1994

Note: West Germany until 1991; all Germany thereafter.
Source: Graphs derived from data from OECD: Historical Statistics

If the response of the developed nations to the earlier price rise had been a somewhat hesitant deflation, this time it was to be more wholehearted. Tolerance of inflation had declined; the view that inflation had serious disadvantages and few benefits had gained ground as had the view that unchecked inflation would create self-fulfilling expectations of price rises which could only worsen the problem. Monetary policy was tightened and interest rates everywhere rose sharply. This produced the most severe recession since the end of the Second World War, and in 1982 output in the developed world as a whole showed an absolute fall for the only time since 1945. It also produced a disastrous situation for many developing nations, which saw the price of their oil imports rising while both the price and volume of their exports declined as demand in the developed countries fell. In addition the interest burden on their outstanding debts rose as most of these debts had variable interest rates linked to dollar interest rates in New York or in London. This resulted in what became known as the international debt crisis, as one country after another announced its inability to meet its obligations and sought to reschedule its debts.

This time the anti-inflationary policies in the developed countries were more effective and by 1986 average rates of inflation fell below 3% for the first time in two decades. But if the tolerance for inflation had fallen that for unemployment had risen. In most countries it remained throughout the 1980s more than twice the level that it had been two decades earlier.

The policies of restricting the growth of demand along with the gradual development of less fuel-intensive means of production and of transport curbed the rising demand for oil. At the same time, high oil prices had stimulated the development of new sources of oil, such as the North Sea and the Gulf of Mexico, and had encouraged the development of alternative sources of energy, such as nuclear power. The demand for the oil of OPEC-member states declined and the power of OPEC to act as a cartel waned. In the mid-1980s the oil price collapsed and it has remained at relatively low levels ever since, levels which in real terms are not far from those that prevailed in the early 1970s before the first OPEC-inspired price increase.

The developed economies grew rapidly in the late 1980s but inflation once again became a problem. The response was again one of tight monetary policies and high interest rates, and again this was effective in curbing inflation albeit at the cost of another rise in unemployment.

By the mid-1990s, the developed nations as a group were again achieving growth of 2–3% per annum with low inflation, but there were notable differences between areas. In North America unemployment was down to below 6% of the labour force whereas in Western Europe it remained at nearly twice this level. In Japan, where unemployment has traditionally been low, it had risen to over 3% of the labour force as the economy stagnated due to a high exchange rate of the yen and a financial system burdened by bad debts as a result of rash lending on property in the late 1980s.

With the collapse of communism in Russia and in Eastern Europe, the military threat to the developed nations had been removed and the ideological argument was largely at an end. There was broad agreement among policy-makers and economists alike that some form of mixed economy involving reliance on market mechanisms, but with an important admixture of govern-ment involvement, was the only realistic economic system in current circumstances.

But notwithstanding this and the return to growth with low inflation in both Europe and North America, there appeared little general satisfaction with economic performance. The continuance of high levels of unemployment was disturbing; governments found it difficult to keep up with the growing demands for more health care, better education and wider social-security provision; and serious social problems such as crime and poverty seemed to be without solution.

There were demands by many countries for more aid and for better access to the markets of the developed economies, but at the same time there were many encouraging signs. A number of countries in South-East Asia were growing rapidly and achieving high standards of living, and this growth was spreading with the prospect that virtually the entire region including China itself would be economically transformed within a generation. In Eastern Europe some of the former communist states were starting to see some benefits after several years of attempts to restructure their economies.

Eastern Europe and Russia

The collapse of communism and the opening up of hitherto closed economies enabled everyone to see how inefficient the former communist regimes had been. By dint of devoting large resources to areas of high priority, the former Soviet Union had created an impressive space programme and, together with its Eastern European satellites, had established a vast and powerful military regime. But neither the Soviet Union nor its allies could provide consumer goods in the quantity or of the quality common in the West. They were slow to learn new technologies and largely incapable of putting them into everyday practice throughout the economy. The environment was neglected with a wasteful use of energy and few effective controls on industrial pollution; the cities were shabby with many old buildings in disrepair and many new ones cramped and squalid.

The task after 1990 was to create modern economies with less spending on armaments and with privatized companies operating in markets instead of state-owned industries complying to a greater or lesser extent with the dictates of planners. In Poland, Hungary, the Czech Republic, and Slovenia there was rapid progress with large numbers of companies being privatized. In other countries progress was slower, but with the opening of the economies to Western competition there was pressure to invest and to modernize. At the same time, efforts were made to upgrade road and rail infrastructure and to promote tourism (as a means of earning foreign exchange) and to encourage foreign investment.

The costs of restructuring came through before the benefits and at first output and incomes fell alongside a sudden growth of unemployment. But aided by an inflow of foreign capital (official and unofficial), and also by better export prospects as the economies of Western Europe emerged from recession, a number of countries began to see some rewards for their efforts. In Poland national income grew by nearly 4% in 1993 and by over 4% in 1994. In Hungary and the Czech Republic economic growth began again in 1994 and was predicted to continue.

In Albania, Bulgaria, and Romania reforms started later, but in these countries also there are increasing signs of change and of economic growth. Meanwhile the large Russian economy has continued to contract while the politicians argue about what reforms are necessary. During the three years 1993–95 output fell by around 30% while prices rose tenfold. In the Ukraine and Belarus there have also been falls in output although on a smaller scale. Some Western experts do predict improvements and even growing output, but it seems clear that the transformations of these economies will be difficult and drawn-out.

Latin America

Latin America has always been a diverse region. Its countries vary greatly in size, in population, and in wealth. In the Argentine average incomes are around $8,000 per annum; in Bolivia they are around $800 per annum. In the Argentine and in parts of Brazil economic development began in the nineteenth century and there were expectations that South America would develop successfully as had North America. But it was not to be: most of the countries in the region have suffered from political instability and poor economic management with frequent periods of hyper-inflation. As a result, saving and investment have been low and the growth of output has often barely kept up with the growth in population. The Latin American countries have tended to rely too much on foreign capital and this has resulted in inflows of funds in good times but also rapid outflows of funds and financial crises whenever the confidence of foreign investors has faltered.

During the 1970s there was a rapid development of international banking and funds were readily available. A number of OPEC members were running large current-account surpluses on their balance of payments, something which meant that their domestic savings exceeded their domestic investment. Since the world as a whole cannot save more than it invests, it was a corollary of the OPEC surpluses that other nations would be in deficit. But there remained the 'recycling problem': by what mechanism could the net saving of OPEC members be channelled to those countries with deficient saving?

There was much discussion about this but, in the event, most of the recycling took place through the intermediation of the banks. The OPEC countries deposited much of their surpluses with large international banks who loaned it to deficit countries. They did not lend to the poorest (which were not considered creditworthy) but they did lend to developed countries (including the UK) and to those middle-income countries which were deemed creditworthy. This latter group included most of the Latin American countries. Many billions of dollars were loaned, especially to the larger countries, i.e. Argentina, Brazil, Mexico, Venezuela, Chile, and Peru. With this easy access to funds and with real rates of interest that were low or even negative, most of the countries in the region experienced a decade of rapid growth.

But the banks and the debtor countries themselves, as well as the international agencies and just about everyone else, were slow to realize that the levels of borrowing were not sustainable. It has already been mentioned how the developed nations reacted to the second oil price rise with policies of deflation and tight money. Rates of interest rose to high levels and substantially increased the debt-service costs of the Latin American countries. At the same time oil import bills rose and demand for exports fell, as did the prices of many raw materials.

Almost all Latin American countries were unable to meet their debt obligations and had to begin negotiations with banks about the restructuring of their debts. The debt crisis was not confined to the region: other countries which had borrowed heavily during the 1970s (e.g. Algeria, Nigeria, and the Philippines) also saw themselves obliged to reschedule debt, but the biggest debtors by far were in Latin America.

The consequences were severe. While the debts could be rescheduled, little new lending was forthcoming and the indebted countries had to turn to the

International Monetary Fund for loans which were only granted on the condition of macroeconomic reforms; in particular higher taxes and lower government expenditure. The immediate effect was that national income stagnated and unemployment rose. Over the eight years 1985–93, income per capita actually fell in Brazil and in Peru and rose by less than 1.5% annually in most other South American countries. Only in Columbia (2.3%), Uruguay (3.0%), and Chile (6.1%) did living standards show any appreciable growth. There were further outbreaks of hyper-inflation. In the eight years to 1993, only Chile had an average rate of inflation below 20% per annum; in Brazil it was over 800%. Figures for these countries and others are given in Table 1.5.

Chile stands out as the one country with lower inflation and with a rapidly rising national income. This is usually ascribed to the liberalization of the economy during the 1980s. Tariff and non-tariff barriers were reduced, a programme of privatization was introduced, and, importantly, there was a reform of the national pension arrangements which succeeded in substantially raising domestic saving. A number of other Latin American countries have subsequently begun to adopt similar policies and in the last few years inflation rates have dropped and output has started to rise more rapidly.

South-East Asia

South-East Asia has become the most dynamic region of the world economy. For more than three decades, both Hong Kong and Singapore have achieved regular increases in per capita income of from 5%–10% per annum and, by 1995, both states could boast a per capita GDP higher than that of the UK. In the 1970s other countries followed: first South Korea and Taiwan, and then Malaysia and Thailand began to achieve dramatic increases in output and living standards. In Hong Kong and Singapore, both small states, the growth of production had been mostly in light industry and in services; in South Korea and Taiwan it involved a broadly based industrialization including ship-building, steel, cars, and electronic goods. Malaysia and Thailand are now

Table 1.5. Inflation in Latin America: average annual inflation rates 1985–93, selected countries (%)

Argentina	398
Brazil	823
Chile	19
Colombia	26
Ecuador	49
Mexico	45
Peru	616
Venezuela	35

Note: inflation rates reflect price changes for all goods and services included in GDP.
Source: *World Bank Atlas 1995.*

also developing industries on a broad front including a growing motor industry in Malaysia.

These countries became known as the newly industrialized countries (NICs) or more colourfully as the 'Asian tigers'. Initially their growth was in sharp contrast to the economic stagnation and traditional poverty of many of the neighbouring countries in the region. But in the late 1980s and early 1990s most of these other nations also began to achieve rapid increases in output and in living standards. Most importantly, China, after a programme of economic liberalization and aided by a heavy inflow of foreign investment, began to match the growth rates of its smaller neighbours with output rising by some 8%–10% per annum. Indonesia has also seen a rapid rise in living standards, and recently the Philippines, after years of relative stagnation, has begun to achieve high rates of growth of output.

A feature of growth in South-East Asia is that it has occurred in export-oriented economies; most of the countries in the region are highly dependent on world trade and it has been their ability to sell their goods abroad which has been an important part of their success. This has provided strong support for economic theories of export-led growth as opposed to theories of import substitution, and it has encouraged a number of other developing nations to reduce tariffs and other protective measures and to start to liberalize their economies.

The Indian Sub-Continent and the Middle East

The Indian sub-continent is mainly composed of the three countries India, Bangladesh, and Pakistan. All three figure among the ten most populous countries in the world and all are poor countries with average annual incomes below $300 in India and Bangladesh and below $450 in Pakistan. These figures are calculated on the basis of official exchange rates and understate significantly the real purchasing power of the incomes but, even allowing for this, the standard of living of most of the citizens of these countries remains low.

Table 1.6. Rapid economic growth in South-East Asia: average growth of GNP per capita 1985–93, selected countries (%)

China	6.5
Hong Kong	5.3
Indonesia	4.8
Malaysia	5.7
Singapore	6.1
South Korea	8.1
Taiwan	8.1
Thailand	8.4
Vietnam	4.8

Source: World Bank Atlas, 1995, except for Taiwan where the figure was calculated from data in IMF, *World Economic Outlook*, Oct. 1994.

Agriculture still accounts for between one-quarter and one-third of national income with much of the output produced by small-scale farmers heavily dependent on the weather.

Traditionally, the economies of these three countries have been noted for their large public sectors and extensive government controls domestically, and for important tariff and non-tariff barriers externally. But in all three countries, recent years have seen measures of liberalization with reductions in trade protection, the opening up of the economies to foreign investment, reforms of the tax and financial systems, and the starting of privatization programmes. The reforms are recent and partial and it is too early to judge their success, but the initial evidence is favourable: in all three countries living standards are now rising more rapidly than previously. Pakistan has seen annual growth rates of income of around 6% and India and Pakistan of around 4%–5%.

The economies of the Middle-Eastern states are remarkably diverse. In Saudi Arabia and in a number of small neighbouring states such as Kuwait and the United Arab Emirates, there are relatively small populations and considerable oil reserves. These countries enjoy high standards of living but they are very dependent on the fortunes of the oil industry. Since the mid-1980s the real price of oil has tended to fall and, in consequence, incomes in these countries have grown only slowly or have actually fallen.

Iran and Iraq also have considerable reserves of oil but both have suffered greatly from political instability and war and, in both cases, living standards have fallen. Iraq has also suffered from trade sanctions imposed in 1991 by the United Nations and the country now has few economic contacts with the outside world.

Both Turkey and Egypt are populous states and both experienced some early industrialization but, beyond this, there are few similarities. Turkey is well endowed with natural resources and has, throughout the twentieth century, made regular attempts to modernize its economy and its society. It has recently entered into an agreement allowing free trade with the EU and it enjoys a standard of living above that of a number of East European states. In Egypt living standards are lower and the economy has long been dominated by a large public sector, generally perceived as inefficient. In recent years there has been a slow series of reforms but, in spite of this and of the injection of large amounts of foreign aid, the growth in output has only been marginally in excess of the growth in population.

Syria and Jordan have traditionally been regarded as middle-income countries with per capita incomes that would be around $3,000–$4,000 if account was taken of the real purchasing power of their currencies; but both have suffered from the political instability of the region and Jordan has lost its important trade with Iraq due to the UN sanctions. Both countries have seen living standards fall in recent years. Meanwhile Israel, which has the economic status of a developed country, has continued to achieve annual increases in output of 2–3%.

Africa

For purposes of economic analysis, Africa is usually divided into North Africa—the Arab countries along the Mediterranean coast—and sub-Saharan Africa—comprised of the rest of the Continent.

Of the Arab states, Egypt has been briefly mentioned above, Libya is a sparsely populated oil-producing state, and the other three—Tunisia, Algeria, and Morocco—are all classed by the World Bank as middle-income countries. They are all partially industrialized and gain from being close to the markets of Europe. Tunisia and Morocco have achieved modest growth rates in recent years, but Algeria has suffered from serious political unrest and this has led to declines in output.

In sub-Saharan Africa the picture is generally bleak. It is here that many of the poorest countries in the world can be found, many with average incomes (measured on the basis of official exchange rates) of no more than a few hundred dollars a year. Many of the countries suffer from a paucity of indigenous raw materials, while those that do have mineral resources or exportable commodities such as coffee or cocoa have seen prices tending to fall for much of the last 20 years. A few countries in West Africa do have large oil reserves: Nigeria, the most populous country on the Continent, has been able to exploit these to produce a rising national income, but its neighbours, Cameroon and Gabon, despite oil reserves, have still seen serious declines in income.

More generally, around one-half of the sub-Saharan African states have seen their economies contract over the last decade. Agricultural productivity has remained low and production is vulnerable to droughts. Many countries have suffered from extreme political instability degenerating, in a number of cases, into civil war. The French-speaking countries of West and Central Africa have monies linked to the French franc and, prior to a large devaluation in 1994, these monies were seriously over-valued with the result that almost all the nations in question saw declines in national income.

Many African states are heavily indebted to Western governments and to the international aid agencies; a number, in co-operation with the IMF and/or the World Bank, are implementing structural adjustment programmes designed to reduce government fiscal deficits, curb excessive monetary growth, and promote market-oriented reforms. Some sort of reforms are generally accepted to be necessary but the programmes sponsored by the IMF and by the World Bank have been controversial. They have attracted criticism from a number of academic commentators, but have been strongly defended by their sponsors. It is clear that such programmes do not produce quick results, but where countries have persevered with them (e.g. Ghana) and where there has been a resumption of foreign aid, there have been some modest improvements in economic conditions.[5]

---

[5] For a favourable view of these structural adjustment programmes, see the report of the World Bank *Adjustment in Africa—Reforms, Results and the Road Ahead* (Oxford: Oxford University Press 1994). For a more critical account see P. Mosley, T. Subashat, and J. Weeks, 'Assessing Adjustment in Africa', *World Development* (Sept. 1995).

Table 1.7 Economic stagnation in Sub-Saharan Africa: average growth of GNP per capital 1985–93, selected countries (%)

Cameroon	−7.3
Côte d'Ivoire	−5.2
Ethiopia	−1.8
Ghana	1.3
Kenya	0.3
Mozambique	1.9
Nigeria	3.2
South Africa	−1.5
Sudan	−0.2
Tanzania	1.4
Uganda	1.9
Zaïre	−0.8

Source: World Bank Atlas, 1995

1.4. The International Economic Agencies

An important feature of the last half-century has been the continuing attempts at international economic co-operation organized and promoted by a number of international agencies. Although a few such bodies have been in existence since before the Second World War, most have their origins in the years immediately following that conflict.

The Second World War caused loss of life and material damage on an unprecedented scale. In the closing months of the war and in the years that followed, there was a natural desire to try to foster better political and economic conditions in the hope of making future wars on the same scale less likely. In the political sphere, the most notable achievement was the creation, in 1945, of the United Nations. In the economic sphere, the International Monetary Fund and the World Bank were established; the General Agreement on Tariffs and Trade was created; and the agency which was later to become the influential body known as the Organization for Economic Co-operation and Development was set up.

The International Monetary Fund (IMF)

The IMF was created at a conference in Bretton Woods (New Hampshire) in 1944 and started operations in 1947. It is based in Washington. Its objectives were to promote international monetary co-operation, to establish and maintain a multilateral payments system, and to support orderly exchange-rate arrangements among member countries. Initially, the Fund was committed to a system of fixed exchange rates but, after the collapse in 1972 of the post-war international monetary system and the adoption by many countries of floating exchange rates, it adopted a more pragmatic stance.

Member countries (of whom there are now more than 170) pay a quota subscription to the Fund and are entitled to borrow amounts related to the size of their quota. Small loans are supplied without conditions but any substantial lending is only provided on conditions which normally require restrictive macroeconomic policies.

In the past, loans were granted to, and conditions imposed upon, a number of developed nations, including the UK. But the growth of the international banking system and the international bond market has been such that developed countries can, nowadays, borrow large sums from private sources and do not need to turn to the IMF. The applicants for loans now tend to be those developing countries with insufficient creditworthiness to borrow on private markets and the former communist countries.

The IMF has traditionally provided medium-term finance to countries which have serious deficits on their balance of payments and hence are in need of foreign exchange. In exchange, it requires that borrowers adopt policies that will—in time—remove the deficit, and this usually implies a package of measures including devaluation of the exchange rate and tight monetary policies.

As was mentioned above, this is controversial and critics of the Fund accuse it of imposing deflation on what are often very poor countries. There seems to be an element here of shooting the messenger. Any country, whether rich or poor, if it has a serious balance-of-payments problem will have to take steps to deal with it and these steps are likely to involve deflation. The absence of IMF loans would only make such deflation worse.

The World Bank

The World Bank was founded in 1944 at the same conference in Bretton Woods as was the IMF and commenced operations in 1946. Like the IMF, it is based in Washington. Its purpose was to finance post-war reconstruction and economic development but, from as early as 1949, most of its lending was for projects to promote economic development in the Third World. Funds are obtained from the subscriptions of member countries and from issues of bonds on world financial markets.

Initially the World Bank was a unitary organization and had as its official name, the International Bank for Reconstruction and Development (IBRD). Its constitution enabled it to make loans only to national governments or with the guarantee of national governments. This constrained lending to private organizations in a way that soon seemed undesirable and, in 1956, the International Finance Corporation (IFC) was founded as an affiliated organization with the objective of lending to private investors in developing countries.

Although lending by the IBRD was at low rates of interest, it was always intended that the projects financed should be economically sound and that the recipient country should be able to pay the interest and, in time, to repay the loan. But this left little scope for lending to the poorest nations and so, in 1960, the International Development Association (IDA) was established as a second affiliate of the IBRD in order to lend to the very poor countries at concessionary rates of interest.

The IBRD, the IDA, and the IFC, along with an agency providing guarantees for investment in developing countries, constitute the World Bank group. At end-October 1994 nearly 180 countries were members.

During the 1950s and the 1960s, the World Bank financed mainly large-scale projects, such as power plant, dams and other irrigation schemes, as well as infrastructural investment in ports and railways. This attracted criticism as such projects, although supported by the governments of the countries concerned, frequently involved considerable disruption to the lives of ordinary people. The Bank responded to its critics and it now supports many simpler projects using 'intermediate technology'. It has also increased lending for agricultural and rural development and for projects to improve education, health and public hygiene.

More recently, a new line of criticism has emerged: that the World Bank is too expensive and has, perhaps, outlived its usefulness. Although the outstanding loans of the Bank are large, so are the repayments, and this means that the net transfer of funds to developing countries is now low. Furthermore other transfers, notably private investment, have grown in recent years and are now far greater than the contribution of the World Bank. Meanwhile the Bank's administrative expenses remain high and in 1995 amounted to $1.4 billion; a sum which exceeds the entire national income of one-fifth of its member states. The Bank has accepted the need for economies and budgets are being cut and staff numbers reduced, but there still remains some uncertainty over the future role and size of the World Bank group.

The General Agreement on Tariffs and Trade and the World Trade Organization

As part of the post-war effort to create a better international order, there was a desire to return to a more liberal trading order with less tariffs and other obstacles to trade. There were negotiations to establish an International Trade Organization (ITO) and, as an interim measure, 23 countries signed the General Agreement on Tariffs and Trade (GATT) and set up a small secretariat in Geneva to administer the Agreement. The negotiations to establish the ITO proved difficult and the project was abandoned but the GATT secretariat remained in place and over time it grew to fill the role of world trade body.

The original GATT Agreement pledged the signatory countries to the expansion of multilateral trade and to the reduction of tariffs and quotas.

Multilateral trade meant that countries would not enter into separate bilateral deals and that any concession offered to one trading partner would be offered to all others. This principle was covered by what became known as the 'most-favoured-nation clause'.

In furtherance of its objectives, the GATT organized a number of trading rounds, i.e. international negotiations to agree tariffs reductions, and these were successful in that many tariffs were abolished and others were significantly reduced. The number of signatories to the Agreement grew to over 100 by the early 1990s.

There are, of course, problems. Many developing nations felt that the GATT tended to work to the advantage of the developed countries and, in 1964, they established under the auspices of the United Nations the UN Conference on Trade and Development (UNCTAD). This was intended to be a forum where less developed countries could argue for their own trading interests. One particular concern was the most-favoured-nation clause, as it required countries to give equal treatment to all of their trading partners and the developing countries felt they should be given preferential access to the markets of the prosperous western nations. The GATT members responded and, in 1965, agreed that the clause could be waived to allow preferential agreements with developing countries.

A more general problem was that as tariffs were reduced, countries found ways to replace them by other obstacles. These took diverse forms but included special trade regimes (e.g. the Multi-fibre Agreement regulating trade in textiles) and so-called voluntary agreements under which successful exporters were threatened or cajoled into restricting their own exports (as happened with the export of Japanese cars). Furthermore, important areas of economic life were not covered by the original GATT agreement and these included agriculture, services, and most public sector activities.

It was decided to tackle many of these non-tariff obstacles to trade in the Uruguay Round of trade negotiations which opened in 1986. The discussions were long, complex, and frequently acrimonious. They continued intermittently for seven years but agreement was finally reached on a number of issues including reductions in agricultural protection, the phasing out of the Multi-fibre Agreement, reductions in barriers to trade in services such as banking and insurance, and further substantial reductions in tariffs on industrial goods.

The agreement also included the setting up of a new World Trade Organization (WTO) as a successor body to the GATT. The new organization, which came into existence in January 1995, was planned as a body which would not only promote further reductions in tariffs and other obstacles to trade but would also formulate new rules in areas such as the environment, competition policy, and trade in services. Unlike the GATT, the WTO also has a disputes procedure and member states are expected to submit trade disputes to it for arbitration.

The idea of a world of free trade in which tariffs and other obstacles to trade are progressively reduced and where covert subsidies and other forms of protection are outlawed is one which nowadays has widespread support among economic commentators as well as among government ministers and officials. But, in practice, many pressure groups remain, and governments often find it expedient to assist domestic producers in one way or another. How successful the World Trade Organization will be in resisting such tendencies remains to be seen.

The Organization for Economic Co-operation and Development (OECD)

The OECD also began life in the years following the Second World War. Its origins lie in the distribution of American Marshall Aid, in the co-ordination of the European Recovery Programme and of the European Payments Union, all of which were part of the regeneration of the European economies after the devastation of war.

With the return to normality in Europe, the Organization evolved into a think-tank and research institute for the developed economies. In 1961 it adopted its current name and the USA and Canada became full members. Subsequently Australia, New Zealand, and Japan joined and, in 1994, Mexico became the 25th member.

The OECD, which is based in Paris, publishes a wide range of economic statistics and makes regular short-term economic forecasts as well as publishing annual reports on the economies of each of its member countries. It also provides a forum in which the representatives of member countries can meet and discuss issues of common interest. Such meetings usually take place with little publicity and permit an ongoing exchange of views on important issues. They can range from formal negotiations with government ministers in attendance to meetings of experts to explore topics ranging from financial innovation to atmospheric pollution.

Other International Agencies

There are many other international economic organizations, but space precludes anything more than a brief mention of these. The International Labour Organization, based in Geneva, was founded in 1919 but is now affiliated to the United Nations: it aims to improve working conditions throughout the world and to encourage the development of systems of social security. The Food and Agricultural Organization, based in Rome, is a specialized UN agency which is concerned with improving efficiency in the production and distribution of agricultural, forestry, and fishing products. The Bank for International Settlements in Basle was established in 1929 to deal with reparation payments by Germany due under the Treaty of Versailles, but it now operates mainly as a think-tank and as a forum for discussions among central banks. It has, on occasions, helped to co-ordinate foreign-exchange interventions by central banks and it also carries out financial transactions on behalf of other international organizations.

Finally, one should note that there are a number of regional development banks such as the Asian Development Bank, the African Development Bank, and the Inter-American Bank. These institutions raise funds by taking subscriptions from member countries and by selling bonds to private investors. They use the funds raised to make loans for projects to promote economic development within their area. The latest such bank to be created is the European Bank for Reconstruction and Development, based in London, which provides technical assistance and financial aid to Russia and the former communist states of Eastern Europe.

In general, it can be said that international economic organizations promote co-operation between nations and encourage dialogue and discussion and as such they play a valuable role in the world economy. But they are costly and because, in principle, they are answerable to many masters, there is always the risk that, in practice, they become answerable to no one in particular. There have been a number of cases of apparent waste and inefficiency. It is highly desirable that large international organizations should be subject to periodic assessment of their costs and their benefits.

Further Reading

A. Booth, *British Economic Development Since 1945* (Manchester: Manchester University Press, 1995).

N. F. R. Crafts and N. Woodward (eds.), *The British Economy Since 1945* (Oxford: Oxford University Press, 1991).

D. H. Aldcroft, *The European Economy 1914–1990*, 3rd edn. (London: Routledge, 1993).

H. Van der Wee, *Prosperity and Upheaval: The World Economy 1945–1980* (Harmondsworth: Penguin Books, 1987).

International Monetary Fund, *Annual Report* (Washington DC, various dates).

Organization for Economic Co-operation and Development, *Economic Outlook*, published twice a year in June and December.

World Bank, *World Bank Atlas*, 1995.

World Bank, *World Development Report*, published annually.

THE STRUCTURE OF THE ECONOMY

GERAINT JOHNES AND JIM TAYLOR

2.1. Introduction

The structural changes that have occurred in the UK during the last fifty years have been colossal. In 1950 over 40% of the labour force were employed in manufacturing; by 1995 this had fallen to under 20%. This chapter investigates the changes which have occurred in the structure of the UK economy in recent decades—a shift which has been necessitated by developments outside the UK in an increasingly integrated international economy.

Our main concern is to examine not only the shift in the country's productive capacity from manufacturing to services, but also the shifts in activity within these two sectors. The prime focus of this chapter is on the factors causing these major structural changes, which have been extremely rapid and which have profound implications for labour-market flexibility and for the education and training of the workforce. Throughout we shall highlight the role of changes in the stock and distribution of both physical capital (the plant and machinery used in production) and human capital (the skills of the workforce). These issues are crucial in determining the sectors of the economy in which the UK has a comparative advantage and in which the productive efforts of the country will therefore be concentrated.

2.2. The UK and the World Economy

Comparative Advantage

The pattern of a country's international trade depends in large measure on the international pattern of comparative advantage. The UK's comparative advantage has changed radically in recent decades. Two major changes have been apparent. First, there have been shifts in the comparative advantage within the manufacturing sector; and secondly, there has been a major shift in comparative advantage from manufacturing to services. These shifts in comparative advantage have occurred largely as a consequence of the industrialization of the newly industrialized countries (the NICs), which have won increasing shares of world trade in a wide range of manufactured products, particularly consumer durables. However, the UK maintains a revealed comparative advantage in chemicals, non-ferrous metals, and machine and transport equipment (see Table 2.1), and also in high-technology manufacturing.[1] Outside of manufacturing, the growth of the service sector is partly attributable to exports of invisibles, such as financial services due to the pre-eminence of London as a financial centre, and higher education due to the high quality of the UK's university sector which attracts large numbers of overseas students. This growth of services has helped to keep the UK's share of world trade in goods and services constant in the past two decades in spite of increased competition from the NICs (see Table 2.2).

The changes over time in the UK's pattern of comparative advantage may be understood within the context of the product life-cycle approach of Vernon.[2] The competitive advantage conferred upon an economy by the development of a new product (or a new method of production) is temporary. Eventually, production of the new product will transfer to countries in which labour costs are lower. Thus, for example, the advances made in textile production during

Table 2.1. Revealed comparative advantage in manufacturing

Year	Industries with advantage
1913	Rail and ship Textiles Iron and steel Spirits/tobacco
1937	Spirits/tobacco Textiles Rail and ship Finished goods Electricals
1991	Chemicals Machine and transport equipment Non-ferrous metals

Note: Individual industries are identified as having a comparative advantage if an industry's share of world exports is greater than the corresponding proportion for all industries. The analysis has been conducted at too general a level of industrial classification to allow separate identification of high-technology industries.
Source: N. F. R. Crafts and M. Thomas, 'Comparative Advantage in UK Manufacturing Trade 1910–1935', *Economic Journal*, 96 (1986), 629–45, table 4; information for 1991 based upon authors' own calculations using the Crafts and Thomas method and data from the *United Nations International Trade Statistics Yearbook*. Changes in the *International Standard Industrial Classification* mean that the 1991 data are not strictly comparable with those for earlier years.

[1] OECD, *The OECD Jobs Study* (Paris: OECD, 1994).
[2] R. Vernon, 'International Investment and International Trade in the Product Cycle', *Quarterly Journal of Economics*, 80 (1966), 190–207.

Table 2.2. Per cent shares in world trade

Country	Per cent share of world trade			
	1976–9	1980–4	1985–9	1990–4
US	11.8	12.1	11.5	12.4
Japan	7.3	8.1	9.7	9.4
Germany	11.9	10.4	12.3	11.3
France	6.2	5.5	5.9	6.1
Italy	4.3	4.1	4.6	4.9
UK	5.2	5.4	5.3	5.2

Source: Pink Book.

the Industrial Revolution gave the UK a comparative advantage in that sector. But once the technology and expertise became widely available, lower labour costs in the NICs transferred the comparative advantage to some of the latter economies.

Since entering the European Community (now the European Union) in 1973, an increasing proportion of UK trade has been with the countries of mainland Europe. This is demonstrated by the dramatic increase in the proportion of the UK's exports going to the EU, from under 30% in 1970 to over 50% in 1994 (see Table 2.3). Free trade within Europe and the existence of a common external tariff has promoted this development. Likewise the shift in comparative advantage, brought about both by changes in the industrial composition of the UK's stock of physical capital and the skill mix of its human capital, and also by the economic development of other countries, has led to changes in the group of countries with whom the UK conducts the bulk of its trade. The changing comparative advantage of UK industries is therefore partly a response to and partly a cause of the shift in trade that has occurred as a result of the UK's entry into the EU.

With the exception of the early 1980s, when severe recession dampened the demand for imports, the UK's balance of payments on current account (i.e. exports minus imports) has been persistently in deficit (see Table 2.4). This is in sharp contrast to the experience of Japan, where the current account has

Table 2.3. Visible trade patterns (%)

Region	1970		1994	
	Exports	Imports	Exports	Imports
European Union	28.9	28.3	52.6	51.4
Other Western Europe	17.1	14.9	8.4	11.3
North America	15.0	20.9	14.2	13.1
Other OECD	12.0	10.1	4.1	7.0
Oil-exporting countries	5.8	7.2	4.2	2.1

Note: The European Union data for 1970 refer to the Europe of the 9, while those for 1992 refer to the Europe of the 12.
Source: Pink Book.

Table 2.4. Current balances: exports minus imports as a percentage of GDP

Country	1976–9	1980–4	1985–9	1990–5
US	−0.3	−0.8	−2.9	−1.6
Japan	0.8	0.9	3.2	2.5
Germany	0.6	0.2	4.0	−0.3
France	0.3	−0.9	−0.3	0.2
Italy	0.9	−1.2	−0.5	−0.3
UK	−0.1	1.4	−1.7	−1.4
EU	0.0	−0.4	0.6	−0.2

Source: OECD, *Economic Outlook*.

been in persistent surplus. The growth performance of these two countries is also very different, and this raises the question: does the UK's current account deficit impose a constraint on its output growth? If exchange rates are flexible enough to restore a current account balance, then clearly the answer is 'no'. But if the deficit is persistent, so that the country is spending more than it is earning over the medium term, this may be symptomatic of more deeply rooted problems. For instance, the inability of a country to finance its expenditures may result from it having too low a level of investment in relation to its current consumption.

The Exchange Rate

The movement of the sterling exchange rate over time is shown in Fig. 2.1. The long-term fall in sterling against the Deutschmark suddenly went into reverse in the early 1980s as a result of two factors. The first was the very tight monetary policy imposed by the first Thatcher Government in 1980/1 in order to bring down inflation. The second was the advent of North Sea oil as a major export for the UK (see Fig. 2.2). The boost to exports provided by oil, which also benefited from a substantial hike in the price of oil in 1979/80, had a major effect on the current account of the balance of payments. This prevented the pound from depreciating sufficiently to maintain the competitiveness of the UK's manufacturing industry. Oil therefore accelerated the process of deindustrialization. A similar process was experienced by the Netherlands as a result of a sharp increase in gas production in the 1960s. This experience subsequently became known as the 'Dutch disease'.[3] Since the early 1980s, however, sterling has continued its downward trend against the Deutschmark, though at a somewhat slower pace.

From 1986, a strong correlation became apparent between the international value of sterling and that of the Deutschmark. After tracking the Deutschmark closely during 1986–9, the UK formally entered the Exchange Rate Mechanism

[3] P. R. Ferguson and G. J. Ferguson, *Industrial Economics: Issues and Perspectives*, 2nd edn. (Maidenhead: Macmillan, 1994), ch. 10 on 'Deindustrialization'.

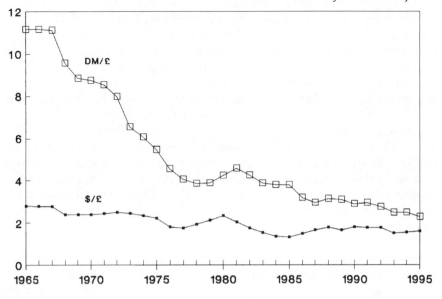

Fig. 2.1. The sterling exchange rate (average daily rates) 1965–1995

Source: Economic Trends.

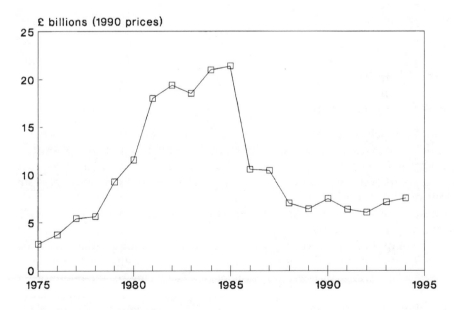

Fig. 2.2. The value of oil exports from the UK, 1975–1994

Source: Pink Book.

(ERM) of the European Monetary System (EMS) on 8 October 1990. Sterling was set at 2.95DM since it had been around the 3DM level over the previous four years despite the existence of a sustained period of current account deficit. This was a short-lived arrangement, however. Following intense speculative pressure, the pound's membership of the ERM was suspended on 16 September 1992. The value of the pound against the Deutschmark has since settled at about 17% below its level during the period of ERM membership.

Subsequent experience indicates that the UK's membership of the ERM during 1990–2 exacerbated the recession which began in 1990. The improved productivity secured in the 1980s in what remained of manufacturing industry after the plant closures and premature scrapping of a large chunk of the manufacturing sector during the first Thatcher Government ensured, however, that the industrial and regional impacts of this recession were very different from those endured ten years earlier.

In summing up this section, we need to emphasize that changes in comparative advantage and the differential impact across industries of exchange rate fluctuations, especially in the early 1980s, are likely to have had a major impact on the development of the UK's industrial structure. Likewise, the inflationary and balance of payments problems that arose as a consequence of the Lawson boom in the late 1980s frustrated hopes that the UK might experience a period of sustained economic growth. In the next section, we consider how the international developments referred to above have affected the composition and growth of output.

2.3. Output

Economic Growth

Simple models of the circular flow of income make clear the identity between national income, national expenditure, and national output. In 1994 Gross Domestic Product (GDP) stood at 579 billion. This is measured at factor cost, which is the value of GDP at market prices less taxes on expenditure plus any government subsidies on expenditure. Table 2.5 shows how these three measures of GDP can be sub-divided into the sources of income, expenditure, and output respectively.

The output of the UK economy grew rapidly in the second half of the 1980s. The recession of the early 1990s has since demonstrated that such apparently spectacular performance was not sustainable. This being so, the boom of the late 1980s has been explained by appeal to a variety of transient conditions. At this time house prices rose rapidly so that existing home owners were able to borrow large sums using their houses as collateral security. Government fiscal and monetary policies were relaxed at the same time, and a consumer-led

Table 2.5. Composition of the Gross Domestic Product in the UK, 1994 (%)

Expenditure method		Income method		Output method	
Consumers' expenditure	72	Employment income	63	Agriculture, forestry, and fishing	2
Investment	20	Private sector profits	16	Production industries	28
Government expenditure	24	Public sector surpluses	1	Construction	6
Net Exports	−2	Rent, self-employment other income	21	Services	64
(Net taxes on expenditure)	−15	(Stock appreciation)	−1		

Note: Figures do not necessarily sum to 100 due to rounding.
Source: NIBB.

boom resulted. By the end of the decade, spare capacity was exhausted. The supply side of the economy proved unable to deliver the required increase in real output and a period of high inflation ensued.

With the exception of the late 1980s, growth of GDP has been somewhat sluggish in the UK by comparison with the rest of the EU, the USA, and Japan (see Table 2.6). Over the very long term, output is determined by the characteristics of the supply side of the economy, and in particular by the growth in its productive capacity. Thus in seeking an explanation for international differences in economic growth over long periods, it is natural to look first at supply-side conditions, such as the level of investment in both physical capital and the skills of the workforce.[4] This is the approach adopted by those who espouse the new models of endogenous growth.[5] These new growth models argue that growth leads to an increased demand for education which, through its positive impact on worker productivity, stimulates future growth. This implies that economic growth stimulates further growth, which

Table 2.6. Growth of real GDP in various countries (% p.a.)

Country	1967–79	1980–4	1985–9	1990–4
US	2.9	1.8	3.1	2.0
Japan	6.4	3.5	4.5	2.2
Germany	3.7	1.0	2.6	2.6
France	4.1	1.5	3.1	1.1
Italy	4.3	1.7	3.1	1.0
UK	2.5	0.8	4.0	0.5
EC	3.8	1.2	3.2	1.4

Source: OECD, *Economic Outlook*.

[4] N. Oulton, 'Supply Side Reform and UK Economic Growth: What Happened to the Miracle?', *National Institute Economic Review*, 154 (1995), 53–70.

[5] P. Romer, 'Increasing Returns and Long Run Growth', *Journal of Political Economy*, 94 (1986), 1002–37.

means that growth is 'endogenous'. The ways in which the pattern of invest-ment in physical and human capital have changed in the UK over the recent past are discussed later in this chapter.

Composition of Output

Almost three-quarters of all expenditure in the UK is accounted for by consumer spending, the remainder being fairly evenly split between private sector investment and government expenditure. These proportions have been fairly stable over recent decades. Consumption is such a large proportion of GDP that autonomous changes in consumers' savings ratios have the potential to produce changes in GDP much greater than those that fiscal policy, acting on taxes or government spending, can produce. For example, while the tax concessions of the 1988 budget no doubt exacerbated the subsequent infla-tionary boom, much more important as a cause of that boom was the coincident autonomous increase in consumer spending. The proportion of consumers' disposable income which was saved fell from 17% to just 3% between the first quarter of 1981 and the last quarter of 1988. The proportion of GDP accounted for by government spending has not changed much in recent years (it was the same in 1993 as in 1951), but over the very long term the role of government has clearly been rising. For example, in 1900 government spending accounted for only 11% of GDP compared to around 25% in 1994.

Employment is by far the most important source of income: almost two-thirds of all income comes from this source. Also important is income from self-employment and rents, which accounts for more than one-fifth of all income. This proportion has been rising in recent years as the number of self-employed workers has risen. In 1979 there were 1.9 million self-employed workers in the UK, but by 1994 the figure had reached over 3 million. These figures should be treated with caution, however, since many workers who have become self-employed in the last decade have their former employer as their main customer. For instance, some construction companies now serve simply to co-ordinate the activities of self-employed building workers, but these same building workers were previously employees of the construction firm itself. This practice increases a firm's flexibility (since it makes it easier to adjust the workforce to the work available), and illustrates an interesting problem—that of defining the boundaries of a firm.[6] Is it appropriate or not to treat the self-employed worker as if he is part of the firm for which he does most of his work?

Services now account for almost two-thirds of output in the UK. This represents a dramatic increase over the last 30 years, most especially at the expense of the production sector. In 1963 the latter accounted for 40% of GDP compared with 27% in 1994. The corresponding figures for services are 50% in

---

[6] R. Coase, 'The Nature of the Firm', *Economica*, 4 (1937), 386–405.

1963 and 64% in 1994. This is indicative of the phenomenon of 'deindustrialization', which is discussed below.

The changes which have occurred in the post-war period in the source of income and in the industrial composition of output have clear implications for the structure of the labour market, which is examined in the next section.

2.4. Employment Trends and the Industry Mix

The industrial structure of the UK economy has undergone radical change in recent decades. In general terms, there has been a continuous decline in employment in manufacturing while the service sector has provided an increasing number of jobs. A more detailed look at the employment data reveals that three main structural changes have occurred since the early 1970s.

First, jobs have shifted between the main industrial sectors. By far the most striking change is the loss of 3.6 million jobs in the manufacturing sector during 1971–94. Employment in manufacturing industries shrank from 8.2 million in 1971 to 4.6 million in 1994 (see Table 2.7). While this process of deindustrialization was happening, industries in the service sector were expanding rapidly. Employment in banking, finance, insurance, and other business services, for example, more than doubled during 1971–94, providing an additional 2 million jobs. The growth of this sector was particularly rapid during the 1980s as the government's deregulation of the financial sector introduced more competition into the UK's financial markets (see Chapter 6). Coupled with a worldwide growth of financial activity, these reforms helped London to become an even more important player in world financial markets, thus benefiting the financial services sector. Other service industries which have expanded rapidly include education, health, business services, and retailing. Since 1980, for example, 1 million extra jobs have been created in the education and health industries. These changes demonstrate just how quickly industrial restructuring has been occurring in the UK.

The second major structural change that has occurred is the rapid growth in the number of self-employed workers. Between 1981 and 1994 the number of self-employed workers increased by over 50%, from 2.1 to 3.2 million. By 1994, 11.5% of UK workers were self-employed, compared to only 7.5% in 1970. This increase in self-employment occurred across a wide range of industries, the largest increases being in the construction and service sectors. Although there was some decline in self-employment in the 1990–3 recession, it seems likely that the long-run underlying trend will continue to be upwards.

The third prominent structural change in the UK labour force in recent decades has been the shift in employment in favour of females. The most rapidly declining industries have been dominated by male jobs while the most rapidly expanding industries have been dominated by female jobs. The high

Table 2.7. Employment by main industry group in the UK, 1950–2000

Industry group	Employees (000s)						
	1950	1960	1971	1980	1990	1994	2000 (forecast)
Agriculture and fisheries	806	610	758	647	583	558	533
Mining and quarrying	857	769	409	365	178	93	91
Manufacturing	8520	8851	8231	7098	5393	4639	4505
Construction	1325	1459	1578	1647	1907	1444	470
Electricity, gas and water	360	378	375	353	277	223	190
Transport and communications	1769	1663	1618	1580	1570	1411	1411
Distributive trades	2130	2833	3592	3900	4278	4073	4364
Insurance, banking, and finance	437	546	575	712	986	911	961
Public administration	1402	1285	1762	1812	1722	1618	1600
Other service industries	3153	4098	5632	7210	9869	10021	11199
Hotels and catering	—	—	814	1083	1436	1398	1603
Other business services	—	—	1224	1526	2735	2839	3302
Education and health	—	—	2865	3575	4373	4539	4821
Other services	—	—	729	1026	1325	1245	1473
Total	20759	22492	24530	25324	26761	24992	26324

Note: Projection for 2000 obtained form Cambridge Econometrics.
Source: *British Labour Statistics*, Historical Abstract; *Regional Economic Prospects*, Cambridge Econometrics.

concentration of females in service industries and the low concentration in the manufacturing sector provides some indication of the reason why employment growth has been much stronger for females than for males. Moreover, many of the new jobs created since the mid-1980s have been part-time rather than full-time. Employers have shifted to part-time workers because of the lower costs and greater flexibility associated with part-time jobs. The majority of women who work part-time take a part-time job because they have children at school. Between 1979 and 1995 the number of females in part-time work in Great Britain increased from 3.4 to 5.1 million compared to an increase from 0.1 to 1.1 million for males (see Table 2.8).

Structural Changes in Employment

Structural changes in the UK economy during the last fifty years have been immense. This is indicated very clearly by the long-run changes in the relative share of employment in each major industry since 1950. The most astonishing trend evident from Table 2.9 is the sharp fall in the proportion of total

Table 2.8. Full-time and part-time jobs by sex in Great Britain, 1979–1995

| | Employment (millions) | | | |
| | Males | | Females | |
	1979	1995	1979	1995
Full-time	14.3	13.0	5.6	6.3
Part-time	0.1	1.1	3.4	5.1

Source: *Labour Market Trends*, Dec. 1995.

employees with jobs in the manufacturing sector, which fell from around 40% in 1960 to 20% in 1990. It is important, however, to be wary of such statistics, since the loss of direct jobs in manufacturing has been associated to some extent with an increase in indirect jobs in non-manufacturing industries which service the manufacturing sector. Manufacturing, for example, may simply be getting more of its service activities provided by specialist companies in business services rather than undertaking these tasks itself. In addition, job losses are often accompanied by productivity increases, which means that manufacturing output has risen while manufacturing employment has fallen drastically since the 1960s. Manufacturing output has in fact been on a gently rising trend since the early 1980s and its share of GDP now appears to have stabilized at around 23% (see Fig. 2.3).

Table 2.9. Employment structure of the UK, 1950–2000

| Industry group | % of employees in each industry | | | | | | |
	1950	1960	1971	1980	1990	1994	2000 (forecast)
Agriculture and fisheries	3.9	2.7	3.1	2.6	2.1	2.2	2.0
Mining and quarrying	4.1	3.4	1.7	1.4	0.7	0.4	0.3
Manufacturing	41.0	39.4	33.6	28.0	20.3	18.6	17.1
Construction	6.4	6.5	6.4	6.5	7.0	5.8	5.6
Electricity, gas, and water	1.7	1.7	1.5	1.4	1.0	0.9	0.7
Transport and communications	8.5	7.4	6.6	6.2	5.9	5.6	5.4
Distributive trades	10.3	12.6	14.6	15.4	15.9	16.3	16.6
Insurance, banking, and finance	2.1	2.4	2.3	2.8	3.7	3.6	3.7
Public administration	6.8	5.7	7.2	7.2	6.5	6.5	6.1
Other service industries	15.2	18.2	23.0	28.5	36.9	40.1	42.5
Hotels and catering	—	—	3.3	4.3	5.3	5.6	6.1
Other business services	—	—	5.0	6.0	10.2	11.6	12.5
Education and health	—	—	11.7	14.1	16.4	18.2	18.3
Other services	—	—	3.0	4.1	4.9	5.0	5.6
Total	100	100	100	100	100	100	100

Note: Forecast for the year 2000 obtained form Cambridge Econometrics.
Source: *British Labour Statistics*, Historical Abstract; *Regional Economic Prospects*, Cambridge Econometrics.

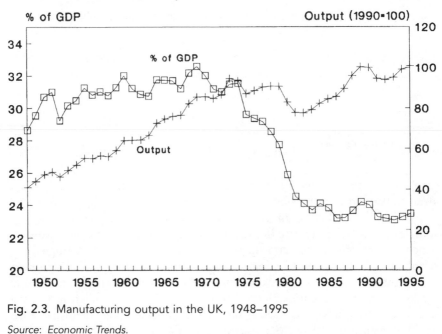

Fig. 2.3. Manufacturing output in the UK, 1948–1995

Source: Economic Trends.

The mirror image of the relative decline of manufacturing jobs has been the incredible expansion in service sector jobs, particularly since the early 1970s. The main contributors to these job gains in the service sector have been business services, education, health, wholesaling, and retailing. Together, these industries have increased their share of national employment from 31% to 46% of the UK jobs total between 1971 and 1994. Although this shift in the job mix from manufacturing to services has taken place incredibly quickly in the UK, it is an employment shift that has been occurring right across the industrialized world. The major reasons are: first, the adoption of capital-intensive methods of production in manufacturing; secondly, the increased competition from the countries of South-East Asia; and thirdly, the steady increase in demand for services as income levels have increased.

2.5. Regional Distribution of Industry

Employment in the UK as a whole was virtually the same in 1994 as it was over twenty years earlier in 1971. The geographical distribution of these jobs between the regions of the UK changed remarkably, however, during this period (see Table 2.10). There are several reasons for these geographical shifts in employment.[7] First, Greater London lost around 20% of its jobs while the rest of the South East gained almost as many, leaving the total for the South East virtually unchanged. The outer South East became increasingly attractive to employers in the South East region partly because the cost of land and premises is lower than in Greater London and partly because of the redistribution of the population out of the metropolis and towards free-standing towns in the outer South East.

Secondly, three regions experienced substantial job gains during 1971–94. East Anglia and the South West increased their employment levels by over 35% and 28% respectively, while the East Midlands experienced a 16% increase. Although it is tempting to attribute the success of these three regions in creating additional jobs to a favourable mix of industries, it can be shown that this was not, in fact, the case. These regions grew rapidly because their industries grew faster than the same industry in other regions.[7] The proximity of the South West, East Anglia, and the East Midlands to the UK's most economically powerful region—the South East—accounts for a significant part of their rapid increase in jobs.

Thirdly, the three main job losers were the West Midlands, the North West, and the North, one of the main reasons for this regional concentration of job losses being the decline of many manufacturing industries, especially heavy industries. The West Midlands and the North West have also suffered because of the high concentration of population in conurbations, which have been

Table 2.10. Employment in the regions of the UK, 1971–2000 (000s)

Region	1971	1980	1990	1994	2000 (forecast)
South East	8124	8286	9037	8073	8450
Greater London	4315	4003	3982	3508	3678
Rest of South East	3809	4282	5055	4565	4772
East Anglia	704	811	987	956	1053
South West	1609	1851	2171	2057	2241
East Midlands	1493	1682	1820	1736	1904
West Midlands	2389	2375	2431	2223	2345
Yorkshire & Humberside	2080	2152	2221	2098	2204
North West	2949	2865	2766	2593	2650
North	1331	1295	1248	1213	1258
Wales	1087	1132	1194	1160	1238
Scotland	2179	2263	2265	2244	2315
Northern Ireland	585	613	622	640	666
Total	24530	25324	26761	24992	26324

Note: Forecast for the year 2000 obtained from Cambridge Econometrics.
Source: Economic Trends; Regional Economics Prospects, Cambridge Econometrics.

[7] R. L. Martin and P. Townroe, 'Changing Trends and Pressures in Regional Development', in R. L. Martin and P. Townroe (eds.), *Regional Development in the 1990s: The British Isles in Transition* (London: Jessica Kingsley, 1992); H. Armstrong and J. Taylor, *Regional Economics and Policy* (London: Harvester Wheatsheaf, 1993).

unpopular with employers looking for places in which to expand their productive capacity due to the high costs of production in densely populated areas.[8] Perhaps rather surprisingly, employment increased in the peripheral areas of the UK. This better than expected performance of the job market in Scotland, Wales, and Northern Ireland can be attributed to a very active inward investment policy (strongly backed by the central government), coupled with the beneficial effects of oil-related activities in Scotland and considerable government spending related to the 'troubles' in Northern Ireland. The continued attractiveness of Scotland and Wales as locations for inward investors suggests that employment will continue to expand in these regions during the 1990s, perhaps to a greater extent than the forecasts to the year 2000 (see Table 2.10) actually indicate. The prospects for Northern Ireland are heavily dependent on the progress towards peace and reconciliation.

These long-term changes in employment, however, conceal the volatility of employment levels over shorter periods. During the 1990–3 recession, for example, the South East lost around 1 million jobs, with Greater London sharing the burden about equally with the rest of the South East. In fact, the 1990–3 recession had a far greater impact on the southern regions than on the northern regions with the result that regional disparities in unemployment narrowed remarkably during the early 1990s. A major reason for this narrowing of unemployment rates between UK regions is the sudden collapse of house prices during 1989–90, a collapse which turned out to be far more serious in the southern than in the northern regions.[9] The collapse of house prices was more severe in the south simply because the preceding house price boom had been greater in southern regions than in northern regions. The subsequent loss of wealth (which took the form of greater debt as house prices collapsed) led to a sharp reduction in consumption which hit the south far more seriously than the north; hence the greater loss of jobs in southern regions during the 1990–3 recession.

2.6. Productivity

As an economy develops, more resources become available for investment. Firms therefore tend to increase their capital/labour ratios over time. This is a self-perpetuating process. As the capital stock increases, labour becomes more productive and demands higher wages, thus making the employment of more

[8] S. Fothergill and G. Gudgin, *Unequal Growth: Urban and Regional Employment Change in the UK* (London: Heinemann, 1982); S. Fothergill, G. Gudgin, M. Kitson, and S. Monk, 'Differences in the Profitability of the UK Manufacturing Sector between Conurbations and other Areas', *Scottish Journal of Political Economy*, 31/1 (1984), 72–91.

[9] S. Bradley and J. Taylor, 'Spatial Disparities in the Impact of the 1990–92 Recession: An Analysis of UK Counties', *Oxford Bulletin of Economics and Statistics*, 56/4 (1994), 367–82.

capital increasingly attractive to firms. It is instructive therefore to examine trends in labour productivity.

Long-run trends since 1960 in output per person-hour in manufacturing industries are shown in Fig. 2.4. These indicate productivity growth of about 2.5% per year during the 1970s and 5.4% per year during the 1980s. In the first five years of the 1990s, productivity in manufacturing has increased by 3.6% per year. The dramatic improvement in productivity between the 1970s and 1980s can be attributed to a number of factors. First, the severe deflationary policies of the early 1980s led to a massive shake-out of labour by manufacturing firms. The number of employees in employment within manufacturing fell by 2 million between mid-1979 and mid-1986; the corresponding figure for all industries was less than this (1.58 million), indicating growth (albeit slow) in sectors other than manufacturing over this period. Inevitably, the most productive firms and the most productive workers were the most likely to survive this shock. Secondly, there were massive redundancies in the (then) nationalized industries; these included coal and steel, where overstaffing was eradicated prior to privatization, and where increased emphasis was put on competitiveness in world markets. Thirdly, the emergence of chemicals, high-technology manufacturing, education, and financial services as industries in which the UK appeared to have a clear competitive advantage, led to increased employment in sectors of industry where labour's productivity is raised by a substantial input of capital—either physical or human. The first two of these

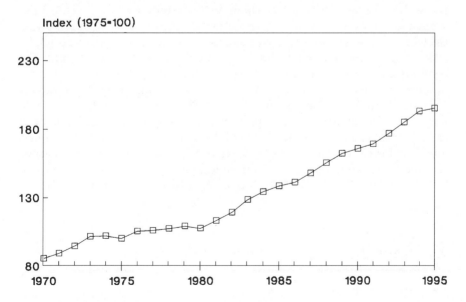

Fig. 2.4. Output per person hour in manufacturing, 1970–1995

Source: Economic Trends.

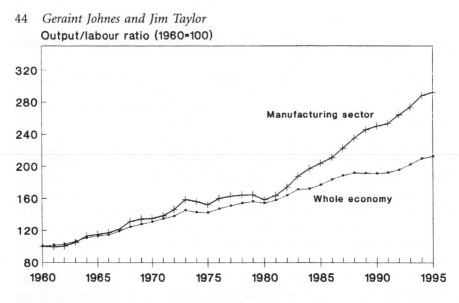

Fig. 2.5. Productivity in the UK: the whole economy and the maufacturing sector, 1960–1995

Source: Economic Trends.

explanations suggest that the productivity growth of the 1980s was a one-off phenomenon.

The last point leads us to study differences in the productivity of labour across the various sectors of the economy. It is readily seen from Fig. 2.5 that production industries, which comprise manufacturing and the utilities (gas, electricity, and water) experienced more rapid productivity growth during the 1980s than other industries (services, agriculture, and construction). This confirms the observation noted above that the labour shake-out had a disproportionate effect on manufacturing firms and on privatized organizations. This was, of course, a once and for all event. The growth of productivity in the long run is dependent upon improvements in the quantity and quality of capital available and upon the quality of the match between workers and their jobs. The former can be secured by investment in physical plant and machinery; the latter refers to the need for education and training—investment in human capital. These issues form the subject-matter of the next section.

2.7. Capital Stock, Investment, and Saving

Growth of Capital Stock

Despite reductions in net investment in times of recession and high real interest rates, the value of the physical capital stock employed by UK industry, determined as it is by long-run considerations, has increased steadily over time. Between 1973 and 1994, for example, gross capital stock increased at a rate of 2.5% per year (at compound rates). This is in line with what we would expect of a growing economy. Since the capital stock normally grows faster than the labour force, the result is an increase in the capital/labour ratio over time. During 1973–94, for example, the UK's capital/labour ratio increased from £61,000 to £104,000 (at 1990 prices). The continuous increase in the capital/labour ratio means that consumption and investment can both increase simultaneously as the economy's productive capacity expands.

The increase in the stock of physical capital is paralleled by an increase in the stock of human capital. As an example of this, we can cite the rise in the numbers of full-time students in higher education in the UK over recent years. In just three years from 1989 to 1992, the numbers increased by over 50%. This represents a substantial increase in the flow of new graduates onto the jobs market. It will, however, be about 40 years before the full labour-market impact of this increase is observed, since only then will workers who did not enter higher education prior to the expansion of the system retire from the labour force. According to this measure, the human capital stock of the labour force is set to increase for decades to come, provided participation in higher education is maintained at its current levels or indeed increased. Nevertheless, the rate of participation of young people in higher education remains lower in the UK than in many other developed economies (see Table 2.11).

Human capital should not be measured simply in terms of academic qualifications. The quantity and quality of provision of vocational education is also an important issue.[10] Consumption benefits of education aside, the appropriate level of investment in each type of human capital within an economy should be determined according to the same rules as are advocated by economists in determining investment in physical capital: 'invest at the margin if the present value of benefits offsets the present value of costs'.

Table 2.11. Percentage of relevant age group entering full-time tertiary education in various countries, 1991

Country	
USA	65
Japan	53
France	44
Germany	43
UK	28

Source: OECD, *Education at a Glance* (Paris: OECD, 1993), Table P15.

[10] S. Prais, *Productivity, Education and Training: Britain and other Countries Compared* (London: NIESR, 1995).

Distribution of the Capital Stock

The distribution of capital across individuals within society has changed markedly in recent years. One example of this concerns the distribution of human capital. The increased human capital stock documented earlier in this section represents a move towards mass further and higher education. The elitism of the past, whereby a relatively small proportion of individuals were helped to gain high-level qualifications, has been eroded.

The increased percentage of people who own (or who are buying) their own homes is another manifestation of a widening distribution of the ownership of capital. As recently as 1971, just under 50% of households owned (or were buying) their own homes. By 1981 the proportion had risen slightly, to 54%, but by 1991 some 67% were living in homes which they owned outright or mortgaged.

Just as the distribution of human and housing capital has become wider, so has the distribution of productive physical capital. While only 7% of the population of Great Britain owned shares in 1981, by 1992 this proportion had increased to 22%. This is, of course, primarily the consequence of the large-scale privatizations of the 1980s. In many cases the companies being privatized were sold at a price below the market valuation, thus making the share offers particularly attractive. In addition, the allocation of shares was in some cases rationed so that only those individuals applying for small numbers of shares would be successful. While a substantial minority of people now own shares, however, the proportion of shares held by individuals (as opposed to institutions) has fallen dramatically. In 1963 some 50% of all shares were in the hands of individuals and only 20% were owned by pension funds and insurance companies. Within 30 years these percentages have been reversed. So while more individuals own shares than ever before, the value of the shares held by the average shareholder has fallen in relation to the size of the market. There is still some way to go before the goal of a property-owning democracy is achieved.

Savings

During the 1980s the ratio of savings to personal disposable income fell dramatically (see Fig. 2.6)—so much so that the rise in consumers' expenditure between 1987 and 1988 exceeded the rise in personal disposable income by 1.7 billion, implying a marginal propensity to consume in excess of unity. As noted earlier, the rapid increase in house prices (due largely to speculation), enabled many consumers to borrow large sums using their homes as security. Owing to the changes noted above, the banking sector must now compete, much more so than in the past, with the housing and equity markets as a

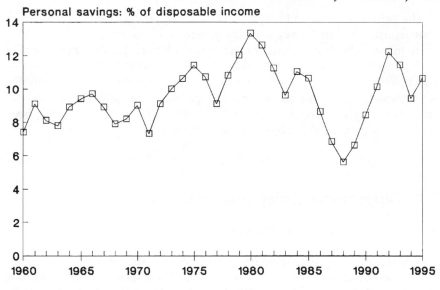

Fig. 2.6. Personal savings ratio in the UK: personal savings as a percentage of disposable income, 1960–1995

Source: Economic Trends.

potential depository for individuals' wealth. These issues are dealt with in greater detail in Chapter 6.

The personal saving ratio should not be confused with the national saving ratio. The latter includes the business sector and the government sector as well as households. As is evident from Table 2.12, gross national saving varies considerably between countries, with Japan far outstripping other industrialized nations with a gross saving rate of around one-third of GDP. Japan's saving rate reflects its continuous surplus in the balance of trade, and it is likely that social custom and practice is a causal factor. The UK's relatively low national saving rate is much more in line with the USA than with its major partners in the EU.

Table 2.12. Gross national saving as a percentage of GDP in various countries

Country	1976–9	1980–4	1985–9	1990–3
US	20.2	19.0	16.6	15.2
Japan	32.1	30.8	32.9	34.1
Germany	22.4	21.0	23.9	22.2
France	24.5	20.5	20.4	20.2
Italy	26.1	22.7	20.9	18.4
UK	17.8	17.0	16.1	13.4
EU	22.7	20.2	20.8	19.8

Source: OECD, Economic Outlook, 1995.

The privatization of industry and of housing capital is symptomatic of a change, over the last 15 years, in the government's perception of its role in economic activity. It is a matter of contention whether the Thatcherite goal of 'rolling back the frontiers of the state' has been achieved. While the government plays as important a part as ever in the workings of the UK economy, the way in which it performs that role has changed very markedly. The influence of its actions on the performance and structure of the economy has been dramatic, and forms the subject of the next section.

2.8. Government Expenditure and Taxation

Privatization and Quasi-Markets

The privatization programme has transferred to the private sector many companies which were formerly nationalized. These include British Telecom, British Gas, British Steel, British Petroleum, British Airways, British Aerospace, the coal industry, and the electricity and water companies. These privatizations are discussed in Chapter 9. In other areas, the government has subjected public sector activities to competitive pressures by various means. These include competitive tendering, where services (ranging from cleaning to consultancy) are bought by public sector organizations (such as the health service, the civil service, local authorities, schools, and colleges) for the best price offered in the private sector. Even in the provision of public goods, a quasi-market can be established in which the government (acting on behalf of final consumers) buys services from private sector providers.[11] For instance, the National Health Service may buy health care from BUPA. This practice does not necessarily reduce government spending, but its advocates argue that it reduces costs while at the same time promoting innovation and competition, and it reduces the number of employees who are directly on the government's payroll.

Sources of Tax Revenue

The Conservative Government elected in 1979 placed great emphasis, in its rhetoric at least, on the supply side of the economy. A major part of the government's effort has accordingly concerned the manner in which the tax and benefits system affects incentives to work. Since income tax reduces take-home pay, its imposition might reduce the number of hours a typical worker chooses to work. Indeed, in extreme cases, income tax might even discourage individuals from working at all. This is especially the case if, by working, the individual loses entitlement to social security benefits. (Benefits are discussed

---

[11] J. Le Grand, 'Quasi-Markets and Social Policy', *Economic Journal*, 101 (1991), 1256–67.

in Chapter 10.) Taxes on expenditure, such as the Value-Added Tax, do not suffer this disadvantage. Accordingly, while reducing the marginal rates of income tax, the government has increased substantially both the coverage of VAT and the rate at which it is charged. In 1978–9, the basic rate of income tax was 33%; it is now (in 1996) 24%. In 1979 the standard rate of VAT was 8%; it is now 17½%. Further evidence of the shift from direct to indirect taxation is evident from Table 2.13. This shows that, as a percentage of the government's total cash receipts, income tax fell from 30 to 27% between 1980 and 1994; over the same period, the corresponding figures for VAT show an increase from 15 to 21%.

Although, as we have seen, taxes on income have a distortionary impact on work incentives, they do have one important advantage over indirect taxes. Income taxes can be used to redistribute income from the rich to the poor. This is an attractive feature if importance is attached to equity as well as to economic efficiency. The contribution of the tax and benefit policies of the last 15 years to the widening of the income distribution is discussed in Chapter 12. It is not possible to make a value-free judgement about the appropriate spread of this distribution, and therefore about the appropriate balance between direct and indirect taxes. Society solves conundrums of this sort—however imperfectly—by conducting general elections in which the electorate can choose between parties with different views about the desirable distribution of income.

The Government Budget Deficit

The Public Sector Borrowing Requirement (PSBR) is charted in Fig. 2.7, which shows that a budget deficit is the norm. There have been exceptions during boom years, such as 1987–90, when tax revenues are high and government spending on welfare benefits is relatively low. This is not, however, untypical compared to other countries, as is evident from Table 2.14.

If investment and savings move in tandem, then there is a close relationship

Table 2.13. Central government tax revenues due to direct taxes and indirect taxes

Year	Taxes on income (% of total cash receipts)		Customs & Excise (% of total cash receipts)		Total cash receipts	
	Total	Income tax[a]	Total	VAT[b]	1994 (£b)[a] prices	% of GDP at factor cost
1960	40.0	20.4	34.7	—	79.1	29.6
1970	41.4	32.2	28.5	—	140.0	40.6
1980	38.7	30.4	28.2	14.9	172.6	39.8
1990	39.1	27.7	29.8	17.7	226.0	41.4
1994	34.9	27.0	33.4	20.5	230.8	39.9

[a] Income tax figures include surtax to 1980.
[b] VAT was introduced on entry to the EU in 1973.
Source: NIBB.

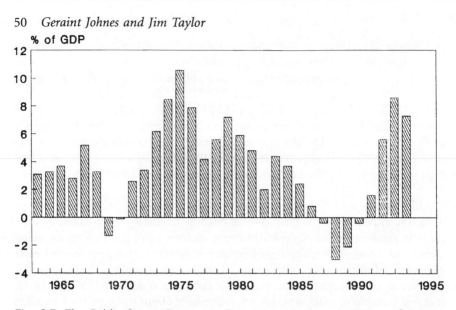

Fig. 2.7. The Public Sector Borrowing Requirement as a percentage of GDP at factor cost, 1963–1994

Source: Economic Trends.

between the PSBR and the balance of payments on current account. A fall in net exports must be accompanied by an increase in government borrowing if product market equilibrium is to be maintained. As we saw earlier, a high current account deficit can dampen economic growth through its impact on the interest rate and on expected future tax rates. A high PSBR can have exactly the same effect. It is for this reason that the government has been anxious to reduce the scale of public sector borrowing in the last few years. In spite of an intention to get public expenditure down since the early 1980s, it is clear from Table 2.15 that this policy has not succeeded. The proportion of GDP accounted for by government spending in the UK, however, is considerably less than for its major partners in the EU.

Table 2.14. General government financial balances as a percentage of GDP in various countries

Country	1978–9	1980–4	1985–9	1990–5
US	0.3	−2.5	−2.5	−2.9
Japan	−5.1	−3.5	0.6	−0.3
Germany	−2.5	−2.9	−1.3	−2.7
France	−1.5	−2.1	−2.1	−4.2
Italy	−10.3	−10.8	−11.2	−9.5
UK	−3.9	−3.1	−0.9	−4.8

Source: OECD, Economic Outlook.

Table 2.15. General government total outlays as a percentage of GDP in various countries

Country	1978–9	1980–4	1985–9	1990–5
US	30.0	32.9	33.0	34.0
Japan	30.6	32.7	31.7	33.8
Germany	47.3	48.2	46.2	48.2
France	44.8	49.7	50.7	52.7
Italy	42.0	46.7	50.7	53.9
UK	41.2	44.3	40.5	42.0

Source: OECD, *Economic Outlook.*

2.9. Conclusion

The change in the UK's industrial structure over the last three decades represents a response to changes in the international economy. The shift from manufacturing to services has necessitated rapid adjustment in the product and labour markets. That the forces of the free market can be so effective in securing major structural change in a relatively short time is impressive. But the change has not been painless. The return of high unemployment has caused immense misery to millions of people, and indicates that the costs of structural change have been borne disproportionately by a relatively small proportion of the population, while others have prospered. In terms of economic efficiency, it is right that an economy should be sufficiently flexible to adapt rapidly to changing circumstances. It is also desirable that the benefits and costs of change should be equitably distributed across the population. This is the challenge that remains to be met.

Further reading

Cairncross, A., *The British Economy since 1945* (Oxford: Blackwell, 1992).

Floud, R. and McCloskey, D. (eds.), *The Economic History of Britain since 1700. iii, 1939–1992* (Cambridge: Cambridge University Press, 1994).

3

THE UK AND THE EUROPEAN UNION

H. W. ARMSTRONG AND M. J. ARTIS

3.1. Introduction

The UK government has had an ambivalent attitude to the EU for many years. Nevertheless, accession in 1973 marked the beginning of a period of fundamental change for the UK economy, a process which will continue in the foreseeable future as further integration occurs. The UK government exerts influence on the nature and pace of integration through its participation in the policy-setting institutions of the EU and through the process by which the budget is set. The institutions and the budget process are considered first in this chapter, before turning to the implications of integration for the UK economy.

The Institutions of the EU

The institutions of the EU are very distinctive. Almost all of the policies of the EU are operated on a day-to-day basis by the member state government bureaucracies, including regional and local government. Indeed, this reliance on lower tiers of government to deliver policies, rather than setting up a strong EU secretariat in each country, is now enshrined in the principle of subsidiarity, which requires that powers be vested in the lower tiers of government wherever possible.

Policy legislation is made by four main institutions. The European Commission is the civil service of the EU. Prior to 1995 it was headed by seventeen Commissioners appointed by the member states. The UK is represented by Leon Brittan and Neil Kinnock. The entry of Sweden, Finland, and Austria in 1995 has led to an increase to twenty Commissioners. Commissioners are allocated policy portfolios, and the bureaucracy of the main policy areas is divided into directorate-generals (DGs).

Traditionally, the size of the civil service supporting these DGs has been small, often compared to that of a UK local authority. It has continuously expanded in recent years, however, as the responsibilities and budget of the EU have expanded. The Commission is far from being a passive bureaucracy. Its importance lies in its power to initiate new legislation and prior to 1995 under the leadership of Jacques Delors it proved to be a formidable engine of change, making hundreds of proposals each year. The main instruments of decision-making are Regulations, Directives, and Decisions. Regulations are immediately legally binding in full on all of the member states and are the most important of the instruments. Directives are also binding, but are more flexible instruments in that while the goal is set, the member states are left discretion on how to achieve it. Decisions apply to specific individuals, firms, or member states. The Commission also generates a constant stream of non-binding recommendations and opinions.

The Council of Ministers is the most powerful of the institutions of the EU and effectively controls EU legislation. Membership is made up of ministerial-level representatives of the member states. The most serious problem facing the Council of Ministers has concerned the voting system. The Council makes its decisions either unanimously, by a simple majority (44 of the 87 votes), or by a weighted voting system in which the smaller member states are protected (qualified majority voting—QMV—requiring 62 of the 87 votes with a blocking minority of 26 votes). The transition from unanimity, which worked quite well when there were only a few member states, to majority voting has been a turbulent one. The Single Market, introduced between 1989 and 1992, has led to a significant increase in the use of QMV, but some decisions are still subject to a unanimity rule. Presidency of the Council is rotated between the member states on a six-monthly basis. The Council has its own support staff, together with the Committee of Permanent Representatives (COREPER) made up from senior representatives of each member state's civil service.

The European Parliament, despite its steady growth in power, remains a surprisingly weak EU institution, giving rise to a great debate on the nature of the 'democratic deficit' in Europe. Prior to 1995 there were 567 MEPs, rising to 626 (87 for the UK) with the entry of Sweden, Finland, and Austria. Although much of its influence is brought to bear through its debates and opinion-forming role, the Parliament also has some significant powers. Traditionally these have included the right to be consulted on legislation and veto power over the budget. Since the 1992 Treaty of Union, the Parliament also has powers on the choice of Commissioners and President.

Finally, there is the European Court of Justice. This is staffed by judges and advocates-general. It plays a key role in interpreting EU legislation and in overseeing its implementation. It has important powers not only over individuals and firms, but also over member state governments themselves. Since the Treaty of Union there has also been a Court of Auditors.

The Budget of the EU

The EU budget is determined annually and is, not surprisingly, an issue of enormous importance to all of the member states. Table 3.1 sets out a summary of the 1995 budget expenditure commitments, together with the preliminary draft 1996 budget. Some EU expenditures, notably agricultural spending, are given priority ('compulsory spending'), as can be seen from the items at the foot of Table 3.1. The table shows that agricultural policy expenditures remain at over half of the full budget, with farm price support spending alone (i.e. spending on 'markets and accompanying measures' in the first row of Table 3.1) at 36.897 billion ECU in 1995 in a total budget of 79.845 billion ECU. Other very large items are the three main structural funds (European Regional Development Fund—ERDF, European Social Fund—ESF, and the Guidance Section of the European Agricultural Guidance and Guarantee Fund—EAGGF).

The expenditure figures in Table 3.1 need to be seen in the context of the financial deal struck by the member states at a Summit of Heads of State at Edinburgh in December 1991. This was the financial package designed to seal the Maastricht Treaty. The Edinburgh Summit envisaged total expenditure

Table 3.1. The general budget of the EU (ECU billion at current prices), 1995 and 1996

Budget heading	1995	1996 (preliminary draft)
1. Agriculture: markets and accompanying measures	36.897	40.828
2. Structural operations		
EAGGF—Guidance	3.567	3.772
Fisheries sector	0.451	0.450
ERDF	10.814	11.884
ESF	6.761	7.146
Community Initiatives	2.224	3.030
Transitional measures and innovation	0.252	0.297
EEA financial mech.	0.108	0.108
Cohesion Fund	2.152	2.444
3. Internal policies		
Research	2.991	3.228
Other agricultural	0.216	0.181
Trans-European Networks	0.381	0.445
Other	1.464	1.412
4. External action		
Central and Eastern Europe	1.172	1.235
Food/Humanitarian Aid	0.858	0.860
Other	2.846	3.062
5. Administration	3.999	4.132
6. Reserves	1.146	1.152
Grand Total	79.845	86.368
of which:		
(a) compulsory	40.392	43.416
(b) non-compulsory	39.453	42.951

Source: *Bulletin of the European Union*, 7/8 (1995), table 14.

commitments rising from 69 billion ECU in 1993 to 84 billion ECU in 1999 (in constant 1992 prices). However, it was envisaged that agricultural price-support spending would fall from 51% to 46% of the total by 1999. Other types of spending would rise, with the structural funds being seen as the major beneficiaries rising from 31% to 36% of the total budget.

EU revenues are also evolving rapidly. Prior to 1970 the EU raised its revenues wholly from member state contributions. Since 1970 the EU has had its 'own resources' in the form of (*a*) levies on agricultural imports (*b*) import duties on other goods, and (*c*) a share of VAT receipts (initially equivalent to the yield of a 1% VAT rate, increased to 1.4% in 1984). Following agreement on the Delors I proposal in 1988 there has also been (*d*) a contribution (the so-called 'fourth resource') based on the size of GNP.

The UK has had a continual problem arising from its inherent tendency to be a net contributor. In the past this has been largely the result of the fact that the agriculture sector in the UK is relatively small, which has meant that receipts from the main spending policy have been relatively low. A series of special arrangements, designed to limit the UK net contribution, have therefore been in existence since 1975. These were most notably strengthened in 1984 under arrangements negotiated by Mrs Thatcher. Table 3.2 shows the UK's gross contributions, gross receipts, and net contributions to the EU budget between 1991 and 1995. Contributions are dominated by the customs duties and VAT revenues collected in the UK and paid over to the EU. Gross receipts are dominated by agricultural fund spending in the UK (EAGGF) and by the various structural funds, of which the regional fund (ERDF) is increasingly important. Overall, the UK remains a substantial net contributor, to the tune of 3.998 billion ECU in 1995.

The EU budget will continue to be a source of continuous disagreement. Problems of fraud, over-spending on agriculture policy, and the demands which extension of membership to Central and Eastern European countries will bring, are all looming issues. In this debate, however, it must be borne in mind just how far the EU budget is from what one would expect in a genuinely federal system of government. The EU budget amounts to only around 1.2% of the annual combined GDP of the EU and is dwarfed by the taxation and spending of the member state governments. The EU also lacks many of the powers which, say, the federal government of the USA has, such as a central income tax system.

3.2. The UK Economy and the EU

The UK economy is one of the 'Big Four' of the countries of the EU, whether measured by population or GNP, as is clear from Figs. 3.1 and 3.2. In terms of population Germany (including the newly incorporated former East Germany) was easily the largest in 1995, with nearly 82 million inhabitants, followed by the UK (58.6 million), France (58.1 million), and Italy (57.4 million). The next most populous of the EU member countries is Spain, with nearly 40 million inhabitants. Fig. 3.1 displays the population data for each of the EU member

Table 3.2. UK contributions to and receipts from the EU budget 1991–1994 (ECU million)

	1991	1992	1993	1994	1995
Contributions					
Agricultural and sugar import levies	28	280	256	260	267
Customs duties	2181	2123	2254	2321	2418
VAT—own resources (before abatement)	5423	5934	6379	5414	5889
Fourth resource payments	1160	1273	2067	3024	2227
VAT and Fourth Resource Adjustments	−768	−431	−697	−1728	371
UK Abatement of VAT	−3563	−2562	−3261	−2230	−1873
Total Contributions	4721	6615	6996	7061	9299
Receipts					
EAGGF Guarantee Sn.	2258	2242	2765	2902	3503
Stock Depreciation	137	131	0	0	0
EAGGF Guidance Sn.	117	92	134	67	90
ERDF	528	757	546	786	831
ESF	883	595	756	414	849
Other receipts	23	34	26	33	28
Total Receipts	3944	3851	4228	4203	5301
Net Contribution	777	2764	2768	2858	3998

Notes:
EAGGF=European Agricultural Guarantee and Guidance Fund; ERDF=European Regional Development Fund; ESF=European Social Fund.
Import duties and levies are collected by the UK and paid over to the EU (net of 10% for collection costs). The Fourth Resource payments are contributions by the member states to the EU budget based on the size of their GNP.
'Receipts' refer only to UK public sector receipts and not payments made to private individuals and firms by the EU (NB costs imposed on private individuals or firms are also ignored in this table).
Figures for 1995 are estimates.
Source: Paymaster General, *Statement on the 1995 EC Budget*, Command Paper 2424, April 1995 (London: HMSO), Table 3.

countries; the figure provides a comparison of the population sizes of the EU with the US and Japan. The size of the EU market, measured in population terms, is clearly the largest of the three.

Of course, market size is not just a matter of population but also of wealth and the level of economic activity. Gross Domestic Product (GDP) is a measure of the latter; though controversial as a measure of economic well-being or welfare, GDP is a reasonable measure of economic output. Fig. 3.2 provides a comparison of the GDP of the EU economies in 1995, based on purchasing power standard (PPS) estimates. These estimates are more reliable for cross-country comparative purposes than figures based on market exchange rates: since exchange rates can often change by as much as 10% (and sometimes even more) in the space of a year, using exchange rates as the basis for comparing one country's GDP with another's can easily be misleading. The PPS approach attempts to avoid these problems.[1]

[1] In the PPS approach, the basic assumption is that the value of output of the same type of good in different countries is the same. A 'Big Mac' in London is worth the same as a 'Big Mac' in Berlin or Paris. The ratio of Big Mac sterling prices to French franc prices or DM prices is less variable than the market exchange rate of the £ in FF or DM. The EU's statisticians employ a generalization of the Big Mac principle to construct their PPS estimates of GDP.

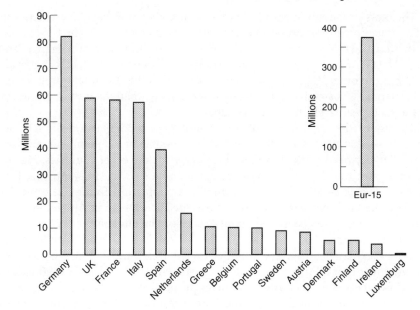

Fig. 3.1. Population figures for members of the European Union, 1995 (000s)

Source: CEC, *European Economy: Annual Economic Report for 1995*, no. 59.

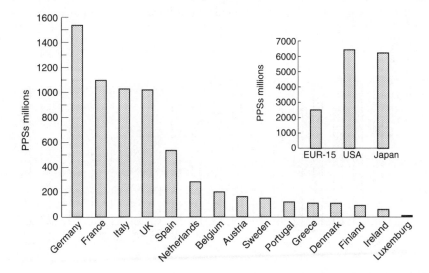

Fig. 3.2. GDP at current market prices for members of the European Union, 1995 (in PPSs)

Source: CEC, *European Economy: Annual Economic Report for 1995*, no. 59.

The units of measurement used in the figures shown in Fig. 3.2 are fictitious 'PPS' units; the important point is the comparisons they yield. The UK appears as the fourth largest economy on this measure, behind Germany, France, and Italy. The German economy, notably, is reckoned to be nearly half as big again as any of the other Big Four. The Figure also shows that the total output of the EU economy was smaller in 1995—by some 3–4%—than the output of the US, but a good deal larger than that of Japan.

Because of the UK's relatively large population, a comparison of GDP per head shows that the UK is well down the league-table of EU member countries, with GDP per head a little less than the average for the other countries. Fig. 3.3 demonstrates this. The three most recent members of the EU—Austria, Finland and Sweden—add about 6% to the EU's population count and some 7% to EU GDP. GDP per head was well above the EU average in Austria in 1995, some 5% below in Sweden and about 8% below in Finland.

The development of trade within the Union is a striking feature of the economic experience of every member except Denmark. Fig. 3.4 shows how the proportion of member countries' exports sent to intra-Union destinations has grown between 1958 and 1993. The proportion for the UK by 1993, at 49.3%, is not far out of line with the proportion found for other members of the Big Four (Germany: 47.6; France: 59.8; Italy: 53.3) having grown from a smaller initial base. The very high proportion of exports going to intra-Union destinations from Belgium and the Netherlands is very noticeable—but this proportion, related to the entrepôt role of these economies, was already over 50% in 1958. A similar story could be told for imports. Aggregating over the EU as a whole, in 1992 over 56% of exports were intra-trade, compared to only just over 37% in 1988. Data like these are simultaneously taken as evidence of

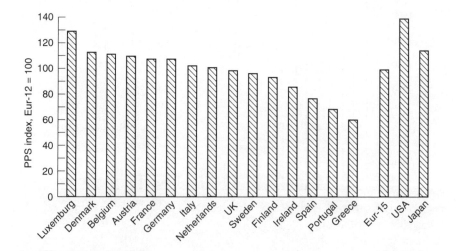

Fig. 3.3. GDP per capita for members of the European Union, 1995 (in PPSs)

Source: CEC, *European Economy: Annual Economic Report for 1995*, no. 59.

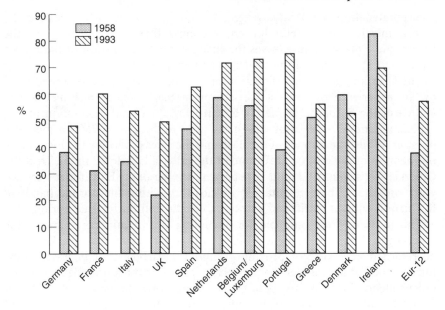

Fig. 3.4. Intra-EU trade as a percentage of total exports: 1958 and 1993

Source: CEC, *European Economy: Annual Economic Report for 1995, no. 60.*

the strength of trade creation in the Union and as evidence of the development of a 'Fortress Europe'. At the level of the EU as a whole, the European countries are probably as 'closed' as the US and Japan. These latter two countries imported 12.9 and 7.3% of their respective GDPs; the total for the EU countries individually was 26.2%—but around a half of this was intra-Union trade.

3.3. The UK and Economic and Monetary Union

In the Treaty of Union negotiated in Maastricht in December 1991 the member states, with the exception of the UK and Denmark, committed themselves to forming an economic and monetary union, that is, creating an area in which a single currency would be used. European Monetary Union (EMU) had been a declared objective at earlier stages of the formation of the Union, but the Maastricht negotiations set out a timetable, criteria for entry into EMU, and statutes for the European Central Bank, which would be charged with the formation of monetary policy for the single currency. Within the UK, the objective of monetary union has never been enthusiastically embraced and this reserve expressed itself in a formal opt-out clause for the UK being incorporated into the Treaty. Where, for other countries which signed the Treaty, meeting the criteria for entry obliges them to participate in the Union, the 'opt-out' clause leaves the final say to the discretion of the British Parliament at the time of the final decision on participation.

The UK's long-standing reservations about monetary union were reinforced by the experience of being a participant in the exchange rate mechanism (ERM) of the European Monetary System (EMS). A brief description of this experience and of the relationship of the ERM to the goal of EMU is therefore in order. Whilst the statutes of the EMS and the rules governing the ERM make no mention of the goal of EMU, one of the criteria laid down in the Treaty of Union is that a country should have been a member of the ERM for at least two years and should have maintained its currency within the normal bands of fluctuation without strain and without a devaluation during that period.

The most obvious rationale for including this requirement among the criteria for entry into monetary union is that participation in the ERM can be regarded as a kind of proving ground for participation in EMU. ERM membership, at least under the pre-1993 regime, meant substantially forgoing independence in monetary policy, just as in EMU, when monetary policy would be made by a European Central Bank. The ERM is an arrangement whereby member countries undertake to maintain their bilateral exchange rates within a band, until September 1993, usually of $\pm 2\frac{1}{4}\%$ around a central parity. From September 1993 that band was greatly widened to $\pm 15\%$, with the aim of deterring speculation. Most countries of the Union had participated in the ERM from the inception of the EMS in 1979, with the principal exception of the UK. With the passage of time, however, the ERM came to prove itself an attractive proposition to UK policy-makers. In particular, it appeared that membership of the ERM offered a way to control inflation on a sustainable basis. The dominant country in the ERM was Germany; with exchange rates (quasi) fixed against the DM, other countries would 'import' Germany's low inflation rate. The UK's adverse inflation experience in the mid–late 1980s made membership of the ERM attractive. The UK joined the system in October 1990 with bands of 6% around the central parity. It was forced out in the speculative crisis of September 1992, along with the Italian lira.

The failure of the UK to stay the pace seems to have been due to a combination of factors. First, the business cycle in the UK was out of phase with that in Germany. As a result while Germany wanted, for domestic reasons, high interest rates, the UK wanted low interest rates. Second, economic forecasters in the UK erred in not fully recognizing the differences in phase of the two cycles and persisted in wrongly forecasting an imminent upturn in the UK economy throughout 1991 and the first eight months of 1992. More realistic forecasts might have led the UK government to arrange an orderly devaluation within the system at an earlier date. Third, the UK joined at too high an exchange rate. Speculators, sensing that the UK government needed lower interest rates than were compatible with continued participation in the ERM, seeing the continued frustration of hopes for a recovery, and having already witnessed the departure of the Italian lira from the system on 12 September, began to sell sterling in large volumes. The Bank of England bought sterling in exchange for DM on a massive scale, with assistance from the Bundesbank. Despite this intervention, however, the pressure continued and sterling was withdrawn from the ERM on 17 September. To the public in the UK the attempt to hang on in the ERM had not only cost a lot of foreign reserves but had postponed the reduction of interest rates and the consequent recovery in output or employment by a year or more. A return to the ERM—which would now take place in the more relaxed wider band of ±15%—is required for EMU. Although the new ERM, with its now much wider bands, represents much less of a risk than the earlier system, a policy of returning to the ERM is still likely to be politically hard to sell in the UK.

The other criteria laid down in the Treaty represent little problem for the UK: they include the two fiscal criteria (a 3% ceiling on the ratio of the budget deficit to GNP; a 60% ceiling on the ratio of government debt to GNP) and criteria relating to the inflation rate (which should be within $1\frac{1}{2}$% of the three best performers) and interest rates (within 2% of the three best inflation performers).

The UK's position with respect to the fiscal criteria contrasts favourably with that of many countries which are keen to participate in EMU: this is illustrated below and discussed in Chapter 7. The UK is also in a good position to qualify in respect of the other criteria. Given the circumstances of other countries it now appears that the relevant part of the timetable laid out in the Treaty of Union is the provision that monetary union should go ahead by 1 January 1999 at latest, on the basis of that set of countries—not necessarily a majority—which meet the criteria by that time. This could still include the UK provided that the UK rejoins the ERM by January 1997 and successfully maintains its position thereafter.

How far is the sceptical position of the UK on EMU justified? Although political arguments are clearly fundamental, economic analysis does reveal why the UK might be less enthusiastic on economic grounds alone, than her continental EU partners. The benefits of having a single currency in place of several different currencies pertain to the removal of the transaction costs involved in changing from one currency to another (these benefits have been estimated at around 0.3–0.4% of EU GDP) and the removal of exchange rate uncertainty. No reliable quantification of the effect of the latter can be made, but it seems likely that a reduction in exchange rate uncertainty would lead to a more efficient location of industry in Europe, probably involving more regional specialization. The cost of participating in a monetary union is essentially the cost of not being able to use an independent monetary policy (as with a flexible exchange rate) to deal with adverse shocks (Fig. 3.5 illustrates the argument that a flexible exchange rate can act as a shock absorber for adverse shocks). On this count, there is now evidence that the UK's business cycle is more closely associated with that of the US and less closely associated with that of Germany, than is the case for most other European Union members; and that the macroeconomic shocks hitting the UK are more idiosyncratic than those hitting the core countries of the Union, which tend to be highly synchronous. These facts might lead one to believe that the UK would not be well off in a monetary union with the principal continental countries; a common European monetary policy might suit Germany or France well enough, but not be suitable for the UK. Over time, the position could well change as the process of integration continues, for this will increase the benefits and may also reduce the costs (if integration makes the UK more like the other EU economies and hence subject to the same shocks and business cycle influences).

3.4. The UK and the Single Market

The Single European Act (SEA) of 1986 marked an important step in the realization, in full, of the objectives of the Treaty of Rome. In the preceding

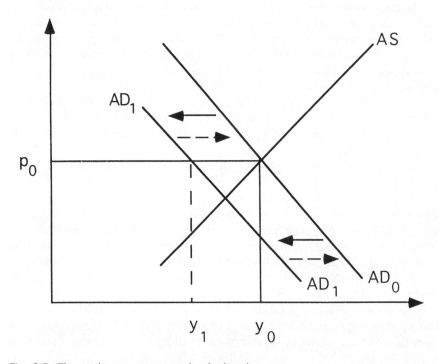

Fig. 3.5. The exchange rate as a shock absorber
A deflationary demand shock disturbs the initial equilibrium at p_0, y_0, driving the aggregate demand schedule to AD_1. If domestic wages and prices are fixed, output will decline to y_1. A devaluation of the exchange rate can increase aggregate demand, shifting the AD-schedule back to its original position.

years much had been done to bring about freer trade within Europe, with the abolition for example of all internal tariffs. The aims of the Single European Act were to take this process further, removing the large number of non-tariff barriers remaining, and taking steps to ensure the free movement of persons and of capital within the Union as well as that of goods. The Act was a response to the perception that the European market still remained fragmented and that, as a result, European industry was not so competitive as it should be and was not able to operate with the optimum size of plant.

Table 3.3 sets out the areas in which directives were needed to realize the Single European Market. The removal of physical barriers to the movement of persons and goods refers to the abolition of customs frontier formalities leading to the goal of passport-free travel within the Union; the removal of technical barriers to the free circulation of goods refers especially to the need to ensure that national standards of safety and quality in goods do not prevent free trade. The procurement policies of public sector agencies traditionally displayed a tendency to favour 'home-produced' goods and services, sometimes favouring a 'national champion': the SEA provided for a levelling of the playing-field in this respect, with open tendering and other arrangements designed to remove the protectionist element in traditional policies. Mutual recognition of professional qualifications is called for—among other items—to promote the free movement of labour within the Union. The SEA also provided for a freeing-up of the market in services, especially financial services, accompanied by the removal of controls over the flow of capital

Table 3.3. Classification of EC directives for the completion of the internal European market

---

1. The removal of physical barriers:

   (a) Those pertaining to the control of trade in goods;
   (b) Those pertaining to the movement of individuals.

2. The removal of technical barriers:

   (a) Those pertaining to the free movement of goods:
   Standard policies;
   Sectoral proposals relating to: (i) motor vehicles; (ii) tractors and agricultural machines; (iii) food law; (iv) pharmaceuticals and high-technology medicines; (v) chemical products; (vi) construction and construction products; (vii) other items;
   (b) Public procurement;
   (c) Free movement of labour and the professions;
   (d) The Common Market for services: (i) financial services (i.e. banking, insurance and securities markets); (ii) transport; and (iii) new technologies and services;
   (e) Capital movements within Europe;
   (f) Creation of suitable conditions for European co-operation;
   (g) The application of Community barriers.

3. The removal of fiscal barriers:

   (a) VAT;
   (b) Excise duties.

Source: G. McKenzie and A. J. Venables (eds.), *The Economics of the Single European Act* (London: Macmillan, 1991).

between the member states of the Union. Finally, as the table shows, the SEA calls for steps to be taken to adjust ('harmonize') rates of indirect taxation so that fiscal barriers will no longer be a significant deterrent to trade. All of these objectives appealed to the liberal free-trading tradition in Britain and the SEA was strongly supported by the British government.

Estimates produced by the European Commission of the eventual effects of the implementation of the SEA were large. The Commission's view that the SEA would eventually result in gains of over 6% of EU GDP, have proved, not surprisingly, controversial. Table 3.4 details the composition of the gains perceived: a large contribution was expected to be made from the greater exploitation of economies of scale made possible by the effective increase in the size of the market and by a decline in 'X-inefficiency'—i.e. a reduction in slackness and consequently in unit costs of production.

The controversy over the size of the gains attributed to the SEA programme essentially reflects a disbelief, on the part of the sceptics, that the fragmentation of the European market (itself not denied) is a product of the type of barriers identified in the SEA programme. That fragmentation could equally well reflect differences in tastes and preferences tied to the cultural diversity of Europe. On this reading, in reality, the gains attributed to the realization of the Single Market are, in some large part, gains that could only be realized with a homogenization of products produced and a reduction in variety; this itself may not be likely to occur quickly and, to the extent that it does, is of questionable benefit.

The timetable of the SEA provided for the Single Market to be completed by the end of 1992—for this reason, the programme is sometimes known as the '1992 project'—but, as Table 3.5 shows, even by mid-May 1995 no country had yet applied 100% of the directives required to realize the Single Market. Despite the broad initial enthusiasm of the British Government for the SEA its implementation has led to consequences not always found to be so congenial by the British Government. The Union's Social Policy arrangements are one example. At the broadest level it was felt that the SEA needed to be accompanied by measures in the social policy field, to counteract the perception that the benefits of the SEA would solely accrue to the business community. The

Table 3.4. Estimates of the economic gains associated with the completion of the internal European market (1985 prices)

Source	% GDP
Cost of barriers affecting trade only	0.3
Cost of barriers affecting all production	2.4
Total direct costs of barriers	2.7
Economies of scale from restructuring and increased competition	2.1
Competition effects on X-inefficiency and monopoly rents	1.6
Total market integration effects	3.7
Total gains	6.4

Source: CEC, 'The Economics of 1992', *European Economy*, 35 (Mar. 1988).

Table 3.5. State of implementation of the internal market White Paper measures: breakdown of situation by member state, 17 May 1995 (%)

Belgium	90.4
Denmark	98.6
France	95.4
Germany	90.0
Greece	86.3
Ireland	89.5
Italy	89.0
Luxemburg	95.9
Netherlands	95.0
Portugal	90.9
Spain	92.7
UK	92.2
EUR 12	92.4

Source: European Commission.

resultant Social Chapter in the Treaty of Union and the UK's negative attitude towards this part of the Treaty is discussed further below. Another consequence has been the emphasis on the objective of Monetary Union: in the minds of many—including the then President of the Commission, Jacques Delors, the full prospective gains of the SEA could only be realized in the context of a single currency, removing exchange rate uncertainty and foreign exchange transactions costs which, after all, can be construed as a barrier to trade.

3.5. The UK and the Key Spending Policies of the EU

The EU is now a many-headed beast. A huge variety of programmes and policies have emerged in recent years. Some, such as environmental policy and transport policy, are clearly destined for a greater role in the future. Others, such as agricultural policy, are under threat and serious attempts are being made to curtail spending. A full examination of all of the EU policies is beyond the scope of this chapter. Instead, attention will be concentrated on the two dominant spending policies: agriculture policy and the structural funds. Between them these two policies accounted for 76% of all EU expenditure in 1995. In each case, having first examined the policy, attention will then be turned to its implications for the UK.

The Common Agricultural Policy

The reasons for the agricultural policy (CAP). The importance of the CAP in the Common Market of the six original member states was partly a reflection of the political 'clout' and economic importance of the agricultural sector in 1958 when the Treaty of Rome was signed, together with basic food availability fears in the aftermath of the Second World War. It must also be recognized that the farming sector faces deep-seated economic problems which would lead to low incomes and large job losses if the sector were left exposed to free-market forces. The main problems faced are:

- the forces of nature mean that actual farm production in a given year can differ enormously from planned output, resulting in very unstable incomes;
- as the EU population has become more prosperous, a diminishing proportion of income is spent on basic foodstuffs, reflecting a low income elasticity of demand for farm products and resulting in a slow growth of farm incomes over time;
- rapid productivity gains and the 'green revolution' in agriculture, combined with the widespread use of subsidies in other parts of the world, such as the USA, have resulted in perennial problems of excess world supply and low prices;
- basic foodstuffs exhibit low price elasticities of demand, giving rise to a steep decline in farm prices as supply increases over time.

The Treaty of Rome committed the fledgling Common Market to a strong agricultural policy. Article 39(1) spelled out clearly the aims of the policy:

1. To increase agricultural productivity. This has certainly been achieved but may well have happened anyway through technological progress.
2. To provide a fair standard of living for those working in the industry. While the CAP has undoubtedly enhanced incomes, those in manufacturing and service industries in the EU have done better over the years since 1958.
3. To stabilize agricultural markets. In this the CAP has certainly been successful.
4. To ensure security of supply. The problem here has, of course, been one of perennial over-supply.
5. To ensure reasonable prices for consumers. The CAP has signally failed to achieve this.

The nature of the CAP.   Governments can help farmers in an enormous variety of ways. One method favoured by the UK prior to its entry to the EU in 1973 involved topping up the price which farmers received for their products by making direct payments per unit of output (a 'deficiency payments' system). Another widely used approach involves protecting farmers from external competition by imposing import levies or import quotas. A third approach involves directly intervening to reduce supplies entering the market (often via purchasing agencies). The agricultural production bought up by the government is then stored (hopefully to be released back into the market when supply is short), destroyed or transformed into some other good such as animal feed, or exported in the form of overseas aid or by giving an export subsidy. A fourth policy involves the transfer of money to farmers in the form of direct subsidies.

Finally, in some cases governments simply impose production quotas on farmers.

The EU agricultural policy which emerged in the years after the Treaty of Rome was a complex one. Arrangements varied from product to product and the failure to establish a common EU currency meant that a complex system of exchange rates ('green currencies') and border taxes and subsidies (monetary compensatory amounts—MCAs) had to be brought in during the 1970s to try to ensure common prices for farm products in each member state.[2]

Despite its day-to-day complexity, EU agriculture policy is still fundamentally a price support (or 'price-floor') policy. Fig. 3.6 illustrates how the CAP operates, by setting a price within the EU (P_d) which is greater than the world price for the agricultural commodity (P_w). Two results inevitably flow from this type of policy. First, farmers respond to the higher prices by expanding supply (while consumers simultaneously cut back their demand) resulting in chronic surpluses of production: in Fig. 3.6 the price support policy increases the surplus from *CD* to *AB*. These added surpluses must be disposed of in some way. They are bought up by intervention agencies. The surpluses are then either stored, destroyed, denatured in some way (e.g. wine to industrial alcohol), given away as foreign aid, or exported (helped along by export subsidies so that they can be off-loaded at lower world prices). A system of

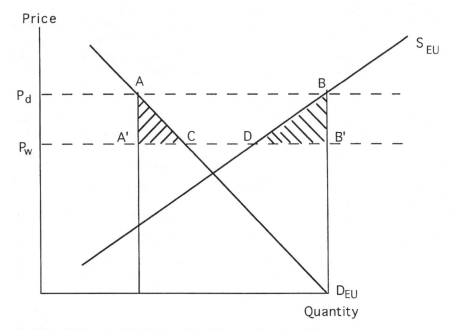

Fig. 3.6. The costs of the EU's Common Agriculture Policy

[2] For a discussion of these see D. Colman and D. Roberts, 'The Common Agricultural Policy', in M. Artis and N. Lee (eds.), *The Economics of the European Union* (Oxford: Oxford University Press, 1994), 96–8.

import levies makes sure that imports from the rest of the world do not drive down the prices which farmers get.

The second inevitable effect of the agricultural price support policy is that it sets up a system of winners and losers within the EU. Taxpayers lose (via the EU budget) since the Guarantee Section of the European Agricultural Guidance and Guarantee Fund (EAGGF) must be used to pick up the tab for intervention buying, storage, and export subsidies. In Fig. 3.6 a measure of the budgetary cost is provided by area $AA'B'B$. Consumers lose because they pay higher prices than they would in a fully free market system with world prices prevailing. This loss can be measured as a loss of consumers' surplus (area P_dP_wCA in the simple case shown in Fig. 3.6). Finally, the farmers and the agribusiness (i.e. producers) gain from the higher prices they enjoy (area P_dP_wDB in Fig. 3.6). Economic analysis indicates that this form of agricultural support gives rise to a net loss of welfare. Deducting the loss of consumers' surplus and the budgetary cost from the gain in producers' surplus leaves a net loss equal to the sum of the two shaded triangles $AA'C$ and $DB'B$.

The problems of the CAP.   The traditional form of CAP which persisted until the 1980s became increasingly criticized as a result of a number of serious problems. The main problems were as follows:

1. The inherent tendency of the policy to produce surpluses proved resistant to repeated attempts to cut it back. The surpluses vary with the degree of protection conferred by the policy, but have been particularly severe for cereals, beef, dairy products, and sugar (from sugar beet). These surpluses proved to be not only unpopular with EU citizens, but also increasingly costly to dispose of.

2. EU consumers gradually became more and more hostile to the higher food prices they have had to bear.

3. Farmers receiving higher prices for products strive to maximize their returns by increasing their total output. Some of the methods the policy encourages create adverse environmental effects. These include the bringing into production of marginal land (e.g. upland areas unsuited to farming, as well as the removal of wetland areas and hedgerows), and the increased use of artificial fertilizers and pesticides.

4. The policy is immensely costly for the EU budget. Typically, in the early decades the CAP absorbed up to three-quarters of the EU budget, with spending being channelled largely through the Guarantee Section of the European Agricultural Guidance and Guarantee Fund (EAGGF). The much smaller Guidance Section of EAGGF, which is used to help in restructuring the farm sector and for investment projects, also adds to budget costs.

5. The widespread use of export subsidies and the giving away as aid of food surpluses has had the detrimental effect of undermining food prices in countries outside the EU. This is a particularly serious problem in developing countries where food deliveries from the EU have undermined the prices received by local farmers, many of whom are already very poor.

6. Because the greatest price protection has been for products such as

cereals, beef, dairy products, and sugar beet, the policy has effectively favoured farmers in the richer northern EU member states. Mediterranean products have been less well protected, yet the Mediterranean farmers are among the EU's poorest.

7. Some member states bear more of the costs of CAP than others. In this respect the UK has been one of the principal losers. Estimating the costs of CAP to a country is a very complex task because in addition to the direct budget cost to the EU budget, consumers in the UK also pay for the policy in the form of higher prices. Table 3.6 shows that the UK has experienced net costs of 3.006 billion ECU. Gains to the UK farming sector of 3.820 billion ECU have been more than offset by higher costs to consumers (4.313 billion ECU) and to UK taxpayers (2.513 billion ECU). Notice that overall the policy has involved a net cost to the EU as a whole of 13.695 billion ECU. The only countries to have enjoyed net benefits from the policy are Ireland, Denmark, and Greece. The producers in all member states (including the UK to the tune of 3.820 billion ECU) are, however, beneficiaries.

The reform of the CAP. In the face of these problems the reform of the CAP became inevitable. The first steps in the reform process took place in a piecemeal fashion in the 1980s. In 1984 attempts were made to rein in the annual price increases for key foodstuffs. In addition, beginning with milk, output quotas were introduced, and attempts were made to control the increasingly complex and costly system of green currencies and MCAs. These changes had only limited effect. In 1988 a new package of reforms was

Table 3.6. Real income effects (gains and losses) arising from the Common Agriculture Policy price support system (ECU million)

	Real income effects			Net gains
	Producer gains	Consumer losses	Budget costs	
Belgium and Luxemburg	859	824	797	−762
Denmark	1072	423	416	233
France	7150	5129	3587	−1566
Germany	4704	4858	4540	−4694
Greece	1108	756	329	23
Ireland	936	330	173	433
Italy	3917	4150	2461	−2694
Netherlands	1758	1172	1161	−575
Portugal	400	516	140	−256
Spain	2895	2513	1213	−831
UK	3820	4313	2513	−3006
EUR-12	28619	24984	17330	−13695

Notes:
 Budget transfers to the EC are distributed among member states according to their VAT contribution.
 Original source is Institute of Agricultural Economics, Copenhagen.
Source: European Commission Directorate-General for Economic and Financial Affairs, 'EU Agricultural Policy for the 21st Century', *European Economy*, 4 (1994), Table 30.

introduced involving an extension of the controls on production, ceilings on the share of the budget devoted to agriculture, and proposals for a 'set-aside' scheme to take land out of production.

Most important of all have been the McSharry Reforms introduced in May 1992. This major reform package was driven not only by the inherent problems of the CAP itself but also as a result of intense pressure from other countries enraged by the effect of the CAP on world agricultural markets. The Uruguay Round negotiations of the GATT proved to be a useful vehicle for pressurizing the EU into new reforms. The McSharry Reforms have taken the form of a combination of cuts in price support with a series of other measures such as production quotas and set-aside schemes designed to reduce over-production. Direct income support for some farmers is also now being used. Whether the reforms succeed in having the desired effect remains to be seen. The CAP remains a major item in the EU budget and EU consumers continue to pay excessively high prices.

The Structural Funds

The EU has three structural funds: the European Regional Development Fund (ERDF), the European Social Fund (ESF), and the Guidance Section of the European Agricultural Guidance and Guarantee Fund (EAGGF). In practice these three funds are closely supported by several other EU financial instruments, notably a new Cohesion Fund set up in the aftermath of the Treaty of Union, the Financial Instrument for Fisheries Guidance (FIFG) designed to help fishing communities, the European Investment Bank (EIB), and the help for coal and steel communities given by the European Coal and Steel Community (ECSC).

The purpose of the structural funds, whose expenditures have been rising rapidly since 1989, is to help firms and individuals to adjust to the rapid pace of integration occurring within the EU. The process of integration inevitably leads to massive structural changes in the economies of the member states. The structural funds are designed to help to smooth the path of this process of change and to 'fire-fight' the many problems for firms and individuals which emerge. The principal goal of the structural funds is to bring about economic and social cohesion. In practice this is to be achieved by tackling five priority objectives:

1. Help for regions whose development is lagging behind. This objective is the responsibility of the ERDF and the ESF working in tandem.
2. Help for regions experiencing industrial decline (ERDF and ESF).
3. Combating long-term unemployment and youth unemployment (ESF alone).
4. Helping workers to adapt to industrial change and new production systems (ESF alone).

5. This objective has two parts:

   5*a*: speeding up the adjustment of agricultural structures (EAGGF- Guidance).

   5*b*: development of rural areas (ERDF, ESF, and EAGGF-Guidance).

With the entry of Sweden, Finland, and Austria a sixth objective has been added: this is designed to allow help to be given to the remote and sparsely populated sub-Arctic areas in Finland and Sweden.

As can be seen, three of the five objectives (1, 2, and 5*b*) are essentially regional *policy* objectives (as is the new sixth Nordic objective). These regional policy aspects of the structural funds will be considered first before turning to the strictly social and agricultural goals (objectives 3, 4, and 5*a*).

Regional policy and the structural funds. Although EU regional policy dates from 1975 when the first ERDF was created, current EU regional policy effectively dates from 1989 when a far-reaching set of reforms was put in place. These reforms were accompanied by a doubling, in real terms, of the size of the budget devoted to regional policy. They were designed to head off regional problems thought likely to arise as a result of the Single Market which was being phased in at that time. The Treaty of Union has led to a further doubling in size of the EU's regional policy budget for the period 1994–9, and a further fine-tuning of the policy.

Regional growth and the need for an EU regional policy. While many arguments can be advanced in support of regional policy, it was the fear that yet more economic integration (i.e. the Single Market and monetary union) would worsen regional problems which underlay the rapid expansion of the regional policy budget in 1989 and 1994.

In reality, considerable controversy surrounds the issue of whether integration and growth in the EU is leading to a narrowing of regional disparities ('convergence') or a widening ('divergence'). Traditional neoclassical economic theory argues that growth leads to convergence of regional disparities. Capital accumulation in the prosperous regions gradually makes them less attractive locations for investment as rates of return fall. Capital then flows from the prosperous regions to the disadvantaged regions to take advantage of the lower wages and higher returns to be had there, while labour migration in the opposite direction reduces the problems faced in the disadvantaged regions. Weaker innovation and technology in the disadvantaged regions in this theory is no problem since technology transfer between regions is very rapid.

Those supporting a divergence view of regional problems in the EU draw on a range of alternative theories. Traditional cumulative growth theory[3] stresses an array of 'backwash effects' tending to widen disparities. Regions with an initial head-start stay in the lead by exploiting economies of scale and agglomeration economies which result in cost savings when firms cluster together. The lead is also maintained by denuding the poorer regions of their

[3] G. Myrdal, *Economic Theory and Underdeveloped Regions* (London: Duckworth, 1957).

capital and their youngest and most active workers. More modern cumulative growth theories such as the Kaldorian model[4] and new growth theory[5] point to other forces which systematically widen regional disparities, such as cumulative productivity gains, skills acquisition, and the application of new technology. New growth theory is particularly interesting in suggesting reasons why the growth process might lead to cumulatively widening regional disparities. The theory stresses the role of new technology and the skills of the workforce in handling the new technology. As Fig. 3.7 shows, a region initially with a capital stock of K_0 whose savings (S) exceed depreciation (D) will accumulate capital. New investment will continuously expand the capital stock. With a skilled workforce and with the flow of new plant and machinery allowing the

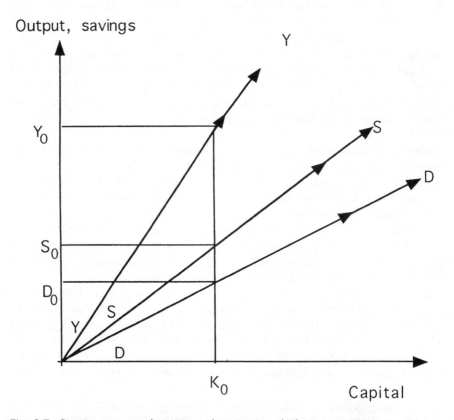

Fig. 3.7. Continuous cumulative growth: new growth theory

Note: D = depreciation of capital.
Source: C. R. Bean, 'Economic Growth', *Economic Review*, Feb. 1994, fig. 6.

---

[4] R. J. Dixon and A. P. Thirlwall, 'A Model of Growth Rate Differentials along Kaldorian Lines', *Oxford Economic Papers* 27 (1975), 201–14.
[5] N. Crafts, 'Productivity Growth Reconsidered', *Economic Policy* 15 (1992), 388–426.

latest state-of-the-art technology to be implemented, there is no reason why income should not continuously accelerate as shown by the arrow on the *Y*-function. Backward regions will be left wallowing in the wake of the leading regions.

Of the two views of the growth process, the available evidence suggests that a process of regional convergence is currently under way within the EU.[6] The process is, however, extremely sluggish, with regional disparities in the EU halving every 35 years. The neoclassical convergence process is so slow that regional policy is necessary if regional problems are to be solved within a reasonable period.

The 'non-regional' objectives of the structural funds.   The structural funds also incorporate non-regional objectives. Objective 3 (long-term and youth un-employment) and objective 4 (helping workers to adapt to change) are primarily social policy objectives relying solely on the ESF. The UK govern-ment is currently resisting applying for objective 4 money and has chosen to take all of its own allocation by way of objective 3. The bulk of this money comes in the form of matching grants for UK training and retraining programmes and for help for special groups such as the disabled and ethnic minorities.

The Guidance Section of EAGGF is harnessed partly for regional policy ends, but also for a special objective of its own (objective 5*a*—speeding up adjust-ment of agricultural structures). This objective has taken on particular sig-nificance in the aftermath of the McSharry Reforms to EU agriculture policy. The money is used for a wide array of initiatives ranging from early retirement schemes for farmers to farm investment and land consolidation.

The UK share of the structural funds.   The EU harnesses all three of its Structural Funds (ERDF, ESF, and the Guidance Section of EAGGF) to tackle regional problems. The UK is not eligible for money from the new Cohesion Fund. Assistance, in the form of grants, is only given if member states provide matching funds of their own. This is done to try to stop member states from substituting EU money for their own spending (the 'additionality' issue). UK disadvantaged regions can also get help from other EU institutions which are not strictly regional policy instruments. In particular, the UK does well from European Investment Bank loans and European Coal and Steel Community grants and loans.

As Fig. 3.8 shows, the UK has a large set of areas designated as eligible for EU help. Three regions are eligible for Objective 1 assistance ('less developed regions' with GDP per capita under 75% of the EU average): Northern Ireland, Merseyside, and the Scottish Highlands and Islands. Objective 1 regions are the poorest in the EU and get the bulk of available help. They comprise 26.6% of

---

[6] H. W. Armstrong and R. W. Vickerman (eds.), *Convergence and Divergence among European Regions* (London: Pion, 1995).

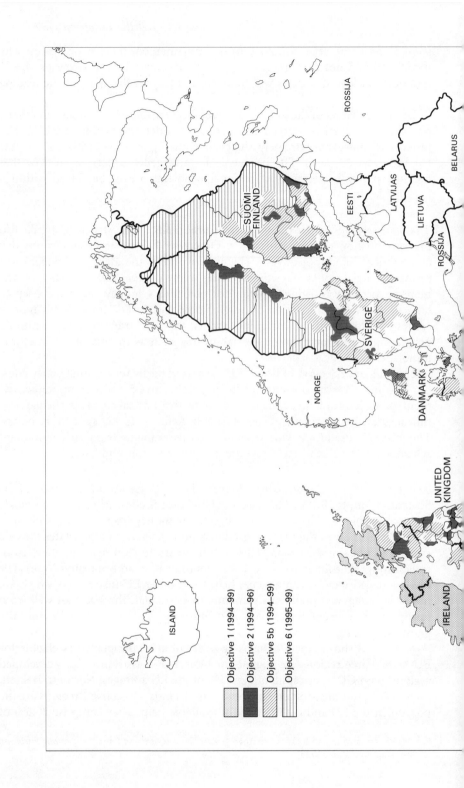

ISLAND

Objective 1 (1994–99)

Objective 2 (1994–96)

Objective 5b (1994–99)

Objective 6 (1995–99)

ROSSIJA

BELARUS

EESTI

LATVIJAS

LIETUVA

ROSSIJA

SUOMI
FINLAND

SVERIGE

NORGE

DANMARK

UNITED
KINGDOM

IRELAND

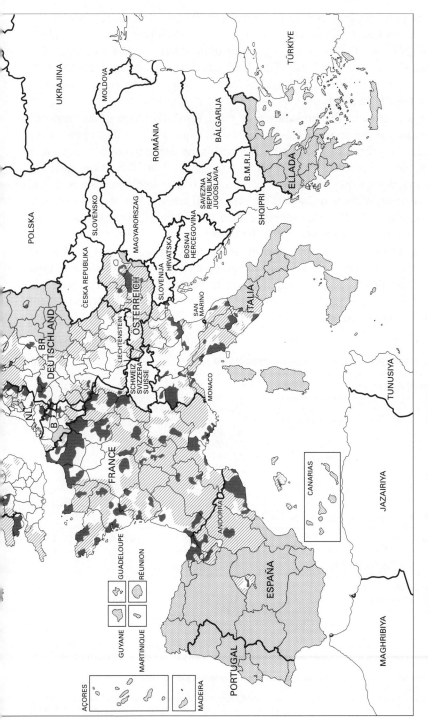

Fig. 3.8. Regions eligible for EU Structural Funds, 1994–1999

Source: European Commission, *Competitiveness and Cohesion: Trends in the Regions: Fifth Periodic Report on the Social and Economic Situation and Development of the Regions of the Community*, Luxemburg, 1994, map 23.

the EU population. In practice, the majority of EU help to the UK comes in the form of Objective 2 money (i.e. for regions with declining industries). These regions comprise 16.8% of the EU population. They include the main disadvantaged areas in the UK. The final category of regional policy help (Objective 5b: problem rural areas) is much smaller. These areas cover only 8.2% of the EU population.

Table 3.7 sets out the breakdown of the UK's 7.2% share of EU regional policy funds for the period 1994–9. The way in which the money is spent in the UK is based on three key principles. The first is the desire to concentrate aid in the most deserving areas (the Objective 1 regions). Over 70% of the total EU budget is given to the Objective 1 regions. Each member state's share of the budget depends on how serious its regional problems are. The second principle is partnership. The EU uses member state governments, local councils, and local development agencies to spend the money and expects its grants to attract matching private sector spending as well. The various partners also get together to draw up a plan for overcoming the local problems. They then carefully monitor its progress and evaluate its success. The third key principle is that of programming. Money is not simply thrown piecemeal at investment projects. Instead, the partners charged with spending the money must put

Table 3.7 The EU Structural Funds, 1994–1999

A. Financial Resources

Year	Ecu million (at 1985 prices)
1994	20,135
1995	21,480
1996	22,740
1997	24,026
1998	25,690
1999	27,400

B. Subdivision of the UK and Overall EU Totals

Objective	UK Share (%)	All Member States (%)
1. Less developed regions	26	74
2. Declining industrial areas	23	6
5b Rural areas	9	5
3,4, and 5a Non-regional objectives	42	15
Total	100	100

Notes:
   The 'non-regional' objectives of the Structural Funds are objective 3 (combating youth unemployment and long-term unemployment), objective 4 (adaptation of workers to industrial change), and objective 5a (agricultural restructuring).
   The objective 2 share is understated in that it refers only to the period 1994–6. In 1996 a further 3-year allocation will be approved.
   Sources: Commission of the European Communities, Community Structural Funds 1994-1999 Luxembourg; (EC, 1993), 16; European Commission, Competitiveness and Cohesion: Trends in the Regions (Luxembourg; (EC, 1994), Table 18.

together coherent programmes designed to tackle specific problems (e.g. derelict land reclamation, stimulating tourism, improving training).

While the majority of EU regional policy money is controlled by the national and local partners, in accordance with the EU's desire for 'subsidiarity' in the way it operates, the Commission does hold back 9% of the budget for a set of pan-European schemes which it controls from the centre. These Community Initiatives (CIs) are designed to tackle regional problems common to the member states or which stretch across member state borders. As Table 3.8 shows, these include many initiatives such as RECHAR and RETEX from which the UK derives a lot of benefit. Note that Table 3.7 gives figures for what the UK can expect to obtain under the 'non-regional' objectives 3, 4, and 5*a* between 1994 and 1999. Some 42% of all of the UK's allocations from the structural funds will come from these sources.

3.6. Conclusion: Issues Facing the UK

The relationship between the UK and the EU remains a stormy one. Actions which are in the best interests of the UK are not always those in the best interests of the EU. While all of the member states experience conflicts of interest, the UK has had more than its fair share of such situations and this seems likely to continue to be the case in the years ahead, with the 1996–7 Intergovernmental Conference being a probable early flashpoint. Each of the

Table 3.8. Main EU community initiatives, 1994–1999 (ECU billion)

Initiative	Focus	Spending
INTERREG	Cross-frontier problems	3.5
LEADER	Rural areas	1.8
REGIS	Extremely remote areas	0.6
NOW, HORIZON, YOUTHSTART, ADAPT	Retraining and skills and adapting to industrial change	3.5
RECHAR, RESIDER, KONVER, RETEX	Coal mining areas, iron and steel areas, textile areas, and conversion of defence industries	2.4
Portuguese Textile Areas		0.4
SME	Small and medium-sized firms	1.1
URBAN	Inner city areas	0.8
PESCA	Fishing communities	0.3
PEACE	Northern Ireland	0.3
Total		14.3

Source: European Commission, *Regional Policy and Cohesion Newsletter*, 23, (Brussels; European Commission, December 1995).

likely key economic issues facing the UK in its relationship with the EU is considered in turn.

The UK and EU Social Policy

The evolution of EU social policy. Social policy, like the CAP, has evolved over the years since the 1958 Treaty of Rome. In the case of social policy, the evolution process has been more complex than most because of the enormous array of issues which can be encompassed under the heading of social policy. Table 3.9, for example, shows just how wide the remit of social policy can be in a modern market economy. In addition to issues related to the workplace (e.g. health and safety, collective bargaining, sex and racial equality), there are also huge issues associated with social welfare, such as schooling, unemployment insurance, and housing.

The Treaty of Rome approached social policy as a means of helping the fledgling Common Market to attain free trade and labour mobility, an approach which implies a concern with employees rather than other groups in society. Social policy has come a long way since those early days. Faced with mounting unemployment and increasing social tensions in the 1970s, the EU

Table 3.9. The scope for social policy in a modern economy

Work	Welfare
Labour-market management and human resource development	*Social transfers*
manpower policy (e.g. retraining)	direct
macroeconomic policy	social insurance
	social assistance
	'universal' grants (e.g. child benefits and citizen entitlements)
Regulation of employment standards and conditions	indirect
health and safety	personal tax allowances and tax reliefs
minimum wages and other employee rights	some producer subsidies
working time and the quality of working life	(e.g. agricultural price support and deficiency payments)
Industrial relations	*Social services*
the framework of collective bargaining	compulsory schooling
workplace/enterprise democracy	health care
social dialogue and policy bargaining	housing policy
	social work
Gender, difference and social inequality	
sex and race discrimination in employment	
the sexual division of labour and other social divisions (e.g. of race, ethnicity, disability).	

Source: D. Purdy and P. Devine, 'Social Policy' in M. Artis and N. Lee (eds.), *The Economics of the European Union* (Oxford: Oxford University Press, 1994), Table 10.1.

responded with a radical Social Action Programme in 1974 and a doubling of social policy funds between 1973 and 1979. The emphasis was placed on retraining, worker mobility, and help for particular disadvantaged groups (especially women, younger unemployed persons, and disabled persons). From 1975 onwards the ESF began to work increasingly closely with the newly-established EU regional policy since social problems are often most severe in regions with high unemployment. In 1983, for example, 40% of ESF money was specifically targeted on the less favoured regions. The 1970s and early 1980s also witnessed an increased flow of new Directives on social policy issues. Once again, however, the emphasis continued to be on the workplace and employee rights rather than society at large.

The Single Market and EU social policy. The advent of the Single Europe Act in 1986 and the gradual phasing in of the detailed Single Market legislation marked a great-turning point in EU social policy. The imminent sweeping away of the remaining barriers to trade, capital mobility, and labour migration posed a great challenge for EU social policy. On the one hand there was the danger of social dumping, the process by which some member states can make themselves attractive locations for larger companies by offering a low cost-low social policy environment for firms. Indigenous firms in countries such as this also enjoy a competitive advantage over other parts of the EU, thus distorting competition. Moreover, the lack of common approaches to social security benefits, conditions of work, and different attitudes to workers' qualifications are themselves formidable barriers to labour migration, thus defeating the whole purpose of the Single Market.

Something clearly had to be done. The first step was a complete reform of the Structural Funds (including the ESF) to ensure that in future they would work more closely together. The budget of the three Structural Funds was doubled in real terms between 1989 and 1993, and has been doubled again in real terms for the period 1994–9. As we have seen, the ESF now works in harmony with the other two Structural Funds with clear common objectives.

The Social Charter and the Social Chapter. The Single Market has also been the catalyst for a fundamental rethink of social policy. The Commission President himself led the way in 1986 by calling for a 'social Europe' to be set in place alongside the Single Economic Market. There has been a rapid shift in emphasis towards regarding social policy as a part of the concept of EU citizenship rather than as something designed purely for employees. A key step along this road was the controversial Social Charter introduced in 1989. This was an attempt to define the principles underlying the new wider view of social policy designed to incorporate issues such as poverty, education, and health and a set of social rights for the citizens of the new EU. The Social Charter was the building-block on which the Social Chapter proposals of the Treaty of Union were based. UK opposition to the whole concept of the Social Chapter has resulted in a complex situation at present. The UK government is in a position to pick and choose among those measures which it wishes to adopt, while the other eleven member states are pushing ahead with a wide social policy agenda. Matters are made more complex as a result of the ability of the Commission to introduce into the UK social policy measures under pre-existing powers (such as health and safety Directives) and by legal decisions of the European Court. These are slowly redefining workers' rights within the UK on issues such as equal treatment for men and women.

Economic dilemmas associated with social policy.   The economic implications of EU social policy are more complex than is at first apparent. As mentioned earlier, the Single Market has triggered a debate within the EU on problems of social dumping. Table 3.10 shows just how widely non-wage costs, principally taxes imposed on payroll to finance social policy, vary among the larger EU member states and also when compared with Japan and the USA. Some caution must be exercised in interpreting these figures, however, for the following reasons.

1. It is one thing for a country to introduce social policy legislation of its own or ratify EU legislation and quite another to effectively enforce it. There are frequent accusations that some member states are paying only lip-service to EU social policy initiatives.

2. The 'informal sector' of the economy tends to operate outside the legal framework of social policy and may comprise up to a quarter of all employees in some countries such as Greece. A growing informal sector not only undermines those domestic companies actively implementing social policy, but also results in one country undercutting firms in other member states.

3. Where markets are highly competitive, the full extent of non-wage cost items such as maternity benefits may not be passed on into final product prices, to the detriment of a company selling across the EU market. In these circumstances, raising the non-wage costs may simply force a compensating reduction in wage costs in countries with active social policies. This serves to protect their external competitiveness to some degree.

4. There is growing evidence that even if a member state such as the UK

Table 3.10. A comparison of selected EU countries with Japan and the USA, 1992

	Non-wage costs (DM per worker)	Unit labour costs (W. Germany=100)
West Germany	19.46	100
France	13.18	84
Italy	17.01	103
Spain	8.86	77
UK	6.85	78
Japan	7.18	89
USA	6.93	88

Source: F. McDonald, 'The Social Chapter and Jobs in the UK', *British Economic Survey*, 231 (Autumn 1993), Table 1. Based on *The Economist*, July 1993 and Institut der deutschen Wirtschaft Koln, 1993.

opts out of social policy provisions it may find that its companies cannot. Many UK firms now also have plants or subsidiaries in other EU countries or are themselves parts of multinationals operating in several member states. As such, they are finding that they are having to abide by EU social policy rules whether they like it or not. Works councils and worker participation on company boards have been a classic example of this in recent years. Many of the UK's top companies are now having to establish these despite the UK opt-out from the Social Chapter. In an integrated Europe they have no choice.

Social policy is now concerned with much more than just the need to create a level playing-field for firms within the EU. The Treaty of Union and the Social Chapter have taken us into the realm of what the social rights of an EU citizen should be. There are strong moral overtones to policies designed to protect the working conditions for employees and the rights of access of disadvantaged groups to the workplace. The UK government argues that issues such as this are the remit of the member states and not the EU. In addition, there is also an external competitiveness issue. Can the EU afford far-reaching social legislation at a time when its industries are under threat from countries such as those in the Pacific Rim? Do workers in permanent jobs within companies with progressive social policies have the right to enjoy these privileges if they are at the cost of others who have lost their jobs or who are confined to part-time and temporary work in a growing dual labour-market situation? These are key issues for the EU in the years ahead.

A 'Two-Tier' Monetary Union

The economics of monetary union are discussed above and some reasons were cited there for the UK's sceptical position on the project for monetary union in Europe. However, a determined effort is being made to realize monetary union in 1999 on the basis of a core group of eligible countries. The Madrid Summit in December 1995 determined that the new single currency would be named the 'Euro', whilst the European Monetary Institute, which was set up by the Treaty of Union to study and find solutions to the problems likely to face the European Central Bank, set out a timetable for the mechanics of introducing a new currency on the supposition that a monetary union is approved in the course of 1998—probably at the March Summit of that year—to begin operations in January 1999. The European Commission issued forecasts in November 1995 illustrating how the member countries were likely to make progress towards satisfying the criteria for entry. Fig. 3.9 shows the position for the difficult and most contentious fiscal criteria: according to these forecasts seven countries (not counting the UK) would satisfy the deficit criterion by 1997, though they would exceed the debt criterion. Although not shown in the Figure, the forecasts also suggest that all seven would satisfy the interest rate and inflation criteria. Although the UK could probably—if it chose to satisfy the ERM criteria for entry into EMU—also qualify as a participant, it does not

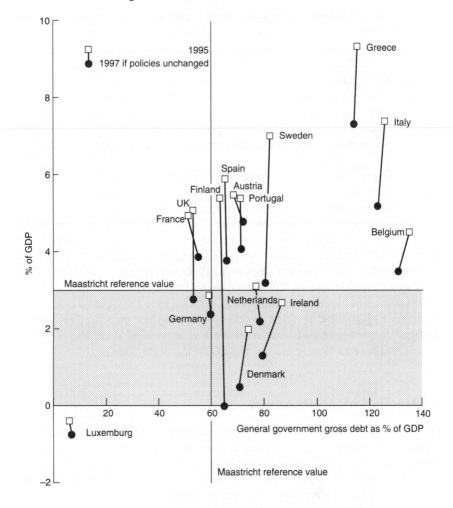

Fig. 3.9. Model for public sector fiscal deficits and debt in EU member countries: general government borrowing as a percentage of GDP

Source: European Commission, Nov. 1995.

appear likely that it will want to do so. We also saw, earlier, that there were some objective economic reasons why the UK might not find the project of EMU such a good one as some other EU member countries. Nevertheless, the prospect that monetary union might be created on a 'two-tier' basis, with a core group forming the initial monetary union and the other group—the second tier of peripheral countries—joining later, raises issues of its own. First and foremost, the UK may need to face the possibility that it cannot afford to be left out. Secondly, there is an issue of how relations between the two tiers should be conducted.

The issue of whether the UK cannot afford to be left out of monetary union, should it occur, comprises two separate sub-issues. First, there is an issue of whether the core group will be in a position to take decisions which unfairly advantage themselves. Second, there is a more general consideration as to whether there will be a 'first mover' advantage accruing to those countries which join monetary union first. On the first of these points, the statutes of the European Central Bank (ECB) make it clear that whilst potential members will be members of the General Council of the ECB, they will have no power to influence the decisions of the ECB directly or even to influence the agenda for decision-making in a formal way. The ability of the outer tier to influence the development of the monetary union seems, formally at least, to be small if not non-existent. This could imply that the founding members might take undue advantage of their position; indeed, it can be argued not only that this would be natural, but that the apprehension of it is a good thing, since it increases the incentive for laggards to adopt the measures necessary to become eligible to join. From the viewpoint of the UK, the scenario seems reminiscent of the earlier lost European opportunities where failure to join the EC at the outset arguably allowed the adoption of policies like the Common Agricultural Policy that made later entry very costly for Britain. There is also a suggestion that there will be a first mover advantage in writing Euro-denominated business, and that whilst it might in principle be possible to participate in this business from the City of London whilst being outside the core Monetary Union, in practice there will be an advantage to being inside the Union. If this is right, then the pre-eminence of the City of London will be lost to the financial centres in the monetary union—Frankfurt, Paris, and Amsterdam. As the provision of financial services has in the past been seen as a revealed comparative advantage of the UK, this is an important consideration. (Table 3.11 shows the proportion

Table 3.11. Proportion of total employment in financial and business services, 1992

	Banking and finance	Total, finance and business services
Belgium	0.03	0.09
Denmark	0.03	0.09
Germany	0.03	0.09
Greece	0.01	0.05
Spain	0.02	0.06
France	0.02	0.10
Ireland	0.02	0.09
Italy	n.a.	0.07
Luxemburg	0.08	0.12
Netherlands	0.02	0.10
Portugal	0.02	0.06
UK	0.02	0.11

Source: CEC, *Employment in Europe*, 1994.

of employment in financial services in the principal EU economies, illustrating the strength of the UK in this respect.)

The second issue would be the nature of the exchange rate system linking the inner core EMU and the centre group. There are two reasons for supposing that some kind of exchange rate system might be considered necessary to regulate this relationship. The first is that, to satisfy the criteria for eventual membership of the EMU, the initially excluded (or, likely, in Britain's case, self-excluded) countries would still need to satisfy the ERM criteria, or a version of them that could be accepted as a substitute in the circumstances. The second is that a degree of exchange rate stability appears necessary to avoid the possibility that two-tier EMU could result in a situation where exchange rate devaluations among the outer fringe countries are seen as purposive actions to gain competitiveness, threatening the achievements of the Single Market. There is indeed some likelihood that a successful inner core EMU would of necessity produce a 'hard' currency, one more likely to appreciate against the excluded countries than the reverse. The complaints from manufacturers in France or Germany that were heard against the devaluation of the pound sterling and Italian lira after 1992 would be repeated in louder volume. The variety of circumstance of the countries liable to be excluded from the initial-stage EMU adds further to the complications of designing a system suitable to all. Despite exercise of the opt-out, monetary union could therefore remain a problem for Britain.

New Accessions

The UK has taken a prominent lead in arguing the case for a widening of the membership of the EU, even if this is at the expense of a deepening of the economic relationships of the existing members (e.g. rapid progress towards monetary union). The entry of Sweden, Finland, and Austria is certainly in the UK interest. These countries, with the exception of Finland which is currently suffering problems resulting from economic collapse in the old Soviet Union, are inherently net contributors to the EU budget. They are all relatively prosperous countries with well established and largely free-trading relationships with the EU. As previous members of EFTA they traditionally had close ties with the UK economy. The high degree of economic integration has been sustained in recent years by the creation of the European Economic Area in which the EU's Single Market was extended to include Austria and the Nordic Countries. While some problems are posed for the UK by the 1995 batch of accessions, such as the need to find money from the Structural Funds for some of the northern regions of Sweden and Finland, the prosperity of the new entrants and the proximity of the UK to the Nordic region mean that their entry is to be welcomed.

It is the possibility of new accessions at the end of the decade of a number of Central and Eastern European countries which poses the biggest problem for the UK. The countries first in line are the Visegrad-4 (Poland, the Czech Republic, Slovakia, and Hungary). Romania and Bulgaria (making up the Visegrad-6) are somewhat further behind in the accession stakes.

The prospects of widening the EU to include at a minimum the Visegrad-4 countries has both attractions and disadvantages from a UK perspective. Apart from the political advantages the UK sees in distracting attention from the objective of 'deepening' the EU, Visegrad-4 entry would have the following effects:

1. The Visegrad-4 countries represent a major new market for UK and other EU countries to gain access to. The Visegrad-4 countries alone had a population of over 64 million in 1992. These countries are currently struggling hard to cope with the need to restructure their economies to achieve freer trade. As a result, their GDP per capita values are low (perhaps only one-third of that of EUR-12) and have also fallen in recent years. This has resulted in a temporary decline in their attractiveness as markets for UK goods. They are, however, now beginning to emerge from their transition phase and future prospects are good.

2. Running counter to the attractiveness of Visegrad markets for UK exporters is the threat they pose to some UK industries. Most Visegrad industries are still in no fit state to compete for domestic UK markets. Some, however, such as textiles, steel, coal, and farm products are already emerging as significant threats and others will no doubt appear as formidable competitors in the years ahead.

3. The Visegrad countries pose an enormous challenge for the EU's budget. Rapid accession would place enormous burdens on the budget and would threaten the receipts which the UK currently enjoys from the EAGGF and the structural funds. Unemployment rates have risen rapidly in the Visegrad countries and GDP per capita values are low. Under present rules all regions in all four countries would be eligible for Objective 1 structural funds assistance. The demands on EAGGF would also be huge, particularly given the size of the Polish agricultural sector. It has been estimated[7] that accession would impose a net budget cost on the EU of 58 billion ECU per annum (dominated by EAGGF and structural funds payments).

Further Reading

Artis, M. J. and Lee, N. (eds.), *The Economics of the European Union* (Oxford: Oxford University Press, 1994).

Bean, C. R., 'Economic Growth', *Economic Review*, 11 (1994), 9–13.

Cecchini, P., *The European Challenge* (London: Gower, 1988).

—— *Community Structural Funds, 1994–1999: Regulations and Commentary* (Luxembourg: European Commission, 1993).

Commission of the European Communities, *Growth, Competitiveness and Employment:*

---

[7] R. Baldwin, *Towards an Integrated Europe* (London: CEPR, 1994).

The Challenges and Ways Forward into the 21st Century, White Paper, Bulletin of the European Communities, Supplement 6/93 (Brussels: European Commission, 1993).

Emerson, M., Aujean, M., Catinat, M., Goybet, P., and Jacquemin, A. *The Economics of 1992* (Oxford: Oxford University Press, 1988).

European Commission, *Competitiveness and Cohesion: Trends in the Regions: Fifth Periodic Report on the Social and Economic Situation and Development of the Regions in the Community* (Luxembourg: European Commission, 1994).

Lintner, V. and Mazey, S., *The European Community: Economic and Political Aspects* (Maidenhead: McGraw-Hill, 1991).

McKenzie, G. and Venables, A. J. (eds.), *The Economics of the Single European Act* (London: Macmillan, 1991).

Swinbank, A., 'The CAP Reform 1992', *Journal of Common Market Studies,* 31 (1993), 359–72.

4

ECONOMIC ACTIVITY AND INFLATION

M. C. KENNEDY

This chapter is concerned with economic instability and inflation in the UK economy. It presents some relatively straightforward explanations of how the economy works and of how its various parts interact with each other to generate recessions, recoveries, and variations in the rate of inflation. These explanations are supported, as far as possible, by statistical evidence. It should be borne in mind, however, that economics is not an infallible guide, and that all hypotheses are open to question. As in other branches of knowledge what seem to be well-established hypotheses remain open to the possibility of refutation or substantial modification. It is essential, therefore, to maintain a critical approach, and to make clear distinctions between hypotheses, value-judgements and statements of fact.

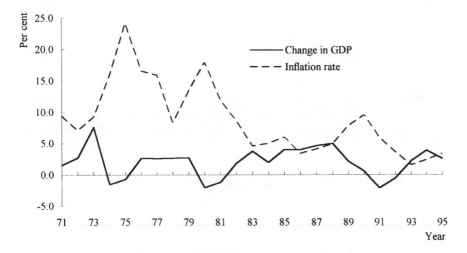

Fig. 4.1. Changes in GDP and retail prices in the UK, 1970–1995

Source: See Appendix Tables 4.A1 and 4.A2.

4.1. The Instability of Total Output

Fig. 4.1 illustrates the instability of total output and prices in the UK since 1970, and the first half of this chapter focuses on output. The figure shows the year-to-year changes in the volume of gross domestic product (GDP), which is the total output of the economy. The main periods of downturn were 1973–5, 1979–81, and 1990–2. Each of these recessions in GDP was accompanied by a fall in manufacturing production and by increases in the percentage rate of unemployment. The main changes are set out in Table 4.1.

Total employment fell in the last two recessions, although not in 1973–5. The employment figures include both part-time and full-time jobs, and since there is no attempt to weight them by the number of hours they represent, they cannot be taken as reliable or consistent indicators of the amount of work done. The effects of recessions on the labour market are more accurately conveyed by the unemployment statistics, which are a count of the number of people claiming benefit and actively seeking work. These figures rose only slightly in 1973–5, and much more seriously in the two more recent recessions. The unemployment problem was particularly severe in the 1980s when the recession coincided with a 'bulge' in the supply of school-leavers and also with what seems to have been a sharp shift in the structure of labour demand towards skilled and qualified workers. Unemployment went on rising from 1979 to 1986 (see Fig. 4.2), when it reached 11.6% of the workforce (3.1 million). In the latest recession it rose from 1.7 million in 1990 to 2.9 million in 1993. But, unlike the previous recession, it began to fall within two years of the low point for output.

4.2. Trend and Actual Output

The depth of a recession may be measured either as the peak-to-trough decline in GDP or as a shortfall from 'trend'. 'Trend output' can be taken as the level of GDP which would have been attained if GDP had grown steadily from its peak level at its peak-to-peak rate of growth: 1.4% per annum for 1973–9 and 2.2%

Table 4.1. Output and employment in three recessions

% change in:	1973–5	1979–81	1990–2
Real GDP	−2.2	−3.1	−2.7
Manufacturing ouput	−7.7	−14.2	−6.1
Employment	+0.2	−5.6	−4.8
Unemployment rate	+0.9	+3.9	+4.0

Sources: see Appendix Tables 4A.1 and 4A.2.

for 1979–90. Trend output (as here defined) must be distinguished from the various measures of 'potential output' which aim to represent the output level attainable with a full use of resources—a level, which in the 1980s and 1990s, would certainly have been much higher.

The estimates of trend output allow us to calculate the shortfall in output, or 'output gap', which measures the loss of the economy's output in all years when it was below trend. Fig. 4.2 illustrates the size of this gap from 1970 to 1995 and compares it with the percentage rate of unemployment, which is clearly related to it.

The size of the gap, or loss of output, was just under 5% in 1975 and about 7% in 1981, 1982, 1992, and 1993. A loss of 7% represents £57 billion (in current prices)—a magnitude which is almost twice the budget of the Department of Health. It must be evident, therefore, that recessions involve a very substantial waste of resources.

This conclusion, however, can be seen in different perspectives. The levels of resource utilization at the peaks of 1979 and 1990 were high enough to promote strong inflationary pressures. Many politicians would accept that it is socially preferable to forgo output and employment in return for the price stability to be gained from a less intensive use of resources. Indeed it can be questioned whether trend output should be estimated as a peak level at all and not at some lower level of utilization such as the 'natural' rate of unemployment (see below). But, whatever the merits of this point of view, it must still be borne in mind that even when GDP was at its peak in 1990, unemployment was 1.7 million (5.8% of the workforce), thus implying that there were plenty of people looking for work and unable to find it. These people could have

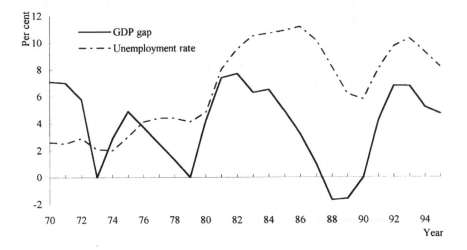

Fig. 4.2. The output gap and unemployment in the UK, 1970–1995

Source: See Appendix Tables 4.A1 and 4.A2.

made a useful contribution to their own well-being as well as to the total output of the economy, if there had been a demand for their services.

4.3. Expenditures and Economic Fluctuations

There is no great mystery about the tendency of the modern industrial economy to lapse into recession. Recessions occur primarily because a large proportion of national output is devoted to the production of capital goods—machines, factories, houses, and even cars. These goods are highly durable, and once purchased, perform their functions for many years. It is theoretically possible, therefore, for the demand for new capital goods to become satiated: firms could reach a point where they are completely satisfied with their existing stock of capital equipment, and want no more. In such circumstances the demand for new capital goods could, at least in principle, be zero. And, whilst this predicament has never occurred for the aggregate of all firms, it is worth recalling that the United States was approaching this position in the depression of 1929–32, when fixed investment expenditure fell by 70%. The demand for capital goods can collapse in a way which is not typical of basic commodities like food, shelter, and clothing.

A major factor in the demand for new investment goods is the progress of technological change. Since this cannot be expected to proceed at an even pace there are bound to be periods when investment opportunities are plentiful and others when they are scarce. In the more prolific periods for innovation there will be investment booms as firms equip themselves with the latest technology. But these will be followed by depressions once the business sector has acquired the new equipment.

A further factor affecting investment expenditure is the presence of uncertainty—as emphasized by J. M. Keynes in the *General Theory*.[1] Investment is undertaken in the expectation of future profits. The predictions of profit have to be made for many years ahead; they are inevitably uncertain, and prone to swings in business mood and confidence.

The effects of innovation, capital satiability, and uncertainty make it natural to look to changes in fixed investment as the prime cause of economic fluctuations. They are inherent in the nature of a capital-intensive economy, and should not be seen as mere accidents or 'shocks' to a fundamentally stable system. It is a misconception of the modern economy to regard it as normally stable and at full employment.

The instability of fixed investment is reinforced by that of stockbuilding—which is the addition to business stocks between the beginning and end of each year. When times are good business firms will stock up with raw materials and

---

[1] J. M. Keynes, *The General Theory of Employment, Interest and Money* (London: Macmillan, 1936).

finished goods in expectation of rising sales. But if demand levels off or falls, firms are forced to cut back their purchases for stock, and this means that production for stock falls too. Changes in stockbuilding (changes in the change in stocks) have always been a major feature of the business cycle—see Fig. 4.5).

Movements in overseas demand and prices are a further source of fluctuation. The depression of the 1930s was initiated by the fall in fixed investment in the USA, but it spread to other countries as a result of the decline in the US demand for imports. In the UK the decline in exports in 1929–32 accounted for almost the whole of the decline in GDP. In recent recessions, however, exports have been of less importance, although it remains true that overseas demand is a major influence on activity in the UK. Overseas price changes can also be important. The boom in oil and commodity prices in 1973 led to a fall in real disposable income in the UK, and thus to a fall in consumer spending.

The factors responsible for the last three recessions are illustrated in Table 4.2, which shows the percentage changes in various expenditure categories during three recession periods, together with the same changes as percentages of GDP. The main change was in fixed investment, which together with stockbuilding, accounted for more than the whole of the decline in GDP in the first two recessions and for most of the third. Exports fell in the 1979–81 downturn, but not in 1973–5 or 1990–2. Consumption fell substantially in 1973–5, when its decline was induced by the oil price rise. Its slowdown in the other recessions was probably brought about by lower disposable incomes as a result of the fall in investment. This is to accept the Keynesian theory of effective demand under which investment, the change in stocks, and exports are seen as the autonomous (or exogenous) causes of change—being independent of the level of income—whereas consumption and imports are directly dependent on income. But consumers' expenditure can also be affected by other factors besides income, most notably tax changes, credit conditions, and changes in world prices.

Table 4.2. Expenditure in cyclical downturns

% change in:	1973–5		1979–81		1990–2	
GDP	−2.2	—	−3.2	—	−2.8	—
Fixed investment	−4.4	(−0.9)	−14.4	(−2.9)	−1.0	(−2.5)
Change in stocks (% of GDP)	—	(−4.7)	—	(−2.8)	(−0.1)	—
Exports	+4.3	(0.9)	−1.0	(−0.2)	+2.1	(0.6)
Government expenditure	+7.3	—	+2.0	—	+2.9	—
Consumers' expenditure	−1.8	(−1.2)	−0.1	(0.1)	−2.2	(−1.6)
Imports	−5.7	—	−6.3	—	+0.5	—

Note: Figures in brackets are % of GDP.
Sources: *ETAS*, 1994; *ET*, Oct. 1995.

Table 4.3. Expenditure in the first year of recovery

% change in:	1975–6	1981–2	1992–3
GDP	2.7	1.7	2.2
Fixed investment	1.7	0.9	0.6
Change in stocks (% of GDP)	2.7	1.4	0.4
Exports	9.1	0.9	0.3
Government expenditure	1.3	0.6	0.3
Consumers' expenditure	0.5	1.8	2.6
Imports	4.8	2.0	2.8

Sources: ETAS, 1994; ET, Oct. 1995.

Table 4.3 shows the main expenditure changes in the first year of each recovery. It indicates that the most general source of recovery was not, as might have been expected, fixed investment, but was the change in stocks, which was generally a swing from negative to positive stockbuilding. Other factors were exports in 1975–6 and 1992–3. Fixed investment has usually taken three to four years to pull back to its pre-recession level.

4.4. The Measurement of GDP from Expenditure

Gross domestic product is essentially a measure of total output—the output of goods and services produced by UK residents. The most familiar measurement, and the one which has already been used in Tables 4.2 and 4.3, is made from the side of expenditure and the change in stocks. The method here is to add together the main expenditures on GDP, and then to add to them any output which is produced during the year but not actually sold. This is done by adding in the change in stocks and work in progress. Thus the expenditure breakdown for 1994 was as follows:

	£bn. at current prices
At market prices:	
Consumers' expenditure (*C*)	428.1
Fixed investment (*I*)	100.1
Value of physical increase in stocks and work in progress (ΔStocks)	3.3
General government consumption (*G*)	144.1
Exports of goods and services (*X*)	173.9
less	
Imports of goods and services (*M*)	−180.1
Factor cost adjustment (*FCA*)	−89.7
equals	
Gross domestic product at factor cost (*GDP*)	579.1

Source: NIBB, 1995

Symbolically, the expenditure identity is:

$$GDP = C + I + \Delta\text{Stocks} + G + X - M - FCA$$

Consumers' expenditure on goods and services consists of expenditure by households and unincorporated businesses. Gross fixed investment comprises all purchases of physical assets by firms and government authorities, including new houses. Both gross domestic product and investment are labelled 'gross' totals because they are not adjusted for capital depreciation. General government expenditure consists of current purchases by both central and local authorities. Imports are deducted because they are produced overseas, and do not, therefore, form part of UK GDP. There are import components in C, I, G, and X, but these are removed by subtracting the import total. The factor cost adjustment is indirect taxes net of subsidies, and is applied in order to bring the valuation of expenditures to a 'factor cost' basis, meaning that GDP is valued as the total (approximately) of factor incomes—mainly wages, profits, and rent. Indirect taxes raise prices above their factor value and subsidies reduce them. GDP may also be valued at market prices, in which case the factor cost adjustment is not applied.

The final item in the GDP identity is the change in stocks. This, as we have seen, plays a significant part in economic fluctuations. Its full title is 'the value of the physical increase in stocks and work in progress', and it is measured initially as the change in the book value of stocks between the beginning and end of the year. But as this figure will include any change in prices within the period, an adjustment has to be made so as to ensure that it is the production value and not the price rise which is being measured: this adjustment is known as the 'adjustment for stock appreciation'.

The change in stocks is not necessarily an 'expenditure'. Stocks can, for example, accumulate simply because firms are unable to sell their products, in which case their change is involuntary. They can also rise because firms want to hold more of them (voluntary stockbuilding). Unfortunately it is not possible to distinguish the voluntary from the involuntary components in the stock-building statistics, and this makes it difficult to interpret their movements. In Table 4.2 the downward swings in the stock change may be only partly voluntary. High levels at the cycle peak may include some involuntary change as demand begins to drop off, whilst a negative stock change may indicate a pick-up in final demand which is being supplied from stock.

The inclusion of the change in stocks along with identified expenditures in the GDP total is an admission that what is produced is not necessarily sold, and, more generally, that total expenditure is not equal to total output. (Theoretical models in which expenditure and output are said to be identical do not allow for stocks, and implicitly assume that all output is immediately sold.)

4.5. Consumers' Expenditure

Consumers' expenditure on goods and services is the largest of the spending categories. After deducting its import content of 21% and indirect taxes of about 15%, it accounts for some 48% of GDP.[2] The most widely accepted theory of consumers' expenditure is that it is determined (and financed) by current income. This makes it interesting to examine the ratio of consumption to personal disposable income—the so-called Average Propensity to Consume (APC)—the behaviour of which is characterized by three main features:

(1) a downward trend over the very long period,
(2) cycles of four to eight years, which, however, do not coincide closely with the GDP cycle, and
(3) great stability from one year to the next.

Table 4.4 presents the long-term behaviour of the APC and the ratio of personal saving to income.

The falling trend over long periods of time is illustrated by the decline from nearly 99% in the 1920s to around 90% in the period since 1970 (Table 4.4)[3] The savings rate has similarly increased from barely 1½% in the 1920s to around 10%.[4] This long-run rise in the savings rate is almost certainly a product of rising real incomes per head, with the result that an increasing

Table 4.4. The APC and savings rate 1920–1994 (%)

	APC	Savings rate
1920–9	98.5	1.5
1930–9	95.2	4.8
1950–9	96.0	4.1
1960–9	91.5	8.6
1970–9	89.9	10.6
1980–9	90.8	9.2
1990–4	89.3	10.7

Sources: C. H. Feinstein, *National Income, Expenditure and Output, 1855–1965* (Cambridge: Cambridge University Press, 1972); *ETAS*, 1994; *ET* Oct., 1995.

[2] *NIBB*, 1988, 29; *NIBB*, 1994, table 1.2.

[3] Early studies of the consumption function, particularly in the USA, were much influenced by the apparent fact that the APC and APS has been stable over the long period, and had not responded to rising real incomes. For a discussion see J. Thomas, 'The Early History of the Consumption Function' *OEP*, Jan. 1989, and A. Spanos, 'Early Empirical Findings on the Consumption Function', *OEP*, Jan. 1989.

[4] The APC, average propensity to save (APS), and savings rate are related as follows:

$$APC = C/Y$$

and

$$APS = S/Y = 1 - C/Y$$

and also that:

$$1 - \% \ APC = \text{savings rate} = 100(S/Y)$$

where C represents consumption, S saving, and Y is personal disposable income.

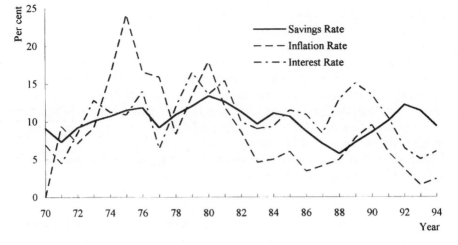

Fig. 4.3. Personal savings rate, inflation, and interest rates, 1970–1994

Note: Savings rate = savings as a percentage of disposable income; inflation rate = increase in RPI; interest rate = Treasury Bill rate.
Sources: *ETAS*, 1995; *ET*, oct. 1995.

proportion of the population has been able to set money aside for old age or other contingencies.

Superimposed on the long-term trend are fluctuations in the savings rate, which for the period since 1970 are illustrated in Fig. 4.3. There were peaks in the savings rate in 1975, 1980, 1984, and 1992.

These movements can be attributed to a number of factors. During the 1970s the savings rate was generally rising, and there was a correlation with the inflation rate which some economists saw as causal. The argument was that inflation eroded the real value of assets such as building society deposits, and that this led people to increase their savings rate in order to rebuild their wealth. For the short period when real interest rates were negative there may have been some substance to this view. But inflation and nominal interest rates normally move together, and interest rates could have been the principal causal factor for much of the time. The pronounced fall in the savings rate in the 1980s, however, was not so much due to interest rates as to the liberal supply of credit at the time; and an additional factor was higher perceived levels of wealth as house prices rose relative to income. The savings rate recovered after 1989 as house prices fell, and by 1992 was higher than it had been for 10 years. The savings rate was still high in 1995.

The third salient feature of the savings rate (and APC) has been its great stability from one year to the next. Taking the whole period since 1950, the change in the rate between successive years has exceeded 2.0% only four times. It has been possible to predict next year's APC from this year's with considerable accuracy—with an average (absolute) error of only 1.2% for the period from 1950 to 1992. It used to be a forecasters' rule of thumb to stick always with the same savings rate unless there were exceptionally good reasons for expecting a change.

These observations seem to corroborate the view that, apart from the influences of credit conditions, interest rates, and wealth, consumption is primarily determined by current income: that the relationship is proportional, but that the proportion rises gently with rising real incomes. The implication is that the MPC is normally likely to be close to the APC, which in turn will not be far off last year's APC.

The view that consumption is determined by current income is often expressed in the form of a linear equation:

$$C = C_0 + c_1 Y$$

where C_0 is a constant term, c_1 the slope of the linear relationship. This form of equation will not be proportional unless the constant term, C_0 is zero. It is, however, a form which can be estimated using the method of ordinary least squares, although it is hazardous to pick too short a time period for the estimate. A long-term example based on the data for 1950–89 is:

$$C = -\text{£}0.60\text{bn} + 0.91 Y$$

where Y again stands for personal disposable income and the figures are in 1990 prices. The equation fits very closely to the data from which it was estimated.[5] The constant term is small, so that the relationship is virtually proportional, and the slope term (which might be taken for the MPC) is close to the APC.

The equation succeeds in predicting consumption for the next five years (1990–4) with an average error of 2.0%. This, however, is still not quite as good as the result of predicting by the rule of thumb that next year's APC will be the same as this year's (where the average error is 1.6%).

One of the questions which is still unsettled is the extent to which consumers follow the so-called 'life-cycle hypothesis' whereby they are presumed to plan their consumption and saving rates by reference to their expected lifetime income. On this view an individual with a life-span of 60 years, of which 45 are spent working and 15 in retirement, might be expected to consume 45/60ths of his income and to set aside 15/60ths in order to finance his retirement. In its extreme form, this hypothesis regards current income as irrelevant to current consumption, except in so far as it forms part of lifetime income. But this assumes a readiness to plan for the future and an ability to borrow on the prospect of future income, which is not really applicable to the whole community.[6] The life-cycle hypothesis is more likely to apply to the

---

[5] The coefficient of determination (r-squared) is 0.999 and the standard error of estimate is 1.5% of the average level of consumption.

[6] The classic references are F. Modigliani and R. Brumberg, 'Utility Analysis and the Consumption Function' in K. Kurihara (ed.), *Post-Keynesian Economics* (London: Allen and Unwin, 1955) and M. Friedman, *A Theory of the Consumption Function*, (Princeton, NJ: Princeton University Press, 1957).

richer and older sections of the population than to the average income earner. The related 'permanent income' hypothesis due to Professor Friedman also assumes that consumers are far-sighted and have ready access to the capital markets. Both hypotheses imply that the path of aggregate consumption is likely to be smoother than that for income. Their advocates can claim that the stability of consumption in 1980–2 and 1975–7—two periods when income was falling—is evidence in their favour. But the truth may be that aggregate consumption behaviour is explained by a combination of the current income and life-cycle hypotheses, with the former playing the dominant role.

4.6. Fixed Investment

Fixed investment, or gross domestic fixed capital formation, has, as we have seen, been a major determinant of recessions in total expenditure and output. It consists of the purchase of capital goods, such as machinery, plant, and vehicles; and it also includes house-building, both by the private and public sectors. Its composition in 1994 (at current prices) was:

	£bn.
Housing investment	21.0
Plant, machinery, and vehicles	48.7
Other buildings and works	30.4
Total fixed investment	100.1

Of these three categories it was house-building which suffered most severely in the last recession, falling by 30% between 1989 and 1991—a decline equivalent to more than 2% of GDP. But other types of investment fell too. Fig. 4.4 shows the main investment trends since 1979.

Whilst a number of theories have been advanced to explain investment it pays to be sceptical of their claims. The acceleration principle makes investment a function of the change in national income:

$$I = a\Delta Y$$

where I stands for investment and ΔY for the change in GDP. It is actually possible to find evidence which appears to support this principle. If, for example, the level of investment in manufacturing industry is compared with the increase in real GDP over the three previous years, the correlation coefficient (for the period 1979–93) is found to be 0.88, implying that 88% of the variation of manufacturing investment around its mean can be statistically accounted for by the change in GDP. Yet it is difficult to believe that the correlation reveals a causal connection. Investment is more likely to be

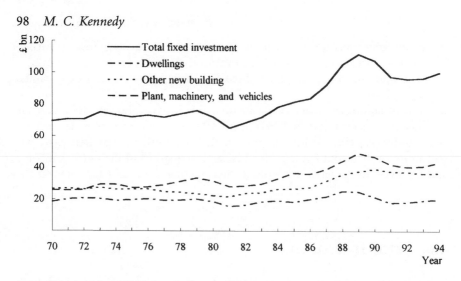

Fig. 4.4. Fixed investment in the UK, 1979–1994

Sources: ETAS, 1994; ET, Oct. 1995.

determined by expectations of future profits, which in turn depend on the stock of investment opportunities, business confidence, the supply prices of capital goods, and interest rates. None of these influences is recognized by the acceleration principle, and the observed correlation is either fortuitous or explicable in other ways. The most likely explanation is that investment tends to peak at the peak of the cycle, when the growth of GDP happens to have been vigorous for several years; and investment tends to be low at the trough of the cycle, after a period of slow or negative growth. It is a characteristic of cyclical movements (e.g. a sine curve) that the level of the curve reaches its turning-point some periods after the rate of change.

The example illustrates the point that correlation does not necessarily spell causation. More specifically, it is difficult to see how there can be a definitive investment function which explains and predicts its level, when on a priori grounds investment has to depend on intangible factors such as the climate of confidence and the state of technological discovery. Economists can point to certain influences on investment, such as interest rates, but it is questionable whether they will ever be in a position to make satisfactory forecasts of investment without the aid of direct surveys of business intentions.

4.7. Stocks and Stockbuilding

Stockbuilding, or investment in stocks, is a change in a level—the level of all stocks held at the beginning of the period. In any one year, stock investment can be positive or negative, whilst the change in stock investment between successive years can, as we have seen, exert a major influence upon GDP.

At the end of 1993 the total value of stocks held in all industries was approximately £117 billion or 21% of the value of GDP in the year. Stocks held by manufacturing industry accounted for £50 billion, and by wholesale and retail business for £41 billion.

Stocks of work in progress are a technical necessity of production, whilst stocks of materials and finished goods are held mainly out of a precautionary motive. They are required as a 'buffer' between deliveries and production; or, more precisely, because firms realize they cannot hope for an exact correspondence between output and sales, or between deliveries of materials and the amount taken into production.

For these reasons it is plausible to assume that firms carry in their minds the notion of a certain optimum ratio between stocks and output. If stocks fall below the optimum ratio, they will need to be replenished; if they rise above it, they will be run down. The reasoning here follows the capital–stock adjustment principle, which although sometimes applied to fixed investment, is more appropriate to investment in stocks. The principle explains investment in stocks as an attempt to adjust inventories from an actual level to a desired level which is dependent on expected output or sales. The model assumes a fixed relationship between output and the appropriate level of stocks, and is expressed by the equation:

$$\Delta ST = aY - ST$$

where ΔST is the desired change in stocks, ST their actual level, a the preferred stock–output ratio, and Y, current output, is a proxy for expected output.

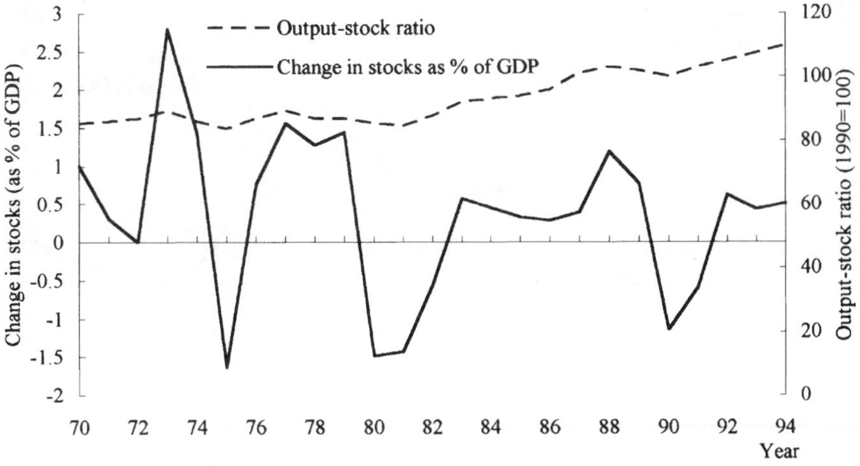

Fig. 4.5. Change in stocks and the output–stock ratio in the UK, 1970–1994

Sources: ETAS, 1994; ET, Oct. 1995.

Fig. 4.5 illustrates the scale of stock changes in relation to GDP. It also shows the stock–output ratio (inverted), the main feature of which is a trend decline which is probably due to a sustained effort by business firms to economize on stocks. There is only a faint correlation between the stock change and the ratio.

The stock-adjustment principle can only be the beginning of an explanation of investment in stocks. It makes no allowance for interest rates or expected future prices, both of which are relevant influences on the preferred stock–output ratio. It applies only to voluntary investment in stocks, and cannot explain involuntary changes, which for finished goods will occur whenever sales deviate from their expected levels.

4.8. Exports and Imports

Exports and imports tend to follow movements in overseas and home demand. Fig. 4.6 takes as its indicator of world demand the total GDP of the OECD countries (which includes the so-called G-7 countries—the USA, Canada, Japan, France, Germany, Italy, and the UK—together with all other major developed economies). On average a rise of 1% in OECD GNP is associated with a rise of slightly more than 1% in UK exports of goods and services. About one fifth of UK exports of merchandise goes to the less developed countries, where the key determinant of real income is the level of primary product prices; and these do not always move with incomes in the developed world. Relative prices are the other main factor in determining UK export

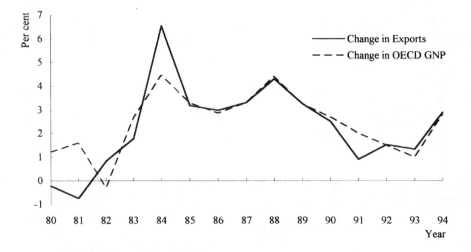

Fig. 4.6. UK exports and change in OECD GDP, 1979–1994

Sources: NIER, Apr. 1995 and earlier; *ETAS*, 1994; *ET*, Oct. 1995.

performance, and help to explain the rise of 12% in UK exports of goods and services in 1992–4, following the UK's departure from the ERM.

Imports are related to demand in the UK, and tend to move with GDP. Over the long period imports have grown much faster than GDP, with a marked upward trend in the import ratio:

	Import ratio (%)
1950–9	15.7
1960–9	17.9
1970–9	21.1
1980–9	25.0
1990–3	31.6

The rise is partly attributable to the liberalization of trade which has affected all countries, but the main factor is likely to have been a gradual loss of competitiveness in terms of price, quality, and delivery dates.

In the shorter run imports are highly sensitive to movements in GDP. Percentage changes in imports tend to exceed the change in GDP by a factor of 2 or 3, pointing to two possible influences at work: (i) a very high income-elasticity of demand, and/ or (ii) an inflexibility of UK supply when demand is rising rapidly (Fig. 4.7). These factors mean that periods of economic expansion are usually associated with a considerable weakening in the balance of payments. There is also some relationship with relative prices, but with over 40% of UK merchandise imports consisting of basic foods, materials, and semi-manufactures, the price elasticity of demand is unlikely to be high.

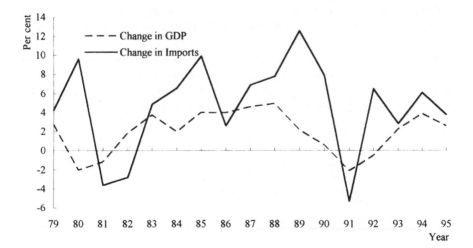

Fig. 4.7. UK imports and change in GDP, 1979–1995

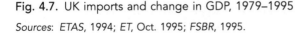

Sources: ETAS, 1994; ET, Oct. 1995; FSBR, 1995.

4.9. GDP by Income

GDP is measured from the side of income by adding up all incomes from production—that is income from employment and self-employment, income from profit, and income from rent. As with the expenditure estimate there is the problem of equating total income receipts to total output when the latter exceeds or falls short of total sales. The problem is resolved by regarding the change in stocks as income in kind, and crediting it to profits. On this definition of terms total 'income' equals total output, and we have an alternative and largely independent estimate of GDP. The income breakdown for 1994 was as follows:

	£bn. at current prices
Income from employment and self-employment	426.4
Profits and trading surpluses *less* stock appreciation	96.4
Rent	56.8
GDP from income	579.6
plus statistical discrepancy	−0.4
GDP from expenditure (at factor cost)	579.1

Note: Detail does not add to total because of rounding.
Source: BB, 1995.

The statistical discrepancy between GDP by income and GDP by expenditure is a reminder that the GDP figures are only estimates. It was small in 1994, but has been as high as 1.7% of GDP.

Personal income is the income of the personal sector, and must be distinguished from income-based GDP. Along with GDP, it includes all income from employment and self-employment. But it includes only the personal sector's share of rent, dividends, and interest. And, unlike GDP, it includes so-called transfer incomes such as student grants, pensions, and social security payments—none of which belong in GDP because they are not payments for production. Thus personal income breaks down as follows:

	£bn. at current prices
Income from employment and self-employment	426.4
Personal receipts of rent, dividends, and interest	72.3
Transfer incomes (Social Security benefits and other grants)	92.4
Total personal income before tax	594.4

It will be clear that the only item to appear in both GDP and personal income is income from employment and self-employment. Personal receipts of rent and profit are only about half as large as the corresponding national receipts. But personal income as a whole is larger than GDP (at factor cost) because of the large sums received in transfer payments.

4.10. The Multiplier

Any increase in GDP will normally give rise to a multiplier process. The initial rise in income leads to higher consumption, higher consumer goods output, and hence to higher GDP. Successive rounds of higher income and consumption will lead to the eventual establishment of an 'equilibrium' level of GDP, this being the level which GDP finally settles at. The multiplier process is the succession of income changes, whilst the 'multiplier' itself is defined as the ratio of the total or cumulative increase in GDP to its initial or 'first round' increase.

In elementary models, the multiplier may be found quite simply because no distinctions are made between GDP and personal income. On these lines it can be seen that an initial increase in GDP of 100 units, combined with a marginal propensity to consume of, say, 0.5, will lead to an eventual increase in GDP of 200 units. This is because personal income rises by the same amount as GDP, so that consumption will then increase (after a time-lag) by 50 units. This leads on to a second-round rise in personal income of 50 units so that consumption in the third round of the multiplier will increase by 25. Each increment of income leads to a rise in consumption half as large as the previous rise, so that the sequence of period-to-period additions to GDP will be:

100, 50, 25, 12.5, 6.25, 3.125 . . . etc.

It is not difficult to see that if all the terms are added together they will eventually sum to 200, which is the equilibrium rise in GDP. And since this is twice the original increase, the multiplier in this example is 2, a value which may also be found from the formula:

$$\Delta Y / \Delta I = 1/1 - MPC$$

where ΔY is the final increase in GDP and ΔI the initial increase.

The multiplier for the UK follows the same principles as the simple model. But it is complicated by the distinction which has to be drawn between personal income and GDP, and by various 'withdrawals' or leakages which do not figure in simple models. A further complication is that expenditure increases at market prices include import and factor cost contents which do not constitute domestic product. Thus a rise of 100 units of fixed investment might have an import content of 34% and an indirect tax (net of subsidies) content of 8%, leaving a domestic product increase of only 58 units.[7]

---

[7] This discussion of the multiplier follows an early paper by W. A. B. Hopkin and W. A. H. Godley, 'An Anaysis of Tax Changes', *NIER*, May 1965.

In expressing the multiplier it is best to relate the eventual rise in GDP (at factor cost) to an initial rise in the domestic-output content of expenditure. This ensures that the multiplier and multiplicand are both expressed in terms of domestic product. A multiplier ratio with GDP as numerator and market price expenditure as denominator does not compare like with like.

Assume now that fixed investment expenditure is raised by £172 million. With import and indirect tax contents of 34 and 8% respectively, this would amount to a rise in GDP of £100 million, and this figure may be taken as the multiplicand.

The first step in the multiplier calculation is to ask how this initial rise in income is likely to be divided between employment income and profits. Since the usual ratio is about 4:1, the best assumption is that employment income rises by £80 million and profits by £20 million. The extra employment income will enter directly into personal income in the form of income from employment and self-employment. Of the £20 million rise in profits, about £7 million will find its way into business saving (undistributed profits) and will not generate an immediate rise in spending; and some part will be paid in corporate taxes (say £6 million). So only about £7 million of the £20 million rise in profits finds its way into personal incomes in the form of dividends.

Falling unemployment as income rises will entail an offset to the rise in personal income on account of lower benefit payments—probably about £4 million for a GDP rise of £100 million. Thus the total increase in personal income will be made up of £80 million for employment incomes, plus £7 million for dividends, but with £4 million subtracted for the fall in transfer incomes—a total rise of £83 million. This is the marginal addition to personal income for a rise in GDP of £100 million; and expressed as a fraction, it is the first in a series of coefficients needed to derive the multiplier (see Table 4.5).

The remaining stages of the calculation involve the marginal rate of direct taxation (including national insurance and pension contributions), the marginal propensity to consume, and the marginal indirect tax and import contents of consumption. Once these are allowed for, it is possible to arrive at the second round increase in GDP, which is the domestically produced element of the rise in consumption.

Table 4.5. Stages in the multiplier estimate

		Assumed marginal relationships
1st round increase in GDP	100	
Increase in personal income	83	$b_1 = 0.83$
Increase in personal disposable income	55	$b_2 = 0.67$
Increase (after a time-lag) in consumers' expenditure at market prices	50	$b_3 = 0.9$
Increase in consumers' expenditure at factor cost	42	$b_4 = 0.82$
Increase in domestically produced consumption at factor cost (equals second-round increase in GDP)	25	$b_5 = 0.61$

The marginal rates of taxation in 1996–7 were 20%, 24%, and 40%, but their average was probably the standard rate of 24%. But national insurance contributions add a further 9% for most incomes, so that the total leakage can be put at about 33% for an across-the-board rise in personal income. As was suggested in Section 4.4, a good central estimate of the marginal propensity to consume is the APC of about 0.9. The marginal rate of indirect tax on consumer goods and services can be taken as equal to the average rate of 0.18. Finally, the marginal import content of consumption (at market prices) has to be put well in excess of the average content—perhaps as much as 0.32.

The upshot of the calculation is that the second-round increase in GDP—which is the domestic output content of the rise in consumers' expenditure—is £25 million, or 0.25 times the initial increase. It follows that the third, fourth, and later increases will each be 0.25 times the previous rise, so that the sequence of period-to-period changes in GDP will be as follows:

£100, 25, 6.25, 1.6, 0.4, 0.1 . . . 0 million

This series sums to a cumulative increase of £133 million, so that the multiplier value is 1.33. This figure is also given by the expression:

$$\frac{1}{1 - 0.25} = 1.33$$

where the coefficient 0.25 can be understood as a marginal propensity to purchase new domestic output. It represents the product of the coefficients b_1, b_2, b_3, b_4, and b_5 in the table. Recall that this multiplier ratio is that of the eventual rise in GDP to an initial rise in GDP. The ratio of the rise in GDP at factor cost (without import content or indirect taxes) to an initial rise in investment at market prices (including import content and taxes) is 133/172 = 0.77.

This discussion takes account of the more important elements in the UK multiplier, and whilst it is not meant to be precise, it should be of about the right order of magnitude. Uncertainties about some of the coefficients suggest that the true figure could be in the range of 1.2 to 1.5. The calculation is, of course, based on the usual multiplier assumptions of unused resources of capital and labour, and of interest rates being held constant through a policy of monetary accommodation. It ignores various side-effects of which the most important is the effect of higher sales on stocks. Stocks will be run down at the start of the process; but their decline is likely to be reversed later as production is stepped up to replenish stocks and to meet the higher level of demand. Finally, it should be recalled that the whole process takes time. Higher output and employment will lead, almost immediately, to a rise in income from employment, but the rise in dividends will be delayed. There will be some time-lag—a month seems a good guess—between higher personal income and higher consumption.

4.11. Inflation and its Measurement

The record of inflation in the UK in the last half-century is one of moderate price increases in the 1950s and 1960s, a quite exceptional inflation in the 1970s, and a return to more moderate rates in the 1980s and 1990s. In the 15 years from 1953 to 1968 the annual rise in the retail price index (RPI) averaged 3.3%, and never exceeded 5%. The pace quickened in the early 1970s, and took off in mid-decade as the result of two main factors: the unprecedented rise in oil and other import prices from 1973 to 1975 (when import prices increased by 112%), and the exceptionally high pressure of demand during and immediately after the 'Barber boom' of 1973. Inflation reached 25% in 1975, and over the 1970s as a whole it averaged 13%. It was not until the deep recession of the early 1980s that inflation came down to a moderate rate. But it picked up again with the 'Lawson boom' of 1987–90, reaching 9½% in 1990, after which it was corrected by the recession of 1990–2. The 1.6% rate of inflation in 1993 was the lowest for 30 years.

In measuring inflation the most usual indicator is the so-called 'headline rate', which is the change in the retail price index (RPI). This index is compiled directly from price data, and registers the prices of a collection of goods and services entering a typical shopping basket. Being a base-weighted index it becomes outdated with the passage of time, and, for this reason, its composition is revised on a regular basis. The index is subject to an upwards bias in times of rapid price inflation because consumers will tend to switch their expenditure towards those goods which are rising least rapidly in price.

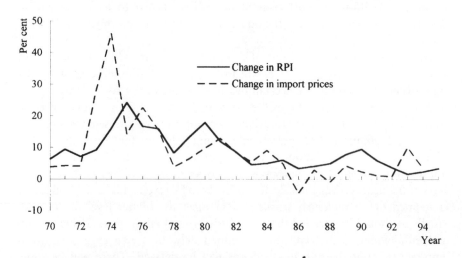

Fig. 4.8. Inflation and import prices in the UK, 1970–1995

Source: See Appendix Tables 4.A1 and 4.A2.

The composition of the RPI is open to the very real objection that it includes mortgage interest payments, which are transfers within the personal sector and not purchases of newly produced goods or services. When mortgage rates are increased, income is simply transferred from borrowers to savers—so that one group of households gains and another loses. Policy-makers can justly complain that, when they raise interest rates to counter inflation, they must accept an immediate increase in the RPI because of the rise in mortgage payments. The official view is that the 'underlying' index, which excludes mortgage interest payments (the 'RPIX'), is a better indicator of inflation, and the government's inflation target is expressed this way.

In practice the differences between the RPI and RPIX have not been large. In the fifteen years since 1979 there have been five occasions when the annual rates of change of the two indices have deviated by more than 1%, and in 1989 the RPI rose by 7.8% compared with 5.9% for RPIX. But, although the underlying rate is the better index in principle, the headline rate is the more relevant to wage claims.

An alternative to these indices is the consumer price index (or CPI). This is a 'deflator', and unlike the RPI and RPIX, is not derived from price data. It is found by dividing the current value of consumers' expenditure by its volume as measured at constant prices, the volume being derived directly from quantity data.

There are various other indices which relate to inflation. The best index of the prices charged for all goods and services produced in the UK economy, but including imports and indirect taxes, is another deflator—the implied deflator for total final expenditure (TFE). This is derived by dividing the value of TFE by its amount at constant prices. If an index is required to measure the prices of goods purchased by UK residents, the best general measure is the implied deflator for total domestic expenditure, since this is the average of prices paid for consumption and investment goods. The GDP deflator, or index of home costs, is another implied index, but is essentially an index of money incomes divided by real output, i.e. wages and profits per unit of output. This index leaves out the effects on market prices of changes in import prices and indirect taxes—except in so far as they influence wages and profits. In this chapter, however, we shall concentrate on the RPI as the principal indicator of inflation.

4.12. The Inflationary Process

The main elements in the inflationary process have been fairly well understood since the 1950s. The chief domestic influence is the pressure of demand on supplies of goods and labour. When demand is high relative to supply there will be upward pressure on wages and profit margins. To this pressure is added the wage-price spiral. Higher wages mean higher industrial costs, which lead to higher prices, which in turn force up earnings in the next round of wage settlements. The process may be damped because wages are only a fraction (about two-thirds) of total variable costs—so that, for example, a 10% increase in wages leads to a less than 10% increase in prices, and so to a less than 10% rise in wages at the next round. But the effects of a boom in home demand in one year will, none the less, be felt for many years after the boom has subsided.

A further influence is the effect of import prices. With imports accounting for roughly one-fifth of total final expenditure and one-third of total variable costs, any rise in import prices will find its way into final prices both directly, and through its effect on industrial costs. With imports that are in competition with home production, the effects may not be so serious, since demand will switch to home output. But a large part of UK imports cannot be made or grown at home, and is in highly inelastic demand. UK prices will also rise if there is an increase in the world price of oil, which, since the late 1970s, has been the UK's main primary product export.[8]

Finally, there is the exchange rate spiral. When the exchange rate is variable, domestic price increases can feed back upon themselves via the exchange rate. A rise in UK prices will tend to put the balance of payments into deficit, leading to a shortage of foreign exchange, and to a consequential fall in the exchange rate for sterling. This entails higher sterling import prices, and hence a further bout of domestic cost and price increases. When this process is at work the wage-price spiral is less effectively damped, and, in principle, a domestic price rise could be self-perpetuating. Thus to illustrate—a 10% domestic price rise could lead to a 10% increase in wages, a 10% fall in the exchange rate, and a 10% increase in import prices. At the next round of the spiral the rate of price change will tend to increase by the full 10% since both the wage and import elements in industrial costs have increased by that

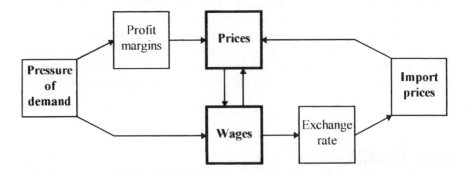

Fig. 4.9. The inflationary process

[8] This account of the inflationary process is closely similar to that described in L. A. Dicks-Mireaux, 'The Inter-Relationship between Cost and Price Changes, 1945–1959', *OEP*, Oct. 1961, and in J. C. R. Dow, *The Management of the British Economy 1945–60*, (Cambridge: Cambridge University Press, 1964).

amount. The process continues with the inflation rate rising by 10% at each round of the wage-price-exchange rate spiral.

The main forces in the inflationary process are illustrated in Fig. 4.9 below.

4.13. The Role of Money and Price Expectations

Two other factors which are frequently claimed to have a major influence on the rate of inflation are the growth of the money supply and price expectations. Inflation will always involve an increase in the transactions demand for money, and can only be sustained if there is a matching growth in the stock of money.[9] If the new money is not forthcoming the inflation can proceed only so long as 'idle balances' (or asset money) are drawn into the active circulation. But once these balances are exhausted the inflation will either come to an end or output will have to fall. It is fair to claim, therefore, that for any sustained inflation or real output expansion to take place, there simply has to be a rise in the stock of money. Growth in the stock of money is a necessary condition of the process. But to maintain, as some economists do, that monetary expansion is the 'cause' of the inflation, is to neglect that the inflation has almost certainly been initiated by some other factor—such as a rise in real demand or an increase in import prices. Monetary expansion *per se* is very seldom an initiating cause of inflation. Thus it seems reasonable to say that the principal 'cause' of inflation is high demand pressure, and that monetary growth is its necessary condition.[10] As D. H. Robertson once put it 'if all parties to any monetary controversy could agree to substitute the words "essential condition" for that elusive word "cause", a good many of the points at issue would tend to disappear'.[11]

The other factor is price expectations, which, in so far as they influence the exchange rate, are potentially important. If, for example, the foreign exchange markets foresee a rapid inflation of UK prices they will sell sterling and the exchange rate will fall. This will raise sterling import prices, and the market's forecast will be self-fulfilling—an outcome which seems possible whether or not there was any real substance in the original forecast. In wage negotiations, however, the dominant influence (contrary to some textbook accounts) is

[9] J. R. Hicks in *Critical Essays in Monetary Theory* (Oxford: Clarendon Press, 1967) argued that the transactions demand for money is better understood as a 'need' than as a demand. There is no real substitute for money as an instrument for effecting transactions—although there are alternatives to money as a store of wealth.

[10] It should also be borne in mind that the money stock is in some measure endogenous, and that central banks, or the governments that control them, are reluctant to allow interest rates to rise in response to a rise in the demand for money.

[11] D. H. Robertson, *Money*, (Cambridge: Nisbet, 1922). Robertson also came near to showing that a rise in the stock of money was a necessary condition of the multiplier process in 'Some Notes on Mr. Keynes' General Theory of Employment', *Quarterly Journal of Economics*, Nov. 1936.

more likely to be the latest rise in the retail price index rather than the expectation of its future rise. The former, after all, is established fact, whilst the latter is a prediction or guess. Price expectations do not play much part in the wage-price spiral.

4.14. Wage Increases and the Pressure of Demand

There is abundant evidence for the hypothesis that the pressure of demand for labour is a major determinant of the rate of inflation. Numerous studies in the 1950s and 1960s showed a strong negative relationship between the rate of change of money wage rates and unemployment. One of the earliest studies of this kind, and certainly the most influential, was published in 1958 by Professor A. W. Phillips.[12] Phillips wrote 'When the demand for labour is high and there are very few unemployed we should expect employers to bid up wages quite rapidly, each firm and each industry being tempted to offer a little above the prevailing rates to attract the most suitable labour from other firms and industries.' He examined unemployment rates and wage increases for nearly a century, and on the basis of data for 1861–1913, suggested that the relationship between wage increases and unemployment was the downward-sloping curve illustrated by Fig. 4.10.

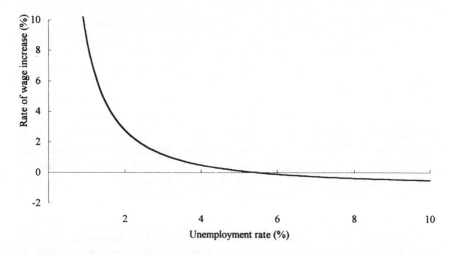

Fig. 4.10. The Phillips Curve

Source: Phillips, 'Unemployment and Wage Rates'.
Note: Curve estimated from data for 1861–1913.

---

[12] A. W. Phillips, 'The Relation between Unemployment and the Rate of Change of Money Wage Rates, 1861–1957', *Economica*, Nov. 1958.

The relationship became known as the Phillips Curve, and implied a wage increase of 8.7% for an unemployment rate of 1.0% and of 1.2% for unemployment at 3.0%—figures which are much too low by today's standards. Phillips estimated that there was a Critical Rate of Unemployment of about 2.4%, at which the rate of wage increase would be equal to the average annual rise in productivity of 2.0%—thus holding wage costs per unit of output at an unchanged level, and exerting no upward pressure on prices.

One of the more remarkable features of the Phillips Curve, and one which distinguished it from many similar studies, both then and later, was that it passed a prediction test. It was able to predict increases in wages well outside its data period of 1861–1913. Phillips showed in his article that wage increases over the 1948–57 period were almost exactly as predicted by his relationship.

The Phillips Curve continued to give accurate predictions of wage increases for a number of years after the study had been published. During the eight years from 1958 to 1965 there was not a single error in excess of 2.5% and the mean error (regardless of sign) was 1.1%[13]—results which would be welcomed by forecasters today.

After the mid-1960s, however, the pure Phillips Curve became increasingly less reliable as a guide to the rate of wage inflation. It underpredicted by about 4.5% per annum in 1967–9, by 10–12% in 1970–3; and by more than 20% in 1974 and 1975.

There were two principal reasons for the breakdown of the Phillips Curve, of which the first was its omission of the rate of price change. Phillips had felt able to neglect price changes because the period from which he started was one of price stability. But as inflation became part of everyday experience, it became increasingly normal for trade-union negotiators to link their wage claims to the rise in prices—thus exposing the Phillips Curve to the criticism that it had omitted a crucial variable. The omission was particularly serious in the period of rapidly rising import prices in the 1970s.

The second principal factor was the failure of the unemployment statistics to register the pressure of demand. Phillips had to use the unemployment series since it was the only available indicator in the period he studied. But other indicators, such as the vacancy rate and the CBI data on labour shortages, have become available since then.

These factors are the main explanations for the Phillips Curve breakdown. They do not alter the main message of the Phillips Curve, which is that wage increases are primarily determined by the pressure of demand. Evidence for this is readily available in the relationship between earnings increases and the vacancy statistics—a series which has a distinct advantage over unemployment in that it points directly to excess demand for labour, and not to excess supply. Wages tend to be flexible upwards but sticky downwards, responding positively

---

[13] For a discussion of the predictive properties of various wage equations see M. T. Sumner, 'The History and Significance of the Phillips Curve' in D. Demery, D. W. Duck, M. T. Sumner, and R. L. Thomas (eds.), *Macroeconomics* (London: Longman, 1984).

to excess demand, but not falling much when a particular market is in excess supply—see below for a further discussion.

Earnings and the Vacancy Rate

The idea of a relationship between the rate of increase in earnings and the vacancy rate can be illustrated, as in Fig. 4.11, by deflating the rise in money earnings by the lagged rise in prices. The lag is six months, with the calendar year rise in prices influencing the end-year rise in earnings. The time-lag between prices and earnings arises because the earnings index is largely dependent on annual wage settlements, and these are made for different bargaining groups at different times of the year. In any particular month (say, December) the index consists of settlements which have been reached throughout the previous twelve months. Only the most recent settlements will take note of the December price index, and the others will have been based on price data published as long ago as the previous January. On average the price data will be 6 months behind the earnings index, implying that the end-year earnings index has to be related to the retail price levels recorded over the twelve months from January to December, i.e. to the calendar year average.

In deflating the earnings index by the rise in retail prices there is an implicit assumption of a one-to-one relationship between the two rates of increase. Whilst this may satisfy the view that workers strive to maintain their real wages, it has to be accepted in practice that some groups will not succeed in

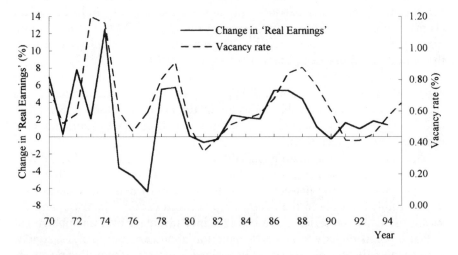

Fig. 4.11. Percentage change in 'real earnings' and the vacancy rate in the UK, 1979–1994

Sources: ETAS, 1986, 1991, 1994; ET, Oct. 1995.
Note: 'Real earnings' are money earnings deflated by the lagged rise in prices: see text.

doing so. To allow for this possibility it is best to take as the dependent variable the rise in money earnings and to relate it to two independent variables— lagged inflation and the vacancy rate.

This procedure was adopted in the two previous editions of this book. Relationships were estimated for the periods 1975–88, which included a period of incomes policy, and for 1980–90. The main conclusion was that the percentage rise in end-year money earnings approximates to:

(1) some 5 to 8 times the vacancy percentage;
(2) plus about 0.7 times the lagged rise in retail prices;
(3) plus or minus a small constant term.

The two estimated equations were:
For 1975–88:

$$W' = -0.74 + 7.68V + 0.74P' -3.00(IP) - 3.00\ (CU)$$

For 1980–90:

$$W' = 1.09 + 5.16V + 0.66P'$$

where W' refers to the rate of increase at end-year (October–March) earnings over a year earlier, V to the annual vacancy rate as a percentage of the workforce and P' to the annual rate of price increase. IP is a 'dummy variable' designed to allow for the effects of incomes policy in 1975–7, and CU is a further dummy to track the 'catch-up' of earnings after the policy had been challenged in 1978–9.

These equations have to be understood as hypothetical propositions. Certain statistical tests were applied to them at the time they were estimated—which they passed quite well.[14] But the relationships cannot be said to have been adequately tested unless they are confronted with observations from outside their data periods. It is an axiom of the scientific method that tests must be reasonably difficult to pass: and merely to compare estimated values with the actuals from which they were calculated is not much of a hurdle—especially when the least-squares technique is itself designed to give the best possible fit to the data.[15]

When put to the more severe test of forecasting outside their estimation periods the equations perform as shown in Table 4.6. The 1975–88 equation (with dummy variable set at zero) predicts with an average error over six years of 1.2%. The 1980–90 equation over four years predicts with an average of 1.1%. These are both good results.

The slight tendency for the equations to overpredict may have been partly due to the government's efforts to hold down wages in the public sector; and possibly to a falling sensitivity to price changes as inflation became more moderate.

---

[14] The standard errors of estimate for the 1975–88 and 1980–90 equations respectively were 0.98 and 0.77%, and the r-squared values were 0.96 and 0.92.
[15] As Phillips realized in 1958, when he was undoubtedly influenced by his colleague at the London School of Economics the late Professor Sir Karl Popper, whose *Conjectures and Refutations* (Routledge and Kegan Paul, 1963) provides an accessible and readable introduction to the philosophy of science.

Table 4.6. Predicted and actual changes in earnings, 1989–1994

	1989	1990	1991	1992	1993	1994	Mean absolute error
Actual changes in earnings, Oct–Mar of year (%)	9.0	9.2	7.5	4.6	3.5	3.8	—
Predicted change from 1975–88 equation	10.9	11.0	6.8	5.1	4.6	5.1	—
Predicted change from 1980–90 equation	—	—	7.1	5.6	4.9	5.3	—
Error from 1975–80 equation	1.9	1.8	0.7	0.5	1.1	1.3	1.2
Error from 1980–8 equation	—	—	0.4	1.0	1.4	1.5	1.1

The trade-off implications of the 1980–8 equation are that the inflation rate for earnings rises by about 1% for each 0.2% rise in the vacancy rate:

vacancy rate (%)	0.3	0.5	0.7	0.9
increase in earnings (%)	2.6	3.7	4.7	5.7

This is the short-run trade-off. But the wage-price spiral will, of couse, result in a steeper long-run trade-off: earnings rose by 9% in the peak years of 1989 and 1990, not by the 5.7% change in the schedule.

The main conclusion is that there is good evidence for a Phillips-type principle in which the rate of change of money earnings is governed by the pressure of demand as indicated by the vacancy rate, but that allowance must also be made for the influence of the lagged inflation rate. Additional factors could be government wages policy, and a factor which has not been considered here, the rate of increase in demand itself (the change in V).

4.15. Price Changes

A preliminary view of prices is that they are determined by a constant mark-up over variable costs, which means that each change in costs would be followed, after a short time-lag, by a change in prices of a given percentage amount. Costs themselves divide into earnings (as an approximation to employment costs) and import prices. These have weights of 0.66 and 0.34, respectively, in total variable costs, so that one method for predicting the change in prices might be to estimate it as (i) 0.66 times the percentage change in employment costs, plus (ii) 0.34 times the percentage change in import prices.[16] But the disadvantage of this method is that profit margins are assumed to remain constant, whereas they probably vary with the state of demand.

A better method is to estimate the change in prices as a function of the

[16] *NIBB*, 1988, 29.

Table 4.7. Predicted and actual changes in retail prices, 1991–1995

Jan–June	1992	1993	1994	1995	Mean absolute error
Actual change in prices (Jan–June from a year earlier, %)	4.2	1.5	2.5	3.4	
Predicted change from 1981-91 equation	3.4	2.9	1.9	3.0	
Error	−0.8	1.4	−0.6	−0.4	0.8

change in import prices, along with the two principal determinants of the change in earnings discussed in the previous section: the lagged vacancy rate and the previous year's price increase. This amounts to substituting the wage equation of the previous section into the price equation, leaving the vacancy rate variable to pick up the effect of demand pressure on both wages and profit margins. The result of doing so for the period from 1981 to 1991 was published in the thirteenth edition of this book, and concluded that the rate of increase in the retail price index for the first half-year could be estimated as:

(1) about 8 times the vacancy rate in the previous calendar year;
(2) plus about 0.6 times the previous year's inflation rate;
(3) plus 0.2 times the rise in import prices for October–March;
(4) plus a constant term.

The estimated equation was:

$$P'_t = -3.91 + 8.00V + 0.62P' + 0.19Pm'$$

where P'_t is the rate of change in retail prices for January to June over the same period a year earlier, V is last year's vacancy rate, P' last year's inflation rate, and Pm' is the October to March change in the unit value index of import prices. The equation fitted its data quite well[17]

The coefficient on the vacancy rate turns out to be stronger than that given for the earnings equations, and this confirms a direct effect of the pressure of demand on profit margins—thus qualifying the crude mark-up hypothesis. The coefficient on lagged prices is about what might be expected, given the wage content of variable costs, and the constant term incorporates the average rise in productivity.

The relationship makes no allowance for changes in indirect taxes or mortgage interest rates, and its coefficient for import prices may be on the low side. Even so, it has been able to predict inflation with reasonable accuracy for several years as shown in Table 4.7.

The equation predicted the rise in the RPI to within 1% of its actual rise in three years out of four.[18]

[17] The standard error of the residuals was 1.1% of the price level, r-squared 0.87.
[18] These 'predictions' are based on true values for the independent variables, and are not comparable with the Treasury's forecast errors which are predicated on forecast values of the relevant variables: the average error from Treasury forecasts over a 10-year period was 1.4% (see Ch. 5).

The Critical Rate and the NAIRU

The equation works well enough to be brought to bear on the question of the critical vacancy rate—the pressure of demand at which the inflation rate is likely to be zero or constant. The question is of much more than technical interest because the vacancy rate is closely related in the short run to unemployment. Unemployment is a lagged indicator of the pressure of demand, and its relationship with vacancies is at its best with a lag of one year. The relationship for 1988–94 is illustrated in Fig. 4.13, and in the first two rows of Table 4.8. Unemployment (lagged one year) tends to fall by about 1.0% for every 0.1% rise in the vacancy rate pressure.[19]

The middle and bottom rows of Table 4.8 set out the short-run trade-off between inflation and unemployment. (But on the assumption of zero inflation in the previous year and stable import prices.) They imply that the critical vacancy rate, at which the rate of inflation is likely to be zero, is in the region of 0.5% of the workforce—which is higher than in the 1991–3 recession, but still a very low pressure of demand. The critical unemployment rate ('non-accelerating inflation rate of unemployment' or NAIRU) looks like being about 9% of the workforce, and at 2.6 million people, indicates the high social cost of containing inflation.

The other implication is that if unemployment for any length of time is held below the NAIRU—or above the critical vacancy rate—then the rate of inflation will tend to increase year by year as each price increase feeds into wages and back again to prices. This is the so-called 'acceleration' result normally associated with theories of the expectations-augmented Phillips curve, but which holds equally well for the wage-price spiral. The table below gives only the 'short-run trade-off' between unemployment and inflation. The feedback coefficient in the equation from the previous year's to this year's inflation is 0.62, so that year 2 inflation will be 0.62 times year 1's rate, and year 3 will be 0.62 times year 2's rate. On the somewhat artificial assumption of no additional interaction through the exchange rate and import prices, the equation suggests that for the comparatively modest vacancy rate of 0.7%, inflation could increase from the 1.7% shown for year 1 to over 4% in year 3. The rate would rise much faster with the exchange-rate-import-price feedback.

Table 4.8. Relationship between vacancies, unemployment, and prices (%)

Vacancy rate	0.3	0.5	0.7	0.9
Associated unemployment rate	11.1	9.2	7.4	5.5
Increase in RPI	−1.5	0.1	1.7	3.3

[19] The r-squared coefficient for unemployment (lagged one year) and the annual vacancy rate for 1988–93 is 0.90. The unemployment values shown in the schedule are obtained from the regression U (lagged) $= 13.89 - 9.31V$ where U and V are the percentage unemployment and vacancy rates; the standard error of U is 0.67 per cent. Quarterly figures suggest that the correlation is at its best with a lag of more than four quarters. See next section for a further discussion.

These quantitative conclusions should, of course, be tempered with the caveat that the statistical analysis on which they are based has to be taken with a margin of error; and also with the hope that as inflation moderates the old sensitivity of wages to prices might decline.

Finally, it should be noted that the NAIRU, although consistent with an equilibrium in the average price level, cannot be accepted as an equilibrium for the labour market, since it represents a huge excess supply of labour in which workers are seeking jobs and not finding them at going rates of pay. The number of vacancies at the NAIRU is substantially less than the number of unemployed, and there is a mismatch between the skills required and the skills of the unemployed. The NAIRU is a labour-market disequilibrium, and bears no resemblance to the full employment, or 'natural' rate (of voluntary unemployment) discussed by Professor Milton Friedman.[20]

4.16. The Pressure of Demand

In the two previous sections it was maintained that the principal domestic generator of inflation in the UK is the pressure of demand for labour. It is normal, since the 'labour market' is an aggregate of individual and mainly local markets for different skills and occupations, to observe excess supply in some markets at the same time as there is excess demand in others. It is, however, the markets with excess demand, not those with excess supply, which are most directly engaged in the inflationary process. This is because excess demand normally generates an increase in money wages, whereas excess supply is much less likely to lead to wage cuts: wages are flexible upwards and sticky downwards. This is why, at least in principle, it makes sense to choose the vacancy rate rather than unemployment as the central variable for analysing wage inflation. Unemployment is a measure of the number of workers claiming benefit and seeking work which they are unable to find; and, as such, it is measurement of excess supply.

In practice, the vacancy figures, unlike those for unemployment, are incomplete. They are reported by employers only if it is worth their while to notify them. Many employers prefer to recruit through local newspapers rather than through job centres; and an employer who has already notified the job centre of vacancies for a particular kind of worker does not need to register new vacancies because the original notice will suffice. The Department of Employment estimates that only about one-third of all new vacancies are reported. This need not invalidate the series, however, since, by most statistical standards, a one-third sample is comfortably large. If the ratio of recorded to unrecorded vacancies remains steady, then the vacancy series can be expected to be a reliable guide to excess demand in the labour market as a whole.

[20] M. Friedman, 'The Role of Monetary Policy', *AER*, Mar. 1968.

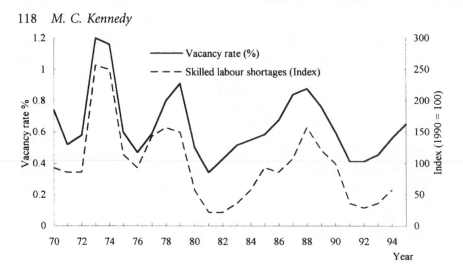

Fig. 4.12. Vacancies and skilled labour shortages

Note: Vacancy rate (%); percentage of firms reporting to CBI that output is limited by shortages of skilled labour averaged over the year and indexed at 1990 = 100.
Sources: ETAS, 1994; *ET*, Oct. 1995.

Support for the vacancy series may be found in its close correlation with another indicator of demand pressure, the CBI's measure of skilled labour shortages (Fig. 4.12). The CBI's quarterly questionnaire asks manufacturing employers whether their output is constrained by shortages of skilled labour. The degree of labour shortage is reflected by the percentage replying positively, and the correlation with the vacancy rate is 0.9—see Table 4.9.

The vacancy rate is also correlated with the output gap for GDP.[21] But, as the table shows, it is not so well related to unemployment over the 23-year period. Even with a lag to allow for the slow response of unemployment to the pressure of demand, the correlation is not strong.

Table 4.9. Correlation coefficients between indicators of the pressure of demand 1970–1993

	Vacancy rate	Skilled labour shortages (CBI)	Output gap (GDP as % of potential)
Skilled labour shortages (CBI)	0.92	—	—
Output gap (GDP as % of potential)	−0.67	−0.68	—
Unemployment rate (lagged one year)	−0.55	0.69	0.31
Unemployment (unlagged)	−0.41	−0.59	0.22

[21] These comparisons for levels of the series are repeated for annual changes: the correlation between the change in the vacancy rate and the change in the CBI series for skilled labour is 0.84.

Table 4.10. Relationship between unemployment and vacancies in the UK (000s)

	Unfilled vacancies		Unemployment	
Demand peaks				
1965–6 (average)	262	(1.0)	346	(1.5)
1973–4 (average)	302	(1.2)	598	(2.1)
1979	241	(0.9)	1,296	(4.1)
1988	249	(0.9)	2,319	(8.4)
Demand lows (vacancies at 0.5–0.6%)				
1962–3 (average)	147	(0.6)	497	(2.2)
1971–2 (average)	139	(0.6)	794	(2.8)
1975–6 (average)	139	(0.5)	1,121	(3.7)
1982–4 (average)	134	(0.5)	3,060	(10.3)
1994	158	(0.6)	2,610	(9.3)

Note: Figures in brackets are percentages

The relationship between unemployment and the vacancy statistics has been changing for many years (see Table 4.10).

In 1965–6 there were about three recorded vacancies for three unemployed people, whereas two decades later, in 1988, and with similar demand pressure, there were nine unemployed people for each vacant job.

This very large rise in unemployment relative to vacancies can probably be attributed to two main sets of factors. First, there has been an increase in the demand for skilled labour relative to unskilled, and this has not been matched by a parallel increase in supply. The CBI's figures of labour shortages at the peaks of the cycle used to show a substantial shortage of unskilled labour, but this is no longer the case (see Table 4.11).

A second factor is the so-called 'hysteresis' or 'ratchet' effect whereby high unemployment tends to perpetuate itself. As unemployment has increased the stigma attached to being without a job has disappeared. The unemployed have discovered the benefit system. Some, especially the lower paid, and those with large families, have been trapped into unemployment by the realization that they are scarcely better off in a job than they are on income support with housing benefit. Others have become demoralized as a result of being repeatedly rejected for jobs in a situation where there are simply not enough jobs to go round.

But, although the *U–V* relationship has changed over the long period, there is

Table 4.11. Vacancy rates and levels of skilled and unskilled labour (%)

	Firms limited by shortages of skilled labour	Firms limited by shortages of unskilled labour	Vacancy rate
1965–6	27	15	1.0
1973–4	36	17	1.2
1979	21	5	0.9
1988	22	4	0.9

Source: ETAS, 1994; CBI

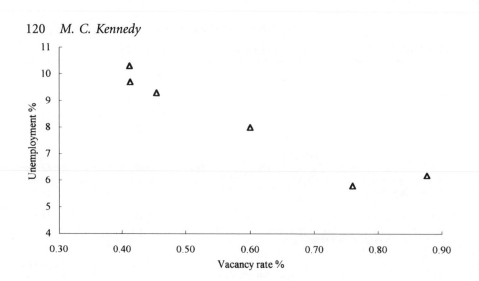

Fig. 4.13. Vacancies and the lagged unemployment rate, 1988–1993

Source: See Appendix Tables 4A.1 and 4.A2.
Note: Unemployment % lagged one year; vacancies as % of workforce.

still a connection over short periods, and one which was particularly close for the 1988–93 period, as illustrated by Fig. 4.13 (correlation coefficient 0.8—see n. 19). This relationship has already been used to indicate the inflation–unemployment trade-off.

Further Reading

See list at end of Chapter 5.

Appendix

Table 4.A1. Indicators of economic activity

	GDP index 1990=100[a]	Manufacturing output 1990=100	Index of employment 1990=100[b]	Unemployment (millions)[c]	GDP as % of trend[d]
1970	64.3	85.6	93.7	0.60	92.9
1971	65.3	84.8	92.5	0.75	93.0
1972	67.1	86.6	92.9	0.84	94.2
1973	72.2	94.6	94.8	0.60	100.0
1974	71.1	93.4	95.2	0.60	97.1
1975	70.6	87.0	94.7	0.94	95.1
1976	72.5	88.6	94.0	1.30	96.3
1977	74.4	90.3	94.1	1.40	97.5
1978	76.4	90.8	94.8	1.38	98.7
1979	78.5	90.6	96.1	1.30	100.0
1980	76.9	82.8	95.4	1.66	95.9
1981	76.0	77.7	92.1	2.52	92.7
1982	77.4	77.6	90.3	2.92	92.3
1983	80.3	79.2	89.6	3.10	93.7
1984	81.9	82.2	91.1	3.16	93.5
1985	85.2	84.5	92.1	3.27	95.1
1986	88.6	85.7	92.3	3.29	96.7
1987	92.7	89.6	93.9	2.95	99.0
1988	97.3	95.9	96.9	2.37	101.7
1989	99.4	100.2	99.3	1.78	101.6
1990	100.0	100.0	100.0	1.66	100.0
1991	97.9	94.6	97.8	2.29	95.6
1992	97.4	94.0	96.3	2.77	93.1
1993	99.6	95.1	95.2	2.90	92.9
1994	103.5	99.1	95.8	2.62	93.6
1995	106.3	101.0		2.31	94.3

Notes: [a] GDP at factor cost, average estimate at constant prices.
[b] Employed labour force.
[c] UK claimant total.
[d] From peak-to-peak trends 1973–9 and 1979–90, growth rates 1.4 and 2.2% p.a. extrapolated to 1995.
Sources: ETAS, 1982 and 1994; *ET* Oct. 1995; *FSBR* 1996–7.

Table 4.A2. Indicators of inflation (%)

	Change in retail prices	Change in average earnings	Change in import prices[a]	Unemployment rate[b]	Unfilled vacancies[c]	Change in exchange rate [d]
1970	6.4	12.1	3.8	2.6	0.74	−1.0
1971	9.4	11.2	4.3	2.5	0.52	−0.2
1972	7.1	12.9	4.1	2.9	0.58	−3.6
1973	9.2	13.5	28.1	2.1	1.20	−9.3
1974	16.0	17.8	46.1	2.0	1.16	−3.1
1975	24.2	26.5	14.1	3.0	0.60	−7.8
1976	16.6	15.5	22.6	4.1	0.47	−14.3
1977	15.9	9.0	15.5	4.4	0.59	−5.4
1978	8.3	12.8	3.9	4.4	0.80	−0.2
1979	13.4	15.5	6.4	4.1	0.91	5.9
1980	17.9	20.8	9.7	4.8	0.50	10.0
1981	11.9	12.8	12.9	8.0	0.34	1.1
1982	8.6	9.4	8.4	9.5	0.43	−4.5
1983	4.6	8.5	5.4	10.5	0.52	−7.4
1984	5.0	6.0	9.0	10.7	0.55	−4.5
1985	6.0	8.5	4.9	10.9	0.58	−0.6
1986	3.4	7.9	−4.6	11.2	0.68	−8.5
1987	4.1	7.8	2.9	10.2	0.84	−1.5
1988	4.9	8.7	−1.0	8.2	0.88	6.0
1989	7.8	9.2	4.3	6.2	0.77	−3.0
1990	9.5	9.6	2.4	5.8	0.61	−1.4
1991	5.9	8.0	1.2	8.0	0.41	0.4
1992	3.7	6.1	0.9	9.7	0.41	−3.6
1993	1.6	3.4	10.0	10.3	0.45	−9.9
1994	2.4	4.0	3.4	9.3	0.56	0.3
1995	3.4	—	—	8.2	0.65	−4.7

[a] Unit value index.
[b] % of workforce.
[c] % of workforce.
[d] Sterling exchange rate index.
Sources: *ETAS*, 1988, 1994; *ET*, Oct. 1995.

MACROECONOMIC POLICY

M. C. KENNEDY

5.1. The Objectives of Policy

The traditional objectives of macroeconomic policy were the maintenance of a low level of unemployment and the avoidance of inflation. Unemployment is largely involuntary in that workers have lost their jobs through redundancy and not through any fault of their own; for the most part they are anxious to find work at the going rate of pay. Being unemployed means a substantial loss of income and self-respect, whilst a prolonged spell of not working can lead to the erosion of work skills and, ultimately, to the loss of a will to work. Unemployment is statistically associated with poor health, suicide, and crime. According to some commentators there is a danger that an underclass is emerging, the members of which are alienated from the rest of society and its values.

The objective of high employment, however, is in conflict with that of price stability. During the 1950s and 1960s this conflict was not severe, and high levels of employment were attained without serious inflation. But as shown in the previous chapter, the inflation problem became acute during the 1970s. The oil shock of 1973 and the rapid inflation that followed led to a shift in priorities, and since 1979 governments have been almost exclusively concerned with the control of inflation. Even now it is not clear that either of the main political parties has a clearly formulated policy for full employment—even though there are periodic statements of good intention.

In this chapter the early sections will discuss the problems of employment policy, whilst the later sections will concentrate on the objective of price stability. In the course of the chapter we shall take up the associated questions of budget balance, the public debt, and balance of payments, and their bearing on the main policy objectives.

5.2. Demand Management

From the 1950s to the early 1970s governments of both the main political parties were deeply committed to the ideal of full employment as set out in the White Paper on Employment Policy (Cmd. 6527) issued in 1944 by the wartime coalition government. The White Paper stated that:

The Government believe that, once the war has been won, we can make a fresh approach, with better chances of success than ever before, to the task of maintaining a high and stable level of employment without sacrificing the essential liberties of a free society.

The White Paper recommended that there should be a permanent staff of statisticians and economists in the Civil Service with responsibility for inter-preting economic trends and advising on policy. The conduct of employment policy was to be examined annually by Parliament in the debate on the Budget, and it was accepted that the budget did not have to be balanced annually, but should be directed to the needs of the economy. There was, however, a commitment to balance the budget over the longer period. The White Paper foresaw that high levels of employment were likely to endanger price stability, and pointed out the need for 'moderation in wage matters by employers and employees' as the essential condition for the success of the policy.

For nearly thirty years the task of maintaining a high level of employment proved to be less difficult and less inflationary than had been feared. Employ-ment levels were higher than the authors of the 1944 White Paper had hoped for, and inflation, at 3% per year in the 1950s and 4% in the 1960s, was moderate.

The demand management system was essentially one of forecasts, targets, and instruments. Shortly before each main budget (which were then in the spring) the Chancellor of the Exchequer was provided with forecasts of GDP, unemployment, inflation, and the balance of payments. These forecasts focused on the fourth quarter of the current year and the first half of the next year—a period which was judged to reflect the limits of the Treasury's ability to predict. On receipt of the forecasts the Chancellor could decide on his preferred level of activity (his target). He might decide that the forecast situation was acceptable, in which case he would bring in a neutral budget. Or, if the outlook was depressed he would attempt to stimulate demand with a cut in the overall level of taxation. If, on the other hand, the outlook was seen as being too inflationary, or if the balance of payments posed problems, the Chancellor would tighten fiscal policy in the budget.

The targets of demand management were not invariant from year to year, but changed according to political and economic circumstances. The balance of payments, the inflation rate, and the timing of elections were all factors which helped to decide the target for GDP and employment. Nevertheless, the system achieved a great deal. Unemployment was held within the range of

1.0% to 2.5% of the workforce up to 1970, not reaching 3.0% until 1975. The inflation rate peaks were 4.5% in 1955, 4.8% in 1965, and 5.4% in 1969; but again with much higher figures after 1970.

The problem of how to attain the target for employment and GDP could be seen as a largely technical one—a matter of forecasting demand and output, and then of adjusting the instruments of policy so as to bring the forecast level up (or down) to the target level. The forecasts were necessary because of the time-lags and delays in the operation of policy instruments. The key statistics of the economy are all out of date by at least one month and, in some cases, much longer; civil servants may take time to advise the appropriate action; Parliament can take months to enact it; and even after the policy is in force, its full economic effects may not appear for some months afterwards. The hope was that with reliable forecasts the problem of the lagged effects of policy could be overcome.

The instruments of policy were primarily fiscal. The Treasury took the view that changing public expenditure was not a suitable instrument for fine-tuning since first, its level was governed by political and social considerations which should not be subordinated to the needs of employment policy, and secondly, it was difficult to monitor the timing of government projects.[1] Thus the more usual instrument of demand management was a change in tax rates, particularly income tax and indirect taxes. For these, a 'ready reckoner' was drawn up to indicate the effects of given changes in tax rates on GDP and other key variables, such as unemployment, the balance of payments, and prices. This enabled the Chancellor to decide by how much taxes should be raised or lowered in order to achieve his target. It followed the lines set out in Section 5.3 below.

The system of demand management improved over the years as a result of developments in economic statistics—particularly the production of quarterly GDP accounts with seasonal adjustments—and some improvement in forecasting methods.

The Shortcomings of Demand Management

There were various shortcomings in the system, not all of them serious. It was often claimed that the Treasury was guilty of 'fine-tuning', meaning that it was excessively precise in its fiscal adjustments. This criticism, however, may itself underestimate the humility of Treasury economists at the time. The forecasts may have been made in precise terms, but they were known to be subject to a margin of error and treated accordingly. The same applies to the Treasury's estimates of the effects of policy changes. Nevertheless some of the tax changes were very small, and in retrospect need not have been made at all.

[1] J. C. R. Dow, *The Management of the British Economy, 1945–60* (Cambridge: Cambridge University Press, 1964), 180–1.

The forecasts were bound to be inaccurate. Both the Treasury and the National Institute made bad mistakes in 1959, when the National Institute's forecast for GDP for the fourth quarter, made in February, was too low by 4.3%, and the Treasury forecast (as far as can be judged) was too low by 4.0%. The effect of the erroneous forecast was to persuade the government to make substantial tax cuts, with the result that the pressure of demand was unduly high in 1960. The Treasury also underpredicted the boom of 1964 and did not properly foresee the mild recession of 1963. The National Institute's forecasts (which were made by similar methods to those of the Treasury) had an average error, regardless of sign, for the period 1959–67 of 1.4%; the Treasury's error was probably about the same. But both sets of forecasts were better than so-called 'naïve forecasts' which simply predicted the average growth rate for the period.[2]

A popular criticism at the time was that the economy was being driven by 'stop-go'. This vaguely formulated criticism reflected the way in which taxes were raised in some years and reduced in others—an almost inevitable consequence of the business cycle and the attempt to control it by tax changes. It also reflected the fact that the economy—even in this period— was not precisely stable. But perfection was hardly to be expected given the inaccuracy of forecasts. The fact that unemployment remained within a very narrow range is evidence itself of commendable stability. Nevertheless, there was a tendency to underestimate the scale of balance of payments problems, with the consequence that the economy had to be reigned back when sterling came under pressure.

It was also claimed that policy was 'destabilizing' in the sense either that it made fluctuations worse than they would otherwise have been or that policy interventions sometimes or generally took the economy further from the government's short-term objective than would have been the case if policy had been neutral. It is still an open question as to whether the various attempts to establish this result were successful.[3]

In retrospect, the most serious shortcoming may have been that over the whole period, and despite warnings from some economists, governments attempted to run the economy at too high an average pressure of demand, with the consequence that inflation, although quite moderate, became endemic and difficult to eliminate. The emphasis on tax changes as the main instrument of control also meant that investment declines tended to be offset by consumption increases, with the result that labour had to switch industries over the cycle, and this may have been inflationary. Keynes and the White Paper of 1944 had put more emphasis on the timing of public investment as the preferred instrument of policy.

[2] M. C. Kennedy, 'How well does the National Institute Forecast?', *National Institute Economic Review* (Nov. 1969), and 'Employment Policy: What went Wrong?', in J. Robinson (ed.), *After Keynes*, (Oxford: Blackwell, 1973). See also the 6th edn. of this book.
[3] M. C. Kennedy, 'Employment Policy: What went wrong?' *op cit.*

5.3. The Accuracy of Economic Forecasts

The first economic forecasts were developed by the Treasury in the late 1940s, and were used as an aid to demand management. Indications of their content were sometimes revealed in Budget speeches, but few details were provided. It was not until 1968 that the GDP forecasts and component expenditures were published; and, since the Industry Act of 1975, the Treasury has been obliged to publish them twice-yearly. The forecasts now published with the November budget extend for a year and a half, and include forecasts for the inflation rate and the balance of payments on current account.

The accuracy of the Treasury's forecasts was of major interest during the period of demand management, and today's forecasts, although they are not used for fine-tuning, still help to inform policy decisions.

Fig. 5.1 compares the Treasury's November forecasts of next year's GDP increase with the recorded actuals. The difference between the forecast and actual change was in excess of 2% in 1984, 1987, and 1988; and from 1985 to 1988 there was a series of underestimates of growth. These encouraged the view that it was safe to make tax cuts and were partly responsible for the 'Lawson boom'.[4] Over the ten years from 1986 to 1995 the forecasts achieved a level of accuracy of 1.6%, this being the average difference (regardless of sign) between the forecast and actual changes in GDP.

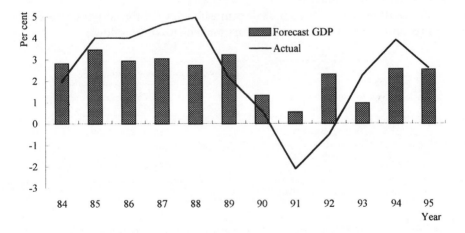

Fig. 5.1. Treasury forecasts of GDP growth, 1984–1995

Note: November forecasts of the percentage change in annual GDP compared with actual change.
Sources: Treasury *Autumn Statements* 1983–1993; *Financial Statement and Budget Report*, Nov. 1994 and 1995.

[4] For a favourable account of Treasury forecasts see T. Burns, 'The Interpretation and Use of Economic Predictions', *Proceedings of the Royal Society*, Series A, 407 (1986), 103–25.

An important question for economists is whether their forecasts succeed in improving on a state of virtual ignorance—since a failure to do so would bring economic knowledge into question. Here the acid test is the comparison with a less informed, or naïve forecaster. Some judgement is needed in deciding what constitutes a naïve forecast, but in the case of GDP forecasts, most people know that GDP tends to grow in most years so that the naïve forecaster might reasonably be assumed to predict the average rate of change of GDP (which for 1985–94 was 2.4%). The mean absolute errors from naïve forecasts of this kind would have averaged 1.9%, compared with the Treasury's 1.6%, so that the Treasury can claim a modest measure of success—improving on the naïve forecasts by 0.3% of GDP.

The fact that the Treasury forecasts are superior to naïve forecasts is of some comfort. But the margin of superiority is not outstanding, and it is disappointing that there has been no perceptible progress in the standard of accuracy compared with earlier years. As we have noted already, the National Institute's forecasts from 1959 to 1967 achieved an average absolute error of 1.4% against a naïve error of 1.8%—a very similar performance to recent Treasury forecasts. Yet the National Institute's forecasts at that time were made using methods which the modern econometrician would regard as primitive and wholly unscientific. They were done without computers and with virtually no use of econometric methods. It seems to be a reflection on the state of economic science that technical progress has not been matched by any obvious gain in knowledge of the economy.

The GDP forecasts are compiled from estimates for the component expenditures and imports, the average errors for which are as follows:

	Average errors (%) from 1986–95
Consumers' expenditure	1.75%
Government consumption	1.25
Fixed investment	3.5
Change in stocks	0.5 (% of GDP)
Exports of goods and services	2
Imports of goods and services	3
GDP	1.5

Source: Treasury, *FSBR 1996–97.*

As the table shows the larger errors have concerned the more volatile elements of demand, such as fixed investment, the stock change, and trade. The errors in the component expenditures tend to offset each other, so that the error on GDP is less than the sum of its parts.

The inflation forecasts are for the change in retail prices from the fourth quarter of the current year to the fourth quarter of next year, and show an average error for 1986–95 of 1.4%. Fig. 5.2 shows that the forecasts were generally quite good, but, like the GDP forecasts, they were consistently

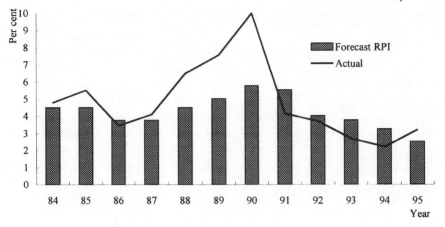

Fig. 5.2. Treasury forecasts of inflation, 1984–1995

Note: November forecasts of the percentage annual change in retail prices (RPI to Nov. 1991, RPIX thereafter) to the fourth quarter of the year compared with actual change.
Sources: As for Fig. 5.1.

optimistic over the period of the 'Lawson boom'. With inflation there is a tendency for one year's inflation rate to be not very far different from the previous year's, so that a naïve forecaster can reasonably be assumed always to predict next year's inflation as the rate recorded up to the fourth quarter of this year. This method would have given an average error of 2.0%, which again is larger than the Treasury's error. Given that the inflation rate has varied from 3% to 10% the Treasury's record has been quite satisfactory.

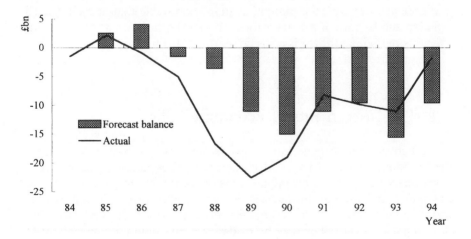

Fig. 5.3. Treasury forecasts of the balance of payments, 1984–1994

Note: November forecasts of next year's balance on current account (£bn.).
Sources: *ETAS*, 1994; *ET*, Oct. 1995.

Table 5.1. Treasury forecasts: summary of performance 1985–1994

Forecast	Mean absolute error	Mean algebraic error (forecast less actual) (bias)	Worst forecast	Mean absolute error from naïve forecasts
GDP: increase between current year and next year	1.6%	−0.1%	2.8% (1992)	1.9%
Inflation: increase in RPI or RPIX, 4th qtr current year to 4th qtr next year	1.4%	−0.6%	−4.3% (1990)	2.0%
Balance of payments on current account	£5.3bn. (1.0% of GDP)	£2.3bn.	£13.1bn. (1988)	£7.4bn. (1.4% of GDP)

Forecasts of the balance of payments on current account are especially prone to error since they relate to the difference between two large totals. Their average error over 1985–94 was £5.3 billion, equivalent to about 1.0% of money GDP. The forecasts for 1988 and 1989 were both optimistic by more than £10 billion. Like the GDP and price forecasts, they managed to improve on naïve forecasts over this period. Here the naïve forecaster is assumed to be so unclear about the outcome that he simply settles for no change. He adopts the rule of thumb in which next year's balance of payments is assumed to be the current account balance for the last known quarter (the second quarter of the year) at a seasonally adjusted annual rate. On this basis he manages an average error of £7.4 billion.

Table 5.1 summarizes the results for the Treasury's three main forecasts. One of the hazards of publishing forecasts is that there is a temptation for the government to present the outlook as more favourable than it really is. The inflation and balance of payments forecasts have both shown a favourable bias over this period, and there is a suspicion that this bias is partly political.

5.4. The Instruments of Economic Policy

Central government expenditure on goods, services, and transfer payments is the equivalent of some 40% of GDP at market prices, and this means that the government has considerable influence over the course of demand, output, and inflation. Any attempt to manage demand or control inflation requires quantitative estimates of the economic effects of policy changes. The effects of changes in fiscal policy may be made using the multiplier analysis of the previous chapter, the main examples to be considered being:

(1) A change in government expenditure on goods and services (ΔG)
(2) A change in government transfer payments (ΔR)

(3) A change in income tax (ΔTy)

(4) A change in indirect taxation (ΔTc)

In each of these cases it is necessary to establish the first impact on the economy, which for an increase in government expenditure on goods and services is a rise in expenditure at market prices. This will include indirect taxes and an import content, the amounts of which will vary according to the type of expenditure. Spending on imported military aircraft will clearly have a much higher import content than expenditure on teachers' pay. But for illustrative purposes, Table 5.2 assumes that both the import and indirect tax contents are at the average levels for government expenditure as a whole: 13% and 6% respectively. Thus if the rise in expenditure is £10.06 billion, the initial rise in GDP at factor cost will be 19% less than this, which is £8.1 billion. This initial change in GDP is, however, raised by the multiplier (estimated at 1.33 in the previous chapter) to £10.8 billion.

An increase in government transfer payments has rather different effects. An addition of £10 billion to pensions, for example, would have its initial impact on personal incomes, which would increase by this amount. The initial effect on GDP is dependent on the various leakages which intervene between a rise in personal incomes and in GDP. The marginal rate of tax can be taken to be 0.25, and, since transfer incomes are not subject to income-related national insurance contributions, the rise in disposable income will be £7.5 billion with a marginal propensity to save of one-tenth, the rise in consumption is £6.8 billion. Indirect taxation and imports take out half of this, so that the initial rise in GDP is only £3.4 billion and the multiplied rise is 1.33 times this.

The effect of a £10 billion reduction in income tax is similar, but with the difference that the initial impact is on disposable income rather than income

Table 5.2. Estimated effects of fiscal policy

	ΔG	ΔR	ΔTy	ΔTc
Initial and impact effects of a £10bn. stimulus on:				
Government expenditure at market prices	10	—	—	—
Indirect taxes on consumption	—	—	—	10
Personal income	—	10	—	—
Real personal disposable income	—	7.5	10	11
Consumers' expenditure at market price	—	6.8	9	9.9
GDP at factor cost	8.1	3.4	4.5	5
Multiplied effect:				
GDP at factor cost	10.8	4.5	6.0	6.6
	(1.8%)	(0.7%)	(1.0%)	(1.1%)
Ratios of eventual GDP change to fiscal stimulus (policy multipliers)	1.08	0.45	0.6	0.66

Notes: Effects of £10bn. increase government expenditure on goods and services (ΔG), in government transfer payments (ΔR), and of a £10bn. decrease in income tax (ΔTy) and VAT (ΔTc). Money GDP at factor cost is assumed to be £615bn.

before tax. This means that there is no initial leakage into taxation, with the result that the initial rise in GDP is larger at £4.5 billion. The multiplied increase is £6.0 billion.

Finally, the effects of a £10 billion stimulus to indirect taxation can be calculated on the principle that it will reduce the prices of consumer goods, and so raise real disposable income. Taking the value of consumers' expenditure to be about £450 billion in a full year, with disposable income at £500 billion, a £10 billion tax cut is equivalent to a fall in prices of 2.2%. Real disposable income will rise from an assumed £500 billion to £511 billion, a rise of £11 billion, and with an MPC of 0.9 consumption rises by about £9.9 billion. With the usual leakages, the initial rise in GDP will be £5 billion, and the multiplied rise £6.6 billion.

These are the effects of lump sum changes. The effects of changes in tax rates can be estimated from the Treasury's estimates[5] of the initial change in revenue, which in the case of 1p on the various rates of income tax is £3.3 billion: the effect would be a multiplied change in GDP of 0.3%. Similarly a 1 percentage point cut in VAT is estimated to cost the revenue £2.35 billion, and would have the effect of raising GDP by about 0.2%.

The table can be used to derive an estimate of the initially balanced budget multiplier. A rise of £10 billion in government expenditure on goods and services has a multiplier effect on GDP of £10.8 billion to GDP, whereas a rise in income taxes of the same amount would reduce GDP by £6.0 billion. Hence the combination of the two might be expected to stimulate GDP by some £4.8 billion. The balanced budget multiplier in this case is 0.48 (4.8 divided by 10), which, it may be noted, is less than the unit multiplier given in the textbooks because of the additional leakages allowed for here, particularly those into taxes and imports.[6]

When discussing the effects of expenditure increases or tax reductions it is important to remember that all changes in the budget balance have to be financed by borrowing, the effect of which may be to raise interest rates. These calculations must assume, therefore, that the supply of money is increased in line with the demand, thus preventing an increase in rates of interest. If there is no monetary accommodation, or if there is an independent and uncooperative central bank, then fiscal expansion will lead to higher interest rates, and some expenditure will be reduced (or 'crowded out').

The estimates assume that there is sufficient slack in the economy for expansion to take place. They make no allowance for time-lags. But as the lag between income and consumption is not likely to be much more than a month, it can be expected that most of the multiplier effect will be felt within only a short period of time. The more complex repercussions include stock changes. A rise in government spending on goods might come initially out of

---

[5] Treasury, *Autumn Statement*, Nov. 1992.

[6] Note that although these estimates begin with an initially balanced change in the budget the increase in incomes will raise revenues and lead to an improved budget position.

Table 5.3. Comparison of multiplier estimate with the main econometric models

Model	% of GDP
Multiplier estimate	1.8
Treasury	1.2
London Business School	1.5
Oxford Economic Forecasting	1.9
National Institute	2.0

Note: The Table shows the effect of a £10bn. increase in government expenditure on goods and services in the first year.
Source: K. B. Church, P. R. Mitchell, P. N. Smith, and K. F. Wallis, 'Comparative Properties of Models of the UK Economy', *NIER* 3/95.

stocks with no immediate effect on production or imports. But as stocks decline, imports and GDP will respond.

In the case of a rise in government spending it is possible to compare the multiplier estimate here with results from the main econometric models—see Table 5.3.

The analytical bases of the econometric models are not entirely comparable with multiplier estimate. They attempt to allow for effects on stocks and fixed investment, and this may be one explanation of the differences between the estimates.

The efficacy of monetary policy is much more difficult to assess than that of fiscal policy. Although monetary policy has multiplier effects, the main problem is to estimate the direct response of investment and consumption expenditure to changes in interest rates. This is not a multiplier problem, so that there is no scope for the kind of direct multiplier estimate which helps to illuminate the action of fiscal policy. The effects have to be estimated from questionnaires to business or by econometric methods. The econometric models of the Treasury and Bank of England estimate the effects of a 1% change in short-term interest rates as shown in Table 5.4.

The models suggest that monetary measures have quite strong effects: a rise of GDP by 0.8% over two years (Bank) is a substantial amount for a 1% change in interest rates. It implies that interest rate policy could be a significant force in regulating the cycle: the output gap has fallen by about 8% in each of the last

Table 5.4. Estimated effects of 1 per cent cut in short-term interest rates

	Year 1	Year 2	Year 3
% change in GDP			
Treasury model	0.25	0.47	0.67
Bank of England model	0.32	0.78	1.10
% change in prices			
Treasury model	−0.60	−0.50	0.04
Bank of England model	−0.77	−0.83	0.03

Source: K. B. Church, P. R. Mitchell, P. N. Smith, and K. F. Wallis, 'Comparative Properties of Models of the UK Economy', *NIER* 3/94

two cycles, so that a 5% reduction in rates might, on these calculations, eliminate as much as 50% of the cycle.

This optimism, however, could be misplaced. The models may not have succeeded in isolating the causal effects of interest rate changes from the cyclical coincidences. When demand slackens interest rates tend to fall, but the rise in aggregate demand that comes later in the cycle may not have been caused by the interest rate reductions. The practice of estimating investment as a lagged response to interest rate changes may encounter the difficulty that the observed association is non-causal, and not, therefore, a response at all. Thus it does not seem possible to accept these estimates without reservation.[7]

5.5. Debt and Deficits

Government fiscal action to expand the economy and to reduce unemployment leads inexorably to a 'deterioration' in the budget balance, and in most circumstances to an enlarged budget deficit. The initial stimulus to demand, whether it is a tax cut or a rise in public expenditure has this effect; and whilst the resulting rise in incomes raises revenue, the increase will not be enough to fully offset the initial rise in the deficit. This means that if, as in the USA, a balanced budget is to be regarded as a goal of economic policy, then there will be a clear conflict with the objective of full employment—except in so far as this can be achieved by monetary policy. Indeed, any sort of target for the fiscal deficit (or the PSBR) will conflict with the employment objective. A difficulty with the Maastricht Treaty concerns its so-called 'convergence conditions', one of which rules that the budget deficit has to be held below 3% of GDP.[8] (A second condition requires the national debt not to exceed 60% of GDP.)

In the UK the most widely discussed measure of the budget deficit is the Public Sector Borrowing Requirement (PSBR) which is the combined deficit of the central government, local authorities, and nationalized industries. In most years the PSBR is a positive amount, although in 1987 to 1990, mainly as the result of privatization receipts, it was negative. Normally, the size of the PSBR tends to reflect the stage of the cycle, and is at its largest in recessions, when tax receipts are reduced by low incomes, and when outlays on unemployment and other social security benefits are at their highest. Its record level over the last 30 years was in 1975–6, when it was 9% of money GDP (at market prices).

More recently the highest level for the PSBR was in 1993–4, when, at £45.5 billion, it was 7% of GDP. This gave rise to considerable alarm at the time, and

---

[7] Monetary institutions and policy are discussed further in Chapter 6.

[8] It needs to be asked what will happen in the event of a recession throughout Europe, when budget deficits everywhere are in breach of the Maastricht condition. Will the members of EMU collectively agree to cut their deficits, thus worsening the recession and passing it on to the USA, Japan and the Third World?

the Chancellor was persuaded to raise taxes in a recession, for which he received acclaim in the City of London and in much of the financial press. But it remains questionable whether budget cutting at the bottom of a recession was the most prudent course for the economy.

The PSBR is normally financed by the issue of gilt-edged securities, which add to the interest-bearing national debt. The debt has been in existence since the foundation of the Bank of England in 1694. It grew rapidly in the eighteenth century, and, in 1821, after the Napoleonic Wars, reached a ratio to estimated national income of 2.9. The ratio fell to about 0.3 just before the First World War, but rose to 2.1 by 1924, and, after the Second World War, to 2.7 in 1947. Since then the ratio has declined, and is estimated to be about 44% of money GDP in March 1996.[9]

Arguments about the national debt become confused if the debt is naïvely seen as being analogous to individual debt. If an individual gets into debt, he or she will know that the debt must be repaid, and that this will impose a burden in the form of more work or less consumption. The national debt, however, does not have to be repaid in the same way, and does not give rise to the same sort of burden. The government will, of course, honour its promises to its creditors, and will repay particular debt issues when they mature. But it can, and normally does, borrow again, so that the total debt is not reduced.

The analogy with private indebtedness is sometimes taken further, so that a government is said to be 'insolvent' if its liabilities exceed the value of its assets. But this too is a fallacy since the government, unlike a private agent, is empowered to raise taxes to pay its debts; and if it has control of its central bank it can finance its deficit by creating money. The term 'insolvency' does not really apply to governments.

The only real exceptions to this conclusion concern the possibilities of unsuccessful wars, revolutions, and debt denominated in foreign currency. In recent years a number of LDCs have defaulted on debt service owed in foreign currency. Whilst governments can usually find ways of raising their own legal tender, they have no power to create foreign currency. There is nothing 'gilt-edged' about a government debt which is payable in foreign currency.[10]

---

[9] This refers to net public debt. The gross debt, which includes public corporations and excludes short-term assets, is estimated to be 51.5%. Recent figures are from *FSBR 1996–97* and historical figures from W. Buiter, 'A Guide to Public Sector Debt and Deficits', *Economic Policy*, Nov. 1985.

[10] The remedy of printing money, however, does not apply if the debt is denominated in terms of a foreign currency. Recent experience in the United States shows that it is possible for an irresponsible legislature to refuse permission to repay debt or to pay debt interest—thereby destroying the gilt-edged character of the government's securities and impairing the government's ability to borrow in the future.

How are Deficits Financed?

In principle, a deficit can be financed either by 'printing money' or by issuing bonds. Monetary finance might be used in the initial stages of a recovery when there is no danger of inflation. But when the target level of employment is reached the main source of finance has to be debt issue. This is because a perpetual growth in the stock of money when the demand for money is constant would lead to a progressive lowering of interest rates, thus raising demand and causing inflation.

In reality, the authorities stay clear of direct monetary financing. The UK Treasury does not ask the Bank of England to print notes for it, or even to grant it an interest-free overdraft. If it borrows from the Bank it does so on a very short-term basis and at the market rate of interest. The old (and curious) tradition in central banks and Treasuries is that all monetary financing is 'inflationary', and this means that budget deficits are almost always bond-financed, with a consequential rise in the interest-bearing national debt.

Any increase in government borrowing puts upward pressure on interest rates. But this can be neutralized by accommodating monetary policy: by open-market purchases of bills and bonds. Thus an increased deficit does not necessarily lead to higher interest rates, and does not normally do so.

Does the National Debt Matter?

A government deficit adds to the national debt, and the question is whether this really matters. Even though high levels of debt have not, in the past, brought any obvious problems in the UK, there are some consequences which in an ideal world we would prefer to be without.

The main problem is that interest on the debt has to be financed from taxation, and this means that there will be a transfer burden. Future generations of tax-payers will have to be taxed in order to make interest payments to the owners of gilt-edged securities. These payments do not involve a loss of national income, but they do entail its redistribution. The interest payments will raise personal income before tax, and personal income will eventually become many times larger than GDP. (The national accounting point here is that personal income includes both incomes from production and transfer payments, of which interest on the national debt is an example—see Chapter 4.)

It may be argued that it is immoral to run a budget deficit when doing so inflicts tax increases on future generations. But, although this is undesirable in itself, account must also be taken of the favourable consequences for today—that the deficit raises total output, incomes, and employment. Many would argue that the transfer consequences of a higher national debt are a small price to pay for these advantages. Furthermore, it is likely that high levels of income for the present generation will have the effect of promoting higher investment in plant and equipment, with the result that future generations will benefit from an enhanced capital stock and higher incomes in consequence.

The transfer problem is at its least worrying if the recession and the deficit are temporary. In this case taxes are initially reduced (or government expenditure raised) in order to compensate for a shortfall in private demand. But when private demand recovers the need for the deficit disappears, taxes can be raised, and the budget can return to balance. The national debt increases on a one-off basis, but does not have to rise year by year.

The more serious case is where the extreme assumption is made that the deficiency of demand is permanent, so that, in order to maintain a reasonable level of employment, the government feels obliged to run a deficit year in and year out. On this assumption the deficit will add a given amount to the national debt each year, and the transfer burden will rise continuously. The question is again whether, and how much, this matters?

In this case the transfer problem becomes larger year by year, and tax rates have to be continuously increased in order to finance the rising volume of debt service. The consequence is that the disposable income of the general taxpayer is progressively reduced in order to pay interest to a small number of bondholders. The process is inequitable, and, given time, could be potentially destructive of the will to work. The government might ultimately be forced to make a choice between the objectives of high employment and a satisfactory distribution of income. So, at least in principle, the burden of the national debt, when properly understood as a transfer burden, is a shortcoming of Keynesian policies for supporting aggregate demand. There is no completely 'free lunch'.

The case against large, continuing deficits is sometimes put in algebraic form. If we define the budget deficit as X, GDP as Y, and the growth rate of GDP in money terms as g then:

$$\text{if } X/Y > g$$

the ratio of government debt to GDP will rise. If it is assumed that the deficit/GDP ratio is maintained indefinitely, the ratio of the national debt to GDP will tend to infinity.

This is sometimes referred to as an 'unsustainable' situation, meaning that the situation cannot continue indefinitely. The deficit may, however, be entirely tolerable for a good many years, and the question of exactly when the deficit becomes unacceptable is not answered by the formula. This kind of analysis has been described by some economists as 'unpleasant arithmetic', although their analysis has been more algebraic than arithmetic.[11]

---

[11] T. J. Sargent and N. Wallace 'Some Unpleasant Monetarist Arithmetic', *Federal Reserve Bank of Minneapolis Quarterly Review*, Fall 1981.

An Illustration

The problem of a continuing deficit is best analysed with the help of some real arithmetic—with concrete examples and figures. Suppose that the PSBR is £50 billion in 1996 (7% of GDP) and that (somewhat unrealistically) it is expected to remain at this percentage of GDP for 20 years—so that the deficit grows at the same rate as GDP. Suppose that the growth rate of nominal GDP is 5.5% a year (3% for inflation and 2.5% real growth), then by the year 2016 we should have an addition to the national debt of:

$$£50(1 + 1.055 + 1.055^2 + \ldots + 1.055^{20}) = £1889\text{bn}.$$

If the interest rate on all new debt is assumed to be 10%, the additional interest payments would amount to £188.9 billion.

Personal income can be expected to grow at the same rate as GDP but with the addition of the extra interest incomes. It would rise, therefore, from its 1996 level of approximately £650 billion to:

$$£650 \ (1.055)^{20} + 188.9\text{bn}.$$

which would bring it to £2085 billion.

On these workings the additional interest payments amount to about 9% of personal income by the year 2016—a burden which is by no means disastrous. Yet this is in the so-called 'unsustainable' case of a 7% deficit and a $5\frac{1}{2}$% growth rate (and with a high interest rate). The deficit would have to continue for many more years before the transfer burden became unacceptable. It would be wrong, therefore, for a government to deflate the economy in reaction to this level of deficit. Deflation might be wise in the event of serious inflation, but a large budget deficit—especially when it is expected for only a year or two—is not, on its own, a good reason for cutting expenditure or raising taxes.

In any event the sustainability formula takes no account of 'bracket creep'—the tendency, when GDP is rising, for tax receipts to rise relative to income as more people move into higher tax brackets. The tax ratio will also rise because the marginal rate of income tax is higher than the average rate. Indeed if the average–marginal rate was 24% then tax revenues would, in this example, increase by more than the rise in personal incomes—so that there would be no question of having to increase actual rates of taxation.

The main conclusion must be that every situation needs to be examined on its merits. The decision to cut back a public deficit should be based, not on arguments about infinite time-series, nor on rules 'golden' or otherwise, but on a careful assessment of the consequences for the economy over a foreseeable time horizon. There is plenty of time for the transfer problem to manifest itself, and if it ever does seem to be unmanageable, then that is the time to take action.

This is where the analysis leads, and although it may not be the received view in the financial markets, or even in the main economic secretariats, it is a position which needs to be stated and discussed. It does not sit comfortably with the convergence guidelines laid down by the Maastricht Treaty.[12]

5.6. Economic Policy and Inflation

Inflation is a much more serious impediment to full employment policy. It does not, at least in a closed economy, reduce the average level of real income, although policies to counter it may have this consequence. In an open economy with fixed exchange rates, a faster inflation than elsewhere will, however, lead to lower output and employment in the export and tradable goods sector—although it might be possible to correct these effects through fiscal and monetary policies or by eventual devaluation. The most serious effect of inflation is that it brings about an arbitrary transfer of real income from some groups to others: from the old to the able-bodied, from those dependent upon non-indexed retirement incomes to those in work, and from members of weak trade unions to members of stronger unions. It distorts relative prices and creates uncertainty about future prices and the exchange rate. It is sometimes described as a 'tax' on cash holdings because, if nominal interest rates are sticky, it reduces their purchasing power. Inflation destroys confidence in the government's ability to manage the economy.[13]

In the period when inflation was merely creeping, it was possible to regard it as a small price to pay for high employment. A gently rising trade-off between inflation and unemployment made the problem of political compromise minimal compared with the situation in the 1970s and after. The oil shock of 1973, and the inflation which followed it, transformed the policy problem. It meant that real incomes were eroded rapidly between wage settlements, and it changed economic behaviour. Economic units learned how to live with inflation and sought to defend their real wages by insisting on full compensation for increases in the cost of living.

For the governments of the 1970s there were two main methods of bringing inflation under control. One was to deflate domestic demand. Demand could have been reduced to such an extent that its depressive effect on wage increases

---

[12] A. P. Lerner, 'Functional Finance and the Federal Debt', *Social Research*, Feb. 1943; repr. in M. G. Mueller (ed.), *Readings in Macroeconomics* (New York: Holt, Rinehart and Winston, 1966) provides an amusing introduction to the problems of debt and deficits—even though his claim that it does not matter how many zeros are added to the figure of the debt may be an exaggeration. See also A. C. Pigou, *A Study in Public Finance*, 3rd edn., (London: Macmillan, 1951), R. A. Musgrave, *The Theory of Public Finance* (New York: McGraw-Hill, 1959) and C. S. Shoup, 'Debt Financing and Future Generations', *EJ*, Dec. 1961. For a recent discussion see Sir Bryan Hopkin and B. Reddaway, 'The Meaning and Treatment of an "Unsustainable" Budget Deficit', *Banca Nazionale del Lavoro Quarterly Review* (Sept. 1994).

[13] For a further discussion of the effects of inflation see W. Eltis, 'How Inflation Undermines Industrial Success', *National Westminster Bank Review* (Feb. 1991), and J. Fender, *Inflation* (Brighton: Harvester Wheatsheaf, 1990).

and profit margins would have been sufficient to offset the influence on wages of earlier price increases. Given that prices were increasing at rates of over 20%, this kind of policy would have necessitated extremely high unemployment or an unbearably long period of correction. In fact there was some deflation in 1974–7 in that the Labour government chose not to counteract the recession of those years. Unemployment reached 3.0% in 1975 and 4.4% in 1977—rates which may not seem much by today's standards but were seen as very high at the time.

The main alternative to fiscal deflation was an incomes policy under which the rate of wage increase was subjected to statutory or firm quasi-statutory control. The Conservative government introduced an incomes policy in 1972–4, opting for a statutory policy after its attempts to negotiate a voluntary policy had failed. The policy led to unrest, chiefly because one trade union, the National Union of Mineworkers, was prepared to go slow and finally strike rather than accept the terms of the policy.[14] One misguided feature of Stage III of Mr Heath's incomes policy was that it provided for the effective indexation of wages to the cost of living. This stage, which came into effect after the election, coincided with a major rise in import prices, and had the unfortunate consequence, therefore, of linking wages indirectly to the inflation of import prices.

The incoming Labour government made the mistake of continuing the indexation provisions of the policy under its 'Social Contract'. For an anxious period of eighteen months it did little to tackle the mounting inflation. Then in July 1975 it introduced a voluntary incomes policy consisting of three stages, the first of which was a maximum increase of £6 per week.

For a while the policy seemed to work very well. The rate of change of money earnings fell from 27% in 1975 to 16% in 1976, and 9% in 1977; and price inflation came down from 24% in 1975 to 16% in 1976, and 9% in 1977 (see Appendix Table 5.A1). Real earnings fell, and for the first time since the 1960s an incomes policy, although helped by the recession, could be said to have made a significant impact upon the rate of wage inflation. It was estimated in the twelfth edition of this book that the effect of the policy was to reduce wages below what they would otherwise have been by about 3% per annum for three years. But the policy was resented by the unions, and in the 'catch-up' after 1977 the estimates suggest that these effects were partly eliminated. Other work has suggested a smaller effect.[15] But whatever the numerical results of incomes policies, the political results have left scars. The Conservatives' incomes policy is often blamed for the election defeat of 1974, whilst the Labour government's policy led to a spate of industrial

[14] See M. J. Stewart, *Politics and Economic Policy in the UK since 1964* (Oxford: Pergamon, 1978).

[15] See also S. G. B. Henry, 'Incomes Policy and Aggregate Pay', in J. L. Fallick and R. F. Elliott (eds.), *Incomes Policies, Inflation and Relative Pay* (Allen and Unwin, 1981), and K. Mayhew, 'Traditional Incomes Policies', *Oxford Bulletin of Economics and Statistics* (Feb. 1983).

disputes in the winter of 1978/9 (the 'winter of discontent'). Since then incomes policies have been rejected by both the main political parties.

The rejection of incomes policy, whilst understandable from a political point of view, has, unfortunately, meant that the conflict between employment and inflation is now completely unresolved. Inflation has come down since the 1970s, but only at the cost of substantial unemployment.

5.7. Counter-Inflationary Policy in the 1980s: The MTFS

The Conservative government which was returned in May 1979 was determined to reduce inflation without recourse to incomes policy. The government was also pledged to reduce income tax, and in the Budget of June 1979, the standard rate was lowered from 33 to 30p in the £. The revenue loss was recouped by an increase in VAT from 8 to 15%, an act of policy which was itself inflationary. It added an estimated 4% to the RPI directly and still more via the wage-price spiral, helping to raise the inflation rate to 18% in 1980.

The chosen method for dealing with inflation was the imposition of monetary targets under the Medium Term Financial Strategy (or MTFS). One-year monetary targets had already been introduced under the Labour government, but it was never clear whether these were real targets or merely forecasts; or, for that matter, whether they were imposed in the genuine belief that they would control inflation. 'Monetarist' ideas were in vogue, but it was not obvious that they were accepted by Labour politicians.

Under the Conservatives there was a clear attachment to the ideas of Professor Friedman and his monetarist followers. Friedman had supported the idea of a steady growth in the money supply since the 1940s, and he also believed, contrary to Keynes, that the real economy was inherently stable along the path of full employment. It was governments and central banks which were to blame for unemployment and inflation. Most of Friedman's monetarism, however, was concerned with the painstaking statistical analysis of correlations between money income or prices and the stock of money, from which he drew the conclusion that monetary factors were the prime cause of inflation, and monetary control the way to cure it.

In point of principle there is some theoretical justification for using the money stock to control inflation. It is the view that if the money stock is held constant, it will after a time act as a constraint on the level of money income. The reasoning is that any increase in nominal income necessitates an increase in the volume of circulating money. Money income and expenditure may rise for a time without any increase in the money stock, but they can do so only because the stock of circulating money is being fed out of idle, or 'asset' balances. Once these give out a rising transactions demand for money can no longer be supplied. The process of rising money income, or of rising prices, must, therefore, come to an end. Thus the conclusion is that any sustained inflation can only take place if the stock of money is rising; and this has the valid implication that if the growth of money stock is reduced towards zero, the rate of inflation will also tend to zero. The money stock can be seen as an anchor for nominal income, and whilst the ship may drift for a while, it cannot drift for ever.[16]

The new approach to inflation control was the Medium Term Financial Strategy (MFTS), which was introduced with the budget of March 1980. It set target rates for the growth of the broad money stock (£M3) over a four-year period, together with a planned reduction in the PSBR (see Table 5.5).

According to Nigel Lawson, the idea of a nominal anchor to the price level was the theory behind the MTFS, and the intention was that the stock of money should function in the same way as the Gold Standard of the nineteenth century. Lawson, then the Financial Secretary to the Treasury, believed that inflation could be squeezed out of the system by insisting on a gradual slowdown of monetary growth. He preferred policy rules to discretion, and devised the MTFS as a self-imposed constraint on policy.[17] Less clear is the extent to which he or the Treasury was influenced by the crude 'monetarist' belief that inflation is caused exclusively by prior increases in the stock of money. But a progressive reduction in the growth of the money stock was seen as a necessary condition for a fall in the inflation rate.

The MTFS also set limits for the PSBR. This was done because the monetary target would put upward pressure on interest rates and tend to 'crowd out' private sector investment unless the demand for funds was cut back elsewhere. Projections for the path of the PSBR were, therefore, included in the policy.

A further idea in the MTFS was the belief that credibility and expectations were of key significance in the policy to control inflation, and that both would be influenced by the expected growth of the money stock. In some quarters, it was even believed that the publication of monetary targets would, through price expectations, be an influence on wage demands. Thus the 1980 FSBR

Table 5.5. Target and actual levels of money supply and PSBR, 1980–1984

| | Financial Year | | | |
	1980/1	1981/2	1982/3	1983/4
Target growth of £M3 (%)	7–11	6–10	5–9	4–8
Projected PSBR as % of GDP	3.75	3.0	2.25	1.5
Actual growth of £M3 (%)	19.4	12.8	11.2	9.4
Actual PSBR as % of GDP	5.6	3.4	3.2	3.2

[16] The doctrine of the monetary anchor can be traced to D. H. Robertson *Money, and Lectures on Economic Principles*, (London: Staples, 1957), R. G. Hawtrey, 'Public Expenditure and the Demand for Labour', *Economica*, Mar. 1925, and to the 'monetary ceiling' in J. R. Hicks, *The Trade Cycle*, (Oxford: Clarendon Press, 1950).

[17] N. Lawson, *The View from No 11* (London: Corgi Books, 1993).

stated that 'the speed with which inflation falls will depend crucially upon expectations both in the United Kingdom and overseas'.

The MTFS gained support from those who realized it would act as a discipline for budgetary policy, ensuring that the recession would not be countered, and would thus, through the Phillips Curve, bring down the rate of wage inflation by creating unemployment. It appealed to those who thought that public expenditure was too high. And for some it represented a way of mastering inflation without effects on employment and output.

In the first two years of the MTFS, the projected PSBR was treated as an inflexible target, and this meant that when unemployment rose by more than had been allowed for in the FSBR projection, the government felt impelled to look either for increases in nationalized industry prices (which made inflation worse) or for cuts in expenditure (which made the recession worse).

There is no doubt that during the period of the MTFS the inflation rate fell. But it did so for three interrelated reasons: first, the recession of 1979–81; second, the MTFS; and third, the high exchange rate. The MTFS helped to make the recession worse than it would otherwise have been, and in this sense it was a factor in the fall of the inflation rate from 18% in 1980 to 5% in 1983. But its contribution came, not from any new 'monetarist transmission mechanism', but from its effect on the pressure of demand for labour and for goods. The vacancy rate in 1981 was lower that it had ever been, and the rate of inflation fell accordingly. The recession made the monetary anchor quite superfluous, whilst the monetary targets were not achieved. They were missed by 8% in 1980/1 and by 3% in 1981/2—an outcome which also put in question the Bank of England's ability to control the stock of money as precisely as the MTFS was hoping for.[18]

After 1983 the MTFS was retained in name but not in substance. The words 'Medium Term Financial Strategy' figured regularly in the Financial Statement and Budget Report, but the content changed. Monetary targets began to be defended less in terms of the monetarist belief that they were a necessary constraint on prices and more on the grounds that the quantity of money was statistically 'related' to nominal income (GDP in money terms). There was a switch in emphasis to technicalities such as the proposition that there is a stable demand for money or a stable velocity of circulation. In 1986 it was admitted that £M3, the target variable, had an unstable velocity of circulation. Its place was taken by M0, the most narrow definition of money, on the grounds of its more stable velocity. But M0, which excludes current accounts, and consists solely of notes, coins, and bankers' balances at the Bank of England, is much too narrow a version of the money stock to count as a strategic magnitude. It amounted to less than one-tenth of £M3, and its

[18] For further discussion, see J. C. R. Dow and I. D. Saville, *A Critique of Monetary Policy* (Oxford: Clarendon Press, 1988), C. Allsopp, 'Monetary and Fiscal Policy in the 1980s', *OREP,* Spring 1985 and C. Allsopp, T. Jenkinson, and D. Morris, 'The Assessment: Macroeconomic Policy in the 1980s', *OREP,* Autumn 1991.

'targeting' was of no real policy significance, although it does function as a statistical indicator of retail sales. But the retention of something that could be called a monetary target helped to preserve the illusion that the old MTFS was still in business.

The steady rise in the rate of inflation from 3% in 1983 to 9.5% in 1990 was associated with the recovery of demand in the economy and the tax reductions of the 'Lawson boom'. During this period the economy expanded steadily and the government took a strangely relaxed attitude to the rising pressure of demand—although its stance can be partly blamed on a series of over-optimistic forecasts. As the inflation problem returned, ministerial discussion moved away from concern with the stock of money to more pertinent variables like the exchange rate, import prices, wage demands—the factors which the Treasury used to believe in before the so-called 'monetarist revolution' (and which were discussed in the previous chapter).

The experience of the MTFS tends to confirm the more traditional view that the crucial variable in controlling inflation is not the money supply, but the pressure of demand in the economy. If this is set right, the money stock will tend to look after itself. And, although the money stock can be seen as an anchor to the level of nominal income, it does not need to be targeted or controlled if the level of demand is properly managed.

5.8. The Inflation–Unemployment Dilemma

Inflation, as argued both here and in Chapter 4, is primarily a matter of the pressure of demand. The dependence of the rate of increase in wage rates (or earnings) upon aggregate demand, and the connection this has with unemployment, has, for many years been taken to signify an important and serious dilemma between the two main policy objectives. It was estimated in Chapter 4 that the critical vacancy rate, at which inflation is zero or constant over time, is about 0.5% of the workforce. This, unfortunately, represents a low point in the cycle and a high level of unemployment, so that the critical rate of unemployment (the non-accelerating inflation rate of unemployment' or NAIRU) must be correspondingly high (see Table 5.6).

Table 5.6 Relationship between vacancies and unemployment, 1980–1994 (%)

	Vacancies	Unemployment	
		Same year	Next year
1980	0.52	10.5	10.7
1981	0.55	10.7	10.9
1993	0.45	10.4	9.3
1994	0.56	9.3	8.2

The NAIRU is probably in the region of 8–9% of the workforce. Hence the cost of achieving price stability is a permanent level of unemployment of 2.2 to 2.6 million people. If, on the other hand, macroeconomic policy is directed towards the reduction of unemployment to acceptable levels, the cost will be positive and increasing inflation—as in the Lawson boom of 1987–9.

This dilemma of price stability versus employment is extremely hard to resolve. One suggested approach is to reduce the NAIRU through supply-side measures. Its advocates recommend a more flexible labour market, improved education and training, a weakening of trade unions, local wage bargaining, and the downward flexibility of real wages. But these measures have been tried for the last 10 years or more, and they have not made it any easier to remove inflation from the system. Whilst admirable in themselves they cannot be expected to reduce unemployment when the labour market as a whole is characterized by excess supply. They are open to the criticism that supply-side medicine cannot cure a demand-side problem.[19]

Another proposal is that the long-term unemployed should be given a job guarantee. The argument is put that the long-term unemployed exert no 'downward pressure' on wages, so that reducing their numbers will have no inflationary effect. But the obvious objection is that, unless there is an increase in the total number of jobs available (and in the demand for labour), any reduction in the long-term workless will be offset by a rise in the short-term unemployed. Furthermore, it is doubtful whether the Phillips Curve is properly understood as unemployment exerting downward pressure on wages—as if to assume that there is always some constant upward force that has to be counteracted if inflation is to be checked. It was argued in the previous chapter that it is labour shortages that lead to wage inflation; and that these can co-exist with high unemployment because of mismatch.

Incomes policy was the older method of resolving the inflation–unemployment dilemma, but is understandably unpopular with the political parties. The policies of the 1970s were, as we have seen, politically embarrassing and seldom effective. Their success depended on consent, and consent was withdrawn. But the climate for such policies could be more favourable now than it was then; and given the severity of the problem there is still a case for trying them—better to try and fail, than not to try at all. Alternatives such as the National Economic Assessment in the Labour Party's 1992 manifesto, which has now been dropped, or the tax-based policy suggested by Professor Layard, could also be considered.[20] But without these or similar policies it is difficult to see how the problem of achieving both low unemployment and price stability is ever going to be solved. As Tinbergen pointed out many years ago, it is seldom possible to attain two objectives without two effective policy instruments.[21]

---

[19] See J. R. Sargent, 'Roads to Full Employment', *NIER* (Feb. 1995).
[20] R. Layard, *How to Beat Unemployment* (Oxford: Oxford University Press, 1986).
[21] J. Tinbergen, *On the Theory of Economic Policy* (Amsterdam: North-Holland, 1952).

5.9. The Balance of Payments

Unlike employment or stable prices, the balance of payments is not an objective of economic policy. There is no particular virtue in running a huge balance of payments surplus or in the accumulation of enormous reserves of gold and foreign exchange. The balance of payments and/or the exchange rate are, however, of major concern because they so often impede the attainment of the two principal objectives—employment and price stability. Their importance arises from the existence of different currencies and the need to hold reserves.

When the economy is on a fixed exchange rate it is not possible to run a deficit on the current account of the balance of payments for any length of time without a strong offsetting balance on the capital account. Countries where there is a high rate of return on inward investment can have current account deficits for long periods of time. An example is Canada in the early years of the twentieth century. But if there is no such strength on the capital account then a current account deficit has, eventually, to be corrected. One method of correction is fiscal deflation which reduces imports by lowering domestic output. But this will jeopardize the government's employment objective. Another is a policy of high interest rates to attract short-term capital from abroad—but this will discourage home investment, and will again reduce employment. The main alternative to these measures is to devalue or float the currency, but this will raise import prices, with consequences for the government's inflation target. Higher import prices will add to product prices, wages will respond, and a wage-price spiral is initiated. Thus balance of payments correction with fixed exchange rates leads either to reduced employment or to increased inflation.

With flexible exchange rates, balance of payments weakness will be manifested as an excess supply of home currency, and this will lead to exchange rate depreciation and the same inflationary consequences as formal devaluation. The main difference between a fixed and a floating exchange rate regime is that in the latter the markets tend to correct the situation automatically, and without giving the government the choice between deflation and devaluation. But the other difference is the greater exposure to speculative activity and the danger that the markets will misjudge the exchange rate with consequential over- and under-shooting. Supply and demand in the foreign exchange market becomes complicated by a speculative element in which the object is to predict what other market traders believe an exchange rate will be, rather than what rate will clear the balance of payments over a period of years.

From 1987 to 1988 the pound was effectively fixed under Mr Lawson's policy of shadowing the Deutschmark at a ceiling rate of DM3.00. In October 1990 the pound entered the European Exchange Rate Mechanism (ERM) at a rate of DM2.95. This was in spite of the current account balance having been in deficit to the tune of £22.5 billion in the previous year, with bank base rate at 15% and inflation at 9.5%. The fall in inflation in 1991 made it possible to reduce interest rates, and there was only a modest fall in the exchange rate. But 1992 was less auspicious, and it became clear that the authorities would prefer to lower interest rates faster than membership of the ERM permitted. Finally, the pound was forced to leave the ERM in September, falling to DM2.45. Since then the pound has been floating. Import prices rose by 11% between the third quarters of 1992 and 1993, but this did not lead to faster inflation as might have been expected because the pressure of demand was so low during the recession.[22]

5.10. Economic Prospects for 1996 and After

By the beginning of 1996 UK economic output was well recovered from the recession of 1992. GDP had reached its previous peak (of the second quarter of 1990) by the end of 1994, and by early 1996 was some 6% higher. But unemployment was still at 8% of the workforce compared with 5.6% in 1990 (second quarter), and employment was also below its peak. The recovery was complete for output but not for employment.

The economic outlook, as portrayed by the Treasury's forecast in November 1995, was for a growth in GDP of 2.6% in 1995–6 and 2.9% in 1996–7. Both rates are probably in excess of the growth rate of productive potential, and, if correct, should have implied some further, if modest, fall in employment during 1996 and 1997.

Table 5.7 shows changes in the main items in the forecast. The Treasury was rather more optimistic than some of the other forecasting bodies, and the projected rise in exports looked particularly sanguine given the signs of weakening demand in Europe.

Table 5.7. Forecast changes in expenditure and GDP

Per cent change in real terms	1995–6	1996–7
Consumers' expenditure	2.4	3.4
Government current expenditure	0.7	0.3
Fixed investment	1.0	4.3
Stockbuilding (as % of GDP)	0.2	−0.1
Exports of goods and services	5.8	7.3
Imports of goods and services	3.8	6.7
GDP at factor cost	2.6	2.9

Source: FSBR 1996–97.

---

[22] It should not have surprised readers of the 12th edn. of this book! The price equation reported there and here reproduced in Chapter 4 predicted inflation rates in the first halves of 1993–5 to within $1\frac{1}{2}$% of the actual rate.

Table 5.8. Treasury forecasts for inflation and balance of payments

	1996	1997
RPIX (4th qtr, excluding mortgage interest payments)	3.0%	2.5%
Balance of payments on current account (full year)	−£6.5bn.	−£5bn.

The Treasury's forecasts for inflation and the balance of payments are shown in Table 5.8.

The main features of the government's macroeconomic policy were the continued pursuit of low inflation and 'sound public finances' with a promise to reduce taxation whenever it appeared 'prudent' to do so. A target for the inflation rate of 1–4% had been set by Norman Lamont, the previous chancellor, in 1992, and the intention was to bring the rate down to $2\frac{1}{2}$% by the end of the current Parliament (in June 1997 at the latest). The Financial Statements of 1994 and 1995 stated that the task of inflation control was 'assigned' to monetary policy, whilst the role of fiscal policy was to achieve a gradual reduction in the budget deficit. The projection was for the PSBR to be £29bn. in 1996–7, and to fall to £22.5bn. and £15bn. in the next two financial years, with a public sector surplus of £2bn. in 1999–2000.

For a government whose sole objective was a low inflation rate, the main criticism is that inflation is primarily determined by the pressure of demand, and that this is much more swiftly and effectively controlled by fiscal than by monetary measures. Thus the assignment of inflation policy to the Bank of England appeared to be a misconception. But if, as seems likely, private sector demand remains sufficiently low, then neither fiscal nor monetary intervention will be needed, and the government will be able to claim credit without doing anything.

The pursuit of fiscal rectitude, although consistent with the Maastricht Treaty, was an anachronism. As pointed out in this chapter it is possible for governments to maintain large fiscal deficits for long periods of years without encountering serious transfer difficulties. But 'sound finance' appeals to City prejudices, and is widely believed to support sterling—albeit at the cost of high unemployment.

From the point of view of a different government altogether—a government with a genuine commitment to high employment as well as to price stability—fiscal 'prudence' would have to be redefined in favour of what is best for the economy. It would involve fiscal and monetary policies of a more expansionary nature, both in the UK and abroad. Inflationary pressures would have to be combated by incomes policies, and the government would be well advised to consider proposals such as Layard's tax-based policy and Lerner's wage-increase permits.[23] They might stand a better chance of working effectively, and with public co-operation, if they are introduced at a time of low inflation. But the only way of telling is to try them. The experience of the 1980s and 1990s has shown that it is relatively easy to achieve a low inflation rate by holding down aggregate demand. But in capital-using economies prone to deficient demand, the real challenge is to achieve low inflation without high unemployment.

[23] Layard, *How to Beat Unemployment* and A. P. Lerner, 'A Wage-increase Permit Plan to Stop Inflation' in A. M. Okun and G. L. Perry (eds.), *Curing Chronic Inflation* (Washington DC, Brookings Institution, 1978).

Appendix

Table 5.A1. Indicators of macroeconomic policy

	Change in retail prices (%)	Unemployment (%)[a]	Change in GDP (%)[b]	PSBR (£bn.)[c]	Balance of payments on current account (£bn.)	Change in exchange rate (%)[d]
1970	6.4	2.6		−0.1	0.8	−1.0
1971	9.4	2.5	1.6	1.3	1.1	−0.2
1972	7.1	2.9	2.8	2.0	0.2	−3.6
1973	9.2	2.1	7.6	4.1	−1.0	−9.3
1974	16.0	2.0	−1.5	6.5	−3.2	−3.1
1975	24.2	3.0	−0.7	10.2	−1.5	−7.8
1976	16.6	4.1	2.7	8.9	−0.8	−14.3
1977	15.9	4.4	2.6	5.4	0.1	−5.4
1978	8.3	4.4	2.7	8.3	1.1	−0.2
1979	13.4	4.1	2.7	12.6	−0.5	5.9
1980	17.9	4.8	−2.0	11.8	2.8	10.0
1981	11.9	8.0	−1.2	10.5	6.7	1.1
1982	8.6	9.5	1.8	4.9	4.6	−4.5
1983	4.6	10.5	3.7	11.6	3.5	−7.4
1984	5.0	10.7	2.0	10.3	1.5	−4.5
1985	6.0	10.9	4.0	7.9	2.2	−0.6
1986	3.4	11.2	4.0	3.1	−0.9	−8.5
1987	4.1	10.2	4.6	−1.7	−5.0	−1.5
1988	4.9	8.2	5.0	−12.4	−16.6	6.0
1989	7.8	6.2	2.2	−9.8	−22.5	−3.0
1990	9.5	5.8	0.6	−1.9	−19.0	−1.4
1991	5.9	8.0	−2.1	8.8	−8.2	0.4
1992	3.7	9.7	−0.5	30.3	−9.8	−3.6
1993	1.6	10.3	2.3	43.9	−11.0	−9.9
1994	2.4	9.3	3.9	38.7	−1.7	0.3
1995	3.4	8.2	2.7			−4.9

[a] % of workforce.
[b] GDP at factor cost, average estimate at constant prices.
[c] For the calendar year.
[d] Sterling exchange rate index.
Sources: ETAS, 1988, 1994; ET, Oct. 1995; NIER 4/95; FT.

Table 5.A2. Calendar of economic events

1986	January	Mortgage lending rises from £26bn. to £36bn.
	March	Budget: income tax cut from 30% to 29%
1987	February	Louvre Agreement. Start of policy of shadowing the DM.
	March	Pre-election budget: income tax cut from 29% to 27%
		Target for M0 only ('notes and coins monetarism').
	May	General election
	October	Stock market crash leading to relaxation of monetary policy
		Base rates down from 10% in August to 8.5% in November.
1988	January	Mortgage lending at £48bn.
	February	Base rate up from 8.5% to 9%
	March	Base rate down 8.5%
	Budget	Tax cuts: another 2p off the standard rate of income tax—to 25p, rates over 40% abolished. Revenue cost with other changes £6.2bn. in full year.
		Ending of mortgage interest relief (long capped at £30,000) for individuals as distinct from properties with a 4-month notice period to 1 August.
	May	Base rate to its lowest for year: 7.5%
1989	March	Budget: employees pay NICs at 2% up to lower earnings limit of £43 p.w. and 9% above it up to £325 p.w. Tax and NICs total cost—£3490 p.a.
		Inflation accelerates reaching 8% in April 1989
	May	Base rate up to 14%
	October	Base rate up to 15%
		Lawson resigned due to differences with Prime Minister.
1990	Budget	Major's first and last budget.
		No change in base rate limit and abolition of composite rate: total change +£955m.
		Mortgage interest relief confined to basic tax at 25%. Thresholds later lowered to 20 and 15% (April 1995).
	October	£ enters ERM. Base rate cut to 14%
	November	John Major succeeds as Prime Minister
1991	Budget	Lamont's first budget. VAT up to 17.5%, cuts in corporation tax; total effect +£1890m.
	May	'Rising unemployment and the recession have been the price that we've had to pay to get inflation down. That is a price well worth paying.' N. Lamont.
	September	Base rate cut to 10.5%
1992	5 January	Lamont states 'Realignment is another word for devaluation. We are not going to devalue the pound.'
	7 February	Maastricht Treaty is signed.
	March	Budget: new lower rate of 20%. Total change in revenue −£2600m.
	May	General election
	July	Cabinet agrees to new spending strategy—gains by one minister have to be offset by cuts for another.
	3 September	UK arranges ECU borrowing facility to support £.
	12 September	Lira devalued by 7% against all ERM currencies
	16 September	Black Wednesday. £ suspended from ERM. £ falls to DM2.45
		Peseta devalued by 5%.
		MLR reduced to 10%
	22 September	MLR 9%

	8 October	Lamont announces 1–4% inflation target at Brighton Conference
	12 October	2½% target suggested to Treasury and Civil Service Committee
	16 October	Base rate cut to 8%
	2 November	£ falls to $1.53
	13 November	Lamont institutes a 1.5% pay ceiling for public sector workers.
1993	February	First meeting of the Treasury's panel of economic advisors.
	March	Lamont's last budget. With fiscal effects of: £490m. for 1993–4, £6725m. for 1994–5, £10,305m. 1995–6. Tax increases for April 1994 and 1995. VAT on domestic fuel and power 8% for 1994–5, 15% 1995–6.
		National insurance contributions: main rate up from 9% to 10%.
		Cancellation of mortgage finance benefits for the unemployed. Those buying houses to buy insurance.
		Announcement of a November budget.
	May	Resignation of Norman Lamont
	August	Parliament ratifies Maastricht Treaty
	30 November	First unified budget; Kenneth Clarke's first budget.
		Employer's NICs reduced by 1%; married couples allowances raised for over-65s to offset higher fuel costs. 2p on wine. Mortgage interest relief cut to 15% in 1995.
		Employees' NICs to rise 10% in April 1995, but 1% cut for those on less than £200 p.w.
		Effect of two budgets is to raise revenue by £15b. or more than 2% of GDP
	December	Treasury and Civil Service Ctee. recommend greater independence for Bank of England
1994	8 February	Base rate cut from 5.5% to 5.25%
	March	No Budget
	12 September	Base rate raised from 5.25% to 5.75%
	27 September	Labour Party seminar on economic policy. Gordon Brown 'Labour will not tolerate the kinds of inflationary and fiscal imprudence which have characterized the past 15 years' and 'our new economic approach is rooted in ideas which stress the importance of macroeconomics, neo-classical endogenous growth theory and the symbiotic relationships between growth and investment in people and infrastructure'.
	19 October	Treasury to be re-structured. Chief Economic Adviser's and Fiscal and Monetary Policy Divisions to become the Macroeconomic Policy and Prospects and Public Finances Divisions with the objective to (1) Deliver permanently low inflation and (2) Maintain sound public finances and affordable public expenditure. 7 Directorates instead of 9.
	29 November	Clarke's 2nd Budget: 20p band widened to £3200 and various other small tax changes.
		NIER of 1/95 puts the effects of all discretionary tax and expenditure changes as:
		1994/5: 14 £bn.
		1995/6: 24 £bn.
		1996/7: 30 £bn.
	6 December	Government defeated over VAT at 17.5% on domestic fuel.
	7 December	Base rate up 0.5% to 6.25%

	8 December	Mini-budget to replace revenue lost by the government's defeat: Alcohol duty up 4%—1p on a pint, 5p on wine. 1p on litre of petrol, 3.7% on tobacco tax—6p on cigs. VAT on domestic fuel and power to remain at 8%.
	December	First National Lottery
1995	3 February	Base rate up 0.5% to 6.75%
	27 February	Collapse of Barings Bank
	5 May	No rise in interest rates after Bank-Treasury meeting taken by some as sign of inflation policy not being credible.
	18 September	5 million public sector workers told by Clarke that their pay increases would have to be financed out of 'efficiency savings' for the third year running.
	28 November	Budget. Standard rate of income tax reduced to 24%. 20p band extended by £700 and basic rate band by £1200. Personal allowance increased by £240.
	December	Major public sector strikes in France over the government's plans to cut social security so as to meet the Maastricht conditions for budget balance.
	13 December	Base rate down 0.25% to 6.5%. Mortgage rates lowest since 1966.
1996	18 January	Base rate down 0.25% to 6.25%.
	8 March	Base rate down 0.25% to 6.0%.

Further Reading

Allsopp, C. J., 'Monetary and Fiscal Policies in the 1980s', *OREP*, Spring 1985.

—— Jenkinson, R. and Morris, D., 'The Assessment: Macroeconomic Policy in the 1980s', *OREP*, Autumn 1991.

Artis, M. and Cobham, D. (eds.), *Labour's Economic Policies, 1974–1979* (Manchester: Manchester University Press, 1991).

Britton, A. J. C., *Macroeconomic Policy in Britain 1974–1987* (Cambridge: Cambridge University Press, 1991).

—— 'Labour Party Policies', *NIER*, Mar. 1995.

Browning, P., *The Treasury and Economic Policy 1964–1985* (London: Longman, 1986).

Central Statistical Office, *United Kingdom National Accounts*, The CSO Blue Book (London: HMSO, 1995).

Charter for Jobs, *We Can Cut Unemployment* (London, 1985).

Connolly, B., *The Rotten Heart of Europe: The Dirty War for Europe's Money* (London: Faber, 1995).

Dow, J. C. R. and Saville, I. D., *A Critique of Monetary Policy* (Oxford: Oxford University Press, 1988).

Fallick, J. L. and Elliott, R. F. (eds.), *Incomes Policies, Inflation and Relative Pay* (London: Allen and Unwin, 1981).

Feinstein, C. H., *Statistical Tables of National Income, Expenditure and Output of the UK 1855–1965* (Cambridge: Cambridge University Press, 1976).

Gardner, N., *Decade of Discontent: The Changing British Economy since 1973* (Oxford: Blackwell, 1987).

Glyn, A., 'Unemployment and Inequality', *OREP*, Spring 1995.

Grieve Smith, J., *Full Employment in the 1990s* (London: Institute of Public Policy Research, 1992).

Hills, J., *Options for Britain* (Aldershot: Dartmouth Publishing, 1995).

Hopkin, Sir B. and Reddaway, B., 'The Meaning and Treatment of an "Unsustainable" Budget Deficit', *Banca Nazionale del Lavoro Quarterly Review*, Sept. 1994.

Jenkinson, P., 'The Assessment: Inflation Policy', *OREP*, Winter 1990.

Lerner, A. P., 'Functional Finance and the Federal Debt', *Social Research*, Feb. 1943; repr. in Mueller.

Mayhew, J., 'Traditional Incomes Policies', *Oxford Bulletin of Economics and Statistics*, Feb. 1983.

Meade, J. E., *Full Employment Regained?* (Cambridge: Cambridge University Press, 1995).

Mueller, M. G., *Readings in Macroeconomics* (New York: Rinehart and Winston, 1966).

National Institute Economic Review.

Sargent, J. R., 'Roads to Full Employment', *NIER*, Feb. 1995.

Stewart, M., *Politics and Economic Policy in the UK since 1964* (Oxford: Pergamon, 1978).

Treasury, *Financial Statement and Budget Report 1996–7* (London: HMSO).

MONEY AND FINANCE

R. L. HARRINGTON

6.1. The Financial System: Overview

Nature and Functions

A financial system is composed of firms and markets which fulfil a variety of economic functions. Central to all is arranging the lending of funds from one economic agent to another. Most other financial services are ancillary to or are derived from this one. The lending of funds from one economic agent to another—from lender to borrower—can be accomplished in many different ways, but all can be classified into just two distinct approaches.

First, the lender can lend directly to the borrower. This is what happens when a person subscribes to a new issue of government stock or buys a share in a public company. Brokers or other agents may assist with the transaction but in each case the person lends direct to the borrower and incurs all the risks that such lending entails. This may be called direct finance.

The second approach, which may be called indirect finance, involves a financial intermediary standing between lender and borrower. The former lends his funds to the intermediary, e.g. a bank or a building society. The intermediary collects funds from many lenders and decides to which borrowers it will lend. There is no direct contact between lender and borrower. Each deals with the intermediary; instead of one transaction there are two.

This form of finance seems at first sight to be more roundabout and to involve the use of more real resources than direct finance. But financial intermediaries are numerous and indirect finance more common than direct finance. What, then, are its advantages? They are many and they derive from the ability of financial intermediaries to use their size and expertise to transform financial claims so that they can offer savers a wider choice of assets than ultimate borrowers are able to do. At the same time they offer borrowers a more varied choice of credit terms than ultimate lenders are able to do.

Consider a large retail bank. Such a bank accepts deposits of all sizes and on a variety of terms. In the UK, the largest banks each have millions of individual deposits, which in the aggregate sum to more than £50 bn. They know that every day many depositors will withdraw money, but that many others will make new deposits. In normal circumstances, the total sum of money deposited will not vary greatly. In consequence, banks can allow depositors the freedom to withdraw deposits at little or no notice while at the same time making loans to borrowers which last for many years. The banks are said to engage in 'maturity transformation', that is, they borrow short and lend long. It is not only banks that do this. Building societies lend on mortgages for periods of up to 30 years while still allowing most depositors to withdraw funds on demand or at short notice.

Financial intermediaries also engage in 'risk transformation'. With direct finance the lender bears all the risks; for instance, it is the shareholders who stand to lose most when a company goes into liquidation. Banks and other financial institutions also stand to lose when borrowers default. But because they have trained staff able to judge to whom it is safe to lend and because they can diversify lending across a range of borrowers they are usually able to keep losses to a small proportion of total sums advanced. And as past experience enables them to estimate the likely amount of bad debts, they can allow for this by adding a risk premium to the interest they charge borrowers. In this way banks, like other intermediaries, can bear risks and absorb losses, while depositors in normal times can know that their deposits are virtually riskless.[1]

Financial intermediaries provide other services. Retail banks provide facilities for deposits to be transferred from one account to another and thereby provide a payments mechanism. Life assurance companies offer policies which provide for long-term saving but which also provide for the payment of a large sum in the event of the policy-holder's premature death.

In fact financial intermediaries perform many functions and it is for this reason that many lenders and borrowers prefer to deal with intermediaries rather than deal direct with each other. This is especially true of small lenders and borrowers for whom the time-and-trouble costs of direct dealing would normally outweigh any gain in terms of a more favourable interest rate. But there is still need for direct finance. Many wealthy persons are prepared to incur the risks of lending direct to private enterprises in the hope of earning extra returns; and many persons, rich and poor alike, are happy to lend direct to the Government as here the risk of default is considered negligible.

During the last thirty years the financial system, both in the United Kingdom and elsewhere, has changed dramatically. New financial instruments have been created, new techniques for lending and borrowing have been devised, and new financial markets have been developed. This process of financial innovation has had a profound impact both on how financial services are provided and on where they are provided. Many factors have combined to

---

[1] Which is not to say that they are actually riskless or that banks never fail. We return to this issue in 6.6 below.

bring about these changes but the dominant cause would seem to be new technology.

Technological Change

Developments in computer technology have had a profound impact on banking as well as on other areas of finance. Not only do modern computer systems permit the automation of hitherto labour-intensive activities such as cheque-clearing and the maintenance of up-to-date records but they enable financial institutions to undertake a much wider range of business. This means that there is now less segmentation of financial markets and more competition.

When calculations were done manually, it was necessary to keep operations simple and this meant undertaking only a narrow range of business. But now that complex calculations can be performed instantaneously, banks and other intermediaries can introduce a more varied range of assets and liabilities; they can deal easily in assets and liabilities denominated in many different currencies (including composite currencies such as the ECU) and they can more readily envisage competing for new types of business. And however complex the balance-sheet, however variegated the assets and liabilities, if a bank has the appropriate computer hardware and software its managers can still keep track of relevant credit exposures, liquidity needs, interest-rate risks etc.

New technology has also transformed dealing in financial markets. Nowadays dealers, whether in foreign exchange, in short-term financial assets, or in securities, have access to screens on which any one of a number of pages of information on interest rates, exchange rates, etc. can be displayed at the touch of a button. Telephone contact with money brokers, with foreign-exchange brokers, and with other banks is also instantaneous, and deals once struck can be recorded in seconds. This considerable mechanization of dealing has facilitated the surge in money-market activity that has occurred over the last three decades both in London and elsewhere.

There have also been considerable changes in payments technology. Many purchases are now made with the aid of credit or debit cards and when cash is required it is more likely to be obtained from an automatic teller machine rather than by means of a cheque passed across a bank counter. Personal customers and small firms can pay bills electronically by sending instructions by telephone direct to their bank's computer. Large corporate customers can also do this but are likely as well to be able to initiate a wider range of transactions including the sale or purchase of foreign currency and the sale or purchase of short-term financial assets. For important clients, banks guarantee fulfilment of their instructions within agreed limits.

It is no exaggeration to say that the new computer technology has revolutionized finance. Financial institutions can compete for new areas of business, they can offer new products and services, and they can offer newer and more convenient ways of carrying out old forms of business. And, a very significant development, they are now better able to compete for business across national frontiers.

Internationalization

The world is shrinking. Modern technology has made communication of all sorts easier and faster. People can travel rapidly by air between different parts of the globe and they can communicate easily and cheaply by telephone, fax, and E-mail. Computer networks can be operated on a worldwide basis and information made instantly available in different countries. For many economic purposes, national frontiers have become of limited significance and it is now possible for large firms to run their operations on a global basis.

Large banks have established networks of offices around the world. These offices can deal actively in local financial markets and still report promptly to head office details of all business done. In consequence, senior officials can monitor the worldwide position of the bank in many different financial markets; and if they wish they can undertake new transactions designed to offset or to complement the activities of offices abroad so as to keep the bank's global balance-sheet in line with what is desired.

New international markets have grown in short-term financial assets, in bank loans and in securities. These markets are worldwide, although they are in practice dominated by trading in some ten or twenty large financial centres. London, with nearly 500 banks, is the largest but other centres are also important and since much business is potentially mobile each international centre is inevitably in competition with all other centres.

In effect, finance has become a highly competitive business as technology has broken down the old barriers caused by distance and by the need for each firm to restrict itself to a limited range of business. This in turn has altered the relationship between private financial institutions and the public authorities. If the latter are concerned about the size of their country's financial industry (and most of them are) they now have to consider carefully how policy actions may affect their national share of what has become an international business.

6.2. Banks, Building Societies, and Money Markets

The Bank of England

The Bank of England was established as a joint-stock company by Act of Parliament in 1694. Over the years, while still a privately owned institution, it came to exercise a number of public functions, notably holding the nation's stock of gold and foreign-exchange reserves; issuing notes and coins; and acting as a lender of last resort to the discount houses. The Bank (as it is known in British financial circles) was nationalized in 1946 and made subject to the authority of the Treasury. It is now a public institution and its main purpose is to carry out a range of public functions, although it continues to provide banking services for a number of private clients comprised chiefly of banks, of members of its staff, and of a small number of old-established clients whose accounts with the bank date back to its days as a private institution.

Of the many functions of the Bank of England, the following are the most important:

(*a*) banker to the government;
(*b*) banker to the clearing banks;
(*c*) holder of the nation's stock of gold and foreign-exchange reserves;
(*d*) manager of the issue of notes and coins;
(*e*) implementation of government monetary policy;
(*f*) supervision of banks and of certain other financial institutions.

The Bank of England as banker to the Government keeps all the main government accounts, receives tax revenues, and facilitates payments in respect of government expenditure. The Bank also arranges borrowing for the Government through the issue of new gilt-edged stock, as well as arranging for the redemption or conversion of previously issued stock due to mature. This is no small task. During the two years 1992 and 1993 (when the Government was running an abnormally large deficit) the Bank sold nearly £89 billion of new stock and redeemed or otherwise purchased nearly £15.5 billion. The Bank also manages Government short-term borrowing and regularly issues and redeems Treasury bills.

The Bank of England is also banker to the clearing banks, i.e. those retail banks which operate the system through which cheques are cleared and monies transferred from one bank account to another. Although the gross sums transferred through clearing, each day, are large, payments due from one bank to another are normally offset, to a great extent, by payments due in the reverse direction, and it is only necessary to settle a relatively small net balance. This is done, each working day, by transfers between bankers' accounts at the Bank of England.

Status of the Bank of England.   The status of the Bank of England and specifically its subordination to the Treasury has recently become a subject of debate. This has arisen in the context of arguments about the causation of inflation and of the credibility of anti-inflationary policies under the control of elected politicians. The view of inflation that dominates current thinking is that it is ultimately a monetary phenomenon and has been largely caused by lax monetary policies introduced by governments seeking to provide a short-term boost to the economy. Supporters of this view regard modern democratic governments as primarily concerned with short-term electoral advantage and see them as having forfeited all credibility as far as monetary stability is concerned. What is needed is to make central banks independent of government and to assign to them the objective of maintaining price stability. The oft-quoted example of how central banks could and should be run is the German central bank: the Deutsche Bundesbank.

The Bundesbank was established in post-war Germany in 1957. For historical reasons it was given considerable independence and it was assigned as its primary task the maintenance of the stability of the currency, something which has been interpreted in practice as an annual inflation rate of not more than 2%. It has not always achieved this, but inflation in Germany has usually been below that of most other industrial countries and well below that of inflation-prone countries such as the UK or Italy. Over the period of thirty-five years from 1959 to 1964 retail prices in Germany rose to somewhat more than three times their original level; in Britain they rose to over eleven times their original level. In 1959 there were 11.7 Deutschmarks to the pound sterling; by 1994 there were only 2.5.

This example of financial rectitude has become very influential as is shown by the fact that under the terms of the 1992 Treaty on European Union (the Maastricht Treaty) the constitution of the proposed European Central Bank has marked resemblances to the Bundesbank. The first objective of the proposed bank is the maintenance of price stability and the bank is to be granted a large degree of independence from political influence. Furthermore the Treaty requires that national central banks should have more independence from their own national governments and a number of European countries have already taken measures to bring this about.

The British Government declined to change the legal status of the Bank of England but has made concessions to the prevailing climate of opinion. Following the withdrawal of the pound from the ERM in September 1992 (this is discussed further in Chapter 11), the government announced a new monetary policy involving an explicit inflation target. This was initially stated to be that the rate of inflation (excluding mortgage interest payments) should be kept within a range of 1–4 % per annum and should be less than $2\frac{1}{2}$% by the spring of 1997.

In an attempt to give the policy a greater degree of credibility the Bank of England was given what is, in effect, a watchdog role. First, the Bank was to publish a regular report on inflation and the report would not be subject to prior vetting by the Treasury. The Bank could, in effect, 'blow the whistle' on government policies that it regarded as inflationary. Second, it was announced that the level of short-term interest rates would in future be decided at monthly meetings between the Chancellor of the Exchequer and the Governor of the Bank of England. The Chancellor still has the last word but from the start of 1994 the minutes of these meetings have been published, thus providing further scope for the Governor of the Bank of England to make known any disagreement with government policy.

The result is that the Bank of England remains unable to pursue independent policies but is now able to criticize openly policies with which it disagrees. This, it is hoped, will make it politically more difficult for governments to embark on opportunist policies designed to produce short-term booms. In consequence this should give the Government's present commitment to low inflation greater credibility.

At the time of writing (Autumn 1995) there have been no large disagreements over policy between the Government and the Bank of England. However during the course of 1995 as the rate of inflation (excluding mortgage interest payments) edged up from 2.4% to 2.8% some modest difference of opinion did emerge. The Bank favoured a small rise in the level of short-term rates of interest (tightening of monetary policy) while the Government took the view that this was undesirable.

Retail Banks and other Banks

Banking is a diverse business and there are different types of bank. In Britain it is common to distinguish four main groups; *retail banks, merchant banks, other British banks, and foreign banks*; and for many purposes it is convenient to count the building societies as a fifth group as much of their business is similar to that of banks. Fig. 6.1 shows for each of these groups, the amount of deposits outstanding both in sterling and in foreign currencies at end 1993.

The *retail banks*, as their name suggests, are banks which offer retail banking services to business and personal clients, both small and large, through a network of branches. Such services traditionally cover the taking of deposits at sight and at notice, clearing cheques, foreign exchange and international remittances, safe-deposit facilities, financial advice, and in some cases, insurance broking. In recent years, banks have been seeking to increase business and new services have been introduced, notably automated teller machines, eurocheques (cheques which may be written in a number of European currencies), long-term mortgage lending, and opportunities for mutual investment in securities through bank-managed unit trusts. Most retail banks either own or have established links with security traders and now also offer facilities for buying and selling securities.

Retail banking is nowadays contrasted with wholesale banking which involves dealing in large sums of money (typically £1 million and over) in both sterling and foreign currencies. A large part of such business is undertaken in organized money markets in international financial centres such as London, New York, Tokyo, and Paris. But the distinction between retail and wholesale banking is conceptual rather than institutional and most of the banks classified as retail banks are, in reality, mixed banks which undertake both types of banking.

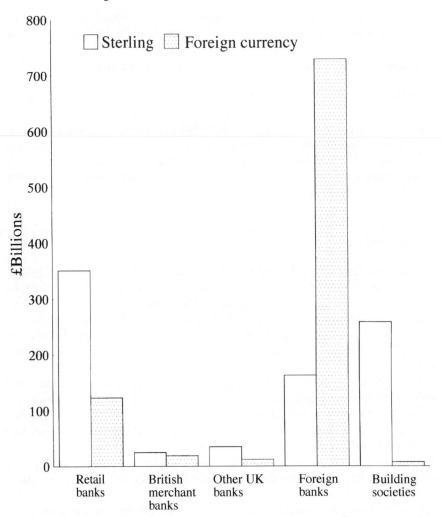

Fig. 6.1. Banks and building societies deposit liabilities, 31 December 1994

Note: Deposit liabilities are defined widely to include both retail and wholesale liabilities, including inter-bank deposits.
Sources: Bank of England Statistical Abstract 1995; Financial Statistics, Aug. 1995.

The main retail banks in the UK are as follows:[2]

Abbey National
Allied Irish Banks
Bank of England, Banking Department

[2] A complete list of all banks in the UK is given each year in the statistical appendix to the February edition of the *Bank of England Quarterly Bulletin.*

Bank of Ireland
Bank of Scotland
Barclays Bank
Clydesdale Bank
The Co-operative Bank
Coutts & Co
Girobank
Lloyds Bank
Midland Bank
National Westminster Bank
Northern Bank
Royal Bank of Scotland
TSB Bank
TSB Bank Scotland
Ulster Bank
Yorkshire Bank

Of these banks, Barclays, Lloyds, Midland, and National Westminster are the main retail banks in England and Wales; Bank of Scotland, Clydesdale Bank, and Royal Bank of Scotland are the main retail banks in Scotland, although the last named also has many branches in England and Wales; Allied Irish Banks, Bank of Ireland, Northern Bank, and Ulster Bank are the main retail banks in both Northern Ireland and in the Republic of Ireland.

A subset of the retail banks, comprising the main English and Scottish banks, owns the Cheque and Credit Clearing Company which manages the daily clearing of cheques. Each bank presents for payment cheques that it has received from clients and receives for payment cheques drawn by its clients and paid into other banks. Banks also present cheques for payment on behalf of other banks which do not participate directly in the clearing. There is a separate clearing system for automated payments (e.g. direct debits and standing orders) and yet a further one, the Clearing House Automated Payment System (CHAPS), which deals with payments of high value transmitted electronically and cleared on the same day. Banks involved in the clearing of payments are known as clearing banks and settle debts between themselves by payments between accounts held at the Bank of England.

The payments system is largely taken for granted but it is something that is vital in any modern economy and which consumes significant amounts of real resources. The numbers involved are large. About ten million cheques are cleared every working day and there is a similar number of automated payments. The total value of all debit and credit items cleared in 1994 averaged approximately £100 billion per working day.[3]

The number of cheques written has been declining for a number of years as more and more purchases are made by means of credit cards and debit cards.

---

[3] Full details of clearing statistics can be found in the *Annual Abstract of Banking Statistics* published by the British Bankers' Association.

The economies of scale in the processing of cheques are large and there is a continuing search for greater efficiency. In 1994 the Co-operative Bank agreed to sub-contract its cheque processing to an American computer manufacturer and in January 1995 the Royal Bank of Scotland announced that it also was to contract out the processing of its cheques.

Merchant banks. These banks combine banking with a number of other financial activities. The banking business is composed largely of wholesale banking: operating in short-term financial markets and catering to large companies and wealthy persons. The retail business is small and only a minority of merchant banks have offices in mainland Britain outside London.

The other financial activities are mainly to do with security trading. A traditional function is that of issuing house, i.e. acting for those who wish to sell large blocks of new or existing securities. It could be that a company wishes to raise funds by selling new shares; it could be that a government wishes to privatize a hitherto publicly owned company. In all cases merchant banks will advise on the terms of the offer and will make the arrangements necessary including preparing a prospectus, receiving applications, and allocating the securities among applicants. Merchant banks also act as fund managers and manage the portfolios of wealthy persons, companies, and pension funds. Many run unit trusts and a number are prominent as financial advisors, notably in the field of corporate mergers and acquisitions.

Following the wholesale reform of security trading in the UK in 1986[4] many merchant banks acquired firms of stock brokers or stock jobbers and became market makers in securities. Reform had become necessary due to the progressive internationalization of security trading and so the merchant banks in their wider role as security dealers found themselves in competition with large American and Japanese security houses and with large German and Swiss universal banks.[5] Over time, size has proved to be important: firms with a large client base can deal more easily in large volumes of securities and therefore are more able to tender successfully for new business. The British merchant banks for the most part have not had a client base comparable to those of many of their foreign rivals. The result has been that most have agreed to be taken over by domestic or foreign banks and now operate as subsidiaries of those banks. In 1995 alone, S. G. Warburg & Co was taken over by Swiss Bank Corporation; Kleinwort Benson was taken over by Commerzbank of Germany, and Baring Brothers & Co, after an astonishing failure in internal controls had enabled their Singapore branch to lose £850 million, was taken over by ING Bank of the Netherlands.

---

[4] For details of this reform see ch. 2 of the 13th edn. of this book.
[5] In Germany and Switzerland, banks have traditionally combined the functions of banking and security trading and have sought to be all-purpose financial institutions, hence the appellation Universal Banks.

Other British banks. This category comprises a large number of banks of varying origins. Some are specialized subsidiaries of other financial institutions, some have more the characteristics of a charitable trust but are obliged to register as banks in order to be able to accept deposits. But for many the main business is that of a finance house: raising money in the wholesale markets and lending to industry, for the purchase of capital equipment, and to persons, for the purchase of consumer durables. Many of these banks are relatively small.

Foreign banks in the UK. On 31 December 1994 there were 336 foreign banks operating in the UK. Most had only one office in or near the City of London. A few have been represented in London since before World War II, but for the most part these foreign banks are relative newcomers. Most arrived during the 1960s and 1970s.

It was during these decades that a new international banking system was developed. This system, often referred to as the eurodollar market, or, more accurately the euro-currency markets, proved a magnet to banks worldwide. All large banks, as well as many medium-sized ones, sought to become involved. And while the euro-currency markets were truly international, with active dealing in many centres in Western Europe and elsewhere, London was, and still remains, the single most important centre. So it was to London that most foreign banks went, when they decided to compete for a share of the new international banking business, although, naturally, the larger banks also established offices in other important centres of the market as well.

The growth and functioning of the euro-currency markets are discussed below. For present purposes it is sufficient to note that virtually all of the foreign banks have as their main business wholesale banking in foreign currencies, and that much of this business is conducted with companies, persons and banks outside the UK.

Banking business in the UK. The combined balance sheet of all banks in Britain as at end May 1995 is given in Table 6.1. This shows all the business, retail, and wholesale on the books of their UK offices. Liabilities and assets are classified according to whether they are denominated in sterling or in foreign currencies. On the liabilities side of the balance-sheet, it can be seen that UK residents hold most of the sterling deposits while overseas residents (which category includes overseas banks), hold most of the foreign-currency deposits. The importance of the interbank market as a source of both sterling and foreign-currency deposits is clear, as is that of the market in certificates of deposit (CDs) and similar short-term paper. CDs are negotiable and hence allow lenders of money to make deposits for fixed periods of, say, three or six months, while having the option to sell the CD if they need funds before the end of the period.

The small item 'notes issued' refers to bank notes issued by those Scottish banks and Northern Irish banks that retain a historic right to issue their own

Table 6.1. Banks in the United Kingdom: balance-sheet at 30 May 1995

Sterling liabilities	(£m)
Notes issued	2215
Deposits	
UK banks	97551
Other UK	356863
Overseas	81910
CDs and other short-term paper	70784
Foreign currency liabilities	
Deposits	
UK banks	108095
Other UK	63914
Overseas	658762
CDs and other short-term paper	70665
Items in suspense and transmission (sterling & foreign currency)	47156
Capital and other funds (sterling & foreign currency)	99489
Total liabilities	1657567
Sterling Assets	
Notes and Coin	3620
Balances with Bank of England (including cash-ratio deposits)	1571
Market loans	
Discount Houses	6474
UK banks (including CDs)	119933
Other UK	6088
Overseas	43054
Bills	
Treasury bills	9424
Eligible bank bills	13188
Other	825
Advances	
UK private and public sectors	394664
Overseas	12037
Banking Department lending to central government (net)	1581
Investments	
UK government stocks	15616
Other	44104
Foreign currency assets	
Market loans and advances: UK Banks (including CDs)	108884
Other UK	82682
Overseas	558175
Bills	10121
Investments	156755
Items in suspense and collection (sterling and foreign currency)	55405
Miscellaneous assets (sterling and foreign currency)	13364
Total assets	1657567
Acceptances outstanding	20065
Eligible liabilities	461804

Note: Minor discrepancies in the additions are due to rounding errors.
Source: BEQB, Aug. 1995, table 3.

notes. The remaining items on the liabilities side cover items held in suspense for whatever reason (e.g. uncertainty as to who is the rightful owner of a deposit); items in transmission between accounts; and the banks' long-term liabilities to shareholders and bondholders.

Bank assets have become very diverse as Table 6.1 shows. Of the sterling assets, first there are holdings of notes and coin (till money) and balances with the Bank of England. Only retail banks hold significant amounts of notes and coin as only they have large volumes of sight deposits convertible on demand into currency. But all banks, other than the very small ones, are obliged to hold a percentage of their eligible liabilities in the form of deposits at the Bank of England. These obligatory deposits account for the greater part of all bankers' deposits held at the Bank. The traditional working balances of the clearing banks are nowadays usually small.

Sterling market loans are sums of money lent in one of several short-term money markets, notably the discount market, the interbank market, and the market for certificates of deposit. These markets are discussed below. The item 'other UK' is comprised mainly of deposits with building societies but also includes a small amount of lending to UK local authorities. Market loans overseas represent for the most part short-term lending to banks abroad.

Banks also make loans by discounting bills. Bills are short-term IOUs issued by the Government (Treasury bills) and by private companies (commercial bills). They are mostly issued for a period of three months and they are sold to banks, discount houses, and other purchasers at a discount on their face value. The discount is calculated so as to give the purchaser a rate of interest in line with current market rates.

Bills are highly marketable, and a bank having made a loan in exchange for a bill is free to rediscount it (i.e. sell it) if it wishes to do so. The Bank of England uses the bill market as a means of influencing the liquidity of the banking system. When it wishes to take money out of the system (and hence raise interest rates), it sells bills. When it wishes to put money into the system (and hence lower interest rates) it buys bills. All Treasury bills are eligible for rediscount at the Bank of England, but eligibility of commercial bills is restricted to those which bear the acceptance of a bank which has fulfilled certain conditions laid down by the Bank of England.

Advances represent the main form of sterling lending to non-bank customers. Almost all of such lending is to the UK private sector; lending by way of advances to the UK public sector is small.

For statistical purposes, the Banking Department of the Bank of England is included within the retail-banking sector. This may seem anomalous, but it will be recalled that the Bank of England, as well as being banker to the Government and to the banks, also has a number of private accounts. Lending by the Banking Department to central government is shown net, and can be either positive or negative.

Foreign-currency assets are dominated by interbank lending (within the UK) and by lending overseas, much of which is to banks abroad, but significant sums are also lent to the UK public sector. 'Acceptances outstanding' and 'eligible liabilities' do not constitute additional actual liabilities. Acceptances relate to bank acceptances of commercial bills. A bank accepts a commercial bill when it puts its own name on the bill as a guarantee that, if the company due to redeem the bill should default, the bank itself will pay all monies due. For this service the bank is paid a fee. As it is only in the case of a prior default by another party that the bank becomes liable, acceptances outstanding represent contingent liabilities rather than actual liabilities.

Eligible liabilities are a subset of total liabilities and are intended to represent, for each bank, total sterling resources available for lending to non-bank borrowers. More formally, eligible liabilities comprise the following:

(1) all sterling deposits from non-bank sources with an original maturity of two years or less;

(2) net sterling interbank borrowing;

(3) sterling CDs issued less sterling CDs held;

(4) any net deposit liabilities in sterling to overseas offices;

(5) any net liability in currencies other than sterling;

less (6) 60% of the net value of transit items.[6]

This magnitude is of importance, as it is the volume of its eligible liabilities that determines for each bank the amount of 'cash ratio deposits' that it must make with the Bank of England. Since August 1981, all banks with eligible liabilities in excess of £10 million have been required to deposit a percentage of these eligible liabilities in a non-interest-bearing account with the Bank. Initially, this was set at 0.5%, but has subsequently been reduced to 0.35%. Cash ratio deposits are not, at present, of significance for monetary policy but are used as a means whereby the Bank of England earns additional income in the form of interest on Government securities and this helps to finance its activities as banking supervisor.

Building Societies

Building societies began as a part of the self-help movement among skilled workers during the nineteenth century. Early societies pooled the savings of their members to finance the building of houses for them. But over time the societies ceased to do their own building and evolved into purely financial institutions taking deposits more widely and making loans for the purchase of houses. In the fifty years since the end of World War II home ownership increased greatly and the building societies grew rapidly.

In spite of this growth, prior to the 1980s the societies continued their business in largely traditional ways. They offered a narrow range of savings deposits and apart from accumulated reserves had no other significant sources of funds, while their lending, apart from the necessary holding of liquid assets, remained exclusively for house purchase. Rates of interest, for the most part, were determined centrally by the Building Societies Association, an organization of which virtually all the large societies were members.

But the 1980s brought many pressures for reform. Many of the societies had

---

[6] These components of eligible liabilities are described in detail in 'Reserve Ratios: Further Definitions', *BEQB*, Dec. 1971.

by now grown beyond their local origins and had developed extensive branch networks which were in direct competition with each other and with the retail banks. The banks themselves, recently freed from official attempts to constrain their growth, had started to compete more effectively for personal deposits and had begun to offer long-term loans for house purchase. Meanwhile the Government with its privatization programme was trying to encourage savers to put more money into shares.

The building societies responded by introducing new types of deposit with higher rates of interest. The power of the Building Societies Association to determine rates began to diminish. In 1986 an Act of Parliament widened the powers of the societies and, notably, enabled them to raise funds in wholesale money markets and to lend limited sums for purposes other than house purchase. This added further impetus to the diversification of activities and for open competition rather than collective agreements on interest rates. Many societies moved fully into the field of money transmission and offered accounts subject to withdrawal by cheque and via automatic teller machines. Many offered credit cards and, in some cases, provided limited facilities for dealing in securities.

But competition brings pressure to keep costs down. The extensive branch networks which had been built up at a time when there was no significant price competition began to appear as a costly extravagance. Equipping all the branches with electronic facilities necessary for a much wider range of business added substantially to costs. There was pressure to merge, to reap economies of scale by spreading the fixed costs over a larger volume of business, and to reduce the number of branches.

The 1986 Act had also given the building societies the right, with the consent of their members, to shed their mutual status and to seek authorization as a bank. Their activities were becoming more and more like those of retail banks and it seemed to many that this would encourage mergers and take-overs not just among building societies but also between building societies and banks and that over time most of the larger societies would seek banking status.

Mergers among building societies did continue to take place but initially only one society, the Abbey National, changed its status to that of a bank. Then in 1994 things began to change more rapidly: the Cheltenham and Gloucester Building Society agreed to a take-over by Lloyds Bank; the Halifax agreed a merger with the Leeds and announced the intention of converting the merged society into a bank; the Abbey National agreed to take over the National and Provincial Building Society. Four of the ten largest building societies were set to become banks or to be merged with banks.

Table 6.2 shows the assets and liabilities of building societies at end March 1995. The figures still include all the societies mentioned in the last paragraph. If all the planned mergers and conversions go ahead then the total shown in Table 6.2 will fall by about 42 per cent.

Table 6.2. Building societies: balance-sheet at 31st March 1995

Liabilities	(£m)
Retail deposits	214590
Wholesale deposits and commercial paper	24363
Certificates of deposit	8384
Bonds	20539
Other liabilities and reserves	34233
Assets	
Bank deposits including CDs	33823
Other liquid assets	9096
First mortgages on owner-occupied property	228250
Other lending	18316
Miscellaneous assets	12624
Total assets = total liabilities	302109

Source: BEQB, May 1995, table 5.2

Measures of Money

Economists usually define money in terms of its functions; 'money is what money does'. Money serves first and foremost as a medium of exchange; that is to say it facilitates the exchange of goods and services. Persons and companies produce goods and services; they sell those to others and they buy from others. But goods do not normally exchange for goods. Goods exchange for money; so that money is the medium of exchange. It also serves as a store of value; that is to say by holding money one can store value—purchasing power—for use at a future date. It need not be a perfect store of value and nowadays most monies lose value over time due to inflation, but for many purposes and especially for short periods of time money remains a convenient means of storing value. Money also serves as a unit of account; it is the means by which we measure value; i.e. prices are expressed in so many Pounds or so many Francs etc.

Money is ubiquitous in modern society and virtually everyone uses it continually. Because of this, the supply of money can have important effects on the aggregate economy and it is easy to see intuitively that increases in the quantity of money mean increases in purchasing power and that this can lead to inflation. It follows that control of inflation necessitates control over the money supply. But this is something which is easier to discuss in theory than to apply in practice.

Given the number of different banks and building societies in the UK and the variety of types of deposit and other liabilities, there can be no unambiguous statistical definition of what constitutes money. Indeed, the notion of the money supply is almost as much an abstraction as the economist's concept of the rate of interest. All one can do is to aggregate different sets of assets and derive different measures of money, and this is what is now done in all developed economies.

The Bank of England has in the past published information on a variety of different monetary series but since 1993 has concentrated on just two: M0 (the monetary base) and M4 (a broad monetary aggregate). It has also begun to publish index numbers attempting to measure a weighted average growth of money: the Divisia indices. The narrowest definition, M0, covers notes and coins in circulation plus banks' operational balances at the Bank of England. These balances exclude the obligatory cash-ratio deposits and are nowadays kept at low levels with the result that M0 is, in practice, close to being just a measure of notes and coin in circulation. In recent years, holdings of notes and coin have, after allowing for a downward trend, tended to move in line with spending and M0 has been seen as a good coincident indicator of aggregate expenditure in the economy. From the 1984 budget onward, the Government set annual targets for the growth of M0 but, after the adoption in Autumn 1993 of an explicit target for inflation, the Government's concern for M0 was re-expressed as a 'monitoring range'. This is currently 0–4%, but given that the annual rate of growth of M0 has exceeded 4% every month since May 1993 it is not clear that the monitoring range has any meaning. M4 comprises the holdings of private-sector residents of note and coin of all sterling deposits (including certificates of deposit) at banks and building societies. Since 1993, the Government has specified a monitoring range for the annual rate of growth of M4 of 3–9%. Until the summer of 1995, recorded growth has remained within this range.

Conventional measures of money, such as M4, add together notes and coin and a range of different types of deposit. It can be argued that if one is concerned to produce measures of money which related to people's actual willingness to spend then one should distinguish between different types of deposit and weight each according to its 'moneyness'. This is the idea behind Divisia indices (named after their originator, Francois Divisia).

It is usual to weight each type of deposit on the basis of its interest rate. Assets (including notes and coin) which earn zero interest have a weight of unity; assets which earn a modest rate of interest have a weight slightly less than unity; assets which earn a high rate of interest have a weight well below unity. The rationale for this is that it is the assets that earn zero interest and which therefore have the highest opportunity cost that will be held chiefly for transaction purposes. They can be viewed as being fully money. Assets which earn interest and which therefore have a lower opportunity cost are more likely to be held for reasons other than making transactions; they can be viewed as being only partially money. If all relevant assets are weighted in this manner and their weighted totals are summed then one derives a Divisia index. In the most recent past calculated Divisia indices have shown some tendency to rise and fall in advance of rises or falls in national income. They are seen as another potential indicator of forthcoming changes in aggregate demand and hence are now compiled by the Bank of England as another aid to forecasting the economy.[7]

[7] For a full discussion of Divisia measures of money, see 'Divisia Measures of Money', *BEQB*, May 1993.

It has to be stressed that there is no one correct definition of money. In a time of financial innovation, the relative attractions of financial assets will be changing and as a result public holdings of any particular category of assets will be likely to change independently of changes in the price level or in real income. It follows that no single definition of money whether narrow or broad, simple or complex, can be treated as an infallible guide to the influence of monetary factors on the level of aggregate demand. This influence may still be strong and it is the case that a rapid expansion of bank credit and bank deposits is likely to be inflationary but to assess this one has to look at a range of statistics and make judgements. As well as exhibiting short-term fluctuations, many monetary series also show long-term trends. Fig. 6.2 shows the change in the ratio to national income of M0, M4, and aggregate Divisia for the years 1977–94.

The Sterling Money Market (Discount Market)

The sterling money market or discount market involves the seven discount houses, other traders in bills, a large number of banks, and the Bank of England. The market plays a central role within the monetary system. Discount houses borrow money, mainly from banks but also from other sources, and invest it in short-term financial assets, notably bills and certificates of deposit. The funds

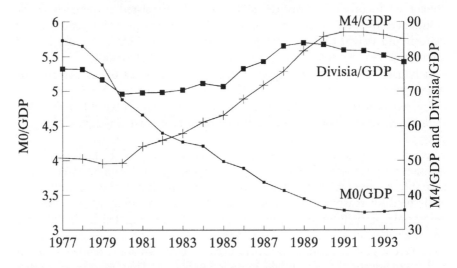

Fig. 6.2. Money-to-GDP ratios: M0, M4, and Divisia

Note: M0 and M4 are actual amounts of money (as defined) outstanding at the end of each year. Divisia is an index with base 100 on 1 January 1977. As with all index numbers, the base is arbitrary and hence so is the absolute level of the series. In the above figure, to facilitate comparisons between the rate of change of the ratios to GDP of M0, M4, and Divisia, we have rescaled the Divisia series at 100 billion.
Source: Figures for the monetary series from BEQB; figures for GDP from NIBB.

they borrow are almost wholly short term, either overnight or at call (i.e. can be recalled without notice) and are secured against the financial assets they hold. Thus, the discount houses provide the banks with a convenient form of liquidity which can be added to, or subtracted from, on a day-to-day basis. Deposits with discount houses earn a competitive rate of interest and, as they are fully secured, any risk is slight. The discount houses also act as market-makers in Treasury bills, commercial bills, and CDs. This ensures that these assets can be easily traded, something which makes them liquid and hence more useful, both for banks and for other market participants.

The Bank of England uses the bill market for purposes of monetary policy, to put money into, or take money out of, the banking system. The operations of the Bank can be summarized as follows. Each day, there are large flows of funds between the commercial banks and the Bank of England. Since the Bank acts as banker to the Government, all payments to the Government involve money flowing from the commercial banks to the Bank. Similarly, all payments by the Government involve money flowing from the Bank to the commercial banks. And the Bank of England will also be making and receiving other payments as well, e.g. on account of foreign-exchange transactions. These movements of money both ways will only exactly cancel out by accident; usually there will be a net balance either way. This will mean that the banking system will normally find itself with either a surplus or a shortage of cash. Whichever is the position, it will quickly be communicated to the discount market, as banks either offer new deposits or call for the repayment of existing ones. When the market is in surplus, the Bank of England will sell bills in order to absorb the surplus. When the market is short of funds, the Bank will announce its willingness to buy eligible bills, but will leave the discount houses individually to decide at what price to offer these. If the Bank is happy with the level of short-term interest rates implied by the offers from the discount houses, it will buy the bills, therefore relieving the shortage of cash. On the other hand, if the Bank is not happy with the interest rates implied by the offers of any discount houses, it can reject these. The discount houses will then have to seek a 'lender-of-last-resort' loan from the Bank and will pay a penal rate for it.

In this way, the Bank of England uses the bill market and the discount houses to smooth out shortages or surpluses of cash in the banking system. Its tactics are designed to avoid always imposing a pattern of interest rates on the market, while leaving itself free to influence rates when it deems this desirable.[8] The Bank's ability to influence rates when it wishes to do so is discussed further in Section 2.7 below. Although the Bank of England may, at times, make loans direct to certain financial institutions, e.g. dealers in government

---

[8] This description of Bank of England operations in the money market is, necessarily, a brief one. For a detailed account, the reader should refer to, 'The Role of the Bank of England in the Money Market', *BEQB*, Mar. 1982, and to 'Bank of England Operations in the Sterling Money Market', Annex 3, 'Bank of England Dealings in the Sterling Money Market: Operational Arrangements', *BEQB*, Aug. 1988.

securities, it is traditionally through the discount market that the Bank deals with the banking system. And whilst, on occasions, the Bank will deal direct with one or more clearing banks, it is still the case that only the discount houses are formally entitled to request loans from the Bank of England as lender of last resort.

Other Short-Term Money Markets

The discount market is the traditional money market in London but, since the 1960s, a number of new markets have been created where short-term financial assets are actively traded. Similar developments have occurred in all other developed financial centres. In London, the main markets for short-term funds are the interbank market, the market in large time deposits from non-bank sources and the market in certificates of deposit (CDs). All these markets include deals in sterling, in dollars and in a number of other currencies. There are smaller sterling markets for deposits with local authorities and with finance houses and, since the 1980s, markets have also existed for short-term deposits denominated in composite currency units such as the ECU and the Special Drawing Rights (SDRs) associated with the IMF. Large companies issue both sterling commercial paper (CP) and dollar or euro-commercial paper (ECP) and there are markets in which outstanding paper is traded.

The interbank market is part of a worldwide interbank market. In the case of sterling, which is not widely held outside Britain, most transactions are between banks in London, but in the case of the dollar or the Deutschmark there is continual dealing between banks in London and banks in other financial centres such as Zurich, Paris, and Frankfurt. Both the interbank market and the market in CDs serve the dual function of providing funds for those (creditworthy) banks which need them and providing remunerative short-term assets for banks with surplus funds. Both functions are a source of liquidity. Banks can regard their short-term assets as being a source of liquidity in the traditional fashion but they can also, quite legitimately, regard their ability to borrow new funds at short notice as an additional source of liquidity.

Most transactions are in large round amounts of £1 million or $1 million or more. Some idea of the size of the sterling markets can be gauged from Table 6.1. At end May 1995, sterling bank assets totalled just over £700 billion and of this total almost £120 billion was accounted for by short-term lending to other banks. With non-sterling markets one needs to consider the worldwide markets. At end 1994, out of total loans outstanding of those banks reporting to the Bank for International Settlements of $8,373 billion, no less than $5,793 or 69% was accounted for by loans between banks.[9]

As markets have grown, both in number and in depth, so banks have become more confident of being able to borrow and lend as they wish,

---

[9] See International Banking Developments, *BEQB*, Aug. 1995

provided, of course, that they maintain their creditworthiness in the eyes of other banks. Liability-management—the continual adjusting of short-term liabilities—has become an accepted part of modern banking and a necessary complement to the more traditional asset management. Non-bank borrowers and lenders have adjusted their behaviour and the finance departments of large corporations now devote considerable resources to monitoring market trends and ensuring that their own borrowing and lending are on the best terms.

Rates of interest are highly competitive and vary continually in accordance with changes in the supply of and demand for funds. The key rate is the London interbank offer rate (LIBOR) for three-month dollars. This is the rate at which banks are prepared to lend for a period of three months and it serves as a base rate for international lending by banks throughout much of the world.

The existence of active markets in a number of different currencies means that banks and other dealers frequently wish to buy or sell particular currencies, so a foreign-exchange market is a necessary complement to these short-term markets. In fact, such is the importance of London as a financial centre, that its foreign-exchange market is, in terms of turnover, the largest in the world. A survey conducted by the Bank of England in April 1995[10] produced estimates of average turnover of $464 billion per day; of which 21% was accounted for by trading between the US dollar and the Deutschmark and 11.5% by trading between sterling and the US dollar. Most trading is between banks and about one third of it is conducted through the intermediation of specialist foreign-exchange brokers. Parallel surveys conducted elsewhere showed New York to be the second largest market in foreign exchange ($244 billion per day) and Tokyo to be the third ($161 billion per day).

The Determination of Short-Term Interest Rates

It was pointed out in the section on the sterling money market that the Bank of England exercises a key role in that market which enables it to influence short-term rates of interest. With many payments made each day between the Government and the private sector, it will frequently be the case that there will be a net balance in favour of the Government. This will mean a net loss of funds to the banking system which will be translated quickly into a shortage of money deposited with the discount houses. Only the Bank of England is in a position to relieve this shortage and it is able to decide the price it will charge for so doing and thereby influence short-term rates of interest in the market.

In the discussion of other short-term domestic markets, it was noted that these were competitive markets where interest rates were set in accordance with supply of and demand for funds. It was partly due to the growing

[10] The results of the survey are given in 'The Foreign Exchange Market in London', *BEQB*, Nov. 1995

importance of these markets that earlier official controls over many rates of interest paid and charged by retail banks were abolished. Since 1971 all banks in Britain have been free to set their own rates and nowadays most rates, even in retail banking, follow the trend of rates in the wholesale markets.

This can sometimes give rise to confusion: is it the case that the authorities set the rates, or is it the case that rates are determined by supply and demand? The position, in fact, is clear. The authorities no longer impose specific rates of interest on particular financial institutions, nor at present do they seek to control long-term rates of interest. Therefore they do not directly control the pattern or structure of relative interest rates. The supply of and demand for funds are free to exert their influence and those intermediaries which are more efficient are free to quote better rates than their rivals.

But the Bank of England, through its own market operations, can alter the supply of funds and hence can push the general level of interest rates up or down. And whilst the Bank normally only operates in the one market, arbitrage ensures that changes in short-term rates there will promptly be mirrored elsewhere. In fact, the Bank's powers are well understood and it only needs a sign that the Bank is ready to see rates move one way or the other for the banks to move their rates into line.

So the position is that it is the authorities, operating through the Bank of England, who effectively determine the general level of short-term sterling rates of interest. It is then up to market forces to determine the pattern of different relative rates of interest. The position is similar in most other developed countries.

The current objective of British monetary policy is to keep inflation low. Accordingly the Bank, in agreement with the Government, will raise short-term interest rates whenever it thinks inflation is likely to rise significantly. This happened in September and December 1994 and in February 1995 when, during a period of rapid expansion of output there were concerns that the rate of inflation would rise. On the other hand, if the authorities believe that inflation is under control and if they are not currently concerned to maintain any particular exchange rate for the pound sterling, they will usually be ready to reduce short-term interest rates.

6.3. The Capital Market

Types of Security

The capital market is a general term which covers the markets in which securities—equity shares, preference shares and bonds—are bought and sold. In principle, the capital market is an example of what we earlier termed direct finance: lenders of funds lending direct to the ultimate borrower, without the intervention of a financial intermediary. In some cases this is so, as for instance when many individuals subscribed to the issue of shares by British Telecom. But, it is by no means always the case. The majority of the securities listed on the British Stock Exchange are now held by institutional investors such as insurance companies, pension funds, unit trusts, and investment trusts. Over the years, many personal holders of securities have chosen to sell out and to entrust their financial wealth to intermediaries; so indirect finance has increased. This has been encouraged by a tax system which has favoured saving via pension funds and (until 1984) life assurance.

Although their detailed terms and conditions can vary widely, most securities fall into three main categories. Firstly, there is the equity share,[11] which represents a share in the ownership of a company; the equity shareholders jointly own the company and have the right to vote at general meetings. If a company makes a profit, that profit belongs to the shareholders and some or all of it may be distributed to them in the form of dividends. But if a company makes a loss, then not only may shareholders receive no dividend, they can also expect to see the market value of their shares fall. Equity shares are risky assets because they represent a claim on a residual: the shareholders own what is left after other creditors have been paid, and if the company cannot pay all its creditors—it becomes insolvent—then the equity shareholders get nothing.

Secondly, there is a somewhat less risky security—the preference share. Preference shareholders are entitled to dividends paid out of profits but only up to a fixed maximum; but, on the other hand, the claims of the preference shareholders take precedence over those of equity shareholders. There is less scope for capital gain and less likelihood of loss. Preference shares do not normally confer voting rights.

Thirdly, there are bonds which, for the most part, are fixed interest securities. Bondholders lend a sum of money for a stated period of time and in exchange are entitled to regular payments of interest and the eventual repayment of the principal sum lent. Beyond this, they have no share in profits but their claims normally have precedence over those of both equity shareholders and preference shareholders.

Both types of share are only issued by commercial undertakings where there is an expectation of profit. Bonds are issued by commercial undertakings and also by governments, by provincial and local authorities and by other public bodies including international organizations.

Not all securities are offered for sale to the public in general or to large institutional investors. Most small companies and a number of not-so-small ones remain as private companies where their shares are held by a limited number of owners and there is no formal means of trading them.

Dealing in securities has changed dramatically over the last 30 years in response to new technology and the progressive internationalization of economic life. The changes have been felt differently in different markets. Equity

---

[11] Equity shares are also known as equities, ordinary shares, and (in America) common stocks.

markets are still largely organized on a national basis and the shares of small and medium-sized companies are still largely owned by domestic investors. But with larger companies, it is now common for significant amounts of the equity to be held by foreign investors and with any large new issue of equity shares it is usual to try to sell these to foreign as well as to domestic purchasers. This has been notable in the case of many recent privatization issues.

In the case of bonds, it is convenient to distinguish the market for government bonds and the more general market for bonds issued by other borrowers. The latter is now a mixture of national markets and the completely international eurobond market. In both the USA and Japan there are vast national markets in which for the most part national firms of security traders issue bonds on behalf of domestic companies. But in Europe, while companies still make modest-sized issues of bonds targeted at domestic investors, most large issues are now in the form of eurobonds and are distributed by international security dealers to both domestic and foreign investors.

The markets for government bonds, like the markets for equities, remain largely organized on a national basis, but there is a trend for the ownership to become more international. A number of governments, including the UK government, issue securities denominated in foreign currencies or in ECU, and in a number of countries the authorities are changing their own markets and procedures to make their issues more attractive to foreign investors.

The Equity Market

New issues of equity can be made in three main ways: a public offer, a private placement, or a rights issue. A public offer of equity shares is usual when a hitherto privately owned company decides to 'go public', i.e. to raise money (for the company or for the existing owners) by offering its shares to the public at large. This is a complicated and costly process: it will usually be managed by one of the larger firms of security-dealers. A prospectus must be drawn up giving detailed information on the company, its directors, and its past and present trading performance including audited profit figures. This prospectus will be distributed to other security dealers, banks, investment managers, and financial advisers in the United Kingdom and (for larger issues) abroad as well. It must also be advertised in a number of national newspapers. The issue will probably be underwritten, that is to say, a number of institutional investors will, for a fee, agree to take up any shares which remain unsold. The managers of the issue have to arrange for applications for shares to be received and checked and shares allocated among would-be purchasers.

A private placing of equities involves their sale direct to a relatively small number of large investors. This is a cheaper method of issue as there is no requirement to publicize a lengthy prospectus and the managers have far fewer purchasers and potential purchasers to deal with. It is used for smaller issues (up to £15 million); as part of a larger issue with the rest being offered publicly (as has happened with many of the UK privatization issues); and as a means of raising modest additional amounts of capital for existing public companies.

A rights issue is an issue of additional shares by an existing public company to its own shareholders. In normal circumstances, the shareholders as the legal owners of a company have first right to subscribe to all new issues of equity but they can, and frequently do, vote at annual general meetings to authorize companies to place a small amount of new shares (not exceeding 5% of issued capital) direct with large investors.

There is no legal requirement on issuers of new equity shares to seek a listing on the Stock Exchange but most do so for the good reason that people are more likely to buy securities of any sort if they know they can sell them again. Neither persons nor corporate bodies can reliably predict their financial circumstances far into the future and neither will wish to be locked into investments for many years. Assets that can easily be resold are more attractive than those which cannot. This is the importance of secondary financial markets. The secondary market in listed equities is organized almost exclusively by the London Stock Exchange.[12] The Exchange is a Recognised Investment Exchange (RIE) under the terms of the Financial Services Act of 1986. Current methods of dealing in securities were introduced by the Exchange in October 1986 as part of the 'Big Bang' reform.[13]

Under the present system, firms which opt to be market makers in specified securities agree to display their prices by means of the Stock Exchange Automated Quotations system (SEAQ) and this makes them accessible on screens to other traders. For widely traded securities, market-makers are committed to dealing, up to published maximum amounts, at the prices displayed; for securities that are less widely traded, the prices displayed are indicative rather than guaranteed. As one would expect, the selling price is slightly above the buying price and market-makers earn income from this difference. They are also free to charge commission on all transactions, but for most large transactions competition has resulted in commission levels of zero or close to zero. Many smaller firms of brokers and provincial brokers have not become market-makers, and continue to act in an agency capacity, buying and selling securities in transactions with market makers on behalf of clients.

Table 6.3 shows the sums raised by offerings of both equity shares and preference shares in the UK for the years 1989–94. Fig. 6.3 below shows the turnover in secondary trading of both equity shares and UK government bonds also for the years 1989–94.

The trading system in London is described as a quote-driven system as it is the market-makers who quote prices at which they are prepared to deal. This

---

[12] A new automated exchange known as Tradepoint is due to come into existence as a rival to the Stock Exchange in late 1995.

[13] For a discussion of these reforms see earlier editions of this book and D. Cobham (ed.), *Markets and Traders* (London: Longman, 1992).

Table 6.3. Funds raised by share offerings in the UK 1989–94 (£ million)

	Ordinary Shares				Preference Shares
	Gross issues		Redemptions	Net issues	
	total	rights issues			
1989	6187	2949	2636	3551	1062
1990	4402	3114	908	3494	728
1991	11140	9129	135	11005	1137
1992	6426	3227	29	6393	624
1993	16536	10891	—	16534	1529
1994	14865	4926	20	13739	402

Source: *Financial Statistics*, various issues

system differs from an order-driven system in which dealers advertise the securities they wish to buy or sell and where there are arrangements for matching buyers and sellers. Other things being equal, a quote-driven system provides a more liquid market as there is no need to match orders: the market-makers themsélves act as counterparties to all sellers and purchasers.

As a consequence of the 1986 reforms much new capital was put into the firms of market-makers with the result that London emerged with a number of large international security traders willing to undertake high-value transactions. A number of firms began to quote prices for the equity shares of larger companies from other European countries. This met with considerable success

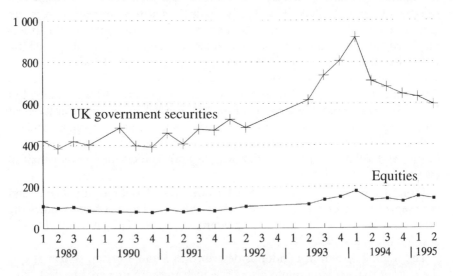

Fig. 6.3. Transactions in equities and UK government bonds, 1989–1994

Notes: Equities include transactions in all equities companies listed in the UK and the Republic of Ireland. The figures include transactions between market makers as well as transactions with clients.
Source: *Financial Statistics*.

and many of the bigger transactions in the shares of such companies are now conducted with market-makers in London. At end March 1993 London dealers were quoting firm prices for over 400 European equities and annual turnover had risen to over £150 billion.[14] This internationalization of equity trading is a new development. It has prompted defensive reform measures in a number of European equity markets, but for the time being at least it appears that London can deal with large transactions more cheaply and more quickly than can other European centres.

The Eurobond Market

The bond market is the most international section of the capital market. It is dominated in Britain and increasingly in many other European countries by the eurobond market, an international capital market in which securities— predominantly fixed-interest securities but also including some variable or floating rate notes (FRNs)—are issued and sold worldwide. Most of the business is handled by some 20–30 international security houses and international banks which act both as issuing houses and market-makers. The main borrowers of funds are international organizations, public corporations, and large well-known companies. Securities are issued in a range of currencies, but the US dollar is the dominant one. There is no physical market-place and the market functions as a worldwide over-the-telephone market. London is the single most important centre.

The issue of new securities involves a lead manager or managers and a syndicate of subscribing banks and security houses. The lead managers arrange the details of the issue: size, currency, duration, interest terms, etc. and then assemble the syndicate of subscribers. Members of the syndicate will intend to place the securities with clients and will subscribe for the amount of securities they feel they can resell. The syndicate will normally be international, and in this way, the securities will end up spread among a wide range of investors in a number of countries. Secondary trading is facilitated by one or more security houses, normally including the original lead manager(s), making a market in the securities, i.e. standing ready to quote prices at which they will buy or sell.

The market is subject to little official regulation; dealers are, of course, subject to laws against fraud and malpractice in the countries where they operate, but they are not subject to long lists of rules such as those which apply to issues of new securities to be listed on the London or New York Stock Exchanges. No lengthy prospectus is prepared for a new issue and there is no requirement to advertise a proposed new issue in national newspapers. This is justified on the grounds that eurobonds are not offered for sale to the general public: they are 'placed' with professional dealers and only sold to a relatively

---

[14] See 'Financial Market Developments', *BEQB*, Aug. 1993.

Table 6.4. Net issues of Eurobonds and Euronotes 1991–93 (£ billion)

	1991	1992	1993	Stock outstanding end 1993
Straight bonds	142.0	115.3	193.7	1389.9
Convertibles	25.0	−19.8	−54.6	196.7
FRNs	3.5	23.7	44.7	263.3
Total Bonds	170.0	119.3	183.8	1849.8
Short and medium-term euronotes	34.9	40.4	72.7	255.8

Note: Figures show new issues i.e. gross issues less redemptions.
   Columns may not sum exactly to the given totals due to rounding errors.
Source: Bank for International Settlements, *Annual Report 1994–95.*

narrow range of professional investors. This argument seems to have been accepted by the UK authorities when framing the 1986 Financial Services Act. The result is that issue costs are low and considerably less than for a public offering of securities. But, at the same time, the scope for worldwide distribution of eurobonds means that large sums of money—often well in excess of $100 million—can be raised.

The market is a flexible one and easily develops new types of financial asset. In addition to straight bonds, there are issues of convertible bonds (with rights to convert into equity at some future date) and FRNs. Moreover, recent years have seen a rapid growth of euromedium-term notes: short-term paper or medium-term bonds issued periodically by large and well-known borrowers within the terms of a pre-established programme. Table 6.4 shows the value of net issues of eurobonds and euronotes for the years 1991–93 and also for the amount outstanding at end 1993. Some two-thirds of all issues originate in London.[15] The US dollar remains the most important currency of issue while the yen and the Deutschmark are also widely used. In recent years sterling issues have raised net annual amounts ranging from some $15 to $40 billion.

The Market for UK Government Bonds

Issues of UK government stock are managed by the Bank of England and are made in three main ways: by auction, by tender, and on tap. In the first two cases, the Bank will publish a short prospectus for an amount of stock of typically £2 billion or more and will invite applications at or above a specified minimum price (in the case of a tender) or without any minimum price (in the case of an auction). With a tap stock the Bank will 'issue' a small amount of stock, typically £100 million or £200 million to itself and will then sell this bit by bit as and when there is demand. In 1995, after a review of debt management, it

---

[15] For further discussion see E. P. Davis, 'The Eurobond Market', ch. 5 of Cobham, *Markets and Traders.*

was announced that in future the Bank would rely primarily on auctions but would also continue to make modest sales of bonds on tap.

The volume of net sales varies greatly from year to year depending on the Public Sector Borrowing Requirement (PSBR). This largely reflects the budget deficit of central government but also includes borrowing on behalf of local authorities and other public-sector agencies as, in Britain, such borrowing is centralized. During the 1970s and the first half of the 1980s, the PSBR was invariably positive and usually large and the Bank of England was a regular net seller of bonds. In the late 1980s the Government had several years of substantial budget surpluses and there were net repayments of debt, but in the early 1990s the more usual pattern of budget deficits reappeared. Fig. 6.4 shows the changing pattern of the PSBR and of net sales of UK government bonds over the years 1985–94.

Secondary trading is organized in ways similar to those for other securities. Specialist gilt-edged market-makers (GEMMs) display on screen the prices at which they are prepared to buy and sell and deals are struck over the telephone. Traditionally, holders of UK government stock have been largely domestic residents, notably British insurance companies and pension funds, but in recent years there has been some tendency for holding of non-residents to grow. At end March 1994, foreign ownership (excluding official holdings) was over 9% of total market holdings. This is part of a general trend. In recent years many governments have needed to borrow heavily and have sought to widen their market by making their bonds more attractive to foreign investors.

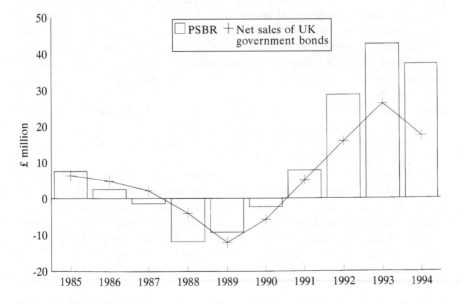

Fig. 6.4. The Public Sector Borrowing Requirement and sales of government bonds.

Source: Financial Statistics.

It can be expected that this trend will continue and that the markets for the bonds of European governments will become more and more integrated into the international bond market.

The Bank of England announced two innovations in UK government bonds for 1996. From the start of the year, there is to be an open repo (repurchase) market enabling all traders to conduct sale and repurchase operations. Later in the year an official strips market will be opened. Stripping a bond involves separating the stream of interest payments from the payment, at maturity, of principal so that the two can be traded separately. This allows investors to choose their cash flows more precisely. When the new market is in operation it will be possible to buy and sell series of interest payments and what, in effect, will be zero coupon bonds. Both these innovations copy features which exist abroad and are designed to increase the attractiveness of UK government stock.

6.4. Derivative Markets

Markets in Financial Futures and Traded Options

Markets in financial futures and in traded options have grown in number and in trading volume in recent years. In Britain virtually all of such trading takes place on the London International Financial Futures Exchange (LIFFE). Financial futures are financial assets such as a three-month bank deposit or a government bond which are traded today for delivery in the future. They are one method of enabling persons and firms to cope with risk. For example, a bond dealer with a portfolio of UK government bonds may fear that interest rates will rise and in consequence the value of his bonds will fall. One way to deal with this risk would be just to sell the bonds straightaway; but bond dealers need to hold a minimum portfolio in order to trade with clients and, in any case, running down the portfolio leaves the dealer at risk if he has guessed wrongly: if bond prices rise and the firm has to repurchase bonds at a later date at a higher price it will lose money.

An alternative strategy is to sell bond futures. That is to say the bond dealer enters into an agreement today to sell a given amount of bonds at a date, say, six months in the future. No money changes hands until the termination of the contract, although both parties are required to put down an initial deposit, usually a small percentage of the value of the contract. Suppose the dealer's expectations are correct and the price of bonds falls by, say, 5%. The value of the dealer's portfolio falls by this percentage but the price of the bond future is fixed. At the expiry of the contract in six months' time, the dealer can buy bonds in the cash market at the now lower price and sell these at the price agreed six months ago and hence make a profit to offset the loss on the portfolio.

This is the position in principle but in practice procedures are simpler. The whole point of having exchange-traded standardized contracts is that it is easy to buy and sell and hence to open up new positions or to terminate (close out) old ones. The bond dealer who sold bond futures for delivery in six months can undertake a contract to buy an equivalent amount of bond futures at any time within the six-month period. The two contracts will cancel each other out and the dealer will receive from or pay to the Exchange the difference in the value of the two contracts. In the example under discussion it was assumed that bond prices fell after the initial future sale and hence the sale price was higher than the price of the subsequent purchase. The bond dealer made a profit on the futures transactions which offset the loss on his portfolio. The dealer had used the futures market to hedge his cash position.

The price of bond futures and the price of cash bonds (i.e. bonds traded for immediate delivery) do not always move precisely in line with one another. Dealing in the one does not provide a perfect hedge for the latter. But they normally move together to a great extent so dealing in the one can be expected, in practice, to be a good hedge for the other.

One can also use futures markets to speculate just as one can use cash markets for this purpose. Anyone who expects bond prices to rise can buy the underlying bonds or can buy bond futures. The advantage of futures is that one only need pay immediately a deposit of a small percentage of the value of the purchase, so the potential gain—and the potential loss—is much greater relative to the amount staked.

Anyone who undertakes a futures contract incurs a liability either to fulfil the contract at the specified time or to undertake an earlier offsetting contract. While the contract is open there is always the possibility of gain or loss. A traded option offers something different. This gives the purchaser the right, but not the obligation, to buy (a call option) or to sell (a put option) a specified amount of a given financial asset at a specified price within a specific period of time. For this right the purchaser pays a premium to the seller of the option.

The premium is the extent of the purchaser's financial commitment; there is no risk of additional loss. Consider the example of the bond dealer discussed immediately above. Another way of hedging his portfolio against a decline in its value would be to purchase options to sell bonds at a given price, close to the existing market price, within, say, the next six months. If bond prices do fall below the price agreed in the option contracts, the bond dealer can purchase bonds in the cash market at the new low price and sell these to the vendor of the options at a profit and so offset the decline in the value of his portfolio. Alternatively, since options are tradable, the purchaser can just sell his options at a profit as the market price will reflect their enhanced value after the fall in bond prices. If bond prices do not fall, there would be no incentive for the bond dealer to exercise the option to sell bonds at a price at or below the current market price. He will allow the options to lapse.

Bond dealers can use both futures and options to hedge their positions—or to speculate. But so can other financial and non-financial companies. Banks can protect themselves against changes in short-term interest rates by buying or selling futures on short-term deposits or by taking out options on these. Industrial companies concerned, for instance, about potential changes in borrowing costs can do likewise.

LIFFE trades futures and options contracts on short-term bank deposits and on long-term government bonds in a number of major currencies. As well as sterling contracts, there are contracts in Eurodollars, Deutschmarks, Swiss Francs, Italian Lire, and in ECU. In fact, the contract on the German government-bond future currently attracts the most business of any contract on LIFFE or on any other European exchange. For all contracts, the total volume of business in 1994 averaged close to 600,000 contracts per trading day. LIFFE, which is the largest such exchange in Europe, now accounts for around 10% of world trading in futures and options.

One should also mention that there is a large volume of dealing in foreign currencies for future delivery and in options on foreign currencies. But although a small part of this business takes place on organized exchanges in the USA, the greater part is conducted between banks and their clients. Attempts by LIFFE to establish futures and options contracts in foreign exchange were unsuccessful. Neither type of contract attracted much interest and all the contracts have ceased to be traded. The provision of forward foreign exchange by banks is discussed further in Chapter 11.

Swaps

Swaps, for the most part, involve the exchange of obligations on debt contracts. A number of different sorts of swap can be arranged: some involve different currencies, some involve different types of interest rate, some involve both. By way of example consider one of the more common types of interest-rate swap. A UK bank wants to borrow $100 million for five years and requires that the loan have a variable rate of interest as this will better match its lending. The bank could raise the funds at (three-month) LIBOR + $\frac{1}{2}$%. The bank does not want fixed-rate funds but it would be able to raise $100 million at a fixed rate of 8%. At the same time we have an industrial company which also wants to borrow $100 million but which seeks fixed-rate money. The company can raise the funds at a rate of 9%. The company does not want a variable-rate loan but its credit-rating is such that it would be able to borrow at LIBOR + 1%.

The bank then wants variable-rate money; the industrial company wants fixed-rate money. If each goes ahead and arranges its financing independently the position will be as follows:

bank interest cost: LIBOR + $\frac{1}{2}$%
industrial company interest cost: 9%

But there is scope for a swap. Suppose the bank borrows money at 8% fixed and the company raises variable rate finance at LIBOR + 1%. Now suppose they each agree to pay the interest costs of the other and in addition the company pays the bank an additional $\frac{3}{4}$% per annum. The net cost to each party now becomes:

bank interest cost: LIBOR + $\frac{1}{4}$%
industrial company interest cost: 8$\frac{3}{4}$%

Each party gets its funds at $\frac{1}{4}$% less than it could have in the absence of the swap.

At first sight it may seem surprising that both parties can gain in this way. It is less surprising when one realizes that the foregoing is just an example of the theory of comparative advantage. The bank has an absolute advantage in that it can borrow cheaper in both markets but it has a comparative advantage in the market for fixed-rate funds while the industrial company has a comparative advantage in the market for variable-rate funds. Just as in international trade, when each party exploits its comparative advantage, there are potential gains to both.

Such transactions are arranged by some 80–100 international swap dealers comprised of large banks and firms of security traders. The market is large and has grown greatly in recent years. The reason for this growth is the great variety of financial markets worldwide and the differing abilities of borrowers to access particular markets. For example, a British company may have a good credit-rating in the UK but may be unknown in the USA. If the company needs dollars, it may be advantageous to borrow sterling on good terms and swap obligations rather than to borrow dollars directly but on unfavourable terms. On the other hand, if the British borrower is well-known abroad but needs sterling (say, for instance, a large building society), it may be possible to achieve a lower interest cost by issuing a eurodollar bond, selling the dollar proceeds in the foreign exchange market and swapping the dollar interest and repayment obligations for obligations in sterling.

Many new bond issues are nowadays related to swaps. Security dealers regularly advise potential borrowers which combination of borrowing and subsequent swap will produce the lowest cost. According to a survey by the International Swap Dealers Association, the total (principal) value of transactions outstanding amounted, at end 1994, to over $11,000 billion.[16] The market is worldwide but London is one of the key centres.

6.5. Other Financial Intermediaries

Life Assurance Companies and Pension Funds

Both life assurance companies and pension funds must be classed as financial intermediaries as both take funds from savers and lend to borrowers. But unlike

---

[16] See 'Financial Market Developments', *BEQB*, Aug. 1995.

most of the institutions previously considered they do not provide short-term financial assets; both offer savers long-term investment possibilities.

The most popular form of life assurance contract nowadays is the endowment policy, although this can come in a number of forms including policies linked to investment in unit trusts. The essential feature of an endowment policy is that the assured pays either a single premium or makes regular payments over a number of years and at the end of this time, the insurance company guarantees to pay a lump sum. This may be just the basic sum assured or it may include additional bonuses or profits depending on the precise type of policy. Should the policyholder die before expiry of the policy, his dependents will receive the sum assured and extra profits (if any). Thus, an endowment policy is a mixed financial instrument. It is largely a straightforward long-term financial contract, in which what is returned reflects what has been paid, an element of accrued interest and, maybe, returns on investments, but it also includes insurance cover against death within the currency of the policy.

There are a number of other forms of life assurance contract, but almost all involve either a single large payment or regular payments by the assured over a number of years in exchange of a guarantee of an eventual lump sum payment to the assured, or to his dependents.

The life assurance companies comprise a number of specialist life companies as well as the large general insurance companies that also offer marine, fire, and accident insurance. The total accumulated funds of all life assurers, the specialist and the general companies, amounted at end 1994 to £419,502. Over half of this sum was invested in domestic and foreign equity shares and somewhat more than 15% in British government securities.

Pension funds are set up to provide pensions for members of a particular occupational group, or for employees of a particular firm or public sector body. The principle is simple: those covered by the fund make regular contributions over a number of years and, upon retirement, are entitled to a regular pension until death. The number and size of pension funds have grown during recent decades as more and more firms have set up funds. In some cases of large firms or public corporations, the pension funds now administer considerable sums of money and are numbered among the largest discretionary managers of funds in the country. At end 1994, total net assets of pension funds amounted to £450,966 million. About two-thirds of total assets are invested in domestic and foreign equity shares and most of the rest is spread over investments on British government securities, in property, and in short-term assets.

Life assurance companies also provide pensions both for individuals (notably the self-employed) and for groups. For many small firms, it is easier to make pension provision for staff through a life assurance company, than to set up one's own fund.

Other Institutions

Unit Trusts and Investment Trusts. There are two forms of mutual investment common in the United Kingdom: unit trusts and investment trusts. The intention of mutual investment is to enable small investors to pool resources in order to gain the benefits of diversification. There are high fixed costs of dealing in securities and a small investor, with say £5,000 to invest would not be able to spread this over a number of different companies. But if 1,000 investors, each with £5,000 to invest were to come together and put their money in a common pool, they would have £5 million to invest. This could be diversified over many companies, so reducing the risk. This is the principle of mutual investment.

Unit trusts are legally constituted as trusts with a trust deed and a trustee. The trustee, usually a bank or an insurance company, holds the assets of the unit trust on behalf of the beneficial owners—the unitholders. The trust is managed by a professional manager who is responsible for decisions about investment policy, subject to the provisions of the trust deed. Units can be sold at any time and the sums raised added to the pool of investible resources. Similarly, units can be sold back to the manager, who is then obliged to sell some investments to repay the unitholder. Investment trusts are not, in fact, trusts in the legal sense. They are limited companies which issue their own shares and use the proceeds to buy the shares of other companies. Thus, anyone who purchases shares in an investment trust automatically purchases a diversified investment. At end 1994 funds managed by unit trusts amounted to over £83 billion, of which the greater part was invested in equity shares, both in the United Kingdom and abroad. The total assets of investment trusts are somewhat smaller and, at end 1994, amounted to nearly £36 billion and again most were invested in ordinary shares.

Finance Houses. There are a number of finance houses and consumer credit companies active in the UK. They tend to be small, as most of the larger institutions have now taken on the status of bank. Many are specialized institutions set up to finance the products of particular manufacturers or retailers. Funds are raised largely by issuing bills and by borrowing from banks. At end 1994, such companies had assets outstanding of £12,853 million, most of which was accounted for by loans to persons and to industrial and commercial companies.

6.6. Regulating the Financial System

Traditionally, financial institutions were governed by a number of different Acts of Parliament, each relating to different aspects of their business but, more recently, Parliament has sought to provide comprehensive regulation within the framework of a limited number of Acts covering specific financial institutions. The 1979 and 1987 Banking Acts cover the activities of all banks; the 1986 Building Societies Act regulates the building societies; and the 1986 Financial Services Act seeks to regulate all trading of securities, of life assurance, and of a wide range of ancillary activity. In addition the European Union has brought forward a series of directives seeking to promote a single market in financial services while, at the same time, maintaining adequate prudential controls over financial institutions.

The 1979 and 1987 Banking Acts require that all firms undertaking banking business be authorized by the Bank of England and lay down detailed conditions for authorization. These include requirements to supply the Bank with regular statistical information, to open one's books for inspection upon request from the Bank, and to respond to any directives given by the Bank. It is apparent that the Acts give considerable power to the Bank of England, although there is provision for any bank refused authorization to appeal to the Treasury. The regulations cover all engaged in banking within the United Kingdom, both British-owned and foreign-owned banks.

The main public efforts of the Bank, to date, have been in the areas of capital adequacy and of liquidity. It has laid down, for all banks, minimum requirements of capital (i.e. equity capital, reserves, and other irredeemable or long-term funds) dependent on both the volume and composition of bank assets. These requirements follow the proposals put forward in 1988 by the Committee on Banking Regulations and Supervisory Practices which is composed of representatives of central banks and supervisory authorities of twelve developed countries[17] and which meets regularly in Basel, Switzerland. These proposals were accepted by the competent authorities in the twelve countries and have since been adopted in whole or in part by many other countries worldwide. The Basel committee worked in close consultation with the European Commission with the result that the 1989 EEC directive on the capital resources of credit institutions closely resembled its own proposals.

The provisions of the Building Societies Act of 1986 have already been touched on above. As well as laying down detailed rules about what activities building societies could and could not engage in, the Act also created a Building Societies Commission with powers over the societies analogous to those of the Bank of England over the banks.

The Financial Services Act of 1986 was a wide-ranging measure designed to regulate the activities of security traders, brokers, agents, and advisers. For all of these it is now necessary to be authorized in order to carry on business and authorization requires compliance with a set of rules of conduct. The Act established a Securities and Investment Board (SIB) with powers of supervision over all firms engaged in financial investment but with power to delegate this

[17] These countries comprise the 'Group of Ten' i.e. Belgium, Canada, France, Germany, Italy, Japan, the Netherlands, Sweden, UK, USA, plus in addition Luxemburg and Switzerland.

supervision to approved regulatory organizations. It was intended that such organizations should be set up for different sections of the industry and that they would include representatives of the firms being regulated, i.e. there would be an element of self-regulation. This was seen as desirable in that much of modern financial activity is complex and almost the only people who understand it well are those actually engaged in the business.

There are, at present, three regulatory organizations. They are:

1. the Securities and Futures Authority (SFA) covering dealers and brokers in securities and in futures and options;
2. the Investment Managers Regulatory Organization (IMRO) covering fund managers; and
3. the Personal Investment Authority (PIA) covering life assurance companies, unit trusts and all agents and brokers dealing with the general public.

Each of these regulatory organizations establishes and publishes its own rules of conduct but these rules have to be approved by the Securities & Investment Board. Thus it is incorrect to say that the system is wholly one of self-regulation: it is a mixed system in which self-regulation is permitted but subject to the ultimate authority of a statutory body. It was the Government's hope that this would produce an effective system of regulation but without the bureaucracy and the legalistic approach believed to be inherent in the American model with a single powerful statutory body; the Securities & Exchange Commission.

The Financial Services Act also established the idea of recognized investment exchanges (RIEs). SIB will recognize an exchange where it is satisfied that it provides an efficient and well-run market with adequate financial resources to safeguard investors. Where firms transact business on an RIE, the requirements on them are less onerous than where transactions are carried out on unrecognized exchanges.

Over the years, the involvement of the EU in financial regulation has grown. The objective of the European Commission is to achieve a single European financial market with financial institutions and their clients able to do business anywhere in the Community unhindered by artificial obstacles and constraints. The Commission has pursued this objective with a three-pronged approach. First, there should be a minimum necessary harmonization of regulations so as to bring about fair competition and ensure adequate consumer protection. Secondly, institutions should not require authorization to do business in each country; once duly authorized by the competent authorities in one member country, they should be free to operate throughout the Community (the principle of the single passport). Thirdly, all activities of each institution should be supervised by the authorities of the country in which its chief office is situated (the principle of home country control).

The Second Banking Co-ordination Directive, which came into force in January 1993, has effectively brought about a single market in banking services. If it did not produce any immediate visible changes in European banking this was chiefly due to the fact that wholesale banking, i.e. dealing in large sums, was already international with most large banks already having offices in the main European financial centres. Retail banking, on the other hand, appears at present to offer little incentive for banks to operate internationally. There are significant economies of scale in operating the payments mechanism and most European markets seem already to be adequately provided for. A number of banks have in the past tried to enter retail banking in other European countries or in the USA and most have given up the attempt. If European economic integration continues, and if Europe does move to a common money, we may see some cross-border mergers of large banks, but, for the time being, retail banking continues to be largely organized on a national basis by domestically owned banks.

Achieving agreement on security trading was more difficult due, in part, to the need to accommodate both the quote-driven market of the UK and the predominantly order-driven markets of the other EU member states. But the Investment Services Directive which removes the legal obstacles to cross-border trade in securities was finally agreed and is due to come into force in 1996. Further directives have promoted a single market for mutual funds (unit trusts) and for life assurance.

But if securing agreement on financial regulation is one problem, enforcing it is another. Several recent well-publicized scandals have provided examples of regulations being ignored both out of deliberate dishonesty and from folly as individual dealers sought to conceal trading losses. In the case of the Bank of Credit and Commerce International (BCCI) it was dishonesty. BCCI was closed down in 1991 when its authorization was withdrawn by the Bank of England and by the supervisory authorities in those other countries where it operated. Following the closure, it became clear that BCCI had been engaged in fraud on a large scale and had disguised this by systematic false accounting. Many depositors lost money. In the case of Barings it was a combination of individual folly and woefully inadequate controls within the Bank. Baring Brothers, one of the oldest banks in the City of London, was sold to the Dutch ING Bank in early 1995 for the sum of £1 after a single trader in Singapore had lost more than the entire capital of the bank in ill-judged speculation on financial futures in both Osaka (Japan) and Singapore. The bank's depositors in this case did not lose money but the shareholders and some bond-holders lost their entire investment.

There have been a number of other examples of fraud and/or folly in the financial area. It is common among journalists and politicians to treat each such case with calls for action: for changes in regulations, for changes in the people who regulate, or for the introduction of whole new regulatory bodies. But one should beware of over-reacting and of action just for the sake of action. Modern financial systems are large and employ large numbers of people and no system of supervision can prevent all improper behaviour. Of course, serious instances of wrong-doing should be studied to see if they could have been prevented and if any loopholes in the regulations could be closed so as to diminish the likelihood of such behaviour occurring in future. But ultimately, financial supervision, like all policing, involves striking a balance between inadequate regulation which fails to stop unlawful activities and excessive regulation which hampers lawful activities.

Suggestions for Further Reading

Bain, A. D. *The Economics of the Financial System*, 2nd edn., (Oxford: Blackwell, 1992).

Cobham, D. (ed.) *Markets and Dealers*, (London: Longman, 1992).

Revell, J. (ed.), *The Changing Face of European Banks and Securities Markets* (London: Macmillan, 1994).

FISCAL POLICY AND THE BUDGET

R. C. BLADEN-HOVELL

7.1. Introduction

This chapter is concerned with the operation of budgetary policy in the United Kingdom. As such it considers the volume and composition of public expenditure, together with the structure of direct and indirect taxation.

The economic functions of government that give rise to public expenditure and/or taxation may be considered as falling into three broad categories. The first function corresponds to the response of governments to breakdowns of the market system in the allocation of economic resources. The type of breakdown, or inefficiency, generally considered in this context relates to the existence of public goods such as, for example, national defence. In their pure form, such goods are characterized by two features: individuals cannot be excluded from consuming a pure public good; consumption of the good by one individual does not prevent anyone else from consuming the good. Together, these characteristics make it difficult for private firms producing public goods to charge individuals for their use. As a consequence, the provision of public goods within a free-market system would generally be less than society desired. Where such goods are considered desirable, a non-market solution to the problem would involve government provision of the good, with funding provided through general taxation.

The second function of government that may involve budgetary considerations is the redistribution of income and wealth. A distribution of income that is solely determined by the market is unlikely to be that most desired by society. In this respect, the ability of government to tax and spend potentially represents a powerful mechanism for changing the distribution of income in the direction that society considers just and equitable.

The final function of government considered here is its potential role in smoothing cyclical fluctuations in the level of economic activity. Tax rates and government expenditure could, for example, be adjusted in order to stimulate aggregate demand during a recession or curb aggregate demand during a boom. The scope to adjust public expenditure and taxation in this way is, however, highly constrained. Government expenditure on, for example, schools, universities, hospitals, and the payment of wages to people who work in these institutions, occurs because society desires that these services be provided centrally. The need to provide such services efficiently, effectively prevents governments from adjusting expenditure programmes frequently in a manner required in order to meet the short-term needs of demand management. Although the government's freedom of action is slightly greater on the tax side, adverse spill-over effects must also be recognized even here. Regular adjustments in corporation tax, for example, may adversely affect investment through the impact on the degree of certainty with which businessmen view future market conditions.

The remainder of this chapter contains six sections. Section 7.2 outlines the aggregate level of general government expenditure and tax receipts for the period since 1965 and compares these levels with budgetary developments in the other Group of Seven (G-7) nations. The structure of the budget is presented in Section 7.3. Details of the volume and composition of government expenditure are provided in Section 7.4, whilst the structure of direct and indirect taxation is outlined in Section 7.5. The surplus or deficit of government transactions is frequently taken to reflect the net impact of government activity on the economy. In Section 7.6, therefore, we examine how the government's need to borrow has varied and discuss the question of the sustainability of fiscal policy. The Chapter is completed by a discussion of the conduct of fiscal policy in the United Kingdom since 1973.

7.2. Background

The measurement of government activity, public expenditure, and taxation is essential to most policy analysis. The relative size of the public sector, the size of the public sector deficit or surplus, and the level of taxation are commonly used indicators of the extent of government intervention in the economy.

Historically, the relative size of the public sector has grown. The public sector in this context is defined as the general government, comprising the central government, local authorities, and public corporations which include the nationalized industries. For the purpose of the current discussion, the central government sector covers the activities of departments and agencies which are answerable to a minister of the Crown or other responsible person, who is in turn answerable to Parliament, together with bodies, such as Regional Health Authorities, which are not administered as government departments but are subject to ministerial or departmental control. Local authorities, on the other hand, are public authorities of limited geographical scope which have the power to raise funds through certain forms of local taxation. They comprise county, district, regional, and borough councils; services run by joint authorities, such as waste regulation, police, and the fire service, are also included.

Public finance relates to the income and expenditure of the public sector of the economy. Income is mainly derived from taxation, national insurance contributions, and the net trading income of public corporations. Expenditure is on the procurement of goods and services, wages and salaries, and current and capital grants in such areas as health, education, defence, welfare, and social security.

One way to show the relative size of the public sector activity in the economy is to present income and expenditure data as a percentage of gross domestic product (GDP). Such information is shown for the period 1965–94 in Fig. 7.1, together with data relating to the Public Sector Borrowing Requirement (PSBR). The PSBR is the difference between public sector payments to and receipts from the domestic private sector and abroad, including net lending, net cash expenditure on company securities (including privatization proceeds), and some minor financial transactions. It indicates the extent to which the public sector borrows from other sectors of the economy and overseas, or runs down its holdings of bank and building society deposits or other liquid assets to finance the balance of expenditure and receipts.

General government expenditure was around one-third of GDP in the early 1960s. It rose to a peak of 48.7% in 1975, fell back for two years, then peaked again in 1982 at 46.1% of GDP. Outturn figures for 1994 show general government spending at 42.7% of GDP. As a percentage of GDP, tax revenues rose with a pronounced cyclical tendency from around 35% of GDP in 1965 to

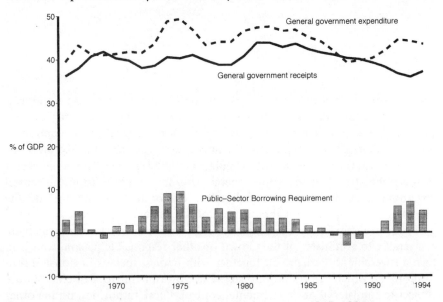

Fig. 7.1. General government expenditure and receipts, 1965–1994

Source: Tables 10.21 and 10.61, *Public Finance Trends 95* (London: HMSO, 1995).

a peak of 44% in 1982. Since then they have fallen steadily; to 36% in 1993/4, before rising slightly to 37% in 1994/5.

The PSBR represents the difference between the government expenditures and receipts shown in the figure. The chart clearly shows the general tendency for government to operate a deficit, i.e. to borrow from the rest of the economy, over the period. The PSBR varies from a high of $9\frac{1}{2}$% of GDP reached in 1975–6 to a low of −3% (a surplus) achieved in 1988–9.

Broadly speaking, these movements mirror similar budgetary developments elsewhere in the world. Table 7.1, for example, presents summary figures for total government outlays and tax receipts, each expressed as a percentage of gross domestic product, for the group of seven (G-7) nations over four different sub-periods, 1960–93. The general tendency for the share of public expenditure and tax revenue to increase over the period is apparent in almost every case. The United Kingdom was the only member to show a marked decline in receipts between 1982 and 1994. This exception aside, the relative size of budgetary outlays and receipts in the United Kingdom corresponds closely to those for Germany, France, and Italy. It is generally larger, however, than the level of budgetary outlays and receipts for the United States and Japan.

7.3. The Budget

The budget is presented annually by the Chancellor of the Exchequer to the House of Commons. Since 1993 the budget has been unified insofar as it presents detailed statements regarding both public expenditure plans and tax legislation for the coming year.[1]

The Government's budgetary policy is set within the context of the Medium Term Financial Strategy (MTFS) which, since 1980, has provided the frame-

Table 7.1. Total government expenditure and receipts: G-7 countries (% of GDP, average figures)

	Government outlays				Government receipts			
	1960–73	1974–9	1980–90	1991–3	1960–73	1974–9	1980–9	1991–3
United States	29.5	32.6	33.0	34.5	27.6	29.8	30.5	30.7
Japan	19.5	28.4	32.1	32.5	20.0	24.6	31.0	34.2
Germany	37.4	47.5	47.1	49.2	37.5	44.0	45.0	46.1
France	38.0	43.3	50.2	52.2	37.7	40.8	48.1	48.5
United Kingdom	36.7	44.4	42.2	42.5	34.8	39.0	40.2	37.0
Italy	33.6	42.9	49.1	54.4	30.2	33.5	38.1	44.7
Canada	31.6	39.2	43.5	49.5	30.0	36.1	39.0	43.0

Source: OECD, *Economic Outlook*, 52 (Dec. 1992) and 55 (June 1994).

[1] Prior to 1993 the budget, delivered in March, dealt with the tax side of the public accounts whilst public expenditure plans were outlined in the November Autumn Statement.

work for monetary and fiscal policy. Details of the strategy are published in the Financial Statement and Budget Report (FSBR) at the time of the annual budget. The MTFS is updated each year, but the defeat of inflation on a lasting basis has remained the central objective. The Government believes that in order to achieve this objective, monetary policy needs to be supported by a firm fiscal stance. The broad aims are those of balancing the budget over the medium term, reducing public spending as a share of national income over time, whilst simultaneously improving the value-for-money of government spending.

Each MTFS presents illustrative fiscal projections for the current fiscal year and for three years ahead. These projections cover the PSBR and its main expenditure and revenue components. The Government, for example, forecast a PSBR of £34.4 billion for 1994–5 and £21.5 billion for 1995–6 in the FSBR published in November 1994. A large part of the current PSBR is attributable to the effects of the economic cycle: in particular, both social security spending and corporate tax receipts lag behind the output cycle.

In preparing the Budget, the Chief Secretary to the Treasury normally leads on behalf of the Chancellor on public expenditure matters, leaving the Chancellor to concentrate on economic, monetary, and tax policies. The preparation goes on throughout the year. The timetable for expenditure decisions in any financial year, summarized in Table 7.2, effectively begins in the February of the previous financial year when the Treasury requests reports from individual departments assessing the priorities and pressure points in their spending programmes. At this point departments seeking to increase spending in particular areas must indicate how they would adjust expenditure

Table 7.2. Calendar of the expenditure decision-making process

Month	Main Events and activities
Financial Year *t*-1	
April	Departments submit position reports.
June	Initial Cabinet discussions of public spending outlook; Confirmation of Control Total ceiling.
July	EDX begins to meet to discuss allocation; Chief Secretary holds bilateral talks with spending ministers and makes recommendations to EDX.
September/November	EDX continues to meet and makes recommendations to Cabinet; Cabinet discusses allocation.
November	Cabinet agrees allocation; Chancellor announces new spending plans as part of a unified budget.
January/February	Detailed scrutiny of Ministerial bids for voted expenditure in financial year (*t*); Publication of departmental reports and statistical supplement to unified budget.
March	Publication of estimates.
Financial Year *t*	
April	Start of financial year.
before end-July	Completion of legislative process on both taxation and spending.

in order to remain within existing programme totals. In early spring Ministers collectively endorse guidance on the conduct of the coming Public Expenditure Survey. The purpose of the Survey, which reviews plans for the next two years and sets them for the new third year, is to review the allocation between programmes of resources within the agreed overall limit to public expenditure. In recent years, the overall level of spending in the period ahead has tended to emerge from a series of compromises on individual departments' programmes reached bilaterally between the Chief Secretary to the Treasury and spending Ministers in July. A Cabinet Committee (EDX), chaired by the Chancellor of the Exchequer, also begins a series of meetings in July to discuss the allocation of resources between programmes within the agreed overall limits. EDX meetings are held throughout the summer and run alongside discussions regarding tax plans for the coming year. The allocation of expenditure is finalized in Cabinet at a meeting held immediately prior to the presentation in November of the budget to the House of Commons.

Detailed scrutiny of individual Ministerial spending programmes by Parliament occurs in the January and February following the budget. Parliamentary control of the budget in this respect occurs because whilst government can propose new areas of tax revenue and expenditure, only Parliament can grant money for departments to spend. Most central government expenditure is approved by Parliament on the basis of detailed statements, known as Supply Estimates, of the estimated expenditure of departments for the year ahead. Some expenditure—such as, for example, entitlements under the National Insurance Fund, payments to the European Union, and interest on government debt—rest on standing authorities given by Parliament. Supply Estimates are typically published in March, immediately prior to the start of the financial year; the legislative process for tax and expenditure being completed when proposals become law before the end of July in the form of a Finance Act.

7.4. Government Expenditure

Control and Outturn

Public expenditure is planned in the context of the Public Expenditure Survey. In order to achieve the objectives for general government expenditure, a more explicitly top-down approach to public spending was adopted in 1992. Under this system, a new spending aggregate—the New Control Total (NCT)—was introduced. Currently referred to as simply the Control Total, this covers over 80% of general government spending. It excludes social security spending which is directly related to unemployment and also central government debt interest. Both are highly cyclical and, if included in the Control Total, could have an undesirable destabilizing effect on other programmes. Although privatization proceeds are officially counted as negative expenditure, spending plans for general government expenditure are generally expressed with them excluded.

Growth in the Control Total is constrained to a rate which ensures that general government spending (excluding privatization proceeds) grows more slowly over time than the economy as a whole. The public spending plans introduced in the FSBR published in November 1994 predicted that Control spending would rise by under 3% a year over the next three years in cash terms with general government spending projected to rise slightly more at an average of 3.25% per annum in cash terms.[2]

The Government's forward expenditure plans are drawn up on the basis of a three-year rolling cycle. Figures for the Control Total and its main components in each of the three years are expressed in cash terms. The figures for year one are translated before the start of the year into detailed spending controls, including cash limits and external financing limits for nationalized industries. The presumption of the medium-term, top-down approach is that these aggregate cash plans should remain unchanged with all departments living within the cash totals previously agreed.

Since the move to cash control in the early 1980s, spending plans are no longer automatically compensated for general inflation. However, they do take account of the impact of inflation on specific areas of spending which are directly linked to price movements, such as index-linked expenditure on social security and pensions. Similarly, the plans also take account of the effect of other economic assumptions such as unemployment on other areas of demand-led expenditure.

The Control Total contains an unallocated reserve. This is intended to cover unforseen policy initiatives, revised estimates of demand-led programmes, and other overruns on spending within the Control Total, where these cannot be absorbed by the spending department concerned. The expenditure plans for 1994–5 include a reserve of £3 billion in a Control Total of £255.7 billion for 1995–6. This increases steadily in years two and three of the expenditure plan, reflecting the increasing uncertainty of future spending plans, rising to a provision of some 3% of the Control Total in 1997–8.

Details of the level of general government expenditure, expressed as a proportion of GDP, sequentially planned since January 1990, together with the published outturn is given in Table 7.3. The date of publication for a particular plan is given in the left-hand column whilst the date to which the plan applies may be read across the top row. Information concerning the planned or actual share of government spending in GDP is then given in each cell of the table: figures located above the broken line relate to the share targeted in a particular plan for a specific year; figures below the broken line indicate the corresponding outturn. Thus reading across any row we may

---

[2] These nominal growth rates translate into a real growth rate of 0.25% per annum for the Control Total and between 0.5 and 0.75% per annum for general government spending.

observe the history of government spending immediately prior to any particular plan together with the planned expenditure over the subsequent three years. Reading down any column we may determine how the target share of government spending changed in a sequence of plans and, for the period till 1994–5, how these plans compare with the final outcome.[3]

Inspection of Table 7.3 indicates that the objective of reducing the share of general government spending is generally preserved within any particular plan. Revision, often substantial, across plans does, however, occur as planned expenditure is adjusted in the light of changing circumstances. The share of government spending in GDP planned for the financial year 1992–3, for example, was originally set at 39.5% in the White Paper published in 1990. This value was revised upwards in each of the subsequent two years to a value of 42% published in the 1992 Supplement. The realized value, published in January 1993, was 45%—i.e. 3% above the level planned only one year earlier.

Local Authority Expenditure. Local authorities account for one-quarter of general government expenditure. In 1994–5, total current and capital spending by local authorities (including debt interest) amounted to £76.9 billion. Expenditure by local authorities can be divided into two categories. The first category corresponds to the provision of main local services. The level, pattern, and standard of these services are determined locally, subject to the financial resources available and, in some cases, subject to regulation and inspection of the service provided. The second category of expenditure relates to other services that are financed almost entirely by central government from specific

Table 7.3. General government expenditure: plans and outturn (share of GDP, excluding privatization proceeds)

	1989–90	1990–1	1991–2	1992–3	1993–4	1994–5	1995–6	1996–7	1997–8
January 1990 White Paper (Cm. 1021)	39.5	40.0	39.75	39.50					
February 1991 Supplement (Cm. 1520)	39.5	40.0	39.75	39.75	39.25				
February 1992 Supplement (Cm. 1920)	40.0	40.0	41.75	42.0	42.0	41.50			
January 1993 Supplement (Cm. 2219)	39.75	40.25	42.25	45.0	45.75	45.0	44.25		
February 1994 Supplement (Cm. 2519)	39.75	40.25	42.25	45.75	45.0	43.75	43.25	42.50	
November 1994 Budget	39.75	40.25	42.0	44.50	44.25	43.5[a]	42.50	41.75	41.0

[a] Estimated value

Source: Financial Statement and Budget Report, 1995–6.

[3] Figures located along the diagonal below the broken line indicate the 'first release' outturn value for the share of government spending in a particular year. Figures below and to the left of these relate to sequentially later publication releases.

grants. Examples of these services include rent allowances and mandatory student grants

Central government control of local authority expenditure is exerted through the concept of Total Standard Spending (TSS). This represents the amount that central government judges appropriate for spending on main services. In 1995–6 this was set at £43.5 billion for local authorities in England, £2.8 billion for Wales, and £6.1 billion for Scotland.[4] The value of the TSS is announced each year at the time of the budget. Like the Control Total for general government expenditure, the announcement takes the form of a three-year rolling plan. This details the aggregate level of TSS together with a breakdown of expenditure on each main service that would be consistent with the overall figure.

Central government control over local authority spending has increased considerably during the early 1990s. In the financial year 1994–5, for example, almost two-thirds of the general purpose local authorities in Great Britain set their budgets equal to an expenditure 'cap' determined by central government. The capping mechanism operates through the power of the central government to limit the tax rates that local authorities set. The process is designed to prevent 'excessive' increases in local expenditure.

Since its introduction in 1984, capping has taken a variety of forms. Until 1991–2 the mechanism was used in a highly selective manner with limits imposed on a small number of authorities designated as excessive spenders. From 1992 onwards, however, capping has been applied universally, with central government announcing a provisional maximum expenditure limit at an early stage of the local budgetary process. Consequently, many local authorities effectively 'cap' themselves by setting their budgets at the limit indicated by the TSS. Changes have also been made in the timing of the cap. Until 1990–1, local authorities deemed to have been excessive spenders were capped in the subsequent year; since 1992, however, capping has applied in the current financial year with the effect that local authorities have been forced to incur the cost of re-billing local residents.

The Private Finance Initiative.   Although the general stance of fiscal policy under the MTFS has been tight, considerable concern has developed in recent years regarding the level of public expenditure and the size of the public sector. The private finance initiative (PFI), launched in November 1992, marks one notable attempt to respond to this concern. The PFI is a government attempt to encourage the use of private finance for what have hitherto been public investment projects. Until 1989, government practice in this respect was directed by the so-called Ryrie rules—named after Sir William Ryrie who chaired a committee in the early 1980s which considered the issue of private finance for nationalized industries. Under the Ryrie rules, the use of private finance would only be allowed if the efficiency gains thereby generated were

---

[4] In Scotland the TSS is referred to as government supported expenditure.

sufficiently large to compensate for the higher cost of private finance, a condition which in practice was never met. These rules were relaxed in 1989 and in 1992, with the result that the government now intends to allow projects to proceed where the private sector takes responsibility and can recoup its costs by charges to the final user.

The motivation underlying the launch of the PFI rests upon two arguments. The first is that private finance may generate incentives for operational efficiency within the public sector and thereby produce desirable welfare effects for society. Second, because private finance does not count towards the PSBR, often taken as a key indicator of the government's performance, the PFI may allow a higher level of infrastructure investment than would otherwise occur. The success of the scheme in generating private finance to date is relatively small—by the end of 1994–5 only around £0.5 billion or 2% of public-sector capital expenditure was planned under the initiative. However, the amount of expenditure involved in this way is growing. By the end of 1995, for example, the programme is likely to involve some £2.5 billion of capital expenditure, including a Docklands Light Railway extension (£100 million), a new Scottish Air Traffic Control Centre (£250 million), and the purchase and leasing of new rolling-stock for London Underground (£400 million). Two further projects—the Channel Tunnel rail link and refurbishment of the West Coast main line railway, which together amount to some £3.1 billion—are under consideration but currently face delays in the tendering process.

Volume and Composition

Government spending accounts for a large part of national income. In the financial year to end March 1994, total expenditure of general government (i.e. central and local government combined) amounted to £283 billion, or 44.25% of gross domestic product. However, not all of this expenditure represented purchases of goods and services by the public sector: nearly one-half was accounted for by transfer payments such as pensions, unemployment benefits, and sickness payments. For many purposes, it is important to distinguish these two categories of expenditure. General government expenditure on goods and services represent a claim on the resources of the country: government hires the services of schoolteachers, policemen, etc., it purchases ambulances from car manufacturers, it pays for the construction of motorways, etc. Transfer payments, on the other hand, involve no direct claim on resources. Government collects the money in the form of taxes and national insurance contributions and redistributes it as cash payments to pensioners, social security claimants, and others. Transfer payments represent a redistribution of income and it is only when the recipients of the pensions, benefits, etc., spend the money that there is an actual claim on resources.

As was seen from Figure 7.1, government spending has grown over time. This is true of expenditure on goods and services and of total expenditure

Table 7.4. General government expenditure, 1950–94 (% of money GDP at market prices)

	Goods and services		Current and capital grants	Debt interest	Net lending	Total
	Final consumption	Gross fixed capital formation				
1950	16.4	3.3	10.4	4.2	0.2	34.5
1955	17.0	3.4	8.1	4.0	1.1	33.5
1960	16.4	3.3	8.7	3.9	2.3	34.6
1965	17.0	4.1	9.5	3.7	2.6	37.0
1970	17.9	4.7	11.5	3.9	2.4	40.4
1975	22.3	4.7	14.2	3.9	3.5	48.7
1980	21.6	2.5	14.8	4.7	1.5	45.0
1985	21.1	2.1	16.6	4.9	−0.5	44.2
1990	20.5	2.3	14.5	3.4	−1.6	39.1
1994	21.5	1.9	16.8	3.3	−0.8	42.7

Source: Economic Trends, Annual Supplement, 1995.

inclusive of transfer payments, both of which have risen in absolute amount and as a share of national income. These trends, which are of long standing and date back to the nineteenth century, continued for much of the period following World War II. This is illustrated in Table 7.4, which shows the total level of general government expenditure, together with its main components, expressed as a proportion of gross domestic product for selected years since 1950. Final consumption comprises expenditure on goods and services and wages and salaries. Since 1950 it has accounted for approximately half of general government spending, rising steadily from 16.7% of GDP to 21.5% in 1994. Since 1993 it includes payments to universities, colleges, and further education institutions which was previously incorporated under grants to the personal sector. Current and capital grants have also increased by a comparable amount since 1950, albeit from a lower base. Current grants to the personal sector, largely made up of social security payments, account for around half of this expenditure. The final item to show some considerable variation over the period is net lending to public corporations, the private sector, and the overseas sector by the general government. Since 1984 this entry has remained negative, reflecting the impact of privatization proceeds which are treated as negative expenditure for the purpose of the government accounts.

The composition of government spending in 1993–4 is shown in Fig. 7.2 and is given in detail for the period 1983–4 in Table 7.5. Together these show that roughly two-thirds of government spending occurs under four headings: social security, health, education, and defence. In 1983 expenditure on defence, health, and education were broadly similar at around 5% of GDP. Social security expenditure stood at 12.9% and other services 16.8%. By 1994 defence expenditure was 3.6% of GDP while social security expenditure had increased by nearly 2% of GDP to 14.7%. Health expenditure had also increased marginally, but education expenditure was at the same level as in

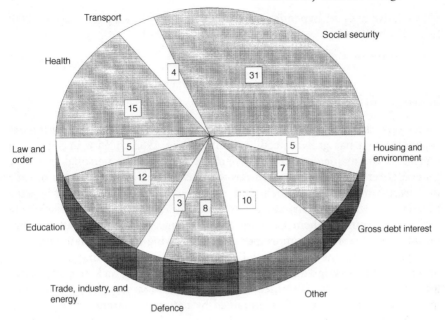

Fig. 7.2. General government expenditure by function, excluding privatization proceeds, 1993–1994 (%)

Source: Financial Statement and Budget Report 1995–96 (London: H.M. Treasury, 1995).

Table 7.5. General government expenditure by category (£m)

	1983	1986	1989	1992	1993	1994	% change 1983–94
General public services	5130	6326	9336	11960	11960	12681	147.2
Defence	15840	19066	20988	24402	24561	23815	50.3
Public order and safety	5326	6826	9433	13854	14434	15049	182.6
Education	16329	19271	24837	31947	33805	36057	120.8
Health	15928	19164	25152	34999	36764	38657	142.7
Social Security	39296	49947	57343	84666	93483	98236	150.0
Housing and community amenities	7422	8066	7996	10604	11083	10591	42.7
Recreation and cultural affairs	1960	2446	3185	4168	4211	4476	128.4
Fuel and energy	523	−1174	−1785	−516	1127	600	14.7
Agriculture, forestry, and fishing	2346	2088	1972	2906	4161	3280	39.8
Mining and mineral resources, manufacturing and construction	2734	1906	1524	1222	1337	1632	−40.3
Transport and communication	5080	3728	7129	6644	6576	6441	26.8
Other economic affairs and services	3328	4128	5049	4488	5228	6320	89.9
Other expenditure	17279	20551	24927	23055	24377	27901	61.5
Total	138521	162339	197086	254604	273113	285736	106.3

Source: Blue Book, 1995.

1983 relative to GDP. Expenditure on other services fell as a percentage of GDP to 13.3% in 1994.

Social Security Spending

Social security is the largest functional component of general government expenditure. It has grown steadily, from 28% in 1983 to 34% in 1994, and represents the major component of current grants to the personal sector by general government. Much of this growth has been caused by factors outside the direct control of government and, on the whole, the generosity of benefits has remained constant in real terms while the number of people who are entitled to claim for them has risen. For instance, an ageing population has meant that there are now more pensioners receiving the basic state pension.

Approximately one half of social security spending, including expenditure on retirement pensions, unemployment benefit, statutory sick pay, and statutory maternity benefit, is termed 'contributory' and is met from the national insurance fund. This fund is maintained by national insurance contributions paid by employers, employees in employment, and the self-employed. Entitlement to these benefits depends partly upon previous contributions to the fund, with the benefits themselves being uprated annually according to movements in the retail price index.

The remaining expenditure on social security benefits is on 'non-contributory' items which are financed from general taxation. The majority of expenditure on non-contributory benefits goes on income-related benefits; that is where the amount of the benefit varies with the recipient's income and circumstances, with benefits not being paid to individuals with resources above a certain level. A prime example of a non-contributory benefit not tied to the recipient's income is Child Benefit; non-contributory benefits tied to the recipient's income include Family Credit and Income Support.

Expenditure on social security has increased as a percentage of GDP since the middle of the 1970s. The increase exhibits a marked cyclical pattern as a large element of the social security budget is related to fluctuations in the level of economic activity. As a percentage of GDP social security expenditure reached a peak of 11.2% in 1982–3 and another peak of 11.4% in 1993–4. Both episodes correspond to periods of economic downturn and an increase in unemployment. Retirement pensions account for the largest single component of the social security budget, though the share has been declining over the last twenty years. In 1975 this item accounted for 52% of the total; by 1994 the share had fallen to 39%. Over the same period expenditure on income support has almost doubled, rising from 13% to 23%. Family benefits, including child benefit, family income support, and maternity grants, have remained stable at between 10 and 12% of the social security budget since the middle of the 1980s.

7.5. Taxation

Taxation is the main source of revenue for the public sector which, when broadly defined to include national insurance contributions, represents around 93% of total current receipts. A summary statement of the proposed tax changes and their effect on Exchequer revenues is presented annually in the FSBR, published immediately after the Chancellor's budget statement to the House of Commons. This document provides details of estimated tax receipts for the past financial year and forecasts of tax receipts for the forthcoming two years. Table 7.6 reproduces the figures given in the FSBR, 1994–5.

As can be seen from the Table, over half the total tax receipts of general government in the financial year 1993–4 were accounted for by receipts collected by the Inland Revenue (broadly speaking, direct taxes) and Customs and Excise (indirect taxes). In addition there were a number of other receipts of which the most important were local authority Business Rates and the Council Tax.[5] National insurance contributions help generate the funds that provide the range of 'contributory' social security benefits. However, the contributions are geared to the income of contributors rather than the expected claims on the fund and in this respect they resemble taxation rather than insurance.

Income Tax

Income tax is the single most important tax raised by the government in terms of the revenue generated. Table 7.6 shows that, in the financial year 1993–4, it yielded £58.4 billion, or just over one-quarter of total tax receipts. Income tax is also one of the oldest taxes, having been introduced to Britain during the Napoleonic Wars and becoming a permanent feature of the tax system in 1842.

The income tax structure is straightforward in principle, but complex in practice. All personal incomes are assessable to tax, but each tax-payer is allowed to earn up to a certain amount before tax is paid. This amount is known as the personal allowance. There are a number of other tax reliefs possible. For instance, expenses necessarily incurred in earning income are not taxable and constitute an additional allowance. Similarly pension contributions and donations to charities may be made before income is assessed for tax. The sum of all allowances is deducted from total income and what remains is taxable income. It is this income that is subject to income tax.

Eligibility for a particular personal tax allowance is usually determined by the individual's circumstances. The value of individual allowances listed in the FSBR, 1995–6, is shown in Table 7.7. The single person's allowance in 1994–5 was £3445, which means that a single man or woman could then earn £287 per

---

[5] Council tax replaced the Community Charge in 1993.

Table 7.6. General government receipts

	£ billion		
	Outturn	Forecast	
	1993–4	1994–5	1995–6
Inland Revenue			
Income tax	58.4	64.2	70.1
Corporation tax	14.9	20.1	26.4
Petroleum revenue tax	0.4	0.7	0.7
Capital gains tax	0.7	0.8	0.8
Inheritance tax and stamp duty	3.0	3.2	3.5
Total	77.5	89.1	101.5
Customs and Excise			
Value added tax	38.9	43.3	49.0
Fuel duties	12.5	14.2	15.6
Tobacco duties	6.5	6.8	7.0
Alcohol duties	5.2	5.4	5.5
Betting and gaming duties	1.1	1.2	1.2
EC own resources	2.2	2.2	2.3
Air passenger duty	0.0	0.1	0.3
Insurance premium duty	0.0	0.2	0.7
Total	66.3	73.2	81.5
Vehicle Excise duties	3.6	3.8	4.0
Business rates	12.6	12.3	13.8
Other taxes and royalties	6.4	6.4	6.3
Total taxes and royalties	166.4	184.9	207.2
Social security contributions	38.7	42.5	44.5
Council tax	8.6	8.8	9.2
Interest and dividends	5.1	4.2	4.6
Gross trading surplus and rent	5.1	5.2	5.7
Other receipts	6.9	6.9	7.6
General government receipts	230.8	252.5	278.9
North Sea revenues	1.2	1.6	2.2

Source: Financial Statement and Budget Report, 1995–6

month or £66 per week before paying tax. For married couples there is an additional allowance of £1720 per annum. The remaining allowances shown in Table 7.7 concern an age-related allowance available for single people or couples with income less than £14,200 a year, and a blind person's allowance.

Income tax in Britain, as in most countries, is a progressive tax. This means that the share of income that is taken in tax rises as income increases. Those with higher taxable income pay a larger proportion of their income as tax. This is usually justified on the principle of ability to pay: those with higher taxable income are presumed to be able to afford to contribute a larger proportion of their income as tax. It is also justified if one accepts the proposition that one purpose of the tax system is to redistribute income among society. Progressivity is achieved by having different tax rates apply to different levels of income. For many years, there were as many as six different tax rates, each applicable to

Table 7.7. Income tax allowances (£)

	1994–5	1995–6
Personal Allowance	3445	3525
Married couple's allowance, additional personal allowance, widows bereavement allowance	1720	1720
For people aged 65–74:		
Personal allowance	4200	4630
Married couple's allowance	2665	2995
For people aged 75 and over:		
Personal allowance	4370	4800
Married couple's allowance	2705	3035
Income limit for age-related allowances	14200	14600
Blind person's allowance	1200	1200
Capital gains tax annual exemption:		
individuals	5800	6000
trusts	2900	3000
Inheritance tax threshold	150000	154000

Source: Financial Statement and Budget Report, 1995–6.

different levels of income. In 1988, however, the majority of these were abolished and the system was simplified to a basic rate of 25% and a higher rate of 40%. In 1992–3 a new lower rate of 20% was introduced. The bands of income to which each of these tax rates apply in the financial year 1994–5 and 1995–6 are shown in Table 7.8.

Tax rates, personal allowances, and the bands to which they apply are announced each year by the Chancellor in the budget speech. Each may be freely varied, but the Chancellor must indicate what uprating would be required in order to compensate for the rate of inflation. This means that proposed tax changes may be assessed on the basis of their real effects as well as their monetary effects. Clearly if money wage rates are increasing at a rate of 10% per annum, but tax allowances only increased by 5%, tax-payers would start to pay tax at a lower level of real income than before. Similarly, if the higher rate threshold were raised by less than 10%, some individuals would find themselves paying the higher rate at lower levels of real income than before. The current budgetary arrangements imply that the Chancellor has complete discretion over whether or not to uprate the tax system in line with inflation, but require him to indicate the full extent to which his policy differs from the inflation-adjusted baseline.

Table 7.8. Bands of Taxable Income (£)

	1994–5	1995–6
Lower rate—20%	0–3000	0–3200
Basic rate—25%	3001–237000	3201–24300
Higher rate—40%	over 23700	over 24300

Source: Financial Statement and Budget Report, 1995–6.

Mortgage Tax Relief. In addition to the system of personal tax allowances, there are also some expenses which are allowable against income tax. The most widespread of these is tax relief granted against mortgage interest payments. This is administered under the MIRAS—mortgage interest relief at source—scheme, whereby the borrower pays interest to the lender net of a specified rate of tax, the tax component subsequently being reclaimed by the mortgagors from the Inland Revenue.

The mortgage relief applies to loans used for the purchase of an individual's main or only residence. Prior to 1974, tax relief was granted on all interest payments on the value of a loan taken out for the purpose of purchasing a house. An upper limit of £25,000 was put on the value of the loan on which tax relief was allowed in that year. Since then the ceiling has increased only once, in 1983, to its current value of £30,000. In 1991 relief was restricted to the basic rate of 25%. This reduced the value of the relief to higher tax-rate payers who had previously been able to claim relief at 40%. In 1994 the value of the relief was further reduced to 20% and reached its current value of 15% in April 1995. With interest rates of 7%, this tax relief is worth £315, i.e. £30,000 × 0.07 × 0.15, to everyone with a mortgage at or above the £30,000 threshold.

The systematic reduction in the rate of tax at which mortgage interest relief is available, together with general reductions in interest rates, has reduced the cost of the MIRAS scheme to the Government. The cost of the scheme reached a peak of £7.7 billion in 1990–1, and this has subsequently fallen to an estimated £2.6 billion in the financial year, 1994–5. This reduction led to calls for MIRAS to be modified in order to boost the depressed housing market. Two proposals have emerged in this respect. The first proposal focuses on first-time buyers in the market and seeks to increase the number of people entering the housing market by raising the relief offered under MIRAS for this category of borrower either by raising the loan ceiling, or by increasing the tax rate at which relief is calculated.

The second proposal is somewhat more complicated and is aimed at helping those individuals who face negative equity in the housing market. Negative equity comes about when falling house prices lead to the value of a property falling below the value of the mortgage outstanding. Selling the house under these circumstances would provide insufficient funds to repay the outstanding debt and, as a result, households in this situation face considerable financial constraints. On current estimates, negative equity affects around 1.2 million households in the United Kingdom, some 11% of the total number of households with a mortgage.

The proposal directed at this problem involves the possibility of individuals being offered the option of giving up their future MIRAS tax entitlements for a cash sum available today. If we assume a discount rate of 7% and a 25-year interest-only mortgage, then the net present value of MIRAS to an individual at its current rate is some £3,670. The potential costs to the Treasury of adopting such a scheme are, however, huge. Even if the proposal were restricted to first-time buyers who bought houses between 1987 and 1989, the potential maximum cost would be some £5.5 billion.

National Insurance Contributions. People who earn income are also liable to pay National Insurance (NI) contributions. These payments are standardized for both employees and the employer with upper and lower limits set, for the income of employees and the profits of the self-employed, below which NI contributions are not imposed, and above which contributions are not increased. Details of the these thresholds and the intermediate rates of contributions for employees and employers as of April 1995 are shown in Table 7.9.

The structure of NI is one area of the British tax system most in need of reform, particularly from the point of view of employers' contributions. The current structure is highly kinked and produces no fewer than four points (at earnings £59, £105, £150, and £205 per week) at which employer's contributions increase by several pounds if the employee earns an additional 1 pence of income. For instance, if an employee earns £149.99 per week, the employer pays NI contributions of £10.50. If the employee's pay increases to £150, the employer's contribution rises to £15.30.

These kinks in the NI structure can create rigidities in the labour market, and the clustering of earnings immediately below the £59 threshold suggests that this problem is particularly acute for the lower paid. In effect employers are reluctant to pay workers slightly higher weekly wages because any production gain is more than offset by the increase in NI contributions. This problem has long been recognized and in both the 1994 and 1995 budgets the Chancellor cut the size of the jumps in the schedule of employer's contributions. However, whilst this reduced the severity of the problem it did not remove it entirely.

Table 7.9. Structure of National Insurance contributions (April 1995)

Weekly earnings	Percentage NIC rate[a]	
	Employees	Employers[b]
Below £59	0	0.0
£59–£104.99	2% of £59	3.0
£105–£149.99	+ 10% of	5.0
£150–£204.99	earnings	7.0
£205–£440	between £59	10.2
Above £440	and £440	10.2

[a] Not contracted-out rate.
[b] Rates apply to all earnings.
Source: *Financial Statement and Budget Report*, 1995–6.

Corporation Tax and Oil Taxation

Corporation tax. Corporation tax was introduced in 1947. As with tax on persons, companies can offset a number of allowances against earnings, and it is the total of profits net of allowances which is assessed for tax. For many years the rate of corporation tax was relatively high at 52% but, at the same time, there were generous provisions whereby much of corporate capital expenditure could be completely offset against earnings. The result was that the yield from corporation tax was very low. In 1984 the government introduced a series of reforms which involved a progressive reduction of the rate of tax to 35% whilst abolishing some of the more generous capital allowances and stock relief. The standard rate of corporation tax was further reduced to 33% in March 1991. This rate applied to companies with profits above £1,250,000, companies with profits below £250,000 being taxed at a lower rate of 25%. Between the two thresholds there is tapering relief which gradually raises the average rate from 25 to 33%.

The tax payable by a company depends upon the level of taxable profits and is unaffected by whether the profits are retained by the company or distributed in the form of dividends to shareholders. But the tax is paid in two parts: advanced corporation tax (ACT) and mainstream corporation tax, and the division between these two does depend on how much is paid to shareholders in the form of dividends. When dividends are paid, they are as net-of-tax payments and the company has to pay tax on behalf of the shareholder at the basic rate of income tax. It is these payments which constitute ACT. The system is best described by an example.

Assume a company has taxable profits of £100 million. Its total liability for corporation tax is £33 million. This is fixed. Now suppose that the company pays to shareholders, dividends of £20 million. Since these payments are regarded as being net of tax, they have to be grossed up in order to determine the shareholders' gross income and the company's liability to ACT. The principle of grossing up is straightforward. If a tax-payer with a marginal tax rate of 50% receives a net-of-tax payment of £500, it can easily be seen that the gross payment must have been £1000: the taxpayer needed to earn £1000 in order to be left with a net payment of £500 after tax. If the marginal rate had been 25% (the basic rate in 1994–5), a net-of-tax payment of £500 would have corresponded to a gross payment of 100/75 × £500 = £666.7. On the same basis, shareholders who have received £20 million net of tax are deemed to have received a gross income of 100/75 × £20 million = £26.7 million, of which £6.7 million is tax due. This is the amount that the company has to pay in ACT. Subsequently it will pay mainstream corporation tax of £33 million less the £6.7 million already paid.

For shareholders liable to tax at the basic rate of income tax, there is no further tax liability. They are deemed to have received a gross income of 100/75 × dividends received and to have had tax paid on their behalf by the company.

For shareholders whose marginal tax rates exceed 25%, additional tax is due on the deemed gross payment. Conversely, shareholders such as pension funds or individuals holding their investment in a Personal Equity Plan, who do not pay tax, can claim a refund of the tax paid on their behalf.

Of the allowances which companies can set against income, the most important are in respect of depreciation. In order to produce, and to generate, profits, all companies require some capital. But capital depreciates in value due to use and due to age. If a company is to remain in business, it has to set aside sufficient funds to be able to replace worn-out plant and machinery. So not all corporate earnings can be viewed as profit, in the sense that they could be distributed and spent by shareholders: some earnings have to be set aside in order to maintain intact the capital stock. This is recognized by the tax authorities and corporation tax is levied on profits after provision for depreciation. To avoid the trouble and expense of trying to assess physical depreciation for each company separately, general rules are laid down. Physical depreciation is translated into accounting depreciation and standard percentage allowances are granted in respect of plant and equipment and in respect of industrial holdings.

In practice, depreciation is calculated by one of two methods: the declining balance method and the straight line method. The difference between the two may most easily be seen by means of an example. Suppose that a depreciation allowance of 20% applied to a machine costing £1000. We could assume that, each year, the machine loses 20% of its existing value. So, in year 1, it loses £200 in value and is then worth £800. In year 2, it loses 20% of £800, i.e. £160, and is then worth £640, In year 3, it loses 20% of £640, i.e. £128, and so on. This is the declining balance method and it results in depreciation allowances being greater in the early period of the life of the capital equipment. Alternatively, we could assume that, each year, the machine loses 20% of its initial value. This would mean that depreciation was a constant £200 each year, and that the machine would be fully depreciated after five years. This is the straight line method. Both methods are used at times by the Inland Revenue.

Oil taxation. Oil taxation involves three separate elements: royalties, petroleum revenue tax (PRT), and corporation tax. Royalties, which are now charged only on certain oil and gas fields, are a direct levy on the value of all production. PRT is a tax levied on the receipts from the sales of oil and gas—above an exempt amount—less operating costs and royalties. Both royalties and PRT are imposed on oil and gas fields individually and apportioned among the participants. Corporation tax is applied normally to the profits of oil and gas producers, but after deduction of royalties and PRT.

This range of taxes was designed to ensure a high yield to the Exchequer from the profitable large fields whilst, at the same time, not overtaxing smaller or more costly fields. To further ensure that taxation should not deter the extraction of oil and gas from marginal fields, the Secretary of State for Energy is given the power to refund royalties and to cancel PRT in cases where the profitability of a field is low.

Total revenues from all royalties and taxes on oil and gas production depend closely on the sterling prices of oil and gas. These depend on world prices expressed in dollars, and on the pound–dollar exchange rate. Receipts were at a peak during the financial years 1984–5 and 1985–6 when they averaged some £12 billion per annum but due, *inter alia*, to a decrease in world oil prices, they have fallen back considerably since then. In the financial year 1994–5, receipts from all royalties and taxes were estimated to be no more than £1.2 billion.

Capital Gains Tax

Tax is levied on capital gains. For persons it is levied at a rate equal to that which would apply if the gain were treated as additional income; for companies it is levied at the corporation tax rate. The case for such a tax is one of equity: why should a person who receives £1,000, in the form of a capital gain, pay no tax, when a person who receives the same sum, in the form of income, has to pay tax? But there is also a case for such a tax on the grounds of efficiency: without it, much energy will be spent on seeking ways to convert income into capital gain, in order to avoid tax. The case for capital gains tax (CGT) is strong.

But there are inherent difficulties in fairly implementing such a tax and, in consequence, the present tax represents something of a compromise between what is desirable in theory, and what is convenient in practice. Many assets are exempt entirely from the tax. These include a person's principal private residence, agricultural property, motor cars, most life assurance policies, assets donated to charities, winnings from gambling, National Savings instruments and government stock, and most corporate fixed-interest securities. There is provision for allowing losses on assets subject to CGT to be offset against gains; and to avoid the high cost of collecting many small amounts of tax, there is an annual personal allowance, whereby gains below a certain amount are exempt from taxation. For the fiscal year 1995–6, this allowance has been set at £6,000 for the individual and £3,000 for most trusts.

A complication of capital gains tax is that gains usually accrue over time and hence it is desirable to distinguish between real and monetary gains. A person who bought a share in company *X* in 1985 for £1,000 and sold it for £2,000 in 1995 made a gain of £1,000 on paper; but since the general price level increased by around 50% over the same period, the real gain was substantially lower. Since March 1982 CGT has been applied on an indexed basis and only real gains have been subject to tax.

Value Added Tax

Value added tax (VAT) is, after income tax and social security receipts, the largest contributor of revenue to the Government. It is intended as a broadly based expenditure tax and was introduced in 1973, following the accession of the United Kingdom to the EEC. VAT had, by then, become part of the process of fiscal harmonization within the Community, although, since for many years there was no attempt to harmonize rates of tax, it remained, at best, only a partial harmonization. Under current arrangements, VAT is rebated on exports but is charged on imports. This means that all goods sold in the United Kingdom are taxed at the appropriate British rate regardless of their origin; all goods sold in France are taxed at the appropriate French rate, etc. This arrangement has enabled the EU to function with widely different VAT rates in different member states although it has relied on border checks and complicated customs formalities. Such formalities have, however, become increasingly difficult to maintain with the formation of the single European market in 1993.

The tax is intended to be non-discriminatory and is levied on producers of intermediate goods as well as on producers of final goods. This raises considerably the costs of collection which fall both on the revenue authorities—the Customs and Excise—and on the tax-payers themselves. But since complete non-discrimination would have undesirable redistributive effects, there are different rates of VAT, so the objective is not achieved in practice.

The tax is levied at all stages of production and is imposed on the value added by each producer. How this works in practice can be illustrated by the following simple example. We assume a VAT rate of 15% which was the standard rate in force in the United Kingdom between 1979 and 1991. A manufacturer purchases raw materials at a price of £115 inclusive of VAT, i.e. the cost of the raw materials is £100 and the tax is £15. This latter is known as the input tax. The manufacturer then uses capital and labour to produce a finished article which he sells to a retailer for £230 including VAT. £30 is the output tax, and the manufacturer has to pay to the Customs and Excise the difference between the output and input taxes, namely £15. So the cost of the product, net of tax, is £200 and tax at the rate of 15% has been paid. The initial supplier of raw materials added value of £100 and so paid £15 in tax; the manufacturer also added value of £100 and so paid the same amount in tax. If, now, we assume that the retailer will earn £20 net on each product he sells, then this sum is the value added at the retail stage, and tax is due on it. The retailer will sell the product at a price of £253; his output tax will be £33, his input tax was £30, so he is liable to pay VAT of £3. The total amount of tax paid (£33) is equal to 15% of the total net-of-tax sale value of the product. It has been collected, at each stage of the production process, by taxing each producer according to his value added.

VAT is costly to collect for the authorities and complex, and therefore costly, for many of those who pay it. Large firms with sophisticated accounting systems cope without difficulty but, for many small businesses, the costs of calculating VAT are high.

The standard rate of VAT was raised to 17.5% in April 1996.[6] This is quite low by European standards. Four countries—Belgium, Denmark, Ireland, and

---

[6] A reduced rate of 8% applies to domestic fuel.

France—have indirect tax rates above 20% and the average across the twelve EU member states is 18.51%. If VAT were levied on all items,[7] it would bear heavily on the poor: unlike income tax, where no tax is payable on low incomes, the full tax would be levied on all expenditures. To prevent this and to introduce some progressivity into the tax, certain items, which form a large proportion of the expenditure of those on low incomes, are zero rated. Not only is no VAT levied on the production and sale of these items, but producers can also reclaim VAT paid by suppliers of intermediate goods. Such commodities include food, children's clothing, and public passenger transport. There is a third category of goods, those that are exempt from VAT. Exemption is not the same as zero rating: producers of exempt goods pay no VAT themselves but cannot reclaim what has already been paid on inputs supplied to them. Exempt goods include health care, rents, and private education. Very small firms with turnover less than a prescribed amount are also exempt from VAT. In financial year 1994–5, this threshold was set at £46,000. It is estimated that zero rating and VAT exemption cost the Government £22,100 million in revenue foregone the same year.

Excise Duties and Customs Duties

Excise duties are duties levied on goods, whether produced domestically or imported, and have as their prime objective the raising of revenue. Customs duties are levied specifically on imported goods and where the objective may be to protect domestic producers, to raise revenue, or both. Following the entry of the United Kingdom into the EEC, and after an initial transitional phase, customs duties have no longer been levied on imports from other member states of the EC; and those that are levied on imports from non-member countries are now determined jointly for all EC members in order to maintain a common external tariff. Receipts of customs duties are regarded as part of the 'own resources' of the Community and remitted to Brussels.

The most significant excise duties, in terms of revenue raised, are clearly those on petrol, tobacco, and alcohol. In 1993–4 these three raised £24.2 billion. It could be asked why one should single out for tax, in what is a highly discriminatory way, these three commodities? The first answer is that all three have inelastic demands, i.e. increases in price have only a small effect on demand, so they are eminently suitable as a means of raising revenue. But other good economic reasons can be advanced. The consumption of tobacco, for example, as a widely accepted cause of cancer, has a very high human cost in terms of suffering and premature death associated with it. Alcohol abuse, which is widespread, has both a high human cost and a high social cost. Motoring has high social costs in terms of congestion, pollution, and the

---

[7] The standard rate of VAT applies to roughly 60% of consumers' total expenditure.

expense of policing while the large number of accidents to which it gives rise have both high human and social costs.

The duties on petrol, tobacco, and alcohol are all stated as fixed monetary amounts. So, unlike VAT—defined as a percentage rate—they are not automatically indexed for inflation. Increases in the duties are regularly made at the time of the budget, and the presentation incorporated in the FSBR records the effects of changing duties from the non-indexed baseline.

Excise duties on alcohol in the United Kingdom are among the highest in the EU. Only Ireland has higher rates on beer, wine, and spirits and raises a higher proportion of total government revenue from this source. The duty differentials between Britain and neighbouring countries creates a large incentive for cross-border shopping which in recent years has inreased significantly. This has consequences for both the Exchequer and domestic producers. Customs and Excise, for example, estimate that the retail value of all alcohol imported into Britain from other EU countries for personal consumption in the twelve months to June 1994 totalled £765 million; lost sales for domestic producers were estimated at £405 million. The impact on government revenue is considerable. Customs and Excise estimate that in the first year of operation, the single European market cost the Exchequer some £200 million in the form of lost tax revenue from cross-border sales of alcohol and tobacco.

The European Commission has proposed that excise duties on tobacco, mineral fuel, and alcohol be harmonized, with all countries moving towards the present average rate of duty in the twelve countries. To date, however, there has been little support for this among the EU member states.

Taxation for environmental purposes has emerged as an important theme of recent budgets. For instance, in November 1994, the Chancellor announced his intention to increase petrol and derv duties by at least 5% in real terms each year, to help the United Kingdom to meet its target of stabilizing carbon dioxide emissions at 1990 levels by the year 2000. Excise duties, in this respect, are being used as a means of correcting a recognized market failure associated with the production of pollution. The failure occurs when firms and individuals do not take the costs of their activities on others into account, and this can lead to an inefficient allocation of resources. Taxation leads to an improvement in welfare by increasing polluters' costs and thereby creating an incentive for individuals and firms to curb pollution.

Local Taxation

Local taxation has long been a controversial and unsatisfactory area of public finance. Until recently the only significant tax raised by local authorities was an annual levy (rates) on immovable property. This tax, which had been in existence for centuries, was levied on housing as well as industrial and commercial property, was much disliked by householders and, in order to keep down the charges made upon them, successive governments increased the grants to local authorities made out of central government revenues. The result was that a rising proportion of local government expenditure was financed not from local rates but from national taxation. In the mid-1950s, some 45% of local authority current expenditure was financed; in 1994/95 the proportion was around 60%. And since much of what was collected in rates was derived from industrial and commercial companies, it meant that local residents, those who voted in local elections, were paying directly only a low and diminishing proportion of the cost of expenditure made in their name. By the mid-1970s, less than 20% of all current expenditure was financed directly by those who voted for the councils which decided the expenditure.[8]

In order to promote local accountability more effectively, the Government replaced the rates system with a new method of local authority taxation, the Community Charge. This change occurred in 1989 in Scotland and in 1990 in England and Wales. The community charge, or the poll tax as it soon became known, was levied at a flat rate, payable by all adults at the level set by the local authority area. Assistance was available to individuals on low incomes, but everyone was required to make a minimum payment of 20% of the new tax. Business rates were also reformed at the same time and removed from the control of local authorities. Instead of each authority setting its own rate, the Government would set a uniform rate which applies to all business premises across the country.

Few taxes are popular, but the Community Charge proved to be exceptionally unpopular and provoked street demonstrations and a widespread compaign of non-payment. The tax was widely seen as being unfair even by those who duly paid it, and it soon became apparent that the cost of collection would be high. It rapidly came to appear as a political liability to the Conservative government that had introduced it, and after the change of leadership in November 1991, the Government announced that the Community Charge would go. There was a period of hasty deliberation and in early 1992 Parliament enacted legislation to abolish the Community Charge and to introduce another tax—the Council Tax—which came into force throughout Great Britain in April 1993. This is primarily a tax on property rather than on persons.

The Council Tax is similar to the old rating system but, unlike the old rating system, it includes a personal element. The property element of the council tax is based upon a new system of banding which is constructed around average property values. Every home in Britain is allocated to one of the eight bands according to its value. The lowest rate of council tax is paid by households living in residences of value of £40,000 or below; the next lowest rate will be paid by households living in residences of value in excess of £40,000 but below £52,000;

---

[8] See N. Hepworth, 'The Reform of Local Government Finance', *Transactions of the Manchester Statistical Society, 1985–86.*

and so on up to the highest rate payable by those occupying properties worth in excess of £320,000.

There is one charge per property and it applies regardless of whether the property is in owner-occupation, is privately let, or is let by the local authority or a housing association. Properties in the same band in a local authority area are assessed to tax on the same basis. The personal element of the tax is introduced via a working assumption that each household contains two adults. Households of three or more adults, however, are not charged extra, while single-adult households receive a discount of 25% of the basic charge. Moreover, unlike the Community Charge, there is no minimum contribution. Individuals on Income Support or equivalent levels of income, are entitled to 100% Council Tax rebate.

In order to lower the amounts due in the final years of the Community Charge and to try to ensure that introduction of the council tax did not involve large increases in tax liabilities for large numbers of people, the Government introduced a further shift in local authority finance away from local taxation to central taxation. Local authorities were compelled to reduce their Community Charge, and subsequently their Council Tax, while direct grants from central government were increased, the increase being paid for out of a rise in VAT from 15% to 17.5%. Announcing this measure in his 1991 Budget, the Chancellor of the Exchequer stated that the net yield from local taxation would fall to £7 billion. In the financial year 1994–5, the yield from the Council Tax had risen slightly to £8.6 billion. This accounted for just 12% of total local authority receipts.

7.6. The Public Sector Deficit

The ways in which the government raises its revenue, and the pattern of expenditure, clearly have an impact on the whole economy. The surplus or deficit on transactions of government or the public sector reflects the net impact of government transactions on the economy and can, under appropriate circumstances, be seen as contributing to growth or inflation.

In most years since the end of World War II, general government revenues from taxation, national insurance, royalties, etc., as well as from the sale of publicly owned assets, have been insufficient to finance total expenditure. In consequence, government has had to borrow. Central government has financed most, if not all, of the borrowing needs of local government and it has also loaned funds to public corporations. In this way the bulk of the borrowing of the public sector has been centralized and managed by the central government. The total need to borrow each year—the public sector borrowing requirement or PSBR—was given a prominent role under the Government's Medium Term Financial Strategy.

The importance of the PSBR, it was argued, had to do with how it was financed. The authorities had a basic choice: they could borrow from the banking system (including, for this purpose, the Bank of England), in which case the money supply would rise; or they could borrow from the non-bank private sector, in which case there would be no increase in the money supply. As it was a central objective of the MTFS to limit the growth of the money supply, there was a clear preference for the latter. But, other things being equal, the more the authorities borrow from the non-bank private sector, the more they will bid up rates of interest. And high rates of interest were seen as undesirable in that, other things being equal, they would be expected to act as a disincentive to capital investment. The unwillingness of the authorities to accept higher interest rates in order to control the money supply implied that the Government had little alternative but to limit its own borrowing; hence the importance of the PSBR.

In its immediate objective, the Government was, for a time, remarkably successful. The PSBR which, during the years 1979–84, had averaged over £10 billion per annum, was greatly reduced in 1985 and 1986 and became a surplus in 1987. In 1988 the surplus was of the order of £14 billion or 3% of GDP and there was a further, if smaller, surplus in 1989–90. These surpluses were used to repay outstanding government debt, hence the term public-sector debt repayment or PSDR.

But public expenditure grew rapidly in 1991 and 1992. This, together with a lower growth in tax revenues due to the recession, brought about a return to substantial public-sector borrowing. These deficits increased rapidly in size until, in 1993–4, the PSBR reached a value of £46.8 billion or some 7% of GDP, before falling back to 5% the following year. Overall, the Government's fiscal objective, reiterated in the 1995–6 FSBR, remains one of bringing the PSBR back into balance over the medium term.

In practice the PSBR is one of three measures of financial deficit or surplus routinely used in the United Kingdom at the current time. The others are the general government financial deficit, GGFD, and the general government deficit on current account, GGCD. Both of these measures are based upon the procedures underlying the construction of the national accounts and, as a result, both are available on an international basis. The key differences between the GGFD, the GGCD, and the concept of the PSBR relate to the fact that the former are measured on an accruals basis—for example, VAT revenue is scored in the period in which the expenditure took place that gave rise to the tax liability, and not when the cash was received, and financial transactions are all considered to be 'below the line'. That is, they finance the surplus or deficit rather than determine its size. The GGCD is further differentiated from the GGFD by excluding capital expenditure or taxes on capital from the calculation. Movements in all three measures, with the PSBR defined so as to alternatively include or exclude privatization proceeds, are shown in Fig. 7.3.

From Fig. 7.3 it is apparent that although the alternative measures of the deficit have tended to move together, the levels of the individual measures have

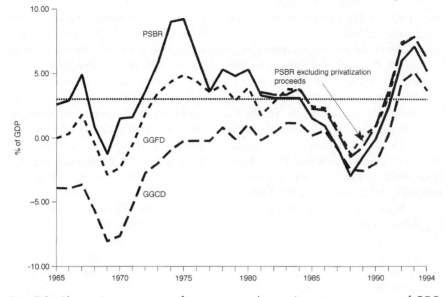

Fig. 7.3. Alternative measures of government borrowing as percentages of GDP, 1965/6 to 1994/5

Source: Tables 10.21, 10.23, and 10.61, *Public Finance Trends 95*.

differed. This was particularly the case during the earlier part of the period when, for example, both the PSBR and GGFD recorded a positive deficit whilst the GGCD recorded a negative deficit value, i.e. a surplus. As expenditure and receipts on the current account have come to dominate general government finances, however, so the measures have tended to converge. In the financial year 1994–5, for example, the three measures lay within a band of a width equivalent to approximately 2% of GDP.

Following the adoption of the Maastricht Treaty in December 1991,[9] particular interest has focused on the GGFD measure of the deficit as one of the convergence criteria for monetary union. Specifically the Treaty set out elaborate procedures to define and deal with 'excessive' budget deficits. The penalties for having an excessive deficit were also made clear: EU countries in this position cannot enter Stage Three of the monetary union.[10] The reference value for the deficit in this respect was set at 3% of GDP; a complementary fiscal criterion, expressed in terms of total debt, established a desired ceiling to the rate of total debt to GDP of 60%. In September 1994 the European Commission concluded that ten EC countries were running excessive deficits and the Council of Europe endorsed that conclusion formally.

In designing the fiscal criteria, two issues appear to have been foremost in

[9] More formally known as the Treaty on European Union. This was adopted by member states on 10 December 1991 and, following ratification, came into effect in November 1993.

[10] Stage Three is characterized by exchange rates between member states being irrevocably locked, the introduction of a single currency, and the transfer of responsibility for the conduct of monetary policy to a new monetary institution.

the minds of the authors of the Maastricht Treaty: the solvency problem and fiscal externalities. The solvency problem is usually expressed in terms of the situation arising when a country operating an excessive public debt is forced to engage in the monetization of its deficits. Although the constitution of the European Central Bank (ECB) forbids lending to any national government, the fear is that a country with an unmanageable public debt problem would create a crisis within the EC which would force the ECB to pursue an expansionary monetary policy. The crisis itself might develop through a variety of mechanisms; through direct political pressure from the country concerned, for example. Pressure is more likely to develop, however, from financial institutions holding the insolvent country's bonds in their portfolio. As the unsustainability of the debt position becomes apparent and the value of the country's bonds begins to fall, these institutions would refuse to roll-over the outstanding debt unless interest rates were raised. In this situation the ECB may find itself having to acquire the country's debt indirectly in order to keep down the interest cost of rolling over the debt. Similar fears of adverse spill-over effects appear to be associated with the issue of externalities. Under irrevocably fixed exchange rates, for example, an excessive deficit in one country will raise interest rates in that country and put upward pressure on interest rates in the other member states.

The fiscal provisions of the Maastricht Treaty are generally recognized as harsh. How harsh may be seen from a simple example. If a country starts with a debt ratio of 100%, runs a budget deficit net of interest payments of 3%, has an interest rate of 4%, and experiences nominal GDP growth of 10%, it will take approximately forty years to bring the debt/GDP ratio down to 60%. Even if the country could balance its budget without depressing growth, the target would still take a full decade to achieve. In 1994 Belgium, Italy, and Greece each had debt ratios in excess of the 100% used in the example. Moreover, their actual deficit position was such that serious fiscal retrenchment would be required before satisfying the fiscal criteria could become a serious prospect.

In the case of the United Kingdom, the situation is more promising. The actual debt ratio has remained comfortably below the 60% Maastricht criterion since the mid-1970s. In contrast, the current deficit position would be considered excessive on the basis of the Maastricht criteria. However, this development is largely seen as reflecting the effect of temporary adverse conditions and the deficit is forecast to fall below the 3% threshold by 1997.

7.7. The Conduct of Fiscal Policy

The overall stance of fiscal policy in terms of whether policy is, or has been, expansionary or contractionary is clearly an important consideration in any evaluation of macroeconomic performance. In many respects, however, conventional measures of the fiscal deficit, such as the PSBR, GGFD, or GGCD described in Section 7.6 are inappropriate from the point of view of such an evaluation. In particular, a common complaint with these measures is that movements in their value reflect not only the effect of discretionary policy action on the part of the authorities, but also the effect of induced fluctuations in government expenditure and tax receipts associated with movements around the business cycle. For this reason, a variety of alternative summary indicators of budgetary policy have been developed. These measures are intended to provide more accurate indications of whether the budget is becoming more or less expansionary than would be obtained by just observing movements of the actual budget balance. The measures may also provide a basis for conducting international comparisons of fiscal policy changes so as to judge, within the context of a policy co-ordination exercise for example, whether fiscal policy has changed over time. In practice, the measures attempt to isolate the effect of discretionary policy by removing the impact of other factors on the measured budget balance. Whilst the potential range of factors that could be removed is large, the most common factor dealt with in this respect is the impact of the cyclical position of the economy.

A summary indicator constructed along these lines, is the fiscal impulse measure constructed by the International Monetary Fund (IMF). Data for this indicator from 1973[11] are shown in Fig. 7.4. Although it is tempting to interpret movements of the fiscal impulse measure as indicating whether policy in a particular year was expansionary or contractionary, considerable care must be taken with this interpretation. The fiscal impulse is defined as the change in the government budget balance resulting from changes in government expenditure and tax policies. Therefore, it is specifically designed to summarize in a single measure the aggregate effects of fiscal policy action on the government's budget balance. Positive values of the measure indicate that the change in the discretionary component of the budget increases. This movement may only be considered expansionary in the narrow sense that the first-round effect of the budget adds to aggregate demand.

On this basis it is readily apparent from Fig 7.4 that the design of fiscal policy has been to restrict the growth of aggregate demand. Following a positive fiscal impulse value in 1973, the indicator remained negative (or positive, but close to zero) until 1978 when the Labour Government then in power attempted to boost the economy in the run-up to the 1979 general election.[12] Fiscal policy remained contractionary, and became increasingly so,

---

[11] Values of the fiscal impulse measure are routinely published by the International Monetary Fund in its *World Economic Outlook*. For a discussion of the method of construction, see P. Heller, R. Haas, and A. Mansur, 'A Review of the Fiscal Impulse Measure', *Occasional Paper No. 44* Washington, DC: International Monetary Fund, 1986.

[12] See M. J. Artis and R. C. Bladen-Hovell (1991), 'A Model-Based Analysis', in M. Artis and D. Cobham (eds.), *Labour's Economic Policies 1974–79*, for a detailed account of fiscal policy in this period.

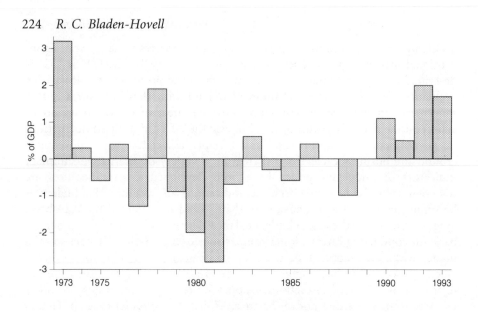

Fig. 7.4. Fiscal impulse as a percentage of GDP, 1973–1993

Source: World Economic Outlook, various issues (International Monetary Fund).

during the early 1980s with the implementation of the MTFS, but became more relaxed in the latter part of the 1980s. In contrast, the indicator suggests that fiscal policy has become expansionary during the 1990s.

Further Reading

A general discussion of the issues involved in public expenditure and taxation in the UK may be found in:

Sandford, C., *Economics of Public Finance*, 4th edn. (Oxford: Pergamon Press, 1992).

Further details of the UK tax structure are provided by:

Kay, J. A. and King, M. A., *The British Tax System*, 5th edn. (Oxford: Oxford University Press, 1990).

James, S. and Nobes, C. (1992), *The Economics of Taxation*, 4th edn. (Englewood Cliffs, NJ: Prentice-Hall).

An extensive discussion of the role of the Treasury and its control of public spending from 1976 to 1993 is given by:

Thain, C. and Wright, M., *The Treasury and Whitehall: The Planning and Control of Public Expenditure, 1976–1993* (Oxford: Clarendon Press, 1995).

INDUSTRY: ITS STRUCTURES AND POLICIES TOWARDS IT

MALCOLM SAWYER

8.1. Introduction

This chapter has, as the title suggests, two main purposes. The first is to describe some of the key features of the industrial landscape in terms of, for example, the sectoral composition of production, the relative size of firms, and the role of multinational (transnational) firms. The second is to outline and evaluate policies towards industry including competition and monopoly policies, and those on technology.

8.2. Sectoral Composition

We begin by considering the composition of output and employment between the major sectors of the economy. Table 8.1 provides a relatively detailed breakdown of output by different sectors in 1990. The primary sector consists of industries which produce raw materials (e.g. minerals, crops), and encompasses agriculture, forestry, and fishing (which for brevity will be hereafter referred to as agriculture), and the extraction of minerals and oil. The historic trend has been that of decline of the primary sector. For example, in Britain, agriculture accounted for 36% of employment in 1801, declining to 22% by 1851, to 9% by the turn of the century: the decline has continued with agricultural employment now less than $1\frac{1}{2}$%. The extraction of minerals and oils has similarly generally declined, with employment in coal-mining falling from nearly three-quarters of a million in the late 1940s to under 10,000 in the mid-1990s. This general trend was temporarily reversed in the 1980s with the

I am grateful to Gary Slater and David Spencer for research assistance on this and the subsequent chapter.

Table 8.1. Distribution of output by sector, 1990

Sector	Share of output (%)
Agriculture, forestry, and fisheries	1.9
Mining and quarrying	2.2
Manufacturing	23.7
Electricity, gas, and water	2.2
Construction	7.2
Distribution, hotels, catering, and repairing	14.2
Transport, storage, and communications	8.4
Financial and business services	18.6
Government and other services	21.7

Source: Economic Trends

exploitation of North Sea Oil, giving rise to a substantial increase in the share of mineral and oil extraction in total output in the early 1980s.

The secondary sector consists of industries which process raw materials, and covers manufacturing, construction, and energy production (gas and electricity). This sector is quite often referred to as industry, and statistics on industrial production ('production' industries) relate to the secondary sector plus mining but minus construction. In the early stages of economic development, the secondary sector grows rapidly, with the primary sector declining in relative importance. Employment in the secondary sector ('industry') peaked at 46% in 1966. The decline in the importance of the secondary sector has generally been referred to as deindustrialization, though sometimes that term is used to refer only to decline in the manufacturing sector: the topic of deindustrialization has been dealt with in Chapter 2.

The tertiary sector covers the distribution of goods and the production of services and is now the predominant provider of employment (and to a lesser degree of output). Whereas in 1981 it accounted for 63% of employees, by 1995 this proportion had risen to over 75%. The growth in this sector's share of employment has been even faster, and one reason for the faster growth of the employment share as compared with the output share is that much of the employment growth in the tertiary sector has been in part-time jobs. Fig. 8.1 provides a more detailed breakdown of the changing sectoral composition of employment. The decline in employment in manufacturing and mining can be clearly seen, as can the notable increase in employment in the business services sector.

8.3. Small and Large Firms

Casual observation of the British economy reveals an enormous range in the size of firms, from one-person businesses through to firms employing over

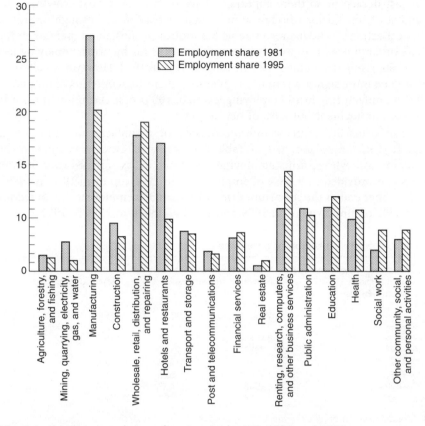

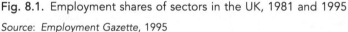

Fig. 8.1. Employment shares of sectors in the UK, 1981 and 1995

Source: Employment Gazette, 1995

50,000 people. Some idea of the range of size of firms can be seen from Table 8.2, which relates to manufacturing industries only.

There is no precise definition of small business, and the promotion of small business is often undertaken on the grounds that today's successful small business is tomorrow's large business. Following the report of the Bolton Committee,[1] independent businesses employing less than 200 people have been regarded as small businesses, though many would regard that size limit as too high, especially when applied outside the manufacturing sector. On that definition, around 128,500 small firms accounted for nearly 34% of total employment in manufacturing. At the other end of the scale, 93 firms each employing over 5,000 workers accounted for over 27% of employment. Over

[1] *Report of the Committee of Inquiry on Small Firms*, Cmnd. 4811 (London: HMSO, 1971), often referred to as the Bolton committee report after the name of the chair of the committee.

the past decade or so there appears to have been a substantial growth in the number of small firms (though some of that increase arises through improved data collection).[2] The figures in Table 8.2 indicate a substantial increase in the share of employment in manufacturing accounted for by firms employing less than 200, rising from under 25% in 1980 to 34% in 1992. However, small firms tend to be more significant in terms of employment than in terms of output: in 1991 manufacturing firms employing less than 100 people accounted for nearly 26% of employment but 20% of net output.

Small firms are more significant outside of manufacturing, and this is indicated in the second part of Table 8.2, where it can be seen that in the economy as a whole, firms employing 10 people or less formed over 90% of firms and provided over 28% of employment in 1991 (up from 19% in 1979). At the other end of the spectrum, firms with over 500 employees accounted for over 35% of employment in 1979 and this had fallen to 27% in 1991.

Table 8.2. Size distribution of enterprises

A. *Size distribution in manufacturing industries, 1980 and 1992a*

Size of enterprise (no. of employees)	Number of enterprises		Share of employment (%)	
	1980	1992	1980	1992
1–99	84944	126366	18.8	27.5
100–199	2437	2150	5.6	6.9
200–499	1479	1364	7.5	9.7
500–999	599	526	6.9	8.4
1000–4999	548	437	18.4	20.1
over 5000	156	93	42.9	27.4

B. *Size distribution of all UK firms*

Employment size band	Cumulative share of total firms		Cumulative share of employment	
	1979	1991	1979	1991
1–2	61.4	64.3	6.6	11.3
3–5	79.2	85.3	12.4	21.2
6–10	89.1	92.5	19.1	28.2
11–19	95.2	96.1	26.7	34.6
20–49	97.8	98.6	33.6	43.6
50–99	98.7	99.3	38.9	50.4
100–199	99.5	99.7	49.1	58.1
200–499	99.8	99.9	57.3	67.2
500–999	99.9	100.0	64.7	73.0
over 1000	100.0	100.0	100.0	100.0

[a] The increase in the number of small businesses between 1980 and 1992 indicated here is inflated through a change in 1984 in the way in which the register of firms for which information was sought was compiled. Sources: Panel A: calculated from *Census of Production*, 1980, 1992; Panel B: 'The UK enterprise population 1979–91', A. McCann, *NatWest Review of Small Business Trends* (June 1993).

[2] For further discussion see P. Dunne and A. Hughes, 'The Changing Structure of Competitive Industry in the 1980s' in C. Driver and P. Dunne (eds.), *Structural Change in the UK Economy* (Cambridge: Cambridge University Press, 1992).

The growth in the importance of small firms in the past two decades reverses previous trends and appears to have occurred in many other industrialized economies.[3]

On one interpretation the trends mark a significant break with the past and offer the opportunity of harnessing new flexible technologies in a more decentralised and small scale system of industrial production, a 'second industrial divide' marking a break away from the mass production industrial culture . . . Other interpretations stress the persistence, if not increased dominance of large-scale producers, the impact of their risk-spreading vertical disintegration in creating a small business sector dependent upon their needs and objectives.[4]

8.4. Concentration

It would be expected that the typical size of firms in an industry would be strongly influenced by the cost conditions under which that industry operates. When there are substantial economies of scale, then it would be expected that there would be a few large firms (since small firms would be at a significant cost disadvantage *vis-à-vis* large firms). Conversely, when there are diseconomies of scale, then a predominance of small firms would be expected.

The theory of perfect competition assumes a large number of firms each of which is a price-taker and free entry into the industry concerned. The profit-maximization condition under perfect competition is the equality between price and marginal cost. The theory of monopoly refers to an industry dominated by one firm, where there are substantial difficulties facing new entrants into the industry. The profit-maximizing condition here is marginal revenue equal to marginal cost, which can be re-written as:

$$p(1 - 1/e) = mc$$

where p is price, e the elasticity of demand, and mc marginal cost.[5] This yields a price of $p = (e/e - 1) \, mc$, which implies that price would be higher (relative to marginal cost) under a situation of monopoly than under a situation of perfect competition. We return later to this comparison of perfect competition and monopoly with a discussion of its policy implications. For our purposes here it is sufficient to note that this view suggests that the structure of an industry is of some significance. The structure of an industry would include

[3] For further discussion see, for example, W. Sengenberger, J. Loverman, and M. Piore, *The Reemergence of Small Enterprises*, International Institute for Labour Studies (Geneva: ILO, 1990).

[4] Quote is from Dunne and Hughes, 'Changing Structure'; for further discussion see Sengenberger *et al.*, *Small Enterprises*.

[5] The profit maximization condition is marginal revenue equal to marginal cost. The marginal revenue is, $\Delta(pq)/\Delta q$ where Δ signifies a small change, which can be expanded as $\Delta pq/\Delta q + p$. This can be written as $p(1 + \Delta pq/\Delta qp)$ which is equal to $p(1 - 1/e)$. Hence $p(1 - 1/e) = mc$.

the number of firms in an industry, the inequality of size amongst those firms, and the ease or difficulty of entry into the industry.

One purpose of measuring industrial concentration is to have some idea of where along the spectrum between perfect competition and monopoly an industry lies. A low level of concentration would indicate the atomistic competition end of the spectrum and a high level the monopoly end. There are numerous measures of industrial concentration which can be used.[6] The simplest, and the one which is used here, is the *n*-firm concentration ratio. This is the share of the largest *n* firms in the industry concerned. The value of *n* is generally determined by data availability rather than any indication from economic theory. In the case of Table 8.3 below, the value of *n* is 5. The share of the largest *n* firms can be measured in a variety of ways, e.g. in terms of sales, employment, or capital stock. Since the concentration ratio is intended to reflect market power within a product market, the use of sales would appear the 'natural' variable to use, but once again data availability often forces the choice.

Concentration can be reported at both the industry (or market) level[7] and at the aggregate level. The discussion above linking concentration measures to the perfect competition/monopoly spectrum would suggest that the industry (market) level would be the appropriate one. But a large firm typically operates in a range of industries, which may enable it to co-ordinate decisions across a range of industries. Concern over the centralization of decision-making in an economy (e.g. over prices, investment, or employment) leads to an interest in aggregate concentration measures. Table 8.3 provides some statistics on the level of concentration in manufacturing industries in 1992. In view of the increasing importance of the tertiary sector it is regrettable that

Table 8.3. Distribution of Five-firm Concentration Ratios, Manufacturing Industries, 1992

Concentration ratio in range (%)	Number of Industries	Share of Employment
0–10	7	15.2
10–20	17	23.9
20–30	19	17.2
30–40	15	19.3
40–50	14	9.0
50–60	10	4.4
60–70	9	5.5
70–80	5	1.2
80–90	3	3.1
90–100	3	1.2

Note: Weighted averages for 102 industries.
Share of largest five firms (ranked by employment): employment = 30.8%; sales = 40.5%; net output = 37.1%.
Source: Calculated from Business Statistics Office, *Census of Production*, 1992 (London: HMSO, 1995)

[6] For further discussion of measures of concentration, see L. Hannah and J. Kay, *Concentration in Modern Industry* (London: Macmillan, 1977) and M. Sawyer, *The Economics of Industries and Firms* (London: Routledge, 1985), chap. 3.

[7] In the text the terms 'market' and 'industry' are used interchangeably.

recent statistics are not available for that sector also. The statistics given refer to the group level (sometimes referred to as the three-digit level). On this basis, the manufacturing sector has 102 groups or industries. Even so, these industries may be too broad for our purposes and contain a number of separate markets (industries). For example, one of these industries is soap and toilet preparations, which covers products such as soaps, soap powder, shampoos, toothpaste, etc.. It could reasonably be argued that a lower level of aggregation would be more appropriate so that, for example, the market for soaps would be treated separately from that for toothpaste.

The lower part of Table 8.3 indicates that on average in 1992 the largest five firms in an industry (when ranked in terms of employment) accounted for 30.8% of employment, and 40.5% of sales. These averages mask considerable variations between industries. In the seven separately identified industries falling within the timber and wooden furniture sector, the largest five firms account, on average, for 15% of employment, whilst in the four metal-manufacturing industries the largest five firms average a share of 63%. The spread of concentration ratios is also indicated in Table 8.3, which shows that there were seven industries where total employment accounted for 15.2% of the total employment in manufacturing industries, in which the five-firm concentration ratio was below 10%. At the other end of the scale, there were six industries (with 4.3% of employment) in which the largest five firms employed over 80% of the industry workforce.

The level of concentration has generally risen during the first sixty years of this century but appears to have levelled off in the past thirty years. This can be conveniently summarized by the course of aggregate concentration.[8] The share of the largest 100 firms in manufacturing net output was estimated to be 16% in the first decade of this century, around 22–4% in the inter-war period, and then rose steadily from a level of 22% in 1949 to 41% in 1968. Since then, the share of the largest 100 firms has been rather steady, and was 36% in 1991 (with the share of employment at 29%).[9]

The average level of concentration in manufacturing fell during the 1980s: the precise figures depend on what weights are applied in calculating the average. Using the relative size of industries in 1980 as weights, the average five-firm concentration ratio declined from 45.3% in 1980 to 42.4% in 1987. Allowing for international trade slightly sharpens the trend, with the trade-adjusted concentration ratio falling from an average of 34.5% in 1980 to 29.8% in 1987.[10] Whilst

---

[8] The trends on industrial concentration are summarized in Sawyer, *Industries and Firms*, chap. 3; for discussion of concentration outside manufacturing see S. Aaronovitch and M. Sawyer, *Big Business* (London: Macmillan, 1975).

[9] There are complications arising from some (rather slight) changes in the definition of the manufacturing sector and from nationalization and privatization of firms. The figures in the text refer to private firms only.

[10] A. Henley, 'Industrial Deconcentration in UK', *Manchester School*, 62. The trade-adjusted figures means making an allowance for imports so that the concentration ratio refers to the share the largest firms have of the domestic market (rather than of domestic production).

only a relatively small part of the decline could be explained, the predominant factor in the decline of concentration was estimated to be a decline in the extent of economies of scale.

8.5. Merger Activity

A major route by which the structure of an industry and the size of firms change is by acquisitions and mergers. There is a technical difference between an acquisition (where one firm takes over another) and a merger (where two or more firms fuse together to form a new company), but in line with common usage we do not make any distinction between acquisition and merger below. Fig. 8.2 illustrates the variation in merger activity in Britain over the past twenty years. The number of firms acquired has averaged around 700 a year, with a total of over 17,500 firms acquired over a 25-year period. Around three-quarters of these acquisitions involve the purchase of independent companies, whilst the remainder involve the sale of subsidiaries by one company to another. Expenditure on acquisitions fluctuates substantially. The number of firms acquired in the most active acquisition year is around three times the number in the least active year. But the variation in terms of the expenditure is much greater. For example, even after deflating for variations in share prices, expenditure on acquiring subsidiaries in 1988 was nearly ten times the value in 1975.

The early years of the period (1968–72) witnessed a merger boom, which was larger than any previous merger boom, but this was followed by a decade during which merger activity was rather subdued. This could be seen as a response to a general disenchantment with the benefits of mergers.[11] However, there was a dramatic upswing in merger activity beginning in 1985 which peaked in 1989. In recent years, merger activity has been at a rather lower, though still substantial, level. The scale of merger activity over the four years 1985–89 well surpassed the levels reached in the last merger boom of 1968–72.

The scale of merger activity can be gauged by comparing expenditure on acquiring subsidiaries with total investment in fixed capital assets (plant, machinery, and buildings). For example, amongst relatively large companies, expenditure on acquiring subsidiaries in 1988 was equivalent to 35% of expenditure on fixed assets.[12] The relevance of this comparison is twofold.

---

[11] The disenchantment was perhaps a reaction to the claims made for the benefits of mergers during the merger boom of 1968–72. The disenchantment was aided by academic work such as G. Meeks, *Disappointing Marriage: A Study of Gains from Merger* (Cambridge: Cambridge University Press, 1977) which strongly suggested that mergers did not on average raise profitability and efficiency. For a survey of recent work see J. Fairburn and J. Kay (eds.), *Mergers and Merger Policy* (Oxford: Oxford University Press), esp. chap. 1.

[12] The source of data is Business Monitor MA3, *Company Finance* (London: HMSO, various years).

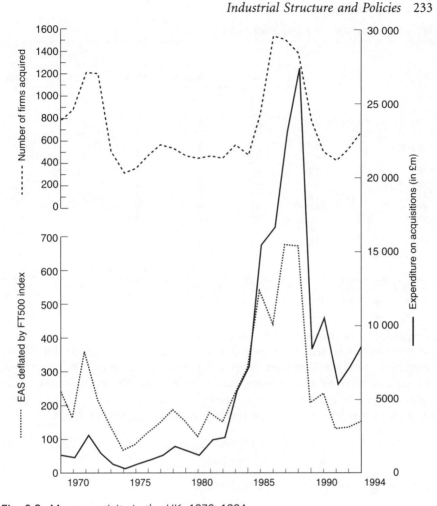

Fig. 8.2. Merger activity in the UK, 1970–1994

Source: Business Monitor; M7; CSO Bulletin; Financial Statistics.

First, the figures for total investment provide an appropriate benchmark and put the large numbers involved in merger activity into perspective. Second, and more important, the comparison draws attention to the use to which firms put their investment resources. Whereas investment in plant and equipment and so on represents the creation of new resources and an addition to the productive potential of the economy, expenditure on acquisitions does not add to productive capacity but rather represents a change of ownership of existing assets.

The direction of merger activity is indicated to some extent by the figures in Table 8.4, which refer to the proposed mergers considered by the Office of Fair Trading as part of mergers policy (see below). These figures refer to relatively large potential mergers, and most large firms are already diversified. A merger

Table 8.4. Proposed mergers classified by type (%)

Year	Horizontal		Vertical		Diversified	
	Number	Value	Number	Value	Number	Value
1970–4	73	68	5	4	23	27
1975–8	65	67	9	8	26	25
1979–82	61	68	6	3	34	30
1983–4	67	76	4	1	29	23
1985–6	64	58	3	3	35	40
1987	67	80	3	1	30	19
1988	58	45	1	1	41	54
1989	60	44	2	3	37	53
1990	75	81	5	3	20	16
1991	88	89	5	5	7	6
1992	93	97	1	0	6	3
1993	90	81	3	1	7	18
1994	88	86	5	11	7	3

Note: 'The allocation of mergers to these three categories involves an element of judgement and this should be kept in mind when interpreting these figures' (Review of Monopolies and Mergers Policy, *A Consultative Document*, Cmnd. 7198 (London: HMSO, 1978).
Source: Annual Reports of the Director-General of Fair Trading

is regarded as horizontal if the two (or more) firms involved are operating in the same industrial sector, whereas it would be regarded as vertical if the firms were in a purchaser–supplier relationship with each other. The diversified merger category covers remaining cases. There is no discernible trend in the figures shown in Table 8.4, with horizontal mergers accounting for two-thirds or more of mergers, and vertical mergers being rather unimportant.

8.6. Transnational Corporations

Most large firms operating in Britain are multinational enterprises (MNEs). In the minority of cases, the firm is owned by foreigners and most of its activities take place outside the United Kingdom. In the other cases, the firm is mainly owned by UK nationals with the larger part of its activities based in Britain. Amongst the largest 100 manufacturing firms in Britain on the basis of employment, 20 are foreign-owned and on the basis of output 29 are foreign-owned, but the vast majority of the remaining largest 100 firms operate internationally.[13]

In 1992, of nearly 130,000 enterprises in manufacturing, 1,507 were foreign-owned, but they accounted for nearly 18% of employment, and produced 24% of net output. Of the foreign enterprises 458 were EC-owned (24.3% of employment in foreign-owned firms) and 1049 non-EC (75.7%), of which

---

[13] For some estimates see K. Cowling and R. Sugden, *Transnational Monopoly Capitalism* (Brighton: Wheatsheaf Books, 1987).

624 were US-owned (47.8%) and 117 Japanese (7.4%, and 7.5% of net output).[14] The proportion of manufacturing net output accounted for by foreign-owned enterprises grew from 19% in 1983 to 24% in 1992. The growth of Japanese-owned enterprises has been quite rapid: in number growing from 24 in 1983 to 117 in 1992, with the share of employment rising from 0.5% to 7.5% (the figures for net output are almost identical). American-owned enterprises have declined in importance: in numbers down from 838 in 1983 to 624 in 1992, and their share of the net output produced by foreign-owned firms down from two-thirds to just over one-half. Across the economy as a whole it was estimated for 1991 that there were 1500 multinationals whose parent corporation was based in the UK and a further 2900 foreign affiliates producing in the UK with parent company based outside of the UK.[15]

Foreign-owned enterprises are probably more capital-intensive than domestically owned enterprises, as suggested by the fact that the share of foreign-owned enterprises in output is greater than their share in employment (as indicated above) and by their relatively high share in net capital expenditure (investment) of nearly 32% in 1992.

Foreign-owned companies are not evenly spread across all sectors of the economy. They tend to be sparsely represented in what could be considered the less dynamic sectors of manufacturing industry. Foreign-owned companies account for less than 10% of employment in textile industries, footwear, and clothing industries and timber and wooden furniture industries. The sectors where foreign-owned companies account for more than 20% of employment are the chemical industry, manufacture of office machinery and data-processing equipment, electrical and electronic engineering, manufacture of motor vehicles and parts thereof, instrument engineering, and processing of rubber and plastics. Employment in foreign-owned manufacturing companies is proportionately much greater in the South-East, West Midlands, and Scotland than in the other regions, and much less in the South-West and East Anglia.

The significance of MNEs regardless of nationality in the British economy can be gauged by some other measures.[16] Production abroad by British-based MNEs has been estimated as equivalent to nearly 130% of exports and 36% of GDP in the period 1980–8. These figures put the UK towards the top end of the scale of involvement with MNEs (especially relative to GDP, where amongst ten countries for which figures are available the UK figure is only exceeded by that for the Netherlands). Much international trade is essentially a movement of goods between one branch of an MNE and another branch: of UK exports in 1981, 30% consisted of such movement within an MNE, of which 16% arose within MNEs of UK origin. Over the period 1980–7 outward

---

[14] Source of information in this and the next paragraph is Business Statistics Office, *Census of Production, 1992*, (London: HMSO, 1995).

[15] United Nations Conference on Trade and Development, Programme on Transnational Corporations, *World Investment Report* (New York: United Nations, 1993).

[16] The source of information in this paragraph is G. Ietto-Gillies, *International Production: Trends, Theories, Effects*, (Oxford: Polity Press, 1992).

direct investment from UK was equivalent to 14.1% of gross domestic fixed capital formation, and inward direct investment was 6.7%.

The arrival of an MNE is often welcomed by the host government. The establishment of a multinational enterprise will generally involve new investment and the creation of employment. But this would not be the case when the multinational enterprise arrives through the acquisition of an established domestic firm. The employment creation effect may be overstated insofar as employment elsewhere in the economy is displaced. Further, multinational enterprises may bring new technology. However, in order to attract multinational enterprises, governments (national and local) often offer substantial investment subsidies, tax exemptions, and the like. The competition between countries and regions of countries tends to lead to a bidding up of the subsidies offered to MNEs, with obvious benefit to the MNEs concerned. Further, decisions on employment, production, etc. are then taken by people based outside the country concerned. A feature of many MNEs is that they are willing and able to move production from one country to another, which would mean that inward investment made in response to the offer of subsidies and other inducements may move out in response to subsidies elsewhere.

8.7. Theories of Industrial Policies

Industrial policies can range from changing the form of ownership of a firm or industry (i.e. nationalization and privatization), and the encouragement or discouragement of mergers through to legislation governing the relationship between firms (e.g. limiting collusion between firms). There are many other policies which influence the behaviour and performance of firms and industries. For example, macroeconomic policies influence the general economic environment within which firms operate, and the price, employment, and investment decisions of firms are likely to be strongly influenced by macroeconomic conditions. Further, taxation and subsidy policies are often designed to influence what firms do. Macroeconomic and taxation policies are discussed elsewhere in this book, so that discussion here is restricted to industrial policy, by which we mean policies designed to change the behaviour and performance of specific firms and industries.

The appropriate role of the state in industrial matters has always been a matter of controversy, and the sharp differences between the role of the state as viewed by the Labour government of 1974–9 and as viewed by the current Conservative government illustrate that controversy. At the risk of over-simplification, it may be useful to consider three broadly defined views of the role of the state in connection with the operation of firms and industries.[17]

---

[17] For further discussion see M. Sawyer, 'On the Theory of Industrial Policy' in K. Cowling and R. Sugden (eds.), *Current Issues in Industrial Strategy* (Manchester: Manchester University Press, 1992); amended version published as chap. 6 of M. Sawyer, *The Market Economy: Theories and Policies* (Aldershot: Edward Elgar, 1996).

These can be labelled the market failure approach, the Austrian school, and the developmental state view. The first of these has been the dominant view amongst economists, whilst the second has had considerable influence on the policies of the current government. The third view has not had as much influence in Britain as in countries such as Japan and France, but some elements of this view can be seen to have been reflected in policies pursued particularly by the Labour governments of 1964–70 and of 1974–9.

8.8. The Market Failure Approach

The market failure approach has two basic elements. The first is the proposition that a system of perfect competition would, under certain assumptions, generate a desirable (Pareto-optimal) outcome. A Pareto-optimal outcome is one from which it is not possible to make some people better off without making others worse off. The second is that when some of those assumptions are not (or cannot) be met, then there is a role for government. This role may be to try to bring about the conditions of perfect competition (e.g. by increasing the number of firms in an industry); or it may be to alleviate the consequences of the impossibility of achieving perfect competition. The discussion now turns to an elaboration of these ideas, along with some examples.

It is convenient to consider an industry in which production takes place subject to constant costs so that average costs and marginal costs are equal. This assumption allows a simplification of the analysis without losing anything of importance for this discussion. With constant costs, the unit costs in an industry are not affected by the number of firms in that industry, and hence the average (and marginal) cost curve can be drawn as a horizontal line without reference to the number of firms. This has been done in Fig. 8.3, where the average cost curve is labelled as *ac*. The demand curve facing the industry is drawn as *D*. If the industry were perfectly competitive, then each firm would equate price with marginal cost (as a condition of profit maximization) and the normal profit requirement would be that price (average revenue) should equal average cost. The output produced, with price equal to marginal cost, would be Q_c.

The outcome of price equal to marginal cost is seen to have some desirable features. The demand curve for a product indicates how much consumers are willing to pay per unit for different quantities. It is intended to represent the consumers' marginal evaluation of the product as the scale of output varies. The marginal cost is the incremental cost of production. In a fully employed economy, greater production of one good requires less production of some other goods. Assuming that the marginal costs of production reflect the opportunity cost of reducing production elsewhere, then the marginal cost is

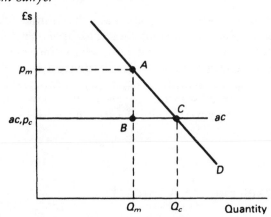

Fig. 8.3. Monopoly welfare loss

equal to the consumers' evaluation of the foregone alternative production. When consumers value the product under consideration more than the alternative, then price exceeds marginal cost, and economic welfare can be increased by shifting resources into its production. This would continue up to the point where price is equal to marginal cost. This argument forms the basis of the idea that perfect competition would generate a desirable outcome, since price would there equal marginal cost.

A situation of monopoly can also be represented in Fig. 8.3. The profit-maximizing position of a monopolist is the equality of marginal revenue and marginal cost, and this would yield an output of Q_m and a price of *pm*. It can be readily seen that price is higher and output lower under monopoly than under perfect competition (when both face the same cost and demand conditions). The loss to consumers of the higher price under monopoly is given (approximately) by the area p_mACBp_c. The basis of this approximation is as follows. Consider a consumer who would have been willing to pay an amount p_a for the good in question. At a competitive price this consumer would gain to the extent of $p_a - p_c$ as the excess of the value of the good to that consumer over the price which is paid. As the price is raised from the competitive level to the monopoly level, a range of consumers withdraw from purchase of this good, and their individual loss is the excess of the price they would have been prepared to pay over the competitive price. This excess summed over all the relevant individuals gives the area p_mACBp_c. This welfare loss can be divided into the rectangle p_mABp_c and the triangle ABC. The former is the monopoly profits (excess of price over average cost times output), and represents a transfer from consumers to producers (as compared with perfect competition). Subtracting this transfer, it is the triangle ABC which represents the net welfare loss of monopoly (again as compared with perfect competition).

The estimates of the size of monopoly welfare loss have ranged from the trivially small to the substantial.[18] The original estimate made by Harberger[19] for the American economy in 1929 was that the loss was less than $\frac{1}{10}$% of GDP, and a number of studies arrived at estimates of a similar order of magnitude. However, some recent estimates have placed the losses at a much more significant level. For example, Cowling and Mueller[20] estimate the welfare loss from monopoly in the range 3% to 7% of gross corporate product for the United Kingdom in the mid-1960s.[21] The implication that the welfare costs of monopoly are (or could be) substantial (as compared with perfect competition) underlies many ideas on anti-monopoly policies. At a minimum, it suggests that situations of monopoly require some monitoring. British monopoly policy is discussed below, but two points should be noted here. First, the discussion here (as usual) has concerned the extreme cases of monopoly and perfect competition, whereas most industries in reality lie somewhere between the two. Monopoly policy in practice is not concerned with firms which are complete monopolists (in the sense of being the only supplier), since there are virtually no firms in such a position, but rather with firms which have a considerable market share (in the British case a share of more than 25%). Second, the only aspect of performance which has been considered has been pricing (and the consequences for output). There are many other dimensions of performance (e.g. technical progress, or advertising) which are important, and in which monopolies and oligopolies may have advantages over atomistic competition. An oligopolist with a reasonably secure market position and a flow of profits may be in a better position to finance and undertake research than a competitive firm in an insecure position with only a competitive level of profits. Research and development (and production in general) may be subject to some economies of scale, providing further advantages for an oligopolistic structure over a competitive one.

The idea that perfect competition has certain desirable properties and the related idea that price should equal marginal cost for an optimal outcome relies on a range of restrictive assumptions, and some of those are now briefly considered. First, the equality achieved by perfectly competitive firms would be between price and marginal private cost, whereas the welfare requirement would be for an equality between price and marginal social cost. The difference between private and social costs arises from the existence of externalities.

---

[18] For a survey of monopoly welfare loss and its estimation see M. Sawyer, *Economics of Industries and Firms* (London: Croom Helm/Routledge, 1985).

[19] A. C. Harberger, 'Monopoly and Resource Allocation', *AER*, 44 (1954), 77–87.

[20] K. Cowling and D. Mueller, 'The Social Costs of Monopoly Power', *EJ*, 88 (1978), 727–48.

[21] There are a number of reasons for the differences in the orders of magnitude of the estimates of Cowling and Mueller (and others) from those of Harberger (and others). Cowling and Mueller assume joint profit maximization and estimate the elasticity of demand from the observed price-cost margin by applying a formula similar to that given in n. 6. Harberger assumed a unit elasticity of demand in all markets. A further major difference arises from the estimation of the competitive level of prices. Harberger used the average rate of profit, with the consequence that some actual prices were below the calculated competitive level. Cowling and Mueller used an estimate of the opportunity cost of capital.

The pollution from a factory is suffered by many people, and some or all of the costs of pollution are borne by people other than the firm which generates the pollution.[22] An extra traveller on a crowded road imposes further congestion on other travellers. Although further discussion of this point falls outside the scope of this chapter, it can be seen that the differences between private and social costs would lead to policy suggestions of imposing taxes and subsidies to remove (or at least reduce) the difference between private and social costs.

Second, there is the presumption of full employment of workers and machinery in the economy. The withdrawal of resources from the industry under consideration is assumed to lead to the use of those resources elsewhere in the economy. Thus redeployment rather than unemployment of resources (including labour) is assumed.

Third, consumers (and indeed firms as well) are assumed to be well informed on the quality of the product which they are buying as well as the price which they are paying. But for many products, their quality can only be judged by use. It may not be possible to judge the safety of a product (e.g. an electrical good) or to know the conditions under which a product was produced (e.g. whether food has been hygienically made). When a product malfunctions and requires repair, most of us are not technically equipped to judge what repairs are necessary (and that applies whether we are thinking of cars or of ourselves). Prices may be quoted in a misleading manner (e.g. the price offered compared with some notional recommended price). Much consumer protection legislation is devoted to imposing minimum standards on products. Codes of practice have been negotiated with a range of industries. The Consumer Protection Act 1987 makes it an offence to give misleading price indications. Thus, much public policy is designed to overcome problems arising from difficulties which consumers face in acquiring necessary information to judge quality and price.

Fourth, unit costs are assumed to be constant (as in our example) or to increase as the scale of production rises. In other words, production is assumed to involve constant or increasing costs. However, in some industries production involves decreasing costs. Industries such as railways, gas, and electricity, which have often been labelled 'natural monopolies', are seen as operating subject to decreasing costs. It would, for example, be wasteful of resources to have two railway lines linking city A with city B unless there was sufficient traffic to warrant both of them.

In a situation of decreasing costs, marginal costs are below average costs and so marginal cost pricing is not viable in the sense that price would be less than average costs and losses would result. Further, perfect competition would not be viable in such a situation for the largest firm would have the lowest costs and be able to undercut its rivals. This would enable the largest firm to expand further, operate subject to even lower costs and eventually reach a monopoly position.

---

[22] This would depend on the nature of the laws governing pollution; e.g. whether those who suffer from pollution can seek legal redress from the polluter.

The dilemma which this presents is clear. Technical efficiency would require a single firm, but one firm would possess monopoly power. There have been a range of policy responses to this dilemma. In Britain as in many other countries (the USA being the notable exception), the 'natural monopolies' of public utilities (postal service, telephone, gas, electricity, water, railways, television and radio) have until recently been under public ownership. The second response, followed in the USA and now for the recently privatized natural monopolies in Britain, has been to subject the firms to regulatory control, especially of prices and profits. The theory of regulation and its application in the UK context are discussed in the next chapter.

The third response, which has been developed in the past decade or so, argues that the number of firms in an industry is largely irrelevant, and that attention should be directed to the ease of entry into and exit from an industry. This line of argument has been associated with the theory of contestable markets, though it can also be linked with the Austrian approach discussed below. The general argument can be illustrated by reference to Fig. 8.3. The implicit assumption in arriving at the conclusion that a monopolist would charge a price of p_m was that its position was not threatened by the prospect of other firms being able to enter the industry. The entry of other firms into the industry would increase total output and reduce prices and profits. The existence of substantial monopoly profits would provide a strong incentive for other firms to seek to enter the industry concerned.

Baumol and his co-workers[23] define a market as perfectly contestable if there are no barriers to entry or to exit. The absence of barriers to entry would mean that any new entrant could compete with the existing firms without any handicap. The absence of barriers to exit would mean that there are no financial or other penalties for leaving an industry. This would mean, for example, that any equipment which was used in that industry could be readily resold for use elsewhere. The relevance of the ease of exit is that firms considering entry into an industry should not be put off by the difficulties of leaving the industry. This leads to the possibility of 'hit-and-run' entry; that is a firm entering an industry briefly, forcing down prices, and then leaving the industry. Baumol and others argue that under conditions of free entry and exit an incumbent firm (even with a monopoly position) would not dare to raise price above the competitive level. For if the firm were to do so, then other firms would immediately enter (seeking the available profits) and that would force down prices. The policy implications of this line of argument are clear, namely that regard should be paid to entry and exit conditions and not to monopoly positions *per se*. A monopolist which seeks to secure its position by raising entry and exit barriers would be condemned.

[23] W. J. Baumol, 'Contestable Markets: An Uprising in the Theory of Industrial Structure', *AER*, 72 (1982), 1–15; W. J. Baumol, J. Panzar, and R. D. Willig, *Contestable Markets and the Theory of Industrial Structure* (New York: Harcourt Brace Jovanovich). For further discussion see Sawyer, *Economics of Industries and Firms*, 250–2.

The final response considered has operated to some degree in commercial television and radio, where the government has begun to auction off the right to operate in a particular market.[24] In the case of commercial television, a franchise to operate has been granted to a single company in each of the television regions, though the granting of the franchise has been based on company plans for programme quality, range of programmes, etc. The basis of this response can again be illustrated by reference to Fig. 8.3. A monopolist would gain profits of $p_m ABp_o$ and a firm would be prepared to pay up to that amount for the right to have the monopoly position. If several firms compete for the right to be the monopolist, then the price paid for that right would be bid up to the level of the monopolist profits. When the price is bid up to that level, in effect the monopoly profits are gained by the firm with the licence but paid over to the government. There would still be some loss of consumer welfare as compared with the atomistic competition case, though with decreasing costs (which underpin the 'natural monopoly' case) atomistic competition would not be viable for the reasons explained above.

8.9. The Austrian School

The view of competition which is embedded in the traditional approach is that of the static equilibrium of atomistic competition with a large number of small firms. In contrast, the Austrian approach views competition as a dynamic process taking place against a background of change and uncertainty. The existence of profits, particularly high profits, is seen as an indicator that the firms concerned are particularly efficient both in terms of productive efficiency and of producing goods which consumers wish to buy. In particular, high profits are not seen as associated with market power, though there may be an association between high market shares and profits. But the link is not from high market share indicating monopoly to high profits, but rather that above-average efficiency generates a high market share and large profits.

The prospect of high profits is seen as the necessary inducement for firms to introduce new ideas, products, and techniques and to pursue efficiency. A firm which is particularly successful will indeed earn high profits. However, high profits are seen as always under threat from the entry of other firms. A firm with high profits may be able to maintain those profits, but only if it can remain more efficient than its rivals (potential as well as actual). It is the threat of new entry into an industry which keeps the incumbent firms on their toes. This leads to an emphasis on the importance of entry conditions into an industry, rather than the number of firms in the industry. One firm in an industry may appear to be a situation of monopoly, but if there are a number of firms ready to enter that

---

[24] See, for example, Home Office, *Broadcasting in the 90s: Competition, Choice and Quality*, Cmnd. 517 (London: HMSO, 1988).

industry if the existing firm allows its prices to rise above their level of costs, then the incumbent firm is highly constrained in its pricing.

In the analysis of monopoly welfare loss, it was implicitly assumed that the excess profits arose from the possession of monopoly power. In contrast, the Austrian approach would argue that the profits were temporary and are the necessary spur to innovation and efficiency. Thus Littlechild[25] considers that an innovating monopolist 'generates a social gain given by his own entrepreneurial profit plus the consumer surplus'.

Another important element of the Austrian approach is the importance of property rights and of the entrepreneur. If the entrepreneur is to seek after profits, then (s)he must have the claim to the profits generated, and hence, it is argued, the property rights to the profits must be assigned to the entrepreneur. The single entrepreneur is seen to be willing to take risks, to strive for lower costs etc., because (s)he will be the beneficiary of any resulting profits. In an organization with a large number of owners, the link between effort and profits is much diluted. The essential difficulty of nationalized industries, workers' co-operatives, and also of large manager-controlled corporations is seen to be that ownership is dispersed.[26]

These lines of arguments can be seen to have influenced the policies of the present government. The stress on property rights, with a strongly implied preference for private ownership over public ownership is reflected in the privatization programme discussed below. The emphasis on competition as a process and the focus on conditions of entry into an industry rather than the number of incumbent firms have influenced monopolies and mergers policies.

8.10. Developmental State

A quite different view of the appropriate roles of private firms, markets, and the state is given by a set of ideas which we include under the heading of the developmental state. The 'market failure' approach discussed above focuses on government intervention when markets in some sense fail, and could also be described in a number of respects as the regulatory view of the state (e.g. regulating monopolies). The developmental state view is seen as complementary with the regulatory view.[27]

Marquand[28] argues that 'the state has played a central part in economic

[25] S. Littlechild, 'Misleading Calculations of the Social Cost of Monopoly Power', *EJ*, 91 (1981), 348–63.

[26] There may be cases such as mutual organizations like building societies where the ownership of the assets of the organization may be very difficult to define.

[27] This distinction is drawn by R. Dore, 'Industrial Policy and How the Japanese do it', *Catalyst* (Spring 1986), and K. Cowling, 'An Industrial Strategy for Britain: The Nature and Role of Planning', *IRAE*, 1 (1987), 1–22.

[28] D. Marquand, *The Unprincipled Society* (London: Fontana Press, 1988).

development in virtually all industrial societies, with the possible exception of early nineteenth century Britain. Even in Britain, moreover, the state played an important facilitating role' in passing a variety of Acts of Parliament which allowed for example the building of the railways and the necessary infrastructure. There are numerous examples of the developmental state in the post-war era, and here three (Japan, France, and Italy) are briefly discussed to indicate the type of policies which a developmental state may follow.

The economic success of Japan in the last four decades is well known. Whilst Japan has operated a market economy, there has been much government influence on the direction of development of the economy. Much of this was undertaken through the Ministry of International Trade and Industry (MITI). The essential objective of industrial policy was to move Japan from a relatively backward economy specializing in labour-intensive products to an advanced industrial power. This meant moving the economy away from the production of goods and services in which it had a comparative advantage to the production of industrial products (initially products such as ships, and steel and later cars and computers). It involved targeting certain key sectors of the economy for development. A barrage of policy devices was used to protect the key sectors and to ensure their development. These included

the extensive use, narrow targeting and timely revision of tax incentives; the use of indicative plans to set goals and guidelines for the entire economy; the creation of numerous, formal and continuously operating forums for exchanging views, reviewing policies, obtaining feedback and resolving differences; the assignment of some government functions to various private and semi-private associations . . . ; an extensive reliance on public corporations, particularly of the mixed public-private variety, to implement policy in high-risk or otherwise refractory area; the creation and use by the government of an unconsolidated 'investment budget'. . . ; the orientation of anti-trust policy to developmental and international competitive goals rather than strictly to the maintenance of domestic competition; government-conducted or government-sponsored research and development (the computer industry); and the use of the government's licensing and approval authority to achieve developmental goals.[29]

Chang[30] reviews the experience of Korea[31] and concludes that 'the Korean state has continued to occupy the economic and moral commanding heights throughout the country's developmental period. State control over credit [was] . . . the most effective means of controlling private firms. . . . In addition to its control over domestic financial flows, the Korean state has maintained tight foreign exchange controls'. Overall, he argues, 'the Korean state played a central role in the country's economic development through its cunning use of state-created rents as an instrument for industrial development.

[29] C. Johnson, *MITI and the Japanese Miracle: The Growth of Industrial Policy, 1925–1975* (Stanford, Calif.: Stanford University Press, 1982).

[30] H.-J. Chang, 'The Political Economy of Industrial Policy in Korea', *CJE*, 17 (1993), 131–57.

[31] On Korea, see also A. Amsden, *Asia's Next Giant*, (Oxford and New York: Oxford University Press, 1989).

Of course, such a result was only possible because the Korean state was a strong state which could discipline firms.'[32]

The route initially followed in France was the use of national plans (which influenced the National Plan drawn up for the UK in the mid-1960s). One feature of the French approach was that the plan 'is at one and the same time comprehensive and passive. The plan provides a co-ordinating structure plus information flows but the planners are left in a peripheral position in relation to crucial strategic decisions.'[33]

One of the intentions of such a national plan is that it presents a consistent economic scenario against which individual firms can make their investment and other decisions. Investment decisions are geared to future growth pro-spects, and one intention of 'indicative planning' is that firms share common expectations about those growth prospects. There is an element of expectations becoming self-fulfilling: the expectation of fast growth becomes translated into a high level of investment which then enables the growth to occur. Another aspect of 'indicative planning' is the identification of constraints on economic growth and the direction of resources to overcome those constraints.

French governments have generally pursued policies of support for 'national champions' in certain strategic, high-technology areas. Assistance has been provided to such industries on a highly selective basis, and can range from provision of subsidies, protection from foreign competition, and the use of public procurement programmes etc.

State-holding companies in Italy (particularly the Institute for Industrial Reconstruction, IRI) have been important instruments in industrial develop-ment. The development of an Italian steel industry and telecommunications industry came largely from the initiative of IRI. There has been a heavy involvement of the public sector in trading activities, and these have included partial ownership of trading companies. In recent years there has been an emphasis on the promotion of investment, research, and innovation through subsidies and other incentives.

The general idea of the developmental state is that the private market will not produce the best possible outcome. It identifies a range of ways by which state intervention can operate to improve the operation of markets.

8.11. Competition and Monopoly Policies

Competition and monopoly policies can be broadly defined as policies designed to influence or change the industrial structure within which firms operate and/or the behaviour of firms (whether towards customers or other

[32] The term 'rent' is being used here in the sense of economic rent, that is a payment for a resource over and above that which is necessary to secure the use of that resource.

[33] Cowling, 'Industrial Strategy'.

firms). From 1948 onwards, British governments have operated, with a varying degree of vigour, evolving competition policies. It is convenient for purposes of discussion to divide these policies into five different types. The first to emerge was monopoly policy (starting from the 1948 Monopoly and Restrictive Practices Act), which originally covered restrictive practices as well. The restrictive practices policy was separated from monopoly policy with the passage of the Restrictive Trade Practices Act 1956. Some control over mergers and acquisitions was added in 1965, and the Office of Fair Trading, created in 1973, is heavily involved in the administration of competition policy.

Monopoly Policy

The previous discussion suggested that a situation of monopoly offered some advantages over a comparable situation of perfect competition but also some disadvantages. A situation of monopoly provides the monopolist with sub-stantial market power. This power could be used to raise prices and lower output (as compared with a situation with more firms). It may enable more research and development to be undertaken and economies of scale to be exploited. In addition, though, the monopolist can in effect take the monopoly profits by allowing costs to rise above those technically necessary.

Monopoly policy since 1973 has had the following structure. A firm (or group of firms acting in concert) can be referred to the Monopolies and Mergers Commission (MMC hereafter) for investigation when its market share is thought to exceed 25%. Thus the statutory definition of monopoly is a market share of 25%. The MMC is required to first investigate whether the firm (or firms) concerned do indeed have a market share of 25%. The major part of its work is to investigate whether the actions and performance of the monopolist have been in the public interest. The public interest is not precisely defined and its interpretation has indeed varied. However, successive Acts since 1948 have indicated that regard should be paid, *inter alia*, to efficient produc-tion and distribution, a balanced distribution of industry and employment within the United Kingdom, increase of efficiency and the encouragement of new enterprise. The only change of significance has been the explicit mention of the desirability of competition *per se* in the Fair Trading Act of 1973.

British monopoly policy operates on a discretionary basis. The Secretary of State for Trade and Industry has discretion over whether a firm (or group of firms believed to be acting together) are referred to the MMC for investigation. In practice, there are many firms with market shares of over 25% which have not been referred for investigation. Further, the MMC has considerable discretion over the interpretation of the public interest. There is no explicit build-up of case law.

In its reports the MMC gives its judgement and usually makes recommenda-tions for changes in the firm's behaviour, though the implementation of any such recommendations is in the hands of the Secretary of State for Trade and

Industry. In the overwhelming majority of cases, the MMC has made some criticisms of the practices of the firms under investigation. Predominant in terms of number of times reported amongst the practices which have been condemned are restriction of sale of competitors' goods, price notification agreements, monopoly pricing and profits, and discriminatory pricing.[34] Most of the practices found to be against the public interest were aspects of behaviour which either operated to make life more difficult for (actual or potential) competitors without benefiting consumers through the supply of 'better' products or the charging of lower prices. These types of behaviour include supplying a retail outlet only if that outlet agreed not to sell competitors' goods and the favouring of some firms at the expense of others by discriminatory pricing. Excessive profits and prices have generally been condemned, particularly when reinforced by entry barriers and restrictions on competition. In the past few years, increasing attention has been given by the MMC to the effects which an existing monopoly or oligopoly position has on competition and on the possibility of new entry into the industry concerned. The majority of those recent MMC reports on monopoly situations which have found activities as against the public interest have included the restriction of competition amongst the activities against the public interest.

In none of their reports did the MMC condemn a monopoly position as such and recommend structural change. The nearest the MMC came to recommending structural change was in the case of roadside advertising services.[35] Ten companies had set up and owned a company called British Posters Ltd., and the MMC made the recommendation, which was carried out, that this company be disbanded. In March 1989 the MMC recommended that brewers be limited to the ownership of 2000 public houses, and six brewers operated more than this number (with Bass operating the most at 7100).[36] However after negotiations between the Department of Trade and Industry and the brewers, an order was made requiring those brewers with more than 2000 tied public houses to release a half of the number in excess of 2000. The Office of Fair Trading continues to monitor the brewers' compliance with a 1989 Beer Order including an undertaking on the number of tied houses.

Merger Policy

Since 1965 a proposed merger which would create or enhance a monopoly position, or which involves the acquisition of assets above a specified size, is evaluated by the government. The definition of a monopoly position is that used in the monopoly policy, i.e. a market share of more than 25%. The size

---

[34] For a summary of practices found against public interest see Review of Monopolies and Mergers Policy, *A Consultative Document*, Cmnd. 7198 (London: HMSO, 1978).

[35] Monopolies and Mergers Commission, *Roadside Advertising Services: A Report on the Supply in the UK of Roadside Advertising Services*, HC 365 (London: HMSO, 1981).

[36] Monopolies and Mergers Commission, *The Supply of Beer* (London: HMSO, 1989).

requirement for a merger to be evaluated was raised to £70 million in February 1994, from the previous level of £30 million which had been maintained since 1984. The initial evaluation of a proposed merger is made by a panel of civil servants (the Mergers Panel), who consider whether there should be a referral of the merger to the MMC for further investigation. The final decision on referral is made by the Secretary of State for Trade and Industry, with advice from the Director-General of Fair Trading (DGFT). A firm contemplating a merger can seek confidential guidance from the OFT on its likely attitude to the proposed merger. The bidding firm can also respond to such guidance by designing the take-over bid in such a way as to reduce the chances of referral of the merger to the MMC. For example, a firm may seek to acquire another but state its intention to resell part of the firm acquired to avoid the creation of a monopoly position. Any investigation by the MMC is normally expected to be completed within six months, during which time the take-over bid usually lapses (under the conditions of the Stock Exchange Take-over Code).

The thrust of the current policy has been described by the then Secretary of State for Trade and Industry (Norman Tebbit) in July 1984 in the following terms. 'I regard mergers policy as an important part of the government's general policy of promoting competition within the economy in the interests of the customer and of efficiency and hence of growth and jobs. Accordingly my policy has been and will continue to be to make references primarily on competition grounds.' The report of this speech continues by saying that '[i]n evaluating the competitive situation in individual cases Mr Tebbit said he would have regard to the international context: to the extent of competition in the home market from non-UK sources; and to the competitive position of UK companies in overseas markets'.[37] Some other aspects of the public interest continue to be taken into account but a recently added consideration is any state-owned company involvement (e.g. a foreign nationalized firm).

The limited impact of merger policy is evident from the proportion of proposed mergers investigated by the MMC. During the period 1965 to 1978, about $2\frac{1}{2}$% of proposed mergers covered by the Fair Trading Act were referred to the MMC for more detailed consideration, with the remainder allowed to proceed. In the period 1979 to 1994, 3654 mergers fell within the scope of the legislation, of which 136 potential mergers were referred to the MMC, amounting to nearly $3\frac{3}{4}$% of total.[38] In the period 1979–94 of the 140 mergers referred to the MMC, 50 were declared against the public interest, 61 were declared as not against the public interest, and 29 were abandoned by the firms involved before the MMC reported and the referral was withdrawn.

---

[37] The quote in the text is taken from a speech by the then Trade and Industry Secretary Norman Tebbit as reported in *British Business*, 13 July 1984, p. 381.
[38] There were a number of instances when a single company was subject to more than one takeover proposal.

Restrictive Practices

Restrictive practices cover matters such as agreement between firms over prices to be charged, over sharing out a market (e.g. agreeing that each geographical area be supplied by only one firm), etc. The major legislation on restrictive practices dates from 1956. There are two notable contrasts between the policy on restrictive practices and policy on monopolies and mergers. The first is that the body which is charged with the operation of the restrictive practices legislation is part of the judiciary, namely the Restrictive Practices Court (hereafter RPC). This means that there is a build up of case law on restrictive practices, in contrast to the situation with monopolies and mergers policy. The second is that there is a presumption in the legislation that restrictive practices are against the public interest unless proved otherwise (whereas the merger legislation has the presumption in favour of mergers). This presumption against restrictive practices has been reinforced by the way in which the RPC has interpreted the legislation. There are eight 'gateways' through which a restrictive practice can pass in order to continue.[39]

Initially the restrictive practices legislation covered only goods, but it was extended to cover services in 1976. The application of the restrictive practices legislation to the operation of the Stock Exchange led eventually to the reorganization of the Stock Exchange in October 1986 in the 'Big Bang' (see Chapter 6). The restrictive practices operated by the Stock Exchange were referred to the RPC, but the matter was taken out of their hands by the government. An act of parliament was enacted to exempt the Stock Exchange from the restrictive practices legislation in exchange for a number of concessions by the London Stock Exchange, the most important of which was the scrapping of minimum commission rates. Agreements between companies continue to be entered into, and each year around 1200 such agreements are submitted to the OFT, of which usually between 500 and 600 are registered.

Resale price maintenance (RPM) is one type of restrictive practice which is separately dealt with under the Resale Prices Act 1976. RPM operates when a supplier makes a condition of supply of goods to retailers that the retailers charge consumers at least some minimum price. Under the Act, such a condition is generally illegal. This legislation contains the presumption against RPM, with the possibility of exemptions being granted by the RPC. Although RPM has declined substantially, firms may resort to practices such as stating recommended prices which can have similar effects. The Office of Fair Trading receives around 35 complaints a year to the effect that producers are imposing conditions on the minimum price to be charged by retailers or wholesalers. In the past few years, investigation of these complaints has led to a few firms

---

[39] These gateways included the defence that removal of the restrictive practice would cause unemployment, or lead to public injury or a fall in exports.

being required to give undertakings to desist from imposing minimum prices to be charged as a condition of supply.

European Union Policies

The EEC has operated (under Articles 85 and 86 of the Treaty of Rome of 1957) a monopoly and mergers policy to which British firms have in principle been subject. The relevant parts of the Treaty of Rome are Articles 85 (dealing with cartels and restrictive trade practices) and 86 (monopoly). These articles refer to inter-state trade, which would appear to exclude any cartels or monopolies affecting only within-country trade, but agreements and actions which serve to limit imports from one EC country to another would be covered by these articles.

The implementation of competition policy is in the hands of the European Commission, with cases which appear to break Articles 85 or 86 being taken to the European Court of Justice. There is a similarity with British policy in the area of cartels and restrictive practices in that there is a presumption that they are against the public interest with the possibility of exemptions being granted. Article 85 covers agreements, decisions, and concerted practices which may affect trade between member states and which have the effect of restricting or distorting competition. The article specifically mentions agreements and practices which fix prices, limit production, share out markets between firms, or which charge discriminatory prices. In practice, the Court and Commission have placed a 'tough' interpretation on Article 85. However, the implementation of the article is subject to a *de minimis* rule under which agreements involving firms with a combined market share below 5% or with a combined annual turnover below 50 million ECU (around £30 million) are excluded from consideration. Firms do not have to register any restrictive trade agreements, but may notify the Commission of agreements. There is an incentive to notify an agreement 'since if they do not do so there can be no question of their agreement being exempted' and if 'the agreement is duly notified it enjoys a provisional or temporary validity'.[40]

Article 86 deals with the abuse of market dominance rather than with monopoly *per se*, and with those abuses which affect trade between member states. In the Article, particular abuses mentioned are:

(*a*) directly or indirectly imposing unfair purchase or selling prices or other unfair trading conditions;
(*b*) limiting production, markets or technical development to the prejudice of consumers;
(*c*) applying dissimilar conditions to equivalent transactions with other trading parties, thereby placing them at a competitive disadvantage;
(*d*) making the conclusion of contracts subject to acceptance by the other parties of

[40] D. Swann, *The Economics of the Common Market*, 6th edn. (Harmondsworth: Penguin Books, 1988).

supplementary obligations which, by their nature or according to commercial usage, have no connection with the subject of such contracts.[41]

The Treaty of Rome does not define dominance but the Court has looked at both market share and actions before arriving at a view as to whether there is dominance in a particular case. A market share as low as 40% has been used as partial evidence of dominance. There is the problem of finding an appropriate definition of the market, and this problem is exacerbated in the EC context since the question arises as to whether the appropriate market area is the whole of the EC or one particular country or region.

Mergers are not explicitly covered by the Treaty of Rome, but the European Court has ruled that Article 86 does cover mergers, partly on the grounds that Article 85 (on restrictive practices) could be side-stepped by firms merging (rather than operating illegal agreements amongst themselves). However, there has not actually been a formal decision of the Court prohibiting a merger. Since late 1990, the European Commission has had jurisdiction over 'concentrations with a Community dimension', which are those where 'the aggregate world-wide turnover of all parties concerned is more than ECU 5 billions; *and* the aggregate Community-wide turnover of each of at least two of the parties concerned is more than ECU 250 million; *unless* each of the parties achieves more than two thirds of its aggregate Community-wide turnover within one and the same Member State'.[42] National authorities may not apply their own competition laws to these mergers except in very limited circumstances.

The conduct of industrial policy (particularly in the realm of subsidies) has probably been more affected by the rules limiting national governments providing 'unfair' advantages to their own firms. Articles 92 to 94 of the Treaty of Rome restrict state aid to firms. The range of state aid which is covered has been defined to be constituted by not only grants 'but also by loans on more favourable terms than are available on the market, guarantees, tax concessions, relief of social security contributions, and by the State putting up new capital for enterprises in circumstances in or on terms which a private investor would not do so'.[43] Part of Article 92 makes state aid which distorts (or threatens to distort) competition by favouring some firms or industries in so far as trade between member countries is affected, incompatible with the common market. Article 93 leads to state aid being kept under constant review, with member countries having to report plans on state aid.[44]

---

[41] Quote is from Article 86 of the Treaty of Rome.
[42] Quote is from Office of Fair Trading, *Mergers* (London: HMSO, 1991).
[43] Commission of the European Communities, *Fourteenth Report on Competition Policy* (Brussels: Office for Official Publications of the European Communities, 1985).
[44] For further details see D. Swann, *Economics of the Common Market.*

8.12. Research and Development Expenditure

Expenditure on research and development (R & D) in Britain amounts to around 2¼% of GDP. The statistics in the first half of Table 8.5 allow some comparisons with other industrialized economies. It can be seen that expenditure in Britain is, relative to GDP, somewhat less than in most of the other countries included in the table, with Italy as the exception. It can also be seen that whilst R & D expenditure has not risen relative to GDP in Britain, it has done so in many other industrialized economies.

Around half of R & D is financed by private industry (52.1% in 1989), with 32.35% financed by government, 3.9% by other national sources (e.g. charities) and the remaining 11.7% financed from abroad (e.g. by multinational enterprises). Business performs 65.9% of the research and development, with 16.5% undertaken in higher education institutions, 13.8% in the government sector, and the remaining 3.8% in non-profit organizations.[45] The involvement of government in the financing of research and development in most industrialized countries is also apparent from Table 8.5. However, the USA and the UK stand out as having particularly high proportions of research and development in areas which are related to defence.

Table 8.5. Statistics relating to research and development expenditure

A. *Overall figures*	Expenditure on research and development as % of GDP		Defence R & D as % of government-financed R & D
	1983	1993	1993
United Kingdom	2.3	2.2	45.1
France	2.1	2.4	33.5
Germany	2.5	2.5	8.5
Italy	1.0	1.3	6.5
Japan	2.4	2.9	6.1
Sweden	2.6	3.1	23.5
United States	2.7	2.7	59.0

Source: OECD, *Main Science and Technology Indicators 1995*.

B. *Composition of government-financed research and development expenditure, 1993/94 (%)*			
	Civil	Defence	Total
Basic	49.8	0	28.6
Strategic	31.1	2.1	18.7
Specific	14.6	24.9	19.0
Experimental	4.4	73.0	33.7

Sources: Cabinet Office, *Forward Look of Government Funded Science, Engineering and Technology Statistical Supplement 1995* (London: HMSO, 1995).

[45] OECD, *Main Science and Technology Indicators, 1995/1* (Paris: OECD, 1995).

The division of research and development expenditure into four categories in Table 8.5 is based on the following distinctions. Basic research is that undertaken primarily to acquire knowledge and with no specific application in mind, whereas strategic research is undertaken with eventual practical applications in mind even though these cannot be clearly specified. Specific research is that which is directed primarily towards identified practical aims or objectives; finally, experimental research is systematic work drawing on existing knowledge to produce new products, processes, etc.

The three approaches to industrial policy suggested above can be applied to the case of research and technology. The 'market failure' approach has to be extended to introduce research and development. Research has a number of key features. First, research is the exploration of the unknown so that calculations on the benefits and costs of an avenue of research are particularly difficult to make. This uncertainty may militate against firms undertaking research, with firms tending to opt for less risky ventures. There are often very long lags between the start of a research programme and the commercial implementation of the fruits of that programme. The combination of uncertainty and long lead times is seen to discourage research and also the provision of finance for research programmes. There may be a transfer of knowledge generated by research programmes so that despite the patent laws firms other than the one undertaking the research benefit from the discoveries made. This line of argument suggests that there will be a systematic tendency for there to be under-investment in research and development. This is reflected in estimates that the rate of return on research and development is much higher than rates of return on other investment projects.[46]

Second, the activity of research is by no means homogeneous: a crude division would be, on the one hand, between basic and strategic research as defined above and, on the other, applied research and development. The former could be seen as research undertaken in the pursuit of knowledge without any thought of commercial or other application, whereas the latter is undertaken for commercial reasons. However, the basic research of one era provides the platform for applied research of the next era. For example, those scientists who discovered the principles of electricity could be seen as undertaking basic research whereas those who have used those principles to develop, say, washing machines are engaged in applied research. The distinction between basic and applied is, of course, not a hard and fast one, though useful for our discussion. Basic research is particularly prone to the difficulties identified above, namely uncertainty of outcome and long lead times. Yet such research is necessary for future progress. Further, the output from basic

---

[46] One estimate puts the social rate of return at 56% on research and development as compared with a private rate of return of 25%, both of which would be above the rate of return on investment in general: see E. Mansfield, 'Measuring the Social and Private Rates of Return on Innovation' in *Economic Effects of Space and Other Advanced Technologies* (Strasbourg: Council of Europe, 1980).

research should be spread as quickly as possible so that it can be drawn into applied research.

Third, knowledge is costly to produce, but once it has been produced it can be spread at very low cost. This sets up the following conflict. An individual will only undertake costly research if the benefits will eventually exceed the estimated costs (of course mistakes are often made). From that perspective, the individual can be encouraged to undertake research by being able to reap the gains. But once the discovery has been made, it would appear beneficial for that knowledge to be passed on to others (since it can be spread at virtually zero marginal cost); in which case the discoverer would not benefit. The patent laws have been seen as an attempt to strike a balance by giving inventors certain rights over the use of their invention for a specified period (generally 16 years in the United Kingdom). The patent holder can be compelled to grant licences for the use of the invention if the patentee is abusing the monopoly position granted by, for example, not working the invention commercially.

The Austrian school draws particularly on the work of Schumpeter.[47] Schumpeter argued that a (temporary) monopoly position often arose out of a successful research programme and the discovery of new products. Hence monopoly profits were often the return to previous research and development, though in turn these profits provide a source of funds for further investment in research and development. But these high profits do not last for ever, for there is a 'perennial gale of creative destruction' which threatens the monopolist's position. The prospect of profits provides the spur to undertake research and development, but competition from others (e.g. development of close substitutes) will eat away at those profits. Thus there is an interplay between a temporary monopoly position (arising from successful innovation) and the background of competition. Schumpeter suggested that the benefits of (temporary) monopoly were to aid the pace of research and development and to more than offset the short-run costs of monopoly in terms of higher price and lower output as suggested in Fig. 8.3. Another element of the Austrian approach (as indicated above) would be the view that '[f]irms themselves are best able to assess their own markets and to balance the commercial risks and rewards of financing R & D and innovation. The Government should not take on responsibilities which are principally those of industry'.[48]

The developmental state perspective would to some degree draw on the arguments outlined, to the effect that the private market will systematically under-invest in research and development. It would further note that competition between firms and between countries in the late twentieth century often takes the form of technical innovation rather than price. This general view is

[47] See, for example, J. Schumpeter, *Capitalism, Socialism and Democracy* (London: Allen and Unwin, 1954).

[48] Department of Trade and Industry, *DTI—the Department for Enterprise*, Cmnd. 278 (London: HMSO 1988).

reflected in the argument that '[t]he Government has . . . a general responsibility to support science and technology because this is fundamental to the social and economic well-being of the country'.[49]

The problem of short termism is thought by many commentators to arise in connection with research and development expenditure (as well as investment expenditure more generally).[50] The general notion of short termism, as the phrase suggests, is that too much weight is in some sense placed on the near future as compared with the more distant future. There are many reasons why individuals and societies would wish to place a lower value on say £1000 to be received in one year's time as compared with receiving it now (and that would still be the case even if inflation was expected to be zero). The extent to which the present is valued over the future is reflected in the rate of discount which we apply to the future: formally a rate of discount r would mean that £1 received in one year's time (valued in today's prices) would be seen as worth the equivalent of $£1/(1 + r)$ today. Hence a discount rate of 5% (i.e. 0.05) would mean a £1 in one year's time equivalent to $£1/(1 + 0.05) = £0.9524$ today.

Particularly for firms who are borrowing money to finance investment projects the rate of discount which they apply to a project will be related to the rate of interest which they have to pay on their borrowings.[51] For if a firm applied a rate of discount lower than the interest rate paid it would find that it was losing money on the projects. Short termism for the economy as a whole would arise when the average rate of discount being applied was higher than the socially desired rate. However, measuring the socially desired rate is highly problematic, but we can make comparisons between countries in the rate of discount which is applied to see whether there is any case for thinking that the rate of discount is particularly high in the UK. One set of estimates of the overall cost of capital (and hence effectively the minimum rate of discount which a firm has to earn) put it at 19.9% in the UK in comparison with 14.7% in Japan, 15.1% in the United States and 15.7% in Germany.[52]

There are (at least) two dimensions to short termism which relate to research and development. The first dimension is that insufficient regard is given to future benefits through the use of a rate of discount which is, in some sense, too high (or requiring a short 'pay off' period[53] for an investment, say of

---

[49] *House of Lords Report of Select Committee on Science and Technology*, HL 20 (London: HMSO, 1986).

[50] For a popular exposition of the problem of short termism and its effects on the UK economy see W. Hutton, *The State We're In*, (London: Jonathan Cape, 1995), especially chap. 6.

[51] An analogous argument would apply if the firm financed its investment out of its retained profits: the rate of interest which it could obtain on lending out those profits would represent the opportunity cost of undertaking the investment.

[52] The estimates relate to the period 1983–91 and were made in the final report for study on international differences in the cost of capital for the European Commision by Coopers and Lybrand in April 1993, as reported in W. Hutton, *State We're In*.

[53] A 'pay off' period of, say, four years would mean that an investment would only proceed if the company expected that the additional profits resulting from that investment over the first four years would be greater than (or equal to) the cost of the investment.

the order of four to five years). 'An implication of short-termism is that there is insufficient investment in projects which have relatively long maturities—some types of projects with positive expected net present value when discounted appropriately both for risk and the pure rate of time preference of investors are systematically rejected'.[54] The second dimension is that the additional profits expected to arise from particular types of expenditure are more heavily discounted than other forms of profits. In the case of research and development expenditure, the benefits may arise in the distant future and be particularly risky and uncertain.

A different angle on the same issue comes from a consideration of the value which the stock market places on a quoted company. This is often viewed in terms of the (present value) of the discounted future dividends of the company concerned. This would obviously involve forming expectations about future dividends (which themselves would be based on the profits of the company as well as the payout ratio). Of particular interest here is the rate at which the future is discounted by the stock market in arriving at the valuation of the company. There has been considerable debate as to whether the stock market tends to under- or over-value research-intensive companies (in effect apply too high or too low a discount rate to the prospective dividends of such companies). Miles[55] concludes that for British quoted companies during the 1980s there 'is apparent evidence of short-termism throughout much of the decade'.

The problem of 'short termism' could be seen as an aspect of 'market failure' (in that the private rate of discount does not correspond to (and is typically greater than) the social rate of discount). But it can also be seen as consistent with the developmental state view in that government action to promote research and development (as part of a more general industrial strategy) is seen as required.

The present government has generally sought to reduce industrial subsidies and assistance, both in terms of selective assistance (much of which went to aerospace, shipbuilding, coal, steel, and vehicle industries) and regional and general industrial support. The overall budget for trade and industry has virtually been halved in real terms during the 1980s, and within that budget there has been a relative shift towards scientific and technological assistance. However, the government's view of its own policy is that 'innovation policy should be focused primarily on the circumstances when research is necessary before commercial applications can be developed, or where the benefits of the research are likely to be widespread, and on technology transfer'.[56]

There are a large number of government programmes which can be placed under the heading of the encouragement and support of industrial research and development. Most of them, however, account for only very small sums of public expenditure. The bulk of public expenditure in this area (as can be seen

[54] D. Miles, 'Testing for Short Termism in the UK Stock Market', *EJ*, 103 (1993), 1379–96.
[55] D. Miles, 'Testing for Short Termism'.
[56] Department of Trade and Industry, *Department for Enterprise*.

from Table 8.5) relates to research in defence-related industries. It has also been estimated[57] that around 30% of Britain's highly qualified scientists and engineers are employed in the defence sector. One particular difficulty which arises here is that the secrecy which surrounds defence-related work limits the spread of knowledge arising from this type of research. The industrial spin-offs benefiting other sectors of industry are then likely to be limited. It has been argued that

technological spin-offs from the military sector, while obviously tangible, are generally few and far between and thus represent a poor return on R & D compared to equivalent civilian outlays. This is partly because Britain's particularly tight security laws inhibit the flow of knowledge from military laboratories, but it stems as much from the qualitative difference between military and civilian technology.[58]

The Civil Aircraft Research and Demonstration Programme (CARAD) is 'part of a national aircraft research effort conducted by industry, government, research establishments, higher education institutes and other agencies. Its objective is to help key sectors of UK aircraft and aerospace industry maintain the technological base needed to compete effectively in world markets'.[59] Much of the research is carried out at the Royal Aerospace Establishment involving public expenditure of nearly £30 million in 1989/90.

In non-defence areas, existing government support of research and development can be conveniently placed under two headings. The first heading is that of collaborative project support. The major programme here has been the ALVEY project, which was designed 'to stimulate [information technology] research through a programme of collaborative pre-competitive projects fitting into the strategies developed for the key technologies of intelligent knowledge based systems (IKBS), the man/machine interface (MMI), software engineering, very large scale integration (VLSI) and computing architectures'.[60] Government funding provided £200 million out of a total of £350 millions. 'UK government policy now puts greater emphasis on support for IT R & D through ESPRIT II'.[61]

The LINK initiative aims to 'encourage pre-competitive research and ensure rapid take-up of research ideas by bringing together industrial and academic workers at the earliest stage of development of new technologies'[62] with the government financing up to half of the cost of each programme. From the start date of 1986 up to 1995, over 570 individual projects worth over £300 million have been initiated with more than 800 companies and 130 science institutions involved. The areas covered include biotechnology, advanced materials, and electronics. The Advanced Technology Programmes (ATPs) are also designed

---

[57] M. Kaldor, M. Sharp, and W. Walker, 'Industrial Competitiveness and Britain's Defence', *LBR*, 162 (Oct. 1986), 31–49.   [58] Kaldor *et al.*, 'Industrial Competitiveness'.
[59] Quote is from *Trade and Industry Expenditure Plans 1991–92 to 1993–94*, (London: HMSO, 1991).   [60] J. Shepherd, 'Industrial Support Policies', *NIER*, 122 (Nov. 1987), 59–71.
[61] Quote is from OECD, *Science and Technology Policy Review and Outlook 1991* (Paris: OECD, 1992).   [62] Quote is from OECD, *Science and Technology*.

to encourage pre-competitive research by industrial companies in new technologies such as computer-aided engineering and high temperature superconductivity.

LINK is a 'cross-government initiative which aims to bridge the gap between the science and engineering base [the research and postgraduate training capacity based in universities and other higher education institutions] and industry.'[63] In March 1995 40 LINK programmes were running, each of which supports a series of projects bringing together at least one science and engineering base partner and one industrial partner.

The EUREKA project was a French-inspired agreement, adopted by eighteen EEC and EFTA nations and the EEC Commission in November 1985. It seeks to encourage industry-led collaborative projects in advanced technologies leading to innovative products, processes, or services. There is no central fund, and each government is responsible for the financial support of its own firms. The British participation is described as designed to 'improve the competitiveness of British firms in world markets in civil applications of new technologies by encouraging European industrial and technological market-led collaboration in R and D'.[64] The extent of government support is 50% of the costs of applied research projects and up to 25% of the costs of development projects. By 1991 there were some 470 EUREKA projects which had been agreed, of which British participants were involved in 115, of which 37 were UK-led.[65]

SMART (Small Firms Merit Award for Research and Technology) is a competition for small firms (50 employees or less) with over 1200 projects having received Stage 1 financial support and half of those receiving stage 2 support, totalling £80 million in grants from the DTI. The prize from the competition was a 75% grant (up to £37500) for a feasibility study lasting up to a year, with further grants for some of the prize-winners. The intention is to encourage the development of high risk projects and the start-up of high technology firms, and the competition looks for the best novel ideas, particularly in biotechnology, information technology, advanced materials technology, and advanced manufacturing technology. SMART and a similiar SPUR scheme are (at the time of writing) being combined to give a programme with a budget of £76 million over three years.

The second heading covers technology transfer, consultancy, advice, and awareness programmes. Technology transfer initiatives provide access for small and medium-sized enterprises to new ideas. These initiatives include Advanced Information Technology (with a £12 million programme over 3 years) and Materials Matter (£2.5 million over 3 years) which provides information on modern engineering materials and their processing methods. Other pro-

---

[63] *Realising Our Potential: A Strategy for Science, Engineering and Technology*, Chancellor of the Duchy of Lancaster, Cmnd. 2250 (London: HMSO, 1993).
[64] Shepherd, 'Industrial Support Policies'.
[65] Source here is OECD, *Science and Technology*.

grammes range from the provision of IT equipment in schools through to business and technical advisory services (BTAS). They are mainly linked to micro-electronics and information technology.

8.13. Small Firm Policies

The present government has placed considerable emphasis on the promotion and formation of small businesses. The Enterprise Allowance Scheme (EAS) began in 1982 to encourage the formation of new businesses by the unemployed. The amount paid as an allowance can now be varied, previously having been £40 a week, with the payment being made for a year with recipients required to provide at least £1000 in start-up capital (which can be borrowed). Up to 1990/1 it was claimed that over 566 000 unemployed had been helped to become self-employed.[66] Estimates based on the earlier years of the scheme estimated that of every 100 aided under the EAS, 57 are still operating after three years, and those surviving firms provide a further 65 jobs. The survival rate six months after the end of the period for which the allowance has been paid was 73% in 1990/1.[67] The estimation of the effect of any policy designed to create or protect employment is fraught with difficulties. The policy may appear to help the creation of jobs which would have been created anyway. Further, the jobs created may be at the expense of jobs elsewhere in the economy. The establishment of a new business will to some degree attract custom from existing firms. The Department of Employment assumes that half of the EAS businesses displace existing business, but admit that there is no firm statistical basis for this estimate.

The Small Firm Loan Guarantee Scheme is designed to fill a perceived gap in the availability of finance for small and medium-sized firms. Application for finance is made direct to a bank which is responsible for the appraisal of the scheme, but subject to final approval by the Department of Employment. In the case of default on the loan, the bank can call on the guarantee provided (on a proportion of the loan) by the Department of Employment. The borrower is charged an interest rate premium (over that which would be charged by the bank). In 1990/1 new loans to a total of £86 million were made to over 3 400 applicants, and the failure rate three years after loan was made was running at 32%.

The Business Expansion Scheme (BES) provides tax relief on money invested in business (with a limit of £500 000 on the total amount invested in a single company within a year). The intention of this scheme is to

[66] Department of Employment, *The Government's Expenditure Plans 1992–1993 to 1994–1995*, Cmnd. 1906 (London: HMSO, 1992); see also National Audit Office, Department of Employment/Training Commission, *Assistance to Small Firms*, HC 655 (London: HMSO, 1988).
[67] Dept. of Employment, Expenditure Plans.

encourage the supply of venture capital and the financing of relatively small firms.

Further Reading

D. Hay and D. Morris, *Industrial Economics, Theories and Evidence* 2nd edn. (Oxford: Oxford University Press, 1991).

M. Sawyer, *Economics of Industries and Firms* (London: Routledge, 1985).

Grazia Ietto-Gillies, *International Production: Trends, Theories, Effects* (Oxford: Polity Press, 1992).

Symposium on Technical Progress, *Oxford Review of Economic Policy*, 4/4 (1988).

Symposium on Competition Policy, *Oxford Review of Economic Policy*, 9/2 (1993).

PRIVATIZATION AND REGULATION

MALCOLM SAWYER

9.1 Introduction

This chapter covers three broad topics. It first considers the policy of privatization, particularly as implemented in Britain in the past fifteen years. The privatization of public utilities has been accompanied by the establishment of regulatory bodies for each of the public utilities, and much of the rest of the chapter is concerned with regulation. The second broad topic of the chapter is the theory of regulation, whilst the third is the practice of regulation. This third topic is divided between the regulation of the public utilities, regulation of transport (where there has been a considerable degree of deregulation over the past 15 years), regulation and consumer protection, and finally the forms of regulation which have been used in respect of the environment.

9.2 Privatization[1]

In this section we consider the privatization programme of the past fifteen years, where privatization is used here to denote the sale of assets previously owned by the state.[2] The extent of public ownership in a range of European countries in 1989 is given in Table 9.1. Since that date, most of the electricity industry, the coal industry, and parts of the railways have been privatized in the UK. The privatization programme of the past fifteen years stands in contrast

---

[1] For evidence on the extent of privatization in a range of European countries see M. Sawyer, 'Industry: Policies and Performance' in David Coates (ed.) *Economic and Industrial Performance in Europe*, (Aldershot: Edward Elgar 1995), and V. Wright (ed.), *Privatization in Western Europe*, (London: Pinter).

[2] The term 'privatization' has sometimes been used to embrace three strands of policy—the sale of assets; the contracting out of the provision to public bodies (government departments, publicly owned hospitals) of goods, and (mainly) services by private firms which had previously been provided by the public bodies themselves; and de-regulation and liberalization.

Table 9.1. Distribution of public enterprises by industry, 1989

| | Per cent of value added in each industry | | | | | | | | | | |
	Post Office	Telecom-munications	Electricity	Gas	Oil	Coal	Railways	Air transport	Road transport	Steel	Ship-building
Austria	100	100	100	100	100	100	100	100	100	100	—
Belgium	100	100	25	25	—	0	100	100	100	50	0
France	100	100	100	100	25	100	100	75	50	75	0
Germany	100	100	75	50	—	50	100	100	25	0	25
Italy	100	100	75	100	—	—	100	100	25	75	75
Netherlands	100	100	75	75	—	—	100	75	50	25	0
Spain	100	50	40	75	—	50	100	100	0	50	75
Sweden	100	100	50	100	—	—	100	50	25	75	75
Switzerland	100	100	100	100	—	—	100	25	0	0	—
United Kingdom	100	0	100	25	25	100	100	0	0	75	50

Note: — = no industry in country concerned
Source: OECD, *Industrial Policy in OECD Countries*, (Paris: OECD 1992), Table 7.

with the previous post-war experience.[3] The major programme of nationalization in the post-war period was undertaken by the Labour Governments of
1945–51. During that period, industries such as coal-mining, railways, part of
road haulage (later de-nationalized), gas, electricity, and the Bank of England
were nationalized. Nationalization in the 1960s and 1970s was concentrated on
industries in long-term decline (such as steel, shipbuilding, and aerospace).
Individual firms, such as British Leyland and part of Rolls-Royce, came into
public ownership more by accident than design as a response by the government to the threat of the extinction through bankruptcy of those firms.[4]

Privatization, as the term suggests, is the transfer of ownership from the
public sector to the private sector.[5] However, privatization in practice involves
rather more than a change of ownership (though some of the changes are
closely related to the change of ownership). The objectives of privatization in
the UK have been variously summarized but would usually be taken to include
the reduction of government involvement in industry; improvement of efficiency in both the privatized companies and what remained of the public
sector; reduction of the Public Sector Borrowing Requirement (PSBR); weakening the power of trade unions in public sector wage bargaining; widening
share ownership; the encouragement of employee share ownership; and the
gaining of political advantages.[6]

The consequence of the changes resulting from privatization can usefully be
considered under a range of headings. First, the transfer of productive assets
from public to private sector means that the sale counts as negative public
expenditure and that the external financing of investment by the company is
no longer counted as part of the Public Sector Borrowing Requirement.

Second, the nature and form of regulation of the company changes. Previously the company, though publicly owned, was managed at 'arms length'
from the government but accountable to and subject to direction by government ministers. Nationalized public utilities were initially instructed to break
even, but forms of marginal cost pricing were introduced in the late 1960s;
these were later superseded by target rates of return (on assets).[7] As will be
indicated below, each of the privatized public utilities is subject to regulation

[3] See M. Chick, 'Nationalization, Privatization and Regulation' in M. W. Kirby and M. B. Rose
(eds.), *Business Enterprise in Modern Britain* (London: Routledge, 1994) for a review of the post-
war history of nationalization and privatization.

[4] For a discussion of the nationalizations in the 1970s see M. Sawyer, 'Industrial Policy' in M.
Artis and D. Cobham (eds.), *Labour's Economic Policies, 1974–1979* (Manchester: Manchester
University Press, 1991).

[5] For further discussion of privatization see, e.g., Symposium on Privatization and After, *FSt*, 5
(1984); J. Kay and A. Silberston, 'The New Industrial Policy—Privatisation and Competition',
MBR (Spring 1984), 8–16; J. Kay and D. Thompson, 'Privatisation: A Policy in Search of a
Rationale', *EJ*, 96 (1986), 18–32; J. Vickers and G. Yarrow, *Privatization: An Economic Analysis*
(Harvard, Mass.: MIT Press, 1988). For a more critical approach see B. Fine, 'Scaling the
Commanding Heights of Public Enterprise Economics', *CJE*, 14 (1990), 127–42.

[6] This listing is based on that given in Wright, *Privatization*, 63.

[7] Chap. 4 of the previous two editions of this book outlines the various ways by which
government in effect regulated the nationalized utilities.

by a newly created regulatory agency with controls over their pricing and other policies.

The third point, which is closely linked to the previous two, is that the privatized public utility would be expected to be run in the interests of its managers and shareholders (subject to the constraints imposed by the regulatory agency), with an emphasis on profits. The nationalized public utilities had a range of other considerations to take into account, including: the provision of employment stability, of social services (e.g. train services in rural areas), and concern with social factors (e.g. the impact of disconnections of water supply), many of which flowed from government policy and/or interventions.

Fourth, the privatized utility can in principle go out of business if it makes losses, though given the monopoly position enjoyed by most of them that would appear unlikely. There is a clear sense in which nationalized public utilities do not face the threat of bankruptcy or of take-over. However, the managers of nationalized public utilities face the threat of dismissal which may place similar pressures on them as the threat of take-over or bankruptcy would.

Fifth, the nationalized public utilities were (generally) statutory monopolies: that is other companies could not enter the industry to compete. There were minor exceptions to this (e.g. the telephone service in Hull was, and still is, provided by a company owned by the local authority and not by British Telecom or its predecessors). In the other direction, the public utilities were generally limited in the range of goods and services which they could provide, and were in the main prevented from operating overseas.[8] Whilst nationalized companies do not have to be statutory monopolies, some of the proponents of privatization argued that the introduction of competition would be less difficult in the context of privatized utilities.[9] Others have criticized the privatization programme for tending to transfer monopoly positions from the public to the private sector without significant change in the competitive environment.

Sixth, the salaries paid to the managers of the public utilities were set by the government and were often closely related to the pay scales of the civil service. The pay of the managing directors (or equivalent) of the public utilities was frequently significantly below the pay for comparable positions in the private sector. The salaries (more accurately the total remuneration package including performance-related pay and share options) for the managers in privatized public utilities are now set in a manner similar to any other private company. At the time of writing, these salaries are the subject of considerable political debate and, as will be seen below, these salaries have tended to increase substantially after privatization.

The scale of the privatization programme in terms of the receipts from sales is indicated in the first part of Table 9.2. It can be seen that in the early 1980s,

---

[8] The obvious exceptions being transport utilities such as British Airways.

[9] For example, M. Beesley and S. Littlechild, 'Privatization: Principles, Policies and Priorities', *LBR*, 149.

the receipts from privatization were relatively modest, but they rose in 1984/5, with the first part of the proceeds from the sale of British Telecom. From 1986/7 onwards the proceeds from privatization have been around £5 billion, and they are projected to remain at around that level for the next few years, though the figure will inevitably drop, as few nationalized industries remain which can be sold. Since the sale of assets is counted as negative public expenditure, these sales were useful for a government committed to the reduction of public expenditure and of the budget deficit. The scope of the privatization programme is also indicated in the second part of Table 9.2, which provides a list of the main asset sales. A further indication of the scale of privatization is that whilst public corporations employed over 2 million people in 1971 and 1867 thousand in 1981, the number fell to 1599 thousand in 1984 and 467 thousand in 1994.[10]

In the first phase of privatization, the companies which were privatized were mainly companies which had been in competition with private sector companies even when nationalized. Some of this privatization was the sale of assets which had been acquired by the National Enterprise Board under the preceding Labour government. In the second phase, the focus shifted to the sale of public utilities, beginning with British Telecom, continuing with British Gas, and then the electricity and water companies.

The issues raised by privatization of companies in competition with other companies already in the private sector are rather different than those raised by the sale of public utilities. The managers of a company operate under a variety of constraints, but two sets of constraints are generally emphasized by economic analysis. The first is that which derives from the nature of the market in which the firm operates. It is generally argued that the more competition the less discretion the managers have and the greater the pressure to strive for maximum profits. The second arises from the capital market and relates to take-overs. The argument is that if the current management fails to make the best use of the assets at their disposal, then the company is likely to become the target of a hostile take-over bid. Others will see that they can put the assets to more profitable use and launch a take-over bid. Suppose that on the basis of the existing management and the expected profits and dividends the stock market values firm A at V_a. Further, suppose that another company (or set of potential owners) believe that the value of firm A would be V_b, then they would be prepared to pay up to V_b for firm A. In order to be successful, a take-over bid has to offer a price substantially above the existing stock-market valuation; and premia of 20–30% are common. There are also significant costs associated with launching a take-over bid (e.g. the cost of advice from a merchant bank, or a press advertising campaign directed to shareholders of the target company).

It is arguable whether most take-overs are of the hostile form which this line of argument would indicate, and also whether the effect of take-overs is to raise the efficiency and profitability of the assets acquired (cf. references given in n. 11

[10] 'Employment in the Public and Private Sectors', *Economic Trends*, June 1995.

Table 9.2. Privatization in the United Kingdom

A. *Proceeds from the sale of public assets* (£bn)

Year	Current £m	Constant (1992) £m
1979/80	377	154.2
1980/81	210	101.4
1981/82	493	266.2
1982/83	455	267.1
1983/84	1139	698.2
1984/85	2050	1320.2
1985/86	2706	1848.2
1986/87	4458	3147.3
1987/88	5140	3783.0
1988/89	7069	5457.3
1989/90	4225	3515.2
1990/91	5347	4871.1
1991/92	7925	7639.7
1992/93	8184	8184.0
1993/94	5460	5547.4
1994/95[a]	6300	6552.0

B. Main Asset Sales by British Government 1979–1994

Sale of shares
  Amersham International
  Associated British Ports
  British Aerospace
  British Airports Authority
  British Airways
  British Gas
  British Steel
  British Telecom
  Britoil
  Cable and Wireless
  Enterprise Oil
  Jaguar Cars
  Electricity companies and Regional electricity boards
  Rolls-Royce
  Regional Water Companies (twelve in number)

Other Sales
  British Coal to RJB Mining and others
  Royal Ordnance and Rover Cars to British Aerospace
  Sealink sold to British Ferries
  National Freight sold to consortium of managers, employees, and
  company pensioners
  National Bus Company (sold as 72 separate companies)
  Girobank sold to Alliance and Leicester Building Society
  British Shipbuilders (warship yards)
  Sale of minority share holdings in British Sugar, British Petroleum, ICL, Ferranti, and British
  Technology Group
  Sale of property etc. of Crown Agents Holdings, Forestry Commission, New Town
  Development Corporation

[a] Estimated.
Source: Public Expenditure Analyses to 1994/95, Cmnd. 2821 (London: HMSO).

of Chapter 8). Initially, for a number of privatized firms the government retained a so-called golden share, which prevented a take-over (or at least one of which the government did not approve), but these so-called golden shares have now generally lapsed. The government argued that 'in certain cases, there is a clear need to protect a business from unwelcome take-over, for example, on national security grounds, or, as a temporary measure, to provide an opportunity to adjust to the private sector'.[11] The privatized public utilities are also large companies which may serve to reduce the possibility of them being taken over (since generally the acquiring firm is larger than the acquired firm). However, there have been significant take-overs of privatized companies. Amongst those which are not regulated Jaguar Cars has, for example, been acquired by Ford, and Rover Cars has been sold by British Aerospace to BMW. But of much more significance have been the take-over bids amongst the regulated companies. During 1995 there was a flurry of take-over bids for regulated companies, notably for the regional electricity companies and the water companies, and we return later to consider the significance of these take-overs for regulation policies.

The nature of the market in which a firm operates is generally seen to place constraints on what the firm can and cannot do. It is, of course, usually argued that a firm in a monopoly position has much more freedom of manœuvre than a firm in a situation of atomistic competition. Many firms which have been privatized, such as the Rover Group, Jaguar, National Freight Corporation etc., were operating in competition with many other firms even when nationalized. The act of privatization has not changed the nature of the market in which they operate.

The setting of the issue price of the shares in the firms which are to be privatized presents a dilemma.[12] The government wishes to secure proceeds from the sale which are as great as possible, but at the same time wishes to ensure that the sale is successful. The spread of share ownership amongst individuals has also been one of the aims of the Conservative government,[13] and this points

---

[11] The Treasury, *Privatisations in the United Kingdom: Background Briefings* (London: HM Treasury, 1990).

[12] In a number of cases (e.g. the sale of the Rover group to British Aerospace) shares were not offered to the public and the company was sold as a going concern to another company. In such cases, the considerations in the text do not apply.

[13] The proportion of shares owned directly by individuals has tended to decline throughout the post-war period, whilst ownership by financial institutions (mainly banks, unit trusts, pension funds, and insurance companies) has increased. This process has continued during the 1980s, with the proportion of shares held by individuals declining from 30.4% at the end of 1981 to 20.3% in 1993 (figures taken from CSO, *Share Register Survey Report* (London: HMSO 1991) and The 1993 Share Register Survey, *Economic Trends,* (Oct. 1993). In 1993 the beneficial owners of the privatized companies were central government 9.2% (compared with 1.4% in all companies), pension funds 27.6% (33.0% in all companies), insurance companies 12.4% (15.7%), unit trusts 4.5% (5.9%), individuals 24.5% (20.3%), overseas 8.3% (12.1%), and others 12.1% (9.6%). One effect of the privatization programme appears to have been to increase the number of shareholders; estimates vary from something of the.order of 5–7% of the adult population to around 20%. However, the impact here of privatization appears to be of shareholders with a small holding of shares in one or two companies.

in the direction of a lower price (to encourage sales). Indeed, the observation that the shares of privatized firms have traded immediately after privatization at levels above the issue price suggests that the issue price has been set too low. The privatized public utilities have been sold with their monopoly position largely intact. This would be expected to lead to higher profits and a higher market valuation as compared with the break-up of the public utilities into competing firms. Thus, striving for a higher price for the firm may well conflict with the aim of increased competition.

Vickers and Yarrow[14] estimated that where the sale was at a set price (rather than by tender offer) the gross proceeds to the government were £16 782 millions. The estimated under-valuation on these sales is £3517 millions (using the share price at the end of the first day of trading for these estimates), i.e. over 20% of the gross proceeds. Curwen and Holmes[15] list the gains in share prices on the day of privatization, which vary considerably but average out at 20%. Table 9.3 provides some further information on the movement in the share prices of a range of companies following privatization as compared with the corresponding movement in the overall share price index.

The evaluation of the impact of the UK privatization programme is not a straightforward exercise. The construction of a counter-factual case (that is, what would have happened otherwise) is problematic: for example, changes in the telecommunications industry owe something (but how much?) to technological change which may well have occurred whatever form of ownership there was in that industry. Some changes (notably the introduction of a degree of competition) may have accompanied privatization which would in principle

Table 9.3. Change in share prices following privatization

Company	Share price rise since flotation (as at 10 June 1993) (%)	FTSE100 since flotation (%)
British Telecom	216	142
British Gas	116	77
British Airport Authority	202	23
National Power	105	16
PowerGen	115	16
Scottish Power	32	13
Scottish Hydro-Power	43	13
Anglian Water	91	22
North West Water	85	22
South West Water	100	22
Thames Water	93	22
Yorkshire Water	100	22
Northumbrian Water	135	22

Source: Financial Times, 14 June 1993.

[14] Vickers and Yarrow, *Privatisation*, 173–80; Table 7.1. (covering sales up to the end of 1987).
[15] P. Curwen and D. Holmes, 'Returns to Small Shareholders from Privatization', *NWBQR*, (Feb. 1992).

have been possible but, some would argue, were in practice unlikely, with a publicly owned firm in place. Further, what would be the relevant indicators of performance? Profitability (e.g. rate of return on assets) and prices (relative to costs) are measures which would often be used as performance indicators. However, prices (and thereby profits) have been regulated (in the public utilities) subsequent to privatization, as discussed below, and were subject to controls under nationalization, and prices were often constrained to aid other economic policy objectives (notably the reduction in the rate of inflation). Hence, performance in terms of profits and prices would reflect the impacts of regulation and controls.

The growth in the productivity of public enterprises had compared favourably with that in manufacturing prior to privatization as illustrated by the figures in Table 9.4. There has been a substantial decline in the employment provided in privatized utilities. This decline continues the trend prior to privatization for, as can be seen from Table 9.4, employment in public enterprises declined continuously prior to 1985.

The remuneration paid to the managers of the privatized utilities became a matter of considerable political controversy in the mid-1990s. Some information on salaries (which relates to a date before the issue became a matter of political debate) is given in Table 9.5. However, it was the income and capital gains accruing from share option schemes which added particularly to the total income of these managers. This was evident from the gains of directors arising from the higher share price coming from a take-over bid: for example three directors in Northumbrian Water 'are set to gain more than £1 million from share options after the £11.79 a share offer from Lyonnaise' (*Guardian*, 24 Nov. 1995).

Table 9.4. Comparative performance of UK public enterprises and manufacturing sector

	Average annual growth rates (%)		
	1951–64	1964–73	1973–85
Public enterprises			
Labour	−0.6	−2.3	−1.2
Labour productivity	3.3	5.0	2.1
Capital	2.3	2.8	0.7
Capital productivity	0.4	0.1	0.2
Total factor productivity	2.4	2.9	1.4
Manufacturing			
Labour	0.7	−1.1	−3.1
Labour productivity	2.5	4.0	2.3
Capital	4.0	3.6	1.4
Capital productivity	−0.8	−0.7	−2.2
Total factor productivity	1.9	2.4	1.1

Source: R. Millward, 'The Nationalized Industries' in M. Artis and D. Cobham (eds.), *Labour's Economic Policies 1974–79* (Manchester: Manchester University Press, 1991).

Table 9.5. Changes in salaries of directors following privatization

Company	Increase in directors' salaries after privatization (%)	
Amersham International	329	(3)
Associated British Ports	67	(2)
British Aerospace	181	(5)
BP	101	(5)
British Telecom	136	(3)
Britoil	36	(2)
Cable and Wireless	352	(3)
Enterprise Oil	215	(2)
National Freight Consortium	93	(2)
British Airways	242	(2)
British Gas	68	(2)

Note: The number in parenthesis indicates the number of years over which the reported change in salary occured. For comparison, the average increase in earnings in the first half of the 1980s was 7.5% p.a.

Source: T. Clarke, The 'Political Economy of the UK Privatization Programme' in T. Clarke and C. Pitelis (eds.), *The Political Economy of Privatization*, (London: Routledge, 1993).

9.3. Ownership and Efficiency

We turn now to the empirical question of whether ownership and control makes any difference to the efficiency of a firm. Making comparisons between the performance and efficiency of private and public sector companies is not a straightforward exercise. There are some general difficulties in making useful comparisons between companies which are in different situations (here of private or public ownership). There may be reasons why the firms are in different situations and those reasons can influence the comparisons. For example, a company may be in the public sector because it failed under private ownership but was judged to be too important to be allowed to go bankrupt. In such a case, a poor performance by a company under public ownership may not be due to the fact that it is in the public sector; rather, it is in the public sector because it is a poor performance company. Comparisons between public sector companies and private sector ones are also complicated by differences in the objectives of the two types of companies. Public sector companies may be required to maintain unprofitable services, be encouraged to maintain employment (particularly in periods of substantial unemployment), and be limited in their range of activities (e.g. British Rail is largely restricted to operating a railway service and is not permitted to diversify into other forms of transport).

Millward and Parker[16] conducted a wide-ranging survey on the available

---

[16] R. Millward and D. M. Parker, 'Public and Private Enterprise: Comparative Behaviour and Relative Efficiency' in R. Millward *et al.*, *Public Sector Economics* (London: Longman, 1983).

evidence and indicate the extensive difficulties in making comparisons between privately owned and publicly owned firms. They conclude that

while the results are rather mixed, there is some evidence that competition does reduce the costs of public firms and regulation raises the costs of private firms. Neither finding is inconsistent with the finding about the effects of ownership on costs namely that there is no general indication that private firms are more cost efficient than public firms.

Ferguson[17] summarized fifteen comparisons of public and private sector efficiency. Eight of these refer to American electricity generation, with the following conclusions. Two studies report no difference between the sectors, three report the public enterprise as more efficient, and one reports private firms as more efficient. One study finds both types of firm with costs $2\frac{1}{2}$% above the competitive level, and the final study reports that private firms sell wholesale electricity at higher prices and buy in at lower prices (than public sector firms). The results of the other seven studies (covering water, rail, and airlines) are similar in tone.

Yarrow[18] concludes that

private sector monitoring [i.e. private ownership] is more efficient where the relevant firm faces strong competition and other forms of product and factor market failure are relatively unimportant. The evidence on comparative performance in cases where product and factor market inefficiencies are substantive is much less clear cut. Indeed, in examples such as electricity supply it tends to point in the other direction, towards better performance by public firms.[19]

9.4. Theory of Regulation

The general analysis of regulation by government (and its agencies) in a market economy arises from the 'market failure' approach.[20] The general ideas on market failure have been discussed in the previous chapter (Section 8.8), and this theme is developed further in this section. The perfectly competitive market model assumes perfect information on the part of both consumers and producers. It is acknowledged that perfect information is something which few of us have, but the question is how significant imperfect information is. It

[17] P. Ferguson, *Industrial Economics: Issues and Perspectives* (London: Macmillan, 1988).

[18] G. Yarrow, 'Privatization in Theory and Practice', *EP* (1986), 324–77.

[19] See also J. Vickers and G. Yarrow, 'Economic Perspectives on Privatization', *Journal of Economic Perspectives*, 5 (1991), 111–32.

[20] For extensive discussion see M. Waterson, *Regulation of the Firm and Natural Monopoly* (Oxford: Blackwell, 1988) and M. Waterson, 'Allocative Inefficiency and Monopoly as a Basis for Regulation' in R. Sugden (ed.), *Industrial Economic Regulation* (London: Routledge). See also D. Helm, 'British Utility Regulation: Theory, Practice and Reform', *Oxford Review of Economic Policy*, 10/3 (1993), 17–39.

can be argued that whilst a consumer may begin in some ignorance of the properties of a particular product, the purchase and consumption of that product will provide the necessary information. An initial purchase of a product may turn out to be a mistake (e.g. the product may be of poorer quality than envisaged), but it is not a mistake which would be repeated. Regulation may be warranted where 'ignorance is not bliss'. To take an extreme example, it would be rather difficult for a consumer to learn through purchase and consumption that an item of food is poisonous. More generally, where the purchase of an item may harm the (relatively ignorant) consumer, regulation of the quality of the product may be indicated. Further, there is generally what is called asymmetric information, that is the information held by one party to the transaction is different from and perhaps superior to that held by the other party. When I take my car to be serviced, the information and knowledge which the garage has is much greater than mine, especially when they have the engine stripped down. When the garage tells me that there is a major fault in the engine, I have little choice but to accept their word. Policies on consumer protection are further discussed below.

One aspect of market failure concerns situations of natural monopoly, that is where there are extensive economies of scale which permit the survival of one firm.[21] The economies of scale (hence declining average costs) mean that marginal costs are below average costs. The economies of scale refer to the long run when all factors are variable, hence the costs refer to long-run costs. But it is often the case that natural monopoly positions involve low short-run marginal costs (e.g. the marginal cost of an additional phone call when there is excess capacity on the phone network). The market failure approach might suggest that regulation should seek to mimic the perfectly competitive market, that is to generate prices in line with marginal costs (whereas the profit-maximizing monopolist would price at marginal cost times $(e/e-1)$, where e is the elasticity of demand as discussed in Section 8.4 above). However, such regulation would run into (at least) three problems. First, marginal cost pricing would involve the regulated firm in losses, since marginal cost is below average cost. Second, how are prices of different services to be priced when the costs of the different services are interlinked? For example, the provision of rail services during peak hours and their provision during off-peak hours may differ in cost (hence justifying differences in prices) but the rolling stock and the rail track are required for both services. Third, the concept of marginal cost is not unambiguous; the simplest example of this is that the length of time over which output can be varied will influence the size of marginal costs.

---

[21] However, there may be many situations of natural monopoly where regulation would be seen as not worthwhile. For example, there are probably declining unit costs in the door-to-door delivery of newspapers or milk, in the sense that the unit costs of one firm supplying all the houses in one street would be lower than the unit costs of two firms. But a duopoly may survive once established if neither of the firms is able to undercut the rival and force them out of business to establish a monopoly for themselves. Further, since there are alternative supplies of newspapers or milk, the natural monopoly may provide little market power to the firm involved.

The argument has been made, particularly by American critics of regulation, that there will be a degree of 'agency capture' by the utility (its owners and managers) of the regulatory agency.[22] The general thrust of this argument is that the regulatory agency will come to reflect the interests of the producers (public utility) rather than the consumers. The number of producers is very small (often one firm) whereas there are numerous consumers. The effects of regulation are likely to be negative as far as the producer is concerned (e.g. profits may be restricted) but concentrated on the few (perhaps one) firm involved. In contrast, the effects for the consumers are likely to be positive but spread over millions of consumers, so that the benefits for any individual consumer are relatively small even if the aggregate benefit is substantial. Thus, the producer has a strong incentive to seek favourable treatment by the regulatory agency. An individual consumer is unlikely to find it worthwhile to lobby the regulatory agency, since lobbying involves costs whereas the (incremental) benefits to the individual are likely to be small.

The personal contact and interchange of personnel between the regulatory agency and the regulated firm can lead the agency to act in the interests of the firm it is formally charged to regulate. The numbers employed by the regulatory agency may be small relative to the numbers employed by the company being regulated and the latter may be able to engulf the former with (perhaps irrelevant) information.

9.5. Modes of Regulation

The rationale for the regulation of 'natural monopolies' arises from their monopoly power, and hence focuses on control of their prices and/or profits. The direct route would appear to be to impose controls on the level or rate of profits, and indeed that has been the mode of regulation generally used with public utilities in the United States under the heading of rate of return regulation (hereafter ROR). In effect, public utilities are there constrained to a maximum rate of return on assets. This mode of regulation was rejected as a model for the UK as it was seen to have some undesirable effects.[23] The basis of the argument was that a constraint on the rate of return provided the managers of public utilities with the wrong incentives. Consider what could happen when a company in a position with the potential to gain a high rate of return is constrained to report a lower rate of return (and that indeed would be the

[22] See, for example, G. Stigler, 'The Theory of Economic Regulation', *The Bell Journal of Economics and Management Science*, 2 (1971); for a critique of that approach see J. Tomlinson, 'Is Successful Regulation Possible: Some Theoretical Issues' in R. Sugden (ed.), *Industrial Economic Regulation*.

[23] See, for example, S. Littlechild, 'Regulation of British Telecom's Profitability', Report to the Secretary of State, Department of Industry (London: HMSO, 1983) and Helm, 'British Utility Regulation'.

purpose of ROR regulation). Such a firm would have incentives to inflate costs (thereby reducing profits) and to increase the size of the assets (thereby allowing more profits in total to be earned from a larger asset base) in order for the reported rate of profit to be brought down to that required by the regulator. The inflation of costs can arise from, *inter alia*, paying higher wages and salaries (including those of the managers themselves) and allowing productive inefficiencies to grow.

The justification for ROR (rate of return) regulation is couched largely in terms of allocative efficiency but its implementation may induce other inefficiencies. For example, it may encourage accounting practices that overstate capital valuations and thus mislead investors. Another drawback is that it requires substantial information about costs and demand to be made available to the regulator. This could induce bureaucratic inefficiencies and may lead to revelation problems. An issue that arises under ROR regulation is rate base selection, what is an appropriate choice for s (the rate of return constraint)? For these and other reasons there has been a shift towards less informationally demanding regulation through what is termed price cap regulatory mechanisms.[24]

The approach to utility regulation in Britain has been described as drawing on three principles: 'the rejection of rate-of-return regulation; the rejection of direct government control; and the rejection of the assumption of monopoly as a permanent feature'.[25] The second principle led to the appointment of regulators who, subject to general specified duties, operate independently of government. The third principle is discussed further below. The first principle led to a general mode of regulation (the precise application of which varies between industries as will be seen below) generally described as RPI$-x$ where RPI refers to the general rate of inflation and x is a figure fixed by the relevant regulatory authority, presumably designed to reflect the productivity potential of the industry concerned relative to that of the wider economy. For example, productivity growth potential is generally viewed as high in the telecommunications industry through the implementation of new technologies, and currently x is set at 7.5% with the view that productivity growth in the telecommunications industry can be at least 7.5% faster than the average elsewhere in the economy.

The RPI$-x$ rule was advocated in the Littlechild Report[26] written by Professor Stephen Littlechild, later Director General of the Office of Electricity Regulation (OFFER), where it was claimed that price-capping regulation (PC) 'dominated ROR regulation in terms of restraining monopoly power, promoting competition, reducing X-inefficiency and by providing incentives for cost reductions'.[27] The term 'X-inefficiency' can be read as technical inefficiency, though it could also include payments to factors of production (notably managers and workers) higher than necessary.

---

[24] C. Doyle, 'Regulating Firms with Monopoly Power' in Sugden, *Industrial Economic Regulation*.   [25] Helm, 'British Utility Regulation'.
[26] Littlechild, 'Regulation of British Telecom'.   [27] Doyle, 'Regulating Firms'.

This approach also suffers from some difficulties. There is a ratchet effect in operation whereby the achieved productivity growth in one period feeds into the target productivity growth for the next period. Information on productivity growth potential is difficult (or perhaps impossible) to acquire, though past performance and that achieved in other countries may provide some guide. If the regulator underestimates the productivity growth potential, then there can be a profit bonanza for the public utility concerned. But if that underestimated potential is achieved (wholly or partly) then the public utility may suffer in subsequent periods through the value of x in the formula being raised, and hence providing some incentive for the public utility to not fully achieve its potential. There is no explicit consideration of quality, and there would be some incentive for the regulated firm to lower quality which would reduce its costs, though it may be able to obtain the same (capped) price for the product. This has led (as discussed further below) to the use of other mechanisms to check on quality, such as levels of services agreements.

The regulatory agency sets rules under which the regulated firm operates, and monitors the degree to which the rules are observed. The relationship between the regulator and the regulated has aspects akin to the principal–agent problem, where one person (or group of people)—the principal—contracts another person (or group of people)—the agent—to undertake a range of activities on their behalf. The principal–agent problem arises since the principal lacks complete information on the possibilities facing the agent, and cannot fully monitor the activities of the agent. In these circumstances, the contract under which the principal employs the agent may easily prove to offer the agent incentives to behave in ways which the principal did not intend and may induce the agent to withhold information. In the context of regulation, this can be illustrated by the rate of return regulation, which may provide incentives for the regulated firm to be 'over'-capitalized.

Helm[28] indicates that shareholders in public utilities have done rather well with 'the returns to shareholders greatly exceed[ing] the cost of capital, and exceed[ing] those in other countries' utility sectors. Shareholders have, in particular, done much better than under rate-of-return regulation'. He also argues that 'there is little positive evidence to suggest outside the telecommunications sector that British utility consumers have fared better than those in other comparator countries [where often utilities have remained nationalized]'.

9.6. Regulation of Public Utilities

When public utilities have been privatized with their monopoly position largely intact, then their activities have been subject to a degree of regula-

---

[28] Helm, 'British Utility Regulation', 29–30.

tion. The major regulatory agencies and their acronyms are Office of Tele-communication (OFTEL), Office of Water Services (OFWAT), Office of Electricity Regulation (OFFER), and Office of Gas Supply (OFGAS).

The Monopolies and Mergers Commission (MMC) can also be involved in regulation, in effect since the regulated companies are generally operating as monopolies. The determination of prices by the regulatory bodies can be subject to appeal to the MMC. The MMC may also investigate a particular monopoly situation, and, as in the case of TransCo (the transportation and storage business arm of British Gas) recommend that the business be subject to price regulation.

For the water industry, (covering England and Wales only), the general formula for the price-cap is described as *RPI* + *K* (in contrast with the *RPI* − *x* rule elsewhere with prices generally falling in real terms). But the formula has been described as RPI − *x* + *q*, where the additional *q* reflects improvements in quality standards. 'In setting price caps the Director General will need to take a view about the appropriate cost of capital for new investment and the return on existing capital'.[29] Initially, in 1989, the cost of capital was set in pre-tax real terms in the range of 7% (for the water and sewerage companies) to 8.5% (for the seven smallest water companies). This was subsequently lowered in 1991 to the range of 5 to 6% in real terms (after business taxes). The translation of the permitted return on existing capital into prices requires not only knowledge of the permitted rate of return but also of the value of the existing capital stock. The valuation of existing capital stock is fraught with difficulties. It could be valued in terms of the historic costs of acquiring the capital stock, but clearly prices paid for capital stock perhaps many years ago are not relevant to current value. Those assets will have depreciated with use and the passage of time: some assets may have turned out to have been poor decisions (and so their value to the company currently is low) or to have been very good decisions (and the value to the company correspondingly high). An alternative valuation of assets is a forward-looking one in terms of the discounted value of the profits which they are expected to earn for the company. There is the obvious problem for the regulator in that the controls of prices and profits which are imposed would themselves influence the value of the assets. A third and related method of valuation would be the share value of the company. This has been adopted for the water industry. The 'Director General [for Water] is minded to adopt, for the water and sewerage companies, the market value based on the share prices averaged over the first 200 days trading as offering the most reasonable measure of initial share value to be remunerated.'[30]

In 1995/6 the *K* element varies from 0.5% to 4.0% for water and sewerage companies, and between −4.1% and 2.5% for water only companies. OFWAT

---

[29]   *Annual Report of OFWAT* (London: HMSO, 1993) 47.

[30]   The share price is likely to reflect market expectations on future profits: thus if the expectations had been for the permitted profits in the water companies to be high, the share price would be relatively high, permitting (with a given rate of return) relatively high profits. Data from *Annual Report of OFWAT* (London: HMSO, 1993), 47.

undertook a periodic review in 1994 which led to the announcement of new price limits for the following decade for the 31 companies in England and Wales. Two companies asked for their price limits to be referred to the MMC for re-determination. 'OFWAT explained its approach [to setting prices] with as much clarity and openness as reasonable. The process of setting prices, however, cannot be mechanistic; the Director General had to have scope to reach his own informed judgements.'[31] The cost of the review was estimated at £6 million. OFWAT claims that the average price limit for the five years 1995–2000 was RPI plus 1.4 based on the new K factors, which was 2.3 percentage points below the average K initially set for this period, and 4.8 percentage points below the average set out in the companies' market plans.

In 1994 OFGAS modified the tariff price formula for the gas industry from RPI−5 to RPI−4: this followed an MMC report[32] which argued that the previous RPI−5 tariff formula (introduced in April 1992) was not in the public interest, 'in that it might be detrimental to the supply of capital to the industry, particularly new investment'.[33] Further, the tariff formula was limited to the supply of gas to those with an annual usage of below 2,500 therms.

The price formula for the telecommunications industry (British Telecom) is of the RPI−x form, where x has been changed from the original 3% at the time of privatization in 1984 until 1988, 4.5% in 1989–91, 6.25% in 1991–3 and 7.5% since August 1993 (to be in place until at least July 1997). This constraint applies to a weighted average of prices charged by BT : within that average, reductions in prices have been concentrated on national peak rate and international calls, and charges for line rentals have increased substantially.[34]

OFFER regulates the prices of the electricity supply industry including the transmission business of the National Grid Company (NGC) and the supply and distribution businesses of the Regional Electricity Companies (RECs) as well as the corresponding businesses of the Scottish electricity companies. 'The original price controls for the RECs permitted their distribution charges to rise at between 0 and 2.5% a year above the rate of inflation'.[35] Changes were proposed in 1994 to include a reduction of between 11 and 17% in real terms in distribution charges from 1 April 1995, followed by real reductions of 2% in each of the following four years. These proposals were thrown into some disarray by information which was revealed during a take-over bid by Trafalgar House for Northern Electric, whose second defence document 'said that the company would make payments of over £5 per share to its shareholders, in part financed by a substantial increase in gearing.' The statement also commented on future operating costs and capital expenditure[36] which supported

---

[31] *Annual Report of OFWAT*, (London: HMSO,1994), 56.

[32] MMC, *Gas – Fair Trading Act 1973*, Cmnd. 2314 (London: HMSO, 1993).

[33] *Annual report of OFGAS*, (London: HMSO, 1994).

[34] Details are given in *Annual Report of Director General of OFTEL* (London: HMSO, 1994), Table 2.   [35] *Annual Report of OFFER* (London: HMSO, 1994).

[36] Ibid. 10.

the views of many commentators that the initial proposals were not severe enough, and that more substantial price reductions were warranted on the basis of cost reductions. The initial proposals were implemented but further tightening of price controls was announced in June/July 1995.[37]

The significance of this episode is twofold. First, it indicates how the initial incorrect setting of x in the RPI $- x$ formula leads over a few years to either massive profits or losses (depending on whether x is too low or too high). Second, it illustrates the difficulties which the regulator may have in securing adequate information on costs (and the potential for reducing costs). In this case, further relevant information became available as a side-effect of a take-over bid after the regulator had set prices.

In 1994 proposals were also made to change the price controls on the distribution businesses of the two Scottish companies: RPI $- 2$ for Scottish Power and RPI $- 1$ for Hydro-Electric and for the supply of RPI $- 2$ in both cases. Whilst ScottishPower accepted the proposals, Hydro-Electric did not and the matter was subject of a reference to the MMC, whose report made proposals which would result in annual price reductions of 2.9% over four years for Scottish Power.[38]

Whilst much attention focuses on the regulation of prices, there are a range of other regulatory functions performed by the various regulatory offices. OFTEL has required British Telecom to produce six-monthly reports on quality of services and some other regulatory bodies produce league tables of dimensions of quality (e.g. speed of response to customer complaints). British Telecom is required to provide a minimum level and coverage of public telephone kiosks even when this would not be profitable for them to do (e.g. in some remote rural areas).

One difficulty for the regulatory authority is that of securing the relevant information. This is illustrated by the following quotation from the Director General of Gas Supply.[39]

Condition 3 of the authorisation stipulates that, at the time of any change in its published tariffs, British Gas must provide OFGAS with a written forecast of the maximum average price per therm, together with its components, for the year in which the change is to take effect and the following year. These forecasts should contain sufficient information as to the assumptions underlying the forecasts to enable the Director General to be reasonably satisfied that the forecasts have been properly prepared on a consistent basis. Initially British Gas refused to provide sufficient information for the Director General to be so satisfied. This resulted in OFGAS giving

[37] The announcement of the further tightening of prices was also surrounded by controversy when information on the new proposals leaked out (after being supplied to the RECs on a confidential basis 24 hours before the formal announcement). This led to a substantial rise in the share prices of the RECs as again the announced price controls were less severe than had been anticipated.

[38] MMC, *Scottish Hydro-electric PLC; Report to the Director General of Electricity Supply,* (London: HMSO, 1995).

[39] Quote from the *Report of the Director General of Gas Supply 1987*, HC 293 (London: HMSO, 1988).

notice in August that it proposed to make an order under section 28 of the Gas Act requiring [British Gas] to produce the necessary information.

Eventually, information was provided and undertakings were given that information would be provided in future.

There is an issue concerning the control of the possible use of monopoly power in areas other than those covered immediately above. This has largely related so far to the prices charged for the supply of gas or telephone services other than those subject to regulatory control. British Gas was referred to the MMC over the pricing and supply of gas to contract customers (broadly speaking non-domestic customers). The MMC concluded that

[w]e have found extensive discrimination by BG in the pricing and supply of gas to contract customers. We believe that this is attributable to the existence of the monopoly situation and operates or may be expected to operate against the public interest. First, BG's policy of price discrimination imposes higher costs on customers less well placed to use alternative fuels or to obtain such fuels on favourable terms. Second, BG's policy of relating prices to those of alternatives available to each customer places it in a position selectively to undercut potential competing gas suppliers. This may be expected to deter new entrants and to inhibit the development of competition in this market. Third, the lack of transparency in pricing creates uncertainty in the minds of customers about future gas prices and renders more risky the business environment in which they operate.[40]

The difficulties which confront the regulatory agency include obtaining the information necessary to perform their function (as indicated above). This may be exacerbated by the relatively small number of staff which they have: 215 in the case of OFFER (concerned with the regulation of electricity generation as well as distribution) and around 150 in the case of OFTEL. A problem which has been identified from American experience is that of agency capture. This simply means that the personal contacts and interchange of personnel between the regulatory agency and the regulated firm as well as deliberate attempts by the regulated firm can lead the agency to act in the interests of the firm it is formally charged to regulate.

The take-over of a regulated public utility raises issues for the regulators. One difficulty is that following a take-over the regulated utility becomes part of a larger company and the calculation of costs and revenues which arise specifically from the public utility becomes more difficult. For example, the merger between North West Water and Norweb (regional electricity company) to form United Utilities may lead to shared overheads in the area of meter readings (and more generally), with the consequent difficulty of allocating costs between the two sets of activities (in this case both are regulated albeit under rather different rules). A further aspect is that the price which the acquiring company was prepared to pay for the acquired utility would generally be much in excess of the previous price, suggesting the potential for

---

[40] Monopolies and Mergers Commission, *Gas*, Cmnd. 500 (London: HMSO, 1988).

increased profits post-acquisition. Finally, some of the proposed acquisitions would in effect undo the vertical separation (see next paragraph) which the government had imposed on privatization of the electricity industry. The bids of PowerGen for Midlands Electricity and National Power for Southern Electricity represented electricity production companies seeking to acquire regional electricity distribution companies. At the time of writing these bids have been referred to the Monopolies and Mergers Commission.

The rationale for regulation is the absence of competition, both actual and potential. There are two features of privatization and the subsequent regulation which are relevant here. The first is that in some public utilities the industry has not been privatized as a single unit but rather has been vertically disintegrated. The two clearest examples of this would be the separation of the electricity industry into the National Grid, electricity production (Power Gen and National Power, plus Nuclear Electric) and distribution (twelve regional electricity companies), and the proposed privatization of the railways into RailTrack (responsible for the track) and regional train companies. The significance of this vertical disintegration is that whilst some parts of the industry are subject to decreasing costs (e.g. the national distribution of electricity), others may not be (e.g. the economies of scale in electricity generation are exhausted at a level of output which is a small proportion of total demand). Thus a natural monopoly may remain in some parts but not in others.

The second aspect has been the introduction of competition into many of the regulated industries under the scrutiny of the regulator. Of the privatized utilities, it is only the water industry where there has not been some entry of new competitors, although to date in the other industries the extent of new entry has been relatively small. The promoters of privatization often regarded regulation as a temporary measure until the dominant monopoly position of the privatized utilities could be undermined by new entrants. In telecommunications, the monopoly of BT moved to a duopoly with the permitted entry of Mercury, where the duopoly was expected to last for seven years with deregulation to follow: but the regulation has continued, with BT retaining a dominant position in the telecommunications market. In the case of gas, the target was set for British Gas to create the conditions under which other suppliers should be able to supply at least 45% of sales to all users of 2500 therms and above by the end of 1995. The intention is for the introduction of competition in the supply of electricity for all customers in 1998. There has been some entry into the electricity generation market, and this accounted for around 7% of total output in England and Wales in 1994. However, the Director-General of OFFER was seeking to create further competition in electricity generation through 'the disposal of existing coal- or oil-fired plant to parties independent of the two major generators [which] is essential for the creation of a more competitive generation market'.[41]

---

[41] *Annual Report of OFFER* (1994), 6.

Competition has been constrained in other directions: for example, BT is prohibited at present from developing into the entertainments market.

9.7. Regulation of Transport

Transport has long been subject to regulation: for example, The Road Traffic Act 1930 brought in the regulation of bus services. Quality was regulated, by, for example, the setting of standards for vehicles and for drivers and this continues. The quantity of bus services was also regulated with licences required to be able to operate a particular route. These restrictions were lifted for inter-city bus services in 1980 and for most other bus services in 1986. The remaining element of regulation is that new service operators need to register with the Traffic Commissioner, giving 42 days notice of their intention to set up a service.

One study on the deregulation of the inter-city services[42] found that prices of express bus services initially fell dramatically with many prices dropping to half their previous level. Prior to 1980 the right to operate many of the most important inter-city routes was held by the publicly owned National Bus Company. Those companies which had previously provided contract coach services provided a ready source of new entrants, helping to generate the substantial price fall. However, the National Bus Company was able to reassert its dominant position in a few years. Prices have since risen, and in many cases prices of express services have returned to close to their level (in real terms, that is relative to the retail price index) prior to deregulation. This study found that there were some gains in efficiency following deregulation.

The government argued that for local bus services, deregulation would bring about reductions in unit costs of up to 30% and viewed the market as 'highly contestable' (see Section 8.8 in the previous chapter).[43] Several changes took place simultaneously including deregulation, compulsory competitive tendering of subsidized services, privatization, and subsidy reduction.[44] Unit costs do appear to have fallen,[45] with some effect coming from falling fuel costs and from extending vehicle life but most from a combination of productivity gains and lower wages. A number of studies[46] have concluded that the bus market is not approaching being perfectly contestable and that issues of monopoly remain. The MMC argued that 'when deregulating the bus market, while the

---

[42] S. A. Jaffer and D. J. Thompson 'Deregulating Express Coaches: A Reassessment', *FSt*, 8 (1986), 45–68.

[43] Department of Transport, *Buses*, Cmnd. 9300, (London: HMSO, 1984).

[44] The special issue of *Journal of Transport Economics and Policy*, 24 (1990) on bus deregulation contains detailed analysis of the various effects.

[45] P. M. Heseltine and D. T. Silcock, 'The Effects of Bus Deregulation on Costs', *Journal of Transport Economics and Policy*, vol. 24, (1990), 239–54.

[46] For a summary see A. Evans, 'Competition and the Structure of Local Bus Markets', *Journal of Transport Economics and Policy*, 24 (1990), 255–81.

Government did not expect direct competition on all routes, it took the view that, because barriers to entry in the bus market were low, all routes would be contestable'.[47] The MMC identified three potential barriers to entry: namely, restricted access to facilities including bus stations, sunk costs which cannot be recovered on exit, and prepaid tickets, though they thought that none of these would be of general significance. However 'local bus markets have remained highly monopolised after deregulation. Active competition is relatively rare, and is probably now well past its peak.'[48] 'We find evidence of competition where small bus operators are involved but little between large operators.'[49] There has been a high rate of take-over activity amongst bus companies. The Monopolies and Mergers Commission[50] report that the market share (by turnover) of the nine major bus companies rose from 12.8% in 1989 to 56.0% in 1994 (and during this period the share of publicly owned companies declined from 30.4% to 7.5% as privatization continued).

Whilst unit costs fell, there was also a decline in bus usage; where there was competition average waiting times fell but uncertainty over timetables increased, as did the lack of co-ordination of the arrival of buses. One study[51] which sought to bring together the various effects concluded that competitive tendering (which operated in London) worked better than deregulation, and there were net gains from the changes in London and metropolitan areas but net losses in the shire counties and in Scotland. Calculations by the MMC for the period 1985/6 to 1995 suggest a 42% decline in real operating costs (that is in costs relative to the retail price index) and with a rise of 24% in vehicle miles run. However, fares have risen by 17% in real terms, with a 27% decline in passenger numbers. The earnings of bus and coach drivers fell by 12% in real terms.

Overall, the picture regarding the impact of deregulation is a mixed one. It is difficult to draw any firm conclusions because of the difficulty in assessing what would have happened if the industry had not been deregulated, and of separating out the impact of the reduction in subsidy which accompanied deregulation.[52]

9.8. Regulation and Consumer Protection

Some other limitations on the activities of firms come from legislation relating to consumer protection, much of which is enforced by the DGFT and by Trading Standards Officers. The DGFT has a duty to collect and assess

---

[47] Monopolies and Mergers Commission, *The Supply of Bus Services in the North-East of England*, Cmnd. 2933, (London: HMSO, 1995).

[48] A. Evans, 'Competition and Structure'.

[49] Monopolies and Mergers Commission, *Supply of Bus Services*.

[50] Monopolies and Mergers Commission, *Supply of Bus Services*.

[51] P. R. White, 'Bus Deregulation: A Welfare Balance Sheet', *Journal of Transport Economics and Policy*, 24 (1990), 311–32.

[52] Monopolies and Mergers Commission, *Supply of Bus Services*.

information on commercial activities, so that trading practices which may affect consumers interests may be discovered. The DGFT has sought to draw up codes of practice in a range of industries (covering, for example, direct selling, double glazing, the motor trade, and credit) and can set in motion procedures which can lead to the banning of specified trade practices. Under the Fair Trading Act 1973, the DGFT can seek assurances on future good conduct when traders persistently disregard their obligations under the law in a manner detrimental to consumers, and if such assurances are not given, or are given and then broken, the DGFT can bring proceedings to obtain a court order (breach of which may result in action for contempt of court). The DGFT has powers to refuse, grant, or suspend licence applications in particular areas of business and trade.

Another area of regulation and consumer protection which is overseen by the Office of Fair Trading is credit licensing. In 1994, 177 notices were served by the OFT on applicants and licensees about their fitness to be granted or to retain a licence to conduct credit business. This aspect as well as the regulation of financial markets in general has already been discussed in Chapter 6. Under the Control of Misleading Advertisements Regulations 1988, the Office of Fair Trading can take action (including court orders) to limit such advertisements.

9.9. Regulation and the Environment

A major rationale for some form of environment regulation arises from market failure in the form of substantial divergences between private costs and social costs and between private benefits and social benefits. Specifically, use of the environment (e.g. the release of pollutants into the atmosphere) may have low or zero private cost whereas there will often be substantial social costs. The costs may be particularly difficult to calculate: either because the scientific (and other) knowledge on the effects of pollutants on, say, the atmosphere is not fully established and/or because putting a price on the damage caused is particularly difficult. Taking an example from a few years ago, it took considerable time before the effects of chlorofluorocarbons (CFCs), widely used in aerosols, refrigeration, and air-conditioning, on the ozone in the stratosphere were discovered.

Regulation of activities which may affect the environment can take a variety of forms. The idea that there is a divergence between private costs and social costs would suggest the levying of a tax which bridges the difference between the two types of costs. The firm or person undertaking the activity would face the social costs of their actions. In a similar vein, a subsidy may be used to bridge the difference between private benefits and social benefits. In this section the main concern will be with those activities which are detrimental to the environment where social costs exceed private costs. Many economists would also seek an optimal level of pollution, where the marginal costs of abatement of pollution equal the marginal benefits of pollution reduction, and which would recognize that some level of pollution may be too expensive to eliminate. However,

neither the marginal costs nor the marginal benefits are typically known: they have to be estimated. The absence of appropriate estimation from virtually all UK environmental regulation is, therefore, surprising. The setting of targets [for reduction of pollutants] is regarded largely a technical matter: economic costs and benefits are, at best, a constraint.[53]

These targets include the reduction of carbon dioxide and other greenhouse gas emissions to 1990 levels by the year 2000, the reduction of sulphur dioxide emissions by 80% on 1980 levels by 2010, and raising standards of drinking water.[54]

The alternative mechanisms for the control of pollution and environmental protection can be usefully divided into two categories. The first is the use of administrative controls and quantity constraints: for example, a limit on the exhaust emissions from cars. The second is the use of the price mechanism, in which some charge is effectively made for the polluting (e.g. a carbon tax) or incentives are provided to adopt more environmentally friendly activities (e.g. the differential tax on leaded and unleaded petrol). The UK government has in principle favoured the latter over the former: for example it has argued that

The [market-based] approach is simply one way for achieving the goals specified by government. It is, however, an effective way, since it allows producers and consumers rather than regulators to decide how best to alter their demands in order to meet environmental needs. Thus has a number of beneficial consequences: freedom of choice is not constrained; those who find it cheapest to reduce emissions will make the biggest reductions; there will be an incentive to develop more efficient technology; there is a continuing incentive not to misuse the environment.

However,

for purposes of policy, the key attribute of full market-based measures is that they provide incentives by establishing prices for environmental services. Modest use has already been made of economic instruments to protect the environment, both here and elsewhere. In most cases these are charges which finance environmental expenditures. It is as yet rare to find a full market-based approach, in which prices reflect all environmental costs and benefits.[55]

However the government then recognized that 'administrative controls will for the foreseeable future remain at the heart of Britain's system of environmental

[53] See D. R. Helm, 'The Assessment: Reforming Environmental Regulation in the UK', *Oxford Review of Economic Policy*, 9 (1993), 1–13.

[54] For a list of key targets, see *This Common Inheritance 1995*, Cmnd. 2822 (London: HMSO, 1995), 13.

[55] *This Common Inheritance: Britain's Environmental Strategy*, Cmnd. 1200 (London: HMSO, 1990), 271.

control'. The use of a market-based approach still raises the issue of who should pay. In other words is the polluter paid not to pollute (on the basis that the previous situation permitted pollution) or should the polluter have to pay: since 1975 it has been the general policy amongst OECD countries for the polluter pays principle to hold.

Similar issues of regulatory failure and capture arise in the context of environmental regulation as with the regulation of public utilities.[56] Further, many public utilities (the water industry being a notable example) are involved in polluting activities and thereby may be regulated both in terms of price and of environmental considerations.

Further Reading

J. Vickers and G. Yarrow, 'Economic Perspectives on Privatization', *Journal of Economic Perspectives*, 5 (1991).
M. Waterson, *Regulation of the Form and Natural Monopoly* (Oxford: Blackwell, 1988).
R. Sugden (ed.) *Industrial Economic Regulation* (London: Routledge).
Symposium on Regulation, *Oxford Review of Economic Policy*, 10/3 (1994).
Symposium on Environmental Regulation, *Oxford Review of Economic Policy*, 9/3 (1993).

[56] See Helm, 'The Assessment', for discussion on this point.

THE LABOUR MARKET

GERAINT JOHNES AND JIM TAYLOR

10.1. Introduction

The problem of unemployment has been one of great concern to economists for generations and rightly so. Unemployment is also of great concern to the public at large, since the consequences of becoming unemployed can be very severe for those affected by it. This chapter aims to provide a better understanding of the nature of the unemployment problem in Britain. In addition, we seek to provide an understanding of the UK labour market more generally. We examine recent labour-market trends as well as many current employment policy issues.

The unsettled nature of the British labour market over the last two decades has led to spectacular swings in unemployment. This is clear from Fig. 10.1,

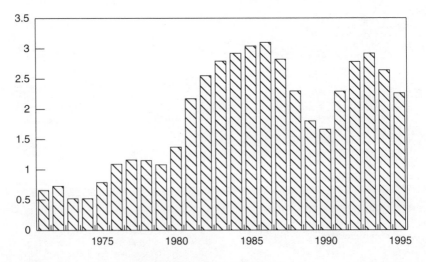

Fig. 10.1. Unemployment in the UK, 1971–1995 (millions)

Source: Employment Gazette; Labour Market Trends.

which shows that in 1974, UK unemployment stood at just half a million but then rose quickly to over 1.1 million by 1978, widely regarded at the time as little short of an economic disaster. The rise in unemployment continued, however, and in 1986 it breached the 3 million mark for the first time since the Great Depression of the 1930s, before subsequently falling to under 1.7 million in 1990. High unemployment then returned with a vengeance in the 1990–3 recession, rising once again to almost 3 million. The strong recovery in 1994–5 was accompanied by another substantial fall in unemployment, which is clearly a very turbulent variable.

High unemployment affects some households profoundly and others not at all. It causes great human misery, and is an inequitable and generally inefficient means of riding a slump in economic activity. This being so, economists have focused on the labour market's apparent imperfections in an effort to improve its functioning. They particularly want to find out why the labour market does not clear, so that it may be possible to devise policies which help to reduce unemployment well below the levels that we have witnessed since the early 1980s.

We begin this chapter, in Section 10.2, with a description of the British labour force, paying special attention to its composition. We aim to examine several aspects of the composition of the workforce such as its sex mix, ethnic mix, occupational mix, hours worked, and participation rates. This is followed in Section 10.3 by a discussion of the incidence and causes of unemployment. Some of the policies used to combat unemployment are discussed in Section 10.4. We then turn our attention in Section 10.5 to a consideration of wages. The factors underlying income differences between individuals are examined and we discuss the system of social security benefits, which provides an income to those who are disadvantaged in the labour market. Finally, we take a look at industrial relations in Section 10.6.

10.2. Employment

The Labour Force

One of the most striking changes in the UK labour market over the past 25 years is the increasing relative importance of female workers. Between 1971 and 1995 the number of females in Great Britain's civilian labour force increased by 40%, from 8.6 million to 12.0 million, while the number of males in the workforce increased by less than 2%. The growth of the British workforce by 3.7 million during 1971–95 was therefore due almost entirely to a greater participation in the labour force of female workers. The growing importance of females in the labour force is vividly demonstrated in Table 10.1, which shows that females increased their share of the workforce from under 36% in 1971 to 44% in 1995.

Table 10.1. The British workforce by sex, 1971–2006

Year	Workforce (in millions)			% of total	
	Males	Females	Total	Males	Females
1971	15.03	8.57	23.60	63.7	36.3
1981	15.31	10.06	25.37	60.3	39.7
1991	15.65	11.66	27.31	57.3	42.7
1995	15.30	12.00	27.30	56.0	44.0
2000[a]	15.60	12.20	27.80	56.1	43.9
2006[a]	15.70	12.70	28.40	55.3	44.7

The increasing importance of females in the workforce is also reflected by the long-run trend in the female activity rate, which is the percentage of females of working age who either have a job or are seeking one. As can be seen from Fig. 10.2, the female activity rate rose from under 44% in 1971 to 54% in 1995 and is expected to rise to over 55% by 2001. In contrast to this, the activity rate for males has moved in the opposite direction, from over 80% in 1971 to 72% in 1995. The gap between male and female activity rates has therefore narrowed remarkably quickly during the past two decades. These statistics demonstrate vividly the increasing dependence of the UK economy on female workers relative to male workers.

The stark contrast in the long-run trends in activity rates between males and females raises an interesting question: why has the male activity rate declined while the female rate has been increasing? The main reason for the downward trend in the male activity rate is a reduction in the retirement age. Table 10.2

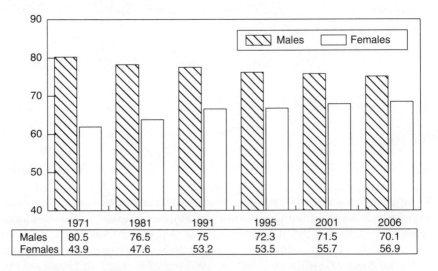

Fig. 10.2. Economic activity rates by sex: Great Britain, 1971–2006 (%)

Source: Employment Gazette; Social Trends.

Table 10.2. Economic activity rates in Great Britain by age and sex, 1971–2001

Age-group	Males				Females			
	1971	1981	1994	2001[a]	1971	1981	1994	2001[a]
16-19	69.4	72.4	62.1	58.0	65.0	70.4	58.7	56.8
20-24	87.7	85.1	84.2	81.0	60.2	68.8	69.4	69.8
25-34	94.6	95.4	94.6	95.3	45.5	56.4	71.0	74.5
35-44	96.2	96.0	93.7	93.7	59.7	68.0	76.9	81.1
45-54	95.7	94.8	90.4	90.2	62.0	68.0	75.4	78.8
55-59	93.0	89.4	76.1	74.6	50.9	53.4	55.7	57.1
60-64	82.9	69.3	51.2	49.9	28.8	23.3	25.6	29.2
60-69[b]	30.4	16.3	14.0	14.3	6.3	3.7	3.3	2.8
70+	10.9	6.5	4.2	3.5	—	—	—	—
All 16+	80.5	76.5	72.6	71.5	43.9	47.6	53.2	55.7

[a] Projected figure.
[b] Includes females aged 70 and over.
Source: Employment Gazette, Apr. 1995, 166.

indicates that this trend is expected to continue into the next century. The opposite is true for females, who are tending to retire later in life.

The reasons for the long-run upward trend in the female activity rate are still the subject of debate, but plausible explanations can be found on both the supply side and the demand side of the labour market.[1] The main explanations on the supply side are that the female activity rate has increased because of:

- a reduction in sexual discrimination in the workplace against females;
- a change in social attitudes towards mothers returning to work after childbirth;
- the rapid growth of nurseries, play-schools, and professional child-minding;
- the introduction of household devices such as the fully-automatic washing machine, the microwave oven, and frozen food.

All these have helped to liberate females (and some males!) from domestic work. In addition, it may even have been the case that husbands have become more tolerant of their wives working, particularly as family income has been boosted as a consequence.

There are three main demand-side explanations for the long-run increase in female economic activity. First, very high levels of labour demand during the 1960s and 1970s led employers to search for additional workers. Secondly, a continuously rising real wage has increased the opportunity cost of not working in paid employment, thereby inducing more women to take a job. Thirdly, in their search for cheaper labour, employers have provided more opportunities for part-time work and this has been found to be particularly popular among married women. Research has tended to support these various explanations of the long-run upward trend in the female activity rate.[2]

[1] J. Mincer, 'Labor-Force Participation of Married Women: A Study of Labor Supply', in H. G. Lewis (ed.), *Aspects of Labor Economics* (Princeton, NJ: Princeton University Press, 1962).
[2] G. Briscoe and R. Wilson, 'Forecasting Economic Activity Rates', *International Journal of Forecasting*, 8 (1992), 201–17.

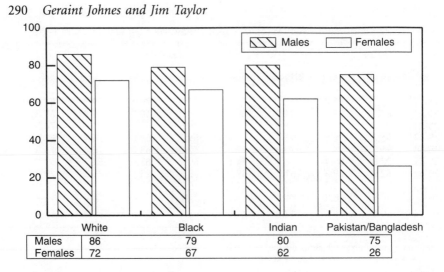

	White	Black	Indian	Pakistan/Bangladesh
Males	86	79	80	75
Females	72	67	62	26

Fig. 10.3. Economic activity rates by ethnic group and sex: Great Britain, Spring 1994 (%)

Source: Employment Gazette.

Differences in economic activity rates occur not only between males and females, and between different age-groups, but also between people from different ethnic groups. This is particularly true for females. The Labour Force Survey, for example, shows that the percentage of females of working age who are economically active is lower for Indian females and very low for Pakistani or Bangladeshi females in the UK compared to white and West

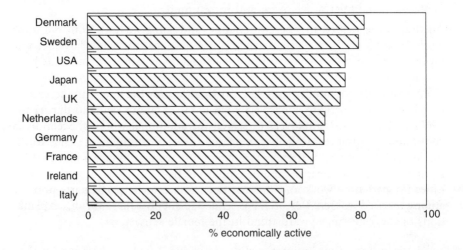

Fig. 10.4. Labour-force activity rates: international comparisons, 1993 (%)

Source: OECD, Economic Outlook.

Indian females (see Fig. 10.3). These differences are probably partly due to differences in custom and practice between ethnic groups, especially among older people, though discrimination in the workplace is also likely to play a part. It will be interesting to see by how much the economic activity rates for different ethnic groups converge over the next decade as younger people from ethnic minorities enter the workforce.

Finally, international comparisons indicate that the UK has a similar activity rate to the USA and Japan and a higher one than most of her European partners (see Fig. 10.4). It is likely that activity rates within the EU will converge during the next two decades as a result of European-wide increases in female activity rates.

Occupations

One of the consequences of the changing industrial structure of the UK economy away from manufacturing and towards services is the sharp fall in the ratio of manual to non-manual jobs and the growth in professional and managerial occupations. There are wide disparities, however, in the types of jobs taken by males and females (see Table 10.3). One in three males are in manual jobs (craft jobs and jobs operating machinery), compared to only one in fifteen females. Managerial and professional occupations are very important for both males and females; and clerical jobs are particularly important for females. The high proportion of females in clerical jobs is not surprising, since many part-time jobs are available in this occupational group.

Hours Worked

Average weekly hours worked in the UK declined sharply from the mid-1950s to the mid-1970s, since which time the trend has been virtually flat. For male

Table 10.3. Distribution of workers between broad occupational categories in Great Britain by sex, 1995

Occupational group	% workers in each category	
	Females	Males
Managers, professionals, technical	31	39
Clerical	25	7
Craft and related	3	20
Personal services	15	6
Selling	11	5
Plant and machinery	4	14
Other occupations	10	7
Total	100	100

Source: Employment Gazette, Dec. 1995, Table 7.6.

workers, average hours worked fell from 49 hours per week in 1955 to under 42 hours per week in the 1980s (see Fig. 10.5). For females, hours worked fell sharply from the mid-1950s to the early 1970s but have been very stable during the past two decades, standing at around 37 hours per week. The long-run downward trend in hours worked now seems to have halted for both males and females.

The almost continuous downward trend in hours worked from the mid-1950s through until the mid-1970s probably reflected an increasing preference for leisure as real income increased. Thus, although an increase in real wages may be expected to induce workers to work longer hours, this was apparently more than offset during 1955–75 by an increase in the desire for more leisure as income increased. Leisure is more useful if income is high enough to enjoy it. During the last two decades, however, the taste for more leisure and less work seems to have evaporated, at least temporarily. The halting of the downward trend in hours worked may also be the result of an increase in employer power in the labour market since the early 1980s.

International comparisons of hours worked provide some very interesting contrasts. Fig. 10.6 shows that the number of weekly hours worked for UK males is the highest in the EU. The opposite is the case for female workers, who work fewer hours per week than most other EU countries. The reasons for the lower hours worked by females may be due to the higher proportion of women in work in the UK, many of whom have part-time jobs.

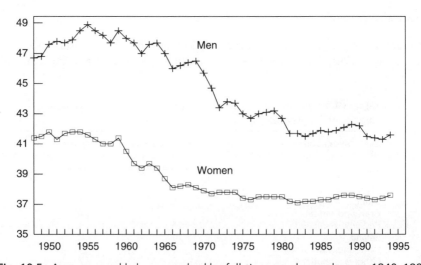

Fig. 10.5. Average weekly hours worked by full-time employees by sex, 1948–1993

Source: British Labour Statistics; Historical Abstract; Employment Gazette; Labour Market Trends.

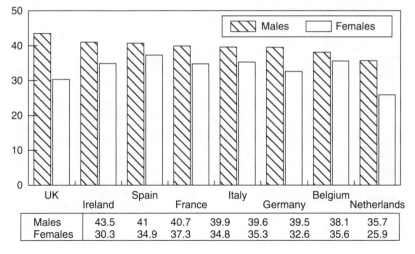

	UK	Ireland	Spain	France	Italy	Germany	Belgium	Netherlands
Males	43.5	41	40.7	39.9	39.6	39.5	38.1	35.7
Females	30.3	34.9	37.3	34.8	35.3	32.6	35.6	25.9

Fig. 10.6. Average weekly hours worked in selected EU countries, 1991

Source: Social Trends, 24.

10.3. Unemployment

Labour Market Stocks and Flows

Unemployment in the UK increased dramatically in the 1980s compared to the golden age of low unemployment in the 1950s and 1960s, when unemployment fluctuated around 2%. Fig. 10.7 shows male unemployment rising to a peak of nearly 14% in 1993, way above the measured female unemployment rate of 5.5%. The long-run upward trend in unemployment has therefore been far more marked for males than for females. In addition, the short-run fluctuations in unemployment have been more severe for males.

These sex differences in the unemployment rate are due to two main factors. First, males and females are unevenly distributed between industries, so that differences between industries in their performance can lead to corresponding differences in their experience of unemployment. Secondly, some women who are out of work are not eligible to claim unemployment benefit and are thus not counted as unemployed even though they would look for work if the job market were more buoyant. According to the Labour Force Survey, for example, there were 842,000 females unemployed in the summer of 1995 whereas there were only 530,000 claiming unemployment benefit. For males, the situation is reversed: 1.69 million males were claiming benefit while only 1.57 million were unemployed according to the Labour Force Survey. The claimant unemployment total therefore seriously understates the true unemployment figure according to official sources.

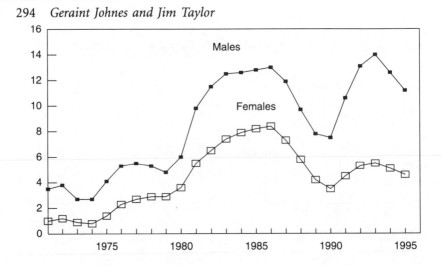

Fig. 10.7. Unemployment rates for males and females in the UK, 1971–1995

Source: Employment Gazette; Labour Market Trends.

There are also those persons who are not looking for a job because they see no prospect of getting one, but who would take a job if a suitable one came along. These 'discouraged workers' could be substantial in number. This applies to males as well as to females. In the winter of 1994/5, for example, there were 1.38 million females and 0.84 million males in this category of 'discouraged workers' (*Employment Gazette*, July 1995, p. LF35). Exactly how many of these would actually take a job if one became available, however, is not known. But it does indicate that the official unemployment figures understate the true level of unemployment in the UK economy, perhaps substantially.

To understand the causes of unemployment, it is useful to begin by examining the relationship between labour-market stocks and flows. Basically, there are three primary stocks: the stock of employed workers, the stock of unemployed, and the stock of those who are not economically active. As Fig. 10.8 shows, the stock of economically inactive persons includes those people of working age who are not in the working population (e.g. students, some mothers with young children, and those who are sick or retired). Each of these three stocks is connected to the other two by means of flows of persons between them. The unemployment stock, for example, is connected to the employment stock because redundant workers flow from the employment stock to the unemployment stock and because some workers voluntarily quit their jobs to look for another one. Unemployed workers who get jobs flow in the opposite direction.

The unemployment stock will increase whenever the inflow into unemployment exceeds the outflow from it, as happens during recessions when firms are releasing more workers than they are taking on. The relationship between these inflows and outflows is shown in Fig. 10.9 for the period 1983–95. Two things

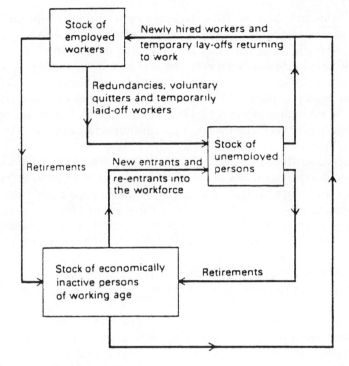

Fig. 10.8. Labour-market stocks and flows

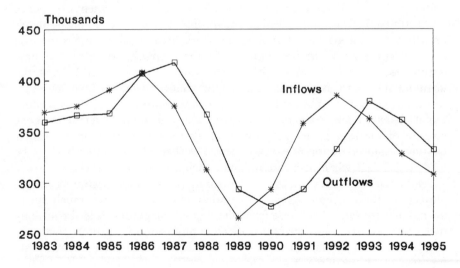

Fig. 10.9. Inflows into and outflows from the stock of unemployed in the UK, 1983–1995 (000s)

Source: Labour Market Trends.

stand out from this diagram. First, the inflows into and out of the unemployment stock are of a similar order of magnitude; they tend to rise and fall together. Secondly, since the flows are very large in relation to the stock, it takes only small differences between the inflow and the outflow to cause a substantial change in the unemployment stock. The outflow exceeded the inflow, for example, during 1986–9, with the result that the unemployment stock fell by 1.3 million (from 3.1 million to 1.8 million). Exactly the opposite occurred during 1990–3 with the result that the unemployment stock increased by 1.25 million.

An analysis of the flows into and out of the unemployment stock raises crucially important questions about the factors which determine the probability that a person will become unemployed. Some people never experience unemployment while others find themselves unemployed for several years at a time or at very frequent intervals; and of those who do become unemployed, some are able to find a job very quickly while others are less fortunate. The question therefore arises whether certain types of people are more likely to become unemployed than others; and if a person does become unemployed, what factors affect the speed at which he or she is able to find a job?

The likelihood of becoming unemployed.   The chances that anyone will become unemployed are strongly influenced by demographic and socio-economic factors. These include a person's age, sex, geographical location, qualifications, skills, and the growth in jobs. In addition, the likelihood of leaving the unemployment stock is closely related to the length of time a person has been unemployed.

The effect of a person's sex and age on his or her unemployment experience is illustrated in Fig. 10.10, which shows that males have a much higher probability of joining the unemployment stock than females. This is the case across all age-groups without exception. Furthermore, the pattern is the same during booms and recessions. It is also evident from Fig. 10.10 that the unemployment rate is generally higher for younger workers than for older workers. This is only to be expected, since younger workers are generally more mobile between jobs than older workers, who are often reluctant to move because of the loss of seniority rights which they have built up with their existing employer. Younger, less experienced workers are also more likely to be made redundant when firms are reducing their employment levels.

Another factor which affects the probability of a person becoming unemployed is ethnic origin. Table 10.4 shows that whites have much lower unemployment rates than those from all other ethnic groups. It is also striking that economic recession adversely affects ethnic minority groups (with the exception of Indians) far worse than it affects whites. The unemployment rate for blacks, for example, increased from 9% to 33% during the 1990–3 recession—a far greater increase than for whites. The generally higher unemployment rates for non-whites probably results from a combination of factors, such as racial discrimination, the concentration of ethnic minority workers in

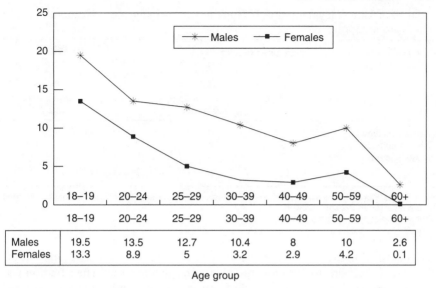

	18–19	20–24	25–29	30–39	40–49	50–59	60+
Males	19.5	13.5	12.7	10.4	8	10	2.6
Females	13.3	8.9	5	3.2	2.9	4.2	0.1

Age group

Fig. 10.10. Unemployment rates by age and sex, October 1995 (%)

Source: Labour Market Trends.

low-skill and less secure jobs, and their residential location. A high concentra-tion of ethnic minorities in economically depressed localities, for example, inevitably leads to higher unemployment for this group of workers.

Age, sex, and ethnic origin are not the only factors which affect the prob-ability of becoming unemployed. A person's educational background, qualifica-tions, and skills also exert a substantial influence. In addition to enhancing a worker's value to employers, more highly educated and better qualified workers tend to be more geographically mobile and therefore have a wider range of job opportunities open to them. This is confirmed by Table 10.5: for white males,

Table 10.4. Unemployment rates in boom and recession by ethnic group, 1990 and 1993

Ethnic group	% unemployed			
	Males		Females	
	Spring 1990	Autumn 1993	Spring 1990	Autumn 1993
White	7	11	6	7
West Indian	13	29	13	19
Black	9	33	11	23
Indian	15	16	24	14
Pakistani / Bangladeshi	12	30	9	29

Source: Employment Gazette, May 1994, 156.

Table 10.5. Unemployment rates in Great Britain by highest qualification level and ethnic group, Spring 1993

Qualification level	% unemployed			
	Males		Females	
	Whites	Ethnic minority groups	Whites	Ethnic minority groups
Higher qualification	5	14	4	9
Other qualification	12	23	7	20
No qualification	19	33	10	19
All	12	24	7	17

Note: Higher qualifications are those above GCE A-level (or equivalent). Other qualifications are those at GCE A-level (or equivalent) or lower.
Source: Employment Gazette, May 1994, 157.

the unemployment rate in 1993 varied from 5% for those with higher educational qualifications to 19% for those with no qualifications. The situation was much grimmer for males in the ethnic minorities. A similar result is obtained for females: those in ethnic minorities suffer from higher unemployment across the qualification spectrum.

Finally, a person's occupation affects the probability of becoming unemployed. This relates to the qualifications possessed by individuals as well as the particular industry to which they are attached. The impact of a person's occupation on the likelihood of being unemployed is shown in Fig. 10.11, which indicates that those in highly skilled occupations (such as the

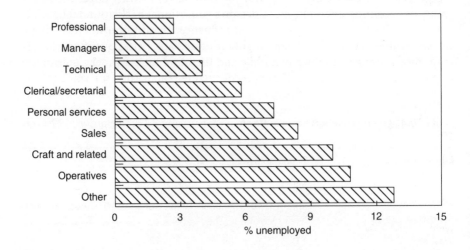

Fig. 10.11. Unemployment rates in Great Britain by occupation, Spring 1995

Note: Unemployment rates refer to previous occupation of the unemployed.
Source: Labour Market Trends.

professions) are less likely to become unemployed than those in manual occupations (such as operatives). In general, the higher the skill level, the lower is the probability of becoming unemployed.

The likelihood of leaving the stock of unemployed. We have shown that the likelihood of becoming unemployed varies considerably between different types of people. Age, sex, occupation, ethnic origin, and location of residence are all important determinants. Similarly, the likelihood of leaving the unemployment stock can be shown to vary according to age, sex, location, and the length of time for which a person has been unemployed.

Young workers, for example, are far more likely to leave the unemployment stock quickly after joining it than are older workers. This is probably because employers generally have a preference for younger workers and because younger workers are often less choosy about their type of job than older workers, who are more likely to be set in their ways.

A further and highly significant factor which affects a person's likelihood of leaving the unemployment stock is the length of time a person has been unemployed. It becomes increasingly difficult to get out of the unemployment stock the longer a person has been in it. There are two reasons for this. First, as the duration of unemployment increases, the unemployed become discouraged and consequently search for a job less enthusiastically. They may even run out of local firms to search. Secondly, employers are more reluctant to hire those who have been unemployed for long periods compared to those who have been unemployed for only a short time. This is partly because employers believe that the long-term unemployed are in some sense inferior; their job applications have already been rejected by other employers, perhaps many times. The long-term unemployed are also less attractive to employers because their skills deteriorate as the duration of their unemployment increases. It is not simply that the unemployed lose their skills but rather that the appearance of new products and new processes require those in jobs to learn new skills. Those in work are constantly updating their skills with the result that the skill gap between the employed and the unemployed widens as the time spent unemployed increases. The consequence of an increase in the duration of unemployment is therefore an increasing mismatch between the skills required by employers and the skills offered by the unemployed.

The distinction between short-term unemployment and long-term unemployment is an important one, since it is long-term unemployment which is generally regarded as being in most urgent need of attention by policy-makers. Long-term unemployment could in principle be reduced without putting upward pressure on inflation. Indeed, the 1994 Budget introduced special incentives to encourage firms to recruit new workers from the ranks of the long-term unemployed. As might be expected, long-term unemployment is more prevalent among some groups of workers than among others. Males, for example, are more likely to be unemployed for long periods than are females once they join the unemployment stock (see Table 10.6); and older persons are

Table 10.6. Duration of unemployment in Great Britain by sex, Spring 1995 (%)

Duration	Males	Females
< 3 months	18.8	31.7
3-6 months	15.1	17.6
6–12 months	16.9	18.3
12–24 months	17.4	14.8
24–36 months	11.4	7.1
Over 3 years	20.4	10.4
All	100	100

Source: Labour Market Trends, Dec. 1995, Table 7.18.

more likely to be unemployed for long periods than are younger persons (see Fig. 10.12). One reason why younger persons are able to get out of the unemployment stock more quickly is their greater mobility and greater flexibility in the eyes of employers.

Some Problems in Measuring Unemployment

The official unemployment count includes only those who are claiming unemployment benefit. These claimants have to be capable of work, available for work, and actively seeking work. It therefore excludes all those seeking work but who are not claiming unemployment benefit. The 'discouraged' workers mentioned in the previous section fall into this category.

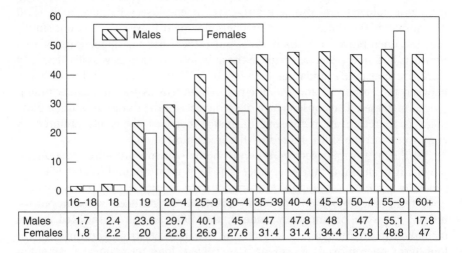

	16–18	18	19	20–4	25–9	30–4	35–39	40–4	45–9	50–4	55–9	60+
Males	1.7	2.4	23.6	29.7	40.1	45	47	47.8	48	47	55.1	17.8
Females	1.8	2.2	20	22.8	26.9	27.6	31.4	31.4	34.4	37.8	48.8	47

Fig. 10.12. Long-term unemployment by age and sex in the UK: percentage unemployed for more than one year, October 1995

Source: Labour Market Trends.

Estimates of unemployment therefore vary substantially according to how the unemployed are counted. The official definition of unemployment was changed several times during the 1980s, leading to a substantial reduction in the official unemployment count. At the 1980s unemployment peak (in 1986), the measured unemployment total stood at around half a million below the level which would have occurred if the administrative changes had not been made. Two changes which were estimated to have reduced the official unemployment count (by 190,000 and 162,000 respectively) are, first, the replacement of the old method of counting all those registering as unemployed at Job Centres by the count based on benefit claimants only; and secondly, the effective lowering of the early retirement age for men to sixty by replacing unemployment benefit by income support (in effect, converting the unemployed into retired persons). A more recent change in the method of counting the unemployed is the removal of all 16–17-year-olds from the unemployment count following the withdrawal of their entitlement to unemployment benefit in October 1988. This reduced the unemployment count by over 50,000—once again by changing the unemployment benefit rules.

Less obvious and less quantifiable changes have occurred in recent years which have affected the unemployment count. First, unemployment benefit offices have tightened up the 'availability for work' tests in order to discourage those claimaints who are not genuinely seeking work. The 1988 Social Security Act specifies that a person has to be 'actively seeking work' in order to be eligible for unemployment benefit. This means that they will be expected to be applying for job vacancies and to be registered with a job agency. In addition, to maintain their entitlement to benefits, those unemployed for over three months have to accept any available job in the area regardless of the person's previous work experience or wage. Secondly, the number of workers on government employment and training programmes has reduced the unemployment total substantially since without access to such programmes many more would be in the unemployment stock.

On the other hand, it has been argued that a substantial number of unemployed people are not interested in finding a job either because they are 'workshy' or because they are supplementing their unemployment benefit by working in the black economy. The latter view is supported by a Department of Employment Survey of 2700 unemployed people in London in 1988 which concluded 'that a significant minority of the capital's 280,000 unemployed were claiming benefit while working in the black economy' (*Financial Times*, 13 Oct. 1988).

In an attempt to remove those not genuinely seeking work from the unemployment stock, the government plans to replace unemployment benefit by the Job Seekers Allowance in 1996. This measure will not only reduce the maximum period of unemployment benefit from twelve to six months, it will also give those officers administering the new scheme the power to penalize anyone claiming the benefit if they do not comply with the advice provided by the Employment Service. The introduction of the Job Seekers Allowance is expected to yield a cut in government spending of around £200 million per year as a result of fewer people claiming benefit even though they may be unemployed according to current definitions.

International Comparisons of Unemployment

Between 1948 and 1968, the annual unemployment rate in the UK averaged 1.8% and never rose above 2.6%. The following two decades witnessed a remarkable change, especially during the 1980s when it reached a post-war record of over 11% (in 1986). More than three million people were recorded as claiming unemployment benefit and about a million others were unemployed but not entitled to benefit and so were not recorded in the unemployment total. After falling back to 5.8% in 1990, the unemployment rate reached another peak in 1993 (10.3%).

The UK was not alone, however, in experiencing high unemployment during the 1980s as can be seen from Fig. 10.13. With the exception of Japan, all of the major industrialized nations experienced substantial increases in their unemployment rates in the early 1980s. An interesting question which is posed by the long-term unemployment trends in Fig. 10.13 is why Japan managed to keep its unemployment rate so low during the 1980s compared to most other industrialized nations. The answer to this question helps to throw some light on the high levels of unemployment experienced by the UK and other European countries during the 1980s, since one of the reasons for the low unemployment rate in Japan is that wages there are far more flexible during recessions than they are in Western European labour markets. This is because large firms offer life-time employment

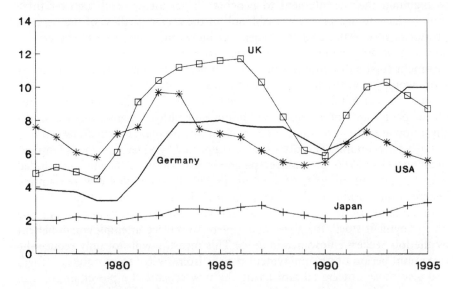

Fig. 10.13. Unemployment rates in selected countries, 1976–1995 (%)

Source: OECD, *Economic Outlook*.

to their employees but, in return, the annual earnings of workers are closely tied to the firm's profitability. The life-time employment system, which flourishes in Japan's major companies, actually requires wage flexibility.

A comparison of US and UK experience suggests that unemployment in the UK has been higher, and employment growth has been slower, than in the US for three reasons.[3] First, income support for the unemployed is more generous in the UK. Not only are fewer people (as a proportion of the workforce) entitled to unemployment benefit in the US, but benefit runs out more quickly, since it terminates after six months, compared to no time-limit on income support in the UK. Unemployed workers in the US are consequently more willing to accept low paid jobs. Secondly, labour markets in the US are more flexible than they are in the UK. US workers are more willing to change jobs (as reflected by higher turnover rates) and are more willing to migrate to other areas in search of a job. The unwillingness of the unemployed in the UK to migrate to find work may be due to the greater availablity of subsidized housing in areas of high unemployment than in areas of low unemployment. The risks associated with moving may simply be too high for the low-skilled unemployed living in subsidized housing in the UK. Thirdly, wages are more responsive to a fall in labour demand in the US, partly because the US labour market is less unionized than in the UK. It has been argued, for example, that UK workers have chosen a high-wage / low-employment combination on the labour demand curve whereas US and Japanese workers prefer higher employment even if this means lower wages.

As far as short-run fluctuations in unemployment are concerned, the predominating influence has undoubtedly been the aggregate level of demand. The early 1980s and early 1990s provide two striking examples of how the government itself can cause an increase in unemployment. The 1980–2 recession was a direct consequence of a contractionary monetary and fiscal policy that was designed to bring inflation down (which it succeeded in doing at the cost of raising unemployment to historically record levels in the mid-1980s). More recently, unemployment has risen sharply during 1990–3 as a direct result of another period of tight monetary control (i.e. high interest rates).

Regional Unemployment Disparities

Regional differences in unemployment have changed dramatically during the past two decades (see Fig. 10.14). The early 1980s witnessed the widest regional differences in unemployment since the 1930s, with the northern regions being more severely affected than the southern regions. The north–south unemployment gap did not begin to narrow until the southern regions ran into severe labour shortages in 1989–90. Then came the 1990–3 recession with a ven-

[3] J. Pencavel, 'British Unemployment: Letter from America', *Economic Journal*, 104 (May 1994), 621–32.

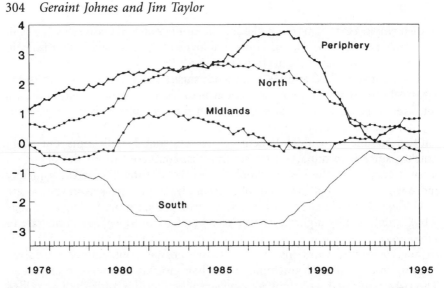

Figure 10.14. Regional disparities in unemployment in the UK: point difference from the UK rate by region, 1976–1995

Note: South = South-East, East Anglia, South-West; Midlands = West Midlands, East Midlands; North = North-West, Yorkshire and Humberside, North; Periphery = Scotland, Wales, Northern Ireland.
Source: Employment Gazette; Labour Market Trends

geance. Past experience suggested that the northern regions would again be hit the hardest. Surprisingly, this failed to happen. It was the southern regions which suffered the worst effects of the 1990–3 recession, with the result that unemployment in the south rose far more quickly than in the north. The fact that the unemployment rate in the South-East actually rose above that of Scotland for the first time since records began speaks for itself. Greater London was particularly hard hit. For once, history was not repeating itself.

The explanation for this totally unexpected regional impact of the recession is to be found in the collapse of the housing market. Just as the rapid rise in house prices had encouraged home-owners in the south to spend more during the late 1980s due to their increased wealth, the rapid fall in house prices in the south during 1990–2 had exactly the opposite effect. Home-owners reduced their spending as their wealth fell and as mortgage repayments rose due to higher interest rates. Not only did the collapse of house prices reduce the wealth of existing home-owners, it actually left many who had bought their house in the boom in serious debt. This fall in wealth and increase in debt led to reduced consumption spending and increased saving, particularly in the south, thus leading to more severe job losses in the south than in the north.[4]

[4] S. Bradley and J. Taylor, 'Spatial Disparities in the Impact of the 1990–92 Recession: An Analysis of UK Counties', *Oxford Bulletin of Economics and Statistics*, 56/4 (November 1994), 367–82; P. Evans and B. McCormick, 'The New Pattern of Regional Unemployment: Causes and Policy Significance', *Economic Journal*, 104 (May 1994), 633–47.

It is important not to become obsessed with the north–south divide. Unemployment black spots exist in all parts of the UK—even in regions where the unemployment rate is relatively low. Parts of the South-East, such as East Sussex and Kent, suffered very badly from the 1990–3 recession, as indeed did many parts of Greater London. The wide disparities in unemployment rates within each UK region can be seen in Table 10.7. These spatial differences in unemployment become even greater as smaller and smaller areas are compared. Inner city areas, for example, usually have the highest unemployment rates, and suburban areas and small towns tend to have lower unemployment rates.[5]

10.4. Policies to Combat Unemployment

Employment policies in the UK are targeted specifically at the unemployed. They are designed to get people out of unemployment and into a job. Since the vast majority of those who become unemployed are able to get back into employment quickly, employment policies are aimed primarily at the long-term unemployed.

The three main types of employment policy are:

- training programmes for the unemployed;
- employment subsidies to firms willing to employ the long-term unemployed;
- the provision of jobs in the public sector (as an employer of last resort).

Employment subsidies and employment in the public sector are normally regarded as being inferior to training programmes. They have come under fire for three main reasons. First, employment subsidies result in a 'deadweight' loss in so far as some of those who get jobs would have got them anyway, in which case the subsidy is wasted. Secondly, firms will substitute subsidized workers for unsubsidized workers. There is no net gain in employment in this case. Thirdly, firms which take on extra workers in order to receive the subsidy may displace employment in firms which do not do so, since they may take work from these latter firms. The net increase in employment may therefore be small.

But all these criticisms assume that the increase in aggregate demand resulting from the subsidy can have no effect on the overall level of activity in the economy in anything but the very long term. The evidence suggests that this is not the case. The whole process of retraining and getting the long-term unemployed back into jobs is designed to increase the productive capacity of the economy, thereby allowing the aggregate demand for goods and services to be raised. The national level of output and employment should be greater as a result of such policies.

[5] H. Armstrong and J. Taylor, *Regional Economics and Policy* (London: Harvester Wheatsheaf, 1993).

Table 10.7. Unemployment rates in the regions and counties of Great Britain, October 1995

Region/county	%	Region/county	%	Region/county	%
South-East	7.7	West Midlands	7.9	North	10.1
Bedfordshire	7.0	Hereford and Worcestershire	6.2	Cleveland	12.3
Berkshire	4.7	Shropshire	5.5	Cumbria	7.0
Buckinghamshire	4.9	Staffordshire	6.6	Durham	8.9
East Sussex	9.6	Warwickshire	5.5	Northumberland	9.4
Essex	8.2	West Midlands Conurbation	9.5	Tyne and Wear	11.1
Hampshire	5.9	East Midlands	7.2	Wales	8.0
Hertfordshire	5.4	Derbyshire	7.7	Clwyd	6.7
Isle of Wight	9.6	Leicestershire	6.0	Dyfed	8.3
Kent	8.1	Lincolnshire	6.9	Gwent	8.2
Oxfordshire	4.4	Northamptonshire	5.4	Gwynedd	9.0
Surrey	—	Nottinghamshire	8.9	Mid-Glamorgan	9.5
West Sussex	4.6	Yorks/Humberside	8.4	Powys	4.2
Greater London	9.6	Humberside	9.3	South Glamorgan	7.9
East Anglia	6.0	North Yorkshire	5.6	West Glamorgan	8.3
Cambridgeshire	5.2	South Yorkshire	10.6	Scotland	7.6
Norfolk	6.8	West Yorkshire	7.7	Borders	4.6
Suffolk	6.0	North-West	8.2	Central	8.0
South-West	6.9	Cheshire	6.2	Dumfries/Galloway	7.5
Avon	7.2	Lancashire	6.1	Fife	9.5
Cornwall	9.1	Greater Manchester	7.9	Grampian	4.3
Devon	7.7	Merseyside	12.4	Highland	8.4
Dorset	6.6			Lothian	6.2
Gloucestershire	5.9			Strathclyde	8.9
Somerset	6.3			Tayside	8.0
Wiltshire	4.8			Orkney Islands	4.2
				Shetland Islands	2.7
				Western Isles	10.7

Note: The unemployment rate for Surrey is not available.
Source: Labour Market Trends, Dec. 1995.

Table 10.8. Government training and enterprise programmes in Great Britain, 1995

Programme	Number of people participating in each programme in August 1995 (000s)	% in each programme
Training for work	82	23
Youth Training	271	77
Total	353	100

Source: Labour Market Trends, Dec. 1995, Table 8.1.

There are currently two main training and enterprise programmes in Britain: Training for Work and Youth Training. The relative importance of these two schemes can be seen from Table 10.8, which shows that Youth Training accounts for around three-quarters of the 350,000 participating in these programmes, while Training for Work accounts for around one-quarter. Current employment policy in the UK is based on the several programmes.

Restart

Restart was introduced in 1986. It requires anyone drawing unemployment benefit for over six months to see a Restart counsellor. The job of the counsellor is to identify possible routes back into employment. These include:

- encouraging the unemployed to search more intensively for a job;
- joining a Job Club in order to learn how to apply for a job and how to contact a potential employer;
- placing a person on a government-financed training scheme;
- finding a person a temporary job subsidized by a government grant.

How effective has Restart been? Immediately after its introduction in 1986, unemployment fell very rapidly and continued to do so until 1990. But this was largely due to a rapid expansion in the level of economic activity throughout the UK economy. Restart may have helped, however, by encouraging the long-term unemployed to search more actively for a job. One of the less desirable consequences of Restart is that many unemployed persons have had to take low-paid jobs rather than improving their skills. Restart may therefore have done little to raise the skill level of the workforce.

Training for Work

Green and Steedman[6] contend that the UK has a poor record on training its workforce compared to France, Germany, and the USA. This is illustrated in

---

[6] A. Green and H. Steedman, *Educational Provision, Educational Attainment and the Needs of Industry: A Review of Research for Germany, France, Japan, the USA and Britain* (London: National Institute of Economic and Social Research, 1993).

Table 10.9. Vocational qualifications of the workforce in selected countries, 1988–1991

Country	% of all economically active persons		
	University degree	Intermediate vocational qualification	No vocational qualification
Britain (1989)	11	25	64
France (1988)	7	40	53
Netherlands (1989)	8	57	35
Germany (1988)	11	63	26
Switzerland (1991)	11	66	23

Source: S.J. Prais, 'Economic Performance and Education: The Nature of Britain's Deficiencies' Keynes lecture to the British Academy, London, Oct. 1993.

Table 10.9 by the low proportion of workers in the UK with vocational qualifications. The importance of improving the skills of the workforce became very apparent in 1988/9 when the UK economy faced severe shortages for skilled labour even though the overall unemployment rate was still around 6% (very high compared to what it had been in the first three post-war decades).

The Training for Work programme was introduced in 1993 (replacing two other programmes—Employment Training and Employment Action). It was seen as a method of relieving skill shortages and reducing unemployment simultaneously, thus aiming at the structurally unemployed. The aim of Training for Work is 'to train the workers without jobs for the jobs without workers'. The problem is seen as one of mismatch between workers' skills and the skills required to fill existing jobs. Training places are available for around 320,000 long-term unemployed. One of the criticisms levelled against the UK's training programmes is that the training period of six months is far too short.[7] It is also argued that the training programme should include a much larger element of direct work experience. This is difficult to achieve, however, when unemployment is high.

It is therefore not surprising that Training for Work (and its predecessors) face major problems. First, many trainees have been unable to find a suitable job (to match their newly acquired skills) after completing their training. Only about one in three people who participate in the programme are in a job six months after leaving the scheme while over 50% are unemployed (see Fig. 10.15). Secondly, the scheme has a drop-out rate of over 40%. The success of any training programme directed at the long-term unemployed depends very heavily upon the growth of the national economy. Training workers for non-existent jobs will help to reduce unemployment only in so far as it takes the unemployed out of the unemployment stock during the period of training. A steady and sustained growth of the national economy is the best guarantee of jobs for the unemployed. Thirdly, only around 40% of those leaving the ET

[7] R. Layard and J. Philpott, *Stopping Unemployment* (London: Unemployment Institute, 1991).

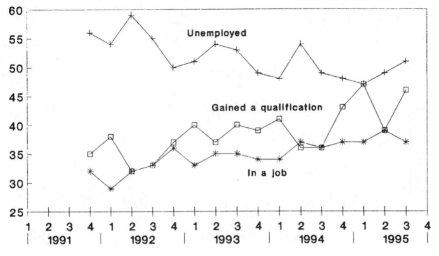

Figure 10.15. Destinations of leavers from the Training for Work programme, 1991–1995 (%)

Source: Labour Market Trends.

programme gain a qualification, though this is on a rising trend—as indeed it needs to be.

The national training programme in the UK is now run by a system of Training and Enterprise Councils (TECs), which are based upon areas with a working population of around 250,000. Each TEC has a budget of about £20 million per year. In addition to providing training schemes for the unemployed and for school leavers, the 82 TECs in England and Wales (and the 22 Local Enterprise Councils in Scotland) administer various business enterprise schemes such as the Enterprise Allowance, the Small Firms Service, and the Business Growth Training Scheme. The TECs are expected to supplement the money they receive from the government by selling their services to local employers who require training schemes for their workers. They have faced a tough task, however, in the early 1990s since firms have generally been unwilling to take on trainees due to the recession.

Youth Training

Youth Training (YT) is by far the largest of the employment and training programmes. This is because a place on YT is guaranteed for all those leaving school at 16 and is now the norm for those not proceeding to further education. The two-year training programme is widely supported by employers because of the large element of government subsidy which it provides.

How successful is the YT programme in getting youths into jobs and in

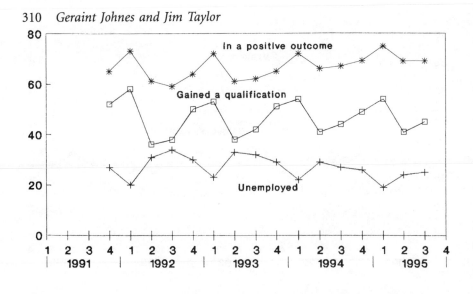

Figure 10.16. Destinations of leavers from the Youth Training programme, 1991–1995 (%)

Source: Labour Market Trends

improving the skills of those who participate in the scheme? Fig. 10.16 indicates that the YT programme is certainly more successful than Training for Work. Around two-thirds of youths proceed to a job or to further training on completion of their YT scheme (indicated in the figure as a positive outcome) and over 40% gain a qualification. Questions therefore need to be asked about why around one-third of youths completing YT do not proceed to a job or to further training, and why nearly 60% fail to gain a qualification. These outcomes indicate that much still needs to be done to the YT programme to make it more effective in raising the skill level of the workforce.

Enterprise Allowance

The Enterprise Allowance is intended to induce unemployed people to create their own business. Anyone unemployed for over two months who has an initial capital of £1000 can obtain a grant of £40 a week for one year if they become self-employed. This scheme, introduced in 1982, contributed considerably to the rapid expansion of self-employment in the UK during the 1980s. The Enterprise Allowance has attracted up to 80 000 unemployed people onto the scheme every year, but it has been estimated that half of these would have become self-employed even if the scheme had not been available.[8] The effect of the Enterprise Allowance on unemployment is therefore likely to have been

[8] Ibid.

relatively small. Whether it has helped to create a more entrepreneurial culture in the UK, its primary objective, has still to be seen.

Employment Policy: Lessons from Abroad?

Can the UK learn from the employment policies of other countries? Layard and Philpott[9] argue strongly in favour of Sweden's employment policy, where unemployment was extremely low compared to other industrialized countries until the early 1990s. The principle underlying Sweden's employment policy is that everyone has the right to work. The policy focuses on making the unemployed employable and this is achieved through a three-pronged strategy:

- training,
- efficient job placement services, and
- work experience schemes.

A further important factor in Sweden's employment policy is that no one can receive unemployment benefit for more than fourteen months. The up-side of this maximum duration of benefits is that all persons are guaranteed a job (often in the public sector) if they have been unemployed for fourteen months. The down-side of the policy is that it is increasingly difficult to find jobs for the long-term unemployed as the unemployment rate itself increases.

The attraction of Swedish-type policies to combat long-term unemployment is becoming increasingly apparent in the UK, where potentially important new policy initiatives (introduced in the 1994 Budget) have been directed at the long-term unemployed. Since employers are generally reluctant to take on the long-term unemployed, the government is offering a substantial employment subsidy (£50 per worker per week for the first six months and £30 for the second six months) on newly recruited workers who have been unemployed for over two years. As yet, however, this scheme is experimental and will be limited to only 5000 long-term unemployed people, a miniscule proportion of the total, during 1995/6. Other policies to help the long-term unemployed include changes to the benefit regulations so that these do not discourage unemployed persons from taking on part-time work in order to get some work experience as a step towards a permanent full-time job. An untaxed back-to-work bonus of up to £1000 is being offered to those willing to use part-time work as a route back into the labour market.

Possible Future Developments in Employment Policy

What could be done to the UK's employment policy to make it more effective? One way forward would be to place greater emphasis on improving the quality

[9] Ibid.

of training. Training courses should lead to a recognized qualification and should include direct work experience, organized through the Training and Enterprise Councils (TECs) which should receive the necessary funding for an expanded programme from the government. Employers in each TEC area should have a major role in determining the training programme and in return they would guarantee employment for a proportion of those completing the programme. The public sector would employ the remainder for, say, a period of six months in order to allow trainees to build up a solid work record.

This policy would cost money. But it has been estimated that the benefits to the economy would far exceed the costs over the medium term.[10] It should not be forgotten that reducing unemployment actually saves the government, and hence the tax-payer, money, since expenditure on unemployment and related benefits will fall when unemployment falls. In addition, the government's revenue will increase, since an increase in employment will raise income tax revenue, national insurance contributions, and value added tax, as national spending increases.

Important as they are, training policies are not the only means by which long-term unemployment can be reduced. The OECD[11] suggests a range of policy options which it believes would help to reduce unemployment levels substantially. These include, first, increasing wage flexibility so that wages respond more quickly to any fall in labour demand. This policy includes encouraging wages to be set locally and not imposing a minimum wage level that harms the employment prospects of the low-skilled. Secondly, non-wage labour costs, such as national insurance contributions, need to be reduced, especially for low wage workers, in order to encourage firms to take on more labour. Thirdly, employment security provisions should be relaxed, since employers have become increasingly reluctant to take on more workers in case they meet a sudden fall in the demand for their products. Fourthly, more investment is needed to improve labour-force skills and competences so that the economy can compete in world markets. Finally, unemployment and related benefits should be set so that they do not remove the incentive to work.

10.5. Income and Earnings

The Determinants of Wage Structure: Occupation, Industry, and Region

Wage structure by occupation.   Suppose all workers are alike and compete in a single labour market which operates perfectly. In such a world, workers engaging in unpleasant tasks would have to be compensated to the extent

---

[10] Ibid.

[11] OECD, *The OECD Jobs Survey: Facts, Analysis, Strategies* (Paris: OECD, 1994).

that they would be indifferent between their present job and more enjoyable but less well-paid jobs. This idea, introduced into economics by Adam Smith, is known as the principle of compensating wage differentials. Compensating wage differentials are to a large extent observed in the world in which we live. Workers can expect wage bonuses in return for working unsocial hours. Workers employed in a dangerous environment can expect to earn higher wages than they would receive in a safer situation.

Reasons other than compensating wage differentials also help to explain the spread of earnings between occupations. First, consider the exceptionally high wages earned by some sports players, musicians, and other entertainers. In general these workers supply non-rival goods. Many people can attend a sports event or concert at the same time, and so the productivity of such workers is very high even though the individual tickets may be relatively inexpensive. This means that high wages can be paid to artists of this kind—they earn a large amount of economic rent by exploiting the scarcity value of their talent. This rent allows them to earn sums over and above what is needed to induce them to stay in their present occupation. Where economic rents are earned, the labour market is imperfect because the uneven distribution of talent across individuals impedes freedom of entry into high-wage occupations.

Second, there may be other factors which prevent competition in the labour market from being perfect. Contracts made between firms and their workers typically restrict wage movements for the duration of the agreement (usually 12 months in the UK). Welfare benefits set a floor below which earnings cannot normally fall; minimum wage legislation can have a similar effect. A world where unions bargain with large firms is far removed from the competitive model of demand and supply—indeed, despite a plethora of theories, there is little consensus about the manner in which wage bargaining takes place. In large organizations, wages are often determined by internal politics, and, where the career path of workers within the firm is clearly defined, wages for some jobs may be set without reference to a worker's earning potential outside the firm.

The spread of average earnings across occupations is very wide. Amongst males, in 1994 the average ranged from £3.88 per hour for kitchen porters to over £20 per hour for marketing and sales managers, financial associate professionals, and senior civil servants. The salary of this latter group reflects the relatively limited supply of talent in this field, and also compensates workers for the long training periods required for this type of work. Average earnings defined across broad occupational categories are reported in Table 10.10. Non-manual workers are on average paid more than manual workers, reflecting the tendency for the former to have sacrificed earnings potential in favour of education and training at an earlier stage in their lives. Moreover, in recent years, pay for non-manual work has been rising at a much faster rate than that for manual work, reflecting long-run changes in the structure of demand for labour. Indeed, the nominal hourly pay of men in personal and protective services actually fell between 1993 and 1994.

Table 10.10. Average gross earnings by occupation, full-time adult men and women, April 1994

Occupational group	Men		Women	
	Weekly (£)	Hourly (p)	Weekly (£)	Hourly (p)
Non-manual				
Managers and administrators	537	1364	368	967
Professional occupations	500	1356	408	1234
Technical occupations etc.	443	1129	333	888
Clerical, secretarial	270	662	230	612
Personal, protective service	296	685	199	500
Sales	310	776	200	517
Manual				
Craft and related occupations	318	695	191	471
Plant, machine operatives	294	618	202	478
Other	251	535	171	423
All non-manual	443	1136	288	775
All manual	291	625	188	455
All occupations	375	897	270	714

Source: New Earnings Survey.

To some extent it is inevitable that inter-occupational differences in earnings are the result of differences in the characteristics of the workforce rather than differences in the nature of the job itself. Pay differences may, to some extent, be due to differences in the job specifications, but it should be borne in mind that differences in the average age, experience, years of education, and sex composition of employees in each occupation can influence average earnings too. Using 1973 data, Shah[12] has estimated that even if all these factors were constant across occupations, judges would, on average, still earn a salary some 70% higher than that of nurses. This reflects, in part, a strong job preference on the part of nurses.

More recently, Blanchflower and Oswald[13] found that between 1983 and 1986 non-manual workers earned 19% more per hour than manual workers. This average estimate is based on a statistical analysis in which personal characteristics, educational background, region of residence, and industry within which they work are all held constant across workers. So even if occupational choice were the only respect in which workers differed, non-manual workers would still be paid 19% more per hour than manual workers. Since the total differential is close to 50%, we may conclude that personal characteristics, education, and so on are important determinants of earnings.

Wage structure by region.   As can be seen in Table 10.11, wages vary substantially across the regions of the UK. Part of this inter-regional variation is due to

[12] A. Shah, 'Professional Earnings in the UK', *Economica*, 50 (1983), 451–62.
[13] D. G. Blanchflower and A. J. Oswald, *The Wage Curve*, Centre for Labour Economics Discussion Paper no. 340 (London: London School of Economics, 1989); summary version published in *Scandinavian Journal of Economics*, 92 (1990), 215–35.

Table 10.11. Earnings by region in Great Britain, full-time men, April 1994 (pence per hour)

Region	Earnings (pence per hour)	
	Manuals	Non-manuals
South-East	664	1303
East Anglia	603	1021
South-West	595	1051
West Midlands	608	1046
East Midlands	603	1002
Yorkshire and Humberside	609	1000
North-West	627	1056
North	626	990
Wales	617	995
Scotland	626	1143

Source: New Earnings Survey.

differences in the industry mix or occupation mix of regions. For example, the relatively high-wage financial sector is strongly represented in the South-East. In 1994, 18.2% of all employees in this region were employed in financial services compared with just 12.5% for Great Britain as a whole.

Blanchflower and Oswald find that, even correcting for industry mix and for other factors, hourly wages outside the South-East were typically between 4 and 8% lower than in the South-East for 23-year-old workers in 1981. High property prices and the considerable costs of travelling long distances to work explain a large part of these disparities. This is a clear example of compensating wage differentials.

Another regional issue concerns the response of wages to local unemployment conditions. Blanchflower and Oswald have, in common with other studies, found that the unemployment elasticity of wages is about −0.1;[14] that is, a region with an unemployment rate of 10% is expected to have wages which are 1% lower than an otherwise similar region with an unemployment rate of 11%. Note that the tendency for the wage to move in a market clearing direction offsets any tendency for employees in high unemployment areas to secure wage compensation for living in a depressed locality; the latter effect might nevertheless go some way towards explaining why the labour market is slow to respond to shocks.

The Determinants of Wage Structure: Worker Characteristics

Many personal characteristics have a role to play in determining an individual's earnings. These include gender, race, family composition, employment history, union membership, health, and education. In this section we deal with each in turn.

[14] D. G. Blanchflower and A. J. Oswald, 'Estimating a Wage Curve for Britain, 1973–90', *Economic Journal*, 104 (1994), 1025–43.

Table 10.12. Relative female/male pay and employment (%)

Year	Full-time workers			Part-time female relative to full-time males	
	Hourly wage rates (W_f/W_m)	Hourly earnings (W_f/W_m)	Employment (F/M)	Hourly earnings (W_f/W_m)	Employment (F/M)
1973	87	64	41	51	10
1976	100	73	42	59	11
1984	100	73	47	58	12
1991	100	78	55	58	13
1993	100	79	58	59	15

Note: W_f is wages or earnings of females; W_m is wages or earnings of males; F and M are, respectively, employment of females and males. Data for part-time workers are expressed as full-time equivalents. The hourly wage data refer to the weighted average of minimum rates of manual workers laid down in collective agreements.
Sources: Z. Tzannatos and A. Zabalza, 'The Anatomy of the Rise of British Female Relative Wages in the 1970s', *British Journal of Industrial Relations*, 22 (1984), 177–94, and authors' own calculations from the *New Earnings Survey*.

Gender.   In 1995, 50% of all employees in employment in Great Britain were females. Of these, almost one-half work part time. Despite their importance in the labour force, women are on average paid substantially less than men. In 1994 some 40% of females but only 21% of males earned less than £4.60 per hour. This is partly the consequence of differences in the type of work that men and women do, but a glance at Table 10.12 shows that even within each broad occupational class men's earnings exceed those of women.

A number of reasons explain these gender differences. First, women tend to be less strongly committed to membership of the labour force than are men, since a large proportion of women drop out of the labour force to have children and then return to work some years later. In the case of graduates, for example, some 28% of women leave the labour force for family reasons within five years of joining it.[15] Work experience is a characteristic which carries a high reward in the labour market since it keeps individuals up to date with new techniques and maintains familiarity with the ways of the workplace.

Second, labour turnover amongst women tends to be higher than is the case amongst men, and this carries penalties for firms employing many women. High turnover rates are costly for firms, both in terms of direct hiring costs and training. These costs may be shifted onto women in the form of lower wages.

Since 1976 the Equal Pay Act has required that women performing similar tasks to men, or performing work of equal value to that of men, must be treated equally to men. The Sex Discrimination Act of 1975 requires that men and women should be guaranteed equality of opportunity. As can be seen from Table 10.12, these Acts had an immediate impact on the minimum rates of pay

---

[15] P. J. Dolton, *The Early Careers of 1980 Graduates: Work Histories, Job Tenure, Career Mobility and Occupational Choice* (London: Department of Employment, 1992).

set in collective agreements (column 1). Their impact on hourly earnings is not so easy to assess, however. Certainly female earnings have risen relative to male earnings. But it is not possible unambiguously to attribute this improvement to the introduction of legislation without first considering alternative explanations.

First, the demand for female workers might have risen during the mid-1970s, thereby pushing wages up. However, a short-run cyclical upswing is not sufficient to explain the figures of Table 10.12, because the hourly earnings ratio remained at historically high levels despite the recessions of the early 1980s and early 1990s. Second, female labour supply might have declined over the 1970s, thereby forcing female wages up. The ratio of female employment to male employment has, however, been rising steadily over the last quarter-century. In the absence of any convincing alternative, it seems fair therefore to conclude that the Equal Pay Act has contributed to the narrowing of gender differentials in rates of pay.

Nevertheless much more remains to be achieved. Female hourly earnings are still well below those of men. This remains the case even if education, experience, hours of work, industry mix, and other variables are held constant across the sexes. Blanchflower and Oswald[16] estimate that 23-year-old women in 1981 earned 23% less per hour than their male counterparts, other things being equal. This might indicate occupational segregation.

Race. Non-whites, like women, suffer from discrimination. Blackaby[17] has estimated that in 1975, other things being equal, non-white males earned approximately 9% less than white males. This estimate holds constant such determinants of earnings as education, experience, family composition, and unemployment history. To the extent that racial discrimination adversely affects employment opportunities among the ethnic minorities, this figure will be an underestimate.

A substantial part of the racial wage gap is due to the fact that non-whites find it difficult to enter occupations which have high wages. The 1982 Policy Studies Institute (PSI) Survey reveals that there is a concentration of ethnic minorities in manual jobs, particularly in semi-skilled and unskilled occupations. 16% of the employed white work force fell into the semi-skilled and unskilled categories compared to 40% for non-whites.[18] This is partly the consequence of ethnic differences in qualifications.

In all regions, white males earn more than non-white males, and the gap is especially pronounced in the North-West and the East Midlands. Overall, the gap in England and Wales amounts to 17%. Comparing this with Blackaby's 9% estimate, it can be deduced that about one-half of the total gap between the earnings of whites and non-whites in Britain is due to such factors as

---

[16] Blanchflower and Oswald, *Wage Curve.*
[17] D. H. Blackaby, 'An Analysis of the Male Racial Earnings Differential in the UK', *Applied Economics*, 18 (1233–42).
[18] C. Brown, *Black and White Britain: The Third PSI Survey* (London: Heinemann, 1984).

education and occupation; this has obvious implications for education policy. The other half is due to pure discrimination.

Education. It is not at all surprising to find that education has a positive influence on an individual's earnings capability. If this were not the case, it would be unlikely that people would sacrifice years of earnings in order to acquire post-compulsory education.

After controlling for other determinants of earnings, Blanchflower and Oswald compare the earnings of 23-year-old workers in 1981 who have no educational qualifications with those who do.[19] As might be expected, it is broadly the case that more education leads to higher earnings. Those workers who have between one and four O-level passes (good GSCE grades) earn an average premium of around 5%. Those with five or more O-level passes earn a premium of 9%. A worker with two or more A-levels earns, on average, 14% more per hour than one with no qualifications, and the premium rises to 18% for those with degrees.

These figures may not seem very high, but it should be remembered that they are based on the assumption that all other determinants of earnings are held constant across all workers. To the extent that highly educated workers tend to enter relatively well-paid occupations, tend to have good promotion prospects, and stable employment histories, the above estimates understate the true differential between the earnings of highly educated workers and others. The usefulness of the estimates lies in the fact that they indicate the extent to which an improvement in education alone (without changes in occupation etc.) can raise earnings.

Family composition. Married male workers tend to earn more than single males, other things being equal. One reason for this is that the responsibility and expense of a family imposes the discipline of a stable work habit. Waldfogel[20] has used National Child Development Survey data to examine male and female earnings at age 33. She found that marriage raises male earnings by around 9% on average, other things being equal, but has a slight negative effect on female earnings. The presence of children has virtually no effect on male earnings, but reduces female earnings by about 10%, other things being equal. For many women, an additional penalty to childbearing is incurred because they forgo labour-market experience; since each year of such experience adds some 3% to female earnings, this penalty can be severe.

Other determinants of earnings. Amongst 23-year-olds in 1981, the following variables were amongst the most important determinants of earnings, other things being equal. First, union membership raised the hourly wage by 7%.

---

[19] Blanchflower and Oswald, *The Wage Curve*.
[20] J. Waldfogel, 'Women Working for Less: A Longitudinal Analysis of the Family Penalty', paper presented to the EMRU/LESG conference, Manchester, 6 July 1993.

(The union mark-up on wages will be discussed at greater length later in this chapter.)

Second, those who work unsocial hours are paid a premium of 11% on average. It is clear that leisure is worth more to people at certain times than at others, and a reduction in the utility of their leisure must be compensated for in the form of higher wages.

Third, if a worker has a history of unemployment experience, his or her wage is, on average, 5% lower than it would otherwise be. Experience of work raises earnings potential whereas periods out of work lead to a depreciation of human capital and hence productivity. A history of unemployment also—rightly or wrongly—sends signals to an employer about a worker's motivation, aptitude, and tenacity.

Fourth, workers who are employed in jobs which are part of a well-established career structure earn a premium of 8%. Such workers might be regarded as members of the 'primary' work force. Firms which fill vacancies in senior positions exclusively from within the ranks of their own work force will be keen to hold on to their best workers. Consequently, wages tend to be higher where a promotion ladder exists.

Fifth, registered disabled people earn, on average, 28% less than other workers. This may in part be the result of inevitable constraints on the type of tasks which they perform and the efficiency with which they can carry out their duties at work. Although the earnings of disabled people are lower than the earnings of able-bodied people, the difference in their incomes need not be so great since many of these workers will qualify for disability benefit.

Changes in Earnings Over Time

Fig. 10.17 shows the rate of growth of weekly earnings of manufacturing employees. The burst of inflation in 1980 was largely stimulated by an oil price rise, an increase in the rate of value-added tax, and the award of large public sector pay increases. The rate at which earnings were growing fell steadily throughout the first half of the present decade. Labour productivity rose rapidly during the labour shake-out of the early and mid-1980s, but the rate of improvement slowed subsequently. This is shown in Fig. 10.18.

Social Security

Having considered the determinants of earnings, we now consider another important component of total personal income, namely social security. The system of welfare payments comprises numerous types of benefit, including child benefit, unemployment benefit, statutory sick pay, invalidity benefit, and the flat-rate retirement pension. In addition to these, three main types of

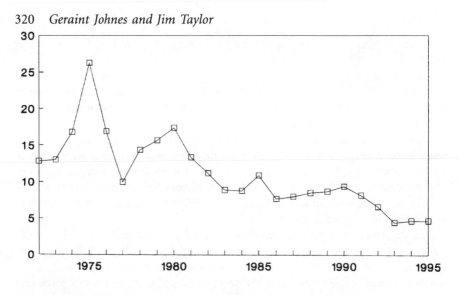

Figure 10.17. Earnings growth in manufacturing in the UK, 1972–1995 (percentage per annum)

Source: OECD *Main Economic Indicators; Labour Market Trends.*

income-related benefit exist; these underwent radical reform and simplification in 1988, and are discussed below.

Housing Benefit. This entitles families on low incomes (and with wealth of less than £16 000) to claim up to 100% of their rent. No assistance is provided

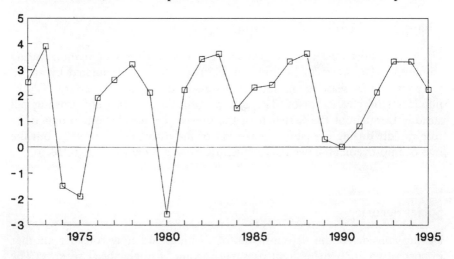

Figure 10.18. Annual rate of growth of output per person employed in the UK, 1972–1995 (%)

Source: Employment Gazette; Labour Market Trends.

with mortgage interest payments for those who are buying their own homes. Such individuals may, however, be able to claim financial help under the Income Support scheme. The Housing Benefit Scheme uses a taper system to ensure that as net income rises entitlement to support declines gradually. Up to a critical level of net income (which depends on family composition) the applicant is entitled to maximum support levels. If net income exceeds the critical level, then assistance with rent is reduced by 65% of the difference.

Family Credit. Family Credit is available to low-income families in full-time work who have children. Claimants receive an adult credit plus an additional credit for each child. The size of these credits depends on the age of the children. No Family Credit is payable if the claimant's wealth exceeds £8000. A taper system (in this case 70% of any excess) operates to ensure that Family Credit entitlements are reduced gradually as income net of disregards rises. The critical level of net income is £3728 per annum for the tax year 1994/95 (to rise to £3910 in 1996/7).

Income Support. This is available to low-income families not working 24 hours or more per week. Income Support is not payable if savings exceed £8000. Claimants receive a personal allowance which rises with the number of dependants. Families with children, single parents, the old, sick, and disabled are entitled to premiums in addition to their personal allowances. Claimants who are unemployed may also be entitled to unemployment benefit, which in the tax year 1994/5 amounts to £45.45 per week for a single person (rising to £48.25 in 1996/7).

The benefits discussed above make up an intricate patchwork of welfare payments to which minor modifications are periodically made. Past experience suggests that as the system becomes more complicated, anomalies such as the 'poverty trap' can occur. This arises where a worker loses more in tax paid and benefits forgone than he gains in pay by working an extra hour per week. The 1988 reforms were designed to remove poverty traps from the benefits system. They were largely successful in doing so. But marginal tax rates (including benefits forgone) paid by some poor people are still close to 100%.[21]

10.6. Trade Unions, Industrial Relations, and European Social Policy

Trade Unions

Trade union membership in the UK has been declining since 1979, when nearly 13.29 million workers were members. At the end of 1992 there were

---

[21] Hansard, written answers, 2 Nov. 1993, 189–90.

9.05 million union members, representing an overall union density of 35%. Union membership has thus fallen by 32% since 1979, and this warrants more detailed investigation.

The first possible explanation for the decline of union membership is that workers leave unions on becoming unemployed. Unemployment rose by 1.8 million over the years in question, and so it is hardly surprising that fewer workers should now be members of unions. Unemployment can only be a partial answer, though, since the fall in membership of 4.24 million has been greater than the rise in unemployment. It is possible that unemployment has a further indirect effect on union membership, since unions may become unattractive to workers during times of recession if it is believed that they price workers out of jobs.

A second reason for the fall in the number of union members is that there has been a change in the structure of industry (see Table 10.13). Declining industries tend to be more heavily unionized than growing industries, so the proportion of workers who belong to trade unions (i.e. union density) falls over time. Industry mix can, however, offer at best only a partial explanation, since Andrews and Naylor[22] have established that establishments within industries have typically experienced falls in union density.

A third possibility is that a change in the sex mix of employees in employment explains the collapse of union membership. This is not likely to be a major factor, however, since in 1993 the proportion of female employees who were union members, 31%, did not differ much from the corresponding proportion of men (38%).

A further factor which might explain the fall in union membership is political climate. Carruth and Disney[23] find that, other things being equal,

Table 10.13. Union density by industry, 1993

Industry in which most members are deemed to be employed	Density (%)
Agriculture, forestry, and fishing	10
Energy and water	66
Other mineral and ore extraction	40
Engineering, metal goods, and vehicles	33
Other manufacturing	32
Construction	25
Distribution and retail trades	11
Transport and communication	53
Financial services	23
Health, education, and administration	53
Total	35

Source: *Employment Gazette.*

[22] M. Andrews and R. Naylor, 'Declining Union Density in the 1980s: What do Panel Data Tell us?', *British Journal of Industrial Relations*, 32 (1994), 412–31.

[23] A. Carruth and R. Disney, 'Where have Two Million Trade Union Members Gone?', *Economics*, 55 (1988), 1–20.

union density is around 2.5 percentage points lower when a Conservative government is in power than at other times.

Finally, it has been suggested that industrial relations legislation introduced in the 1980s contributed substantially to the decline in trade union membership.[24] Several important reforms have been introduced over the last 15 years, and these are discussed later in this chapter. Amongst other things, these reforms emphasize the right of the individual union member not to participate in collective action, and in the eyes of many workers this has reduced the influence of the unions in bargaining; if the influence of unions diminishes, then so does their attractiveness to the potential membership.

Union density varies markedly across regions of the UK, being highest in the North and in Wales, and being lowest in East Anglia and the South-East. Some, but not all, of this inter-regional variation is due to regional differences in industry mix.[25]

Throughout most of the present century there has been a steady fall in the number of unions. This continued through the 1980s. At the end of 1992 there were 268 known unions in the UK. This is down from nearly 500 in 1975. Over 100 of these 268 unions are very small, however, with less than 1000 members each. These tiny unions include the Society of Shuttlemakers (around 40 members) and the London Society of Tie Cutters. At the other extreme, twenty unions had at least 100 000 members in 1992. These include UNISON (the Public Service Union, with 1.5 million members), the Transport and General Workers' Union (1 037 000 members in 1992) and the Amalgamated Engineering Union (884 000 members in 1992). Just over a quarter of all unions are affiliated to the Trades Union Congress (TUC), but since most of the large unions are affiliated, the TUC represents almost 90% of all union members.

The Union Mark-up

Much recent research has focused on the magnitude of the union:non-union wage differential. This is the difference which two workers would expect to obtain between their rates of pay if they were identical to one another in every respect except union membership. It is, of course, to be expected that union members will receive greater remuneration than non-members, since a major aim of unions is to secure higher wages for their members, and if they failed in this task many members might consider withdrawing their financial support from their union.

Estimates of the union mark-up based on panel data provided by Blanchflower[26] are reported in Table 10.14. Although the differential has varied

[24] R. Freeman and J. Pelletier, 'The Impact of Industrial Relations Legislation on British Union Density', *British Journal of Industrial Relations*, 28 (1990), 141–64.

[25] R. Martin, P. Sunley, and J. Wills, 'The Geography of Trade Union Decline: Spatial Dispersal or Regional Resilience?', *Transactions of the Institute of British Geographers*, 18 (1993), 36–62.

[26] D. G. Blanchflower, 'Fear, Unemployment and Pay Flexibility', *Economic Journal*, 101 (1991), 483–96.

Table 10.14. Estimates of the union mark-up

Year	% union mark-up
1983	11
1984	11
1986	13
1987	9
1989	11
1990/1	7–10

Sources: D. G. Blanchflower, 'Fear, Unemployment and Pay Flexibility', *Economic Journal*, 101 (1991), 483–96, Table 3; D. G. Blanchflower and R. B. Freeman, 'Did the Thatcher Reforms Change British Labour Market Performance', in R. Barrell, *The UK Labour Market* (Cambridge: Cambridge University Press, 1994), n.2.

somewhat from year to year, it generally appears to be of the order of 10%. The mark-up varies, however, across occupations. Stewart[27] finds a larger differential for semi-skilled than for skilled workers, and disaggregates his results by union status. The mark-up also varies considerably across industries;[28] for instance, in 1975 the estimated mark-up varied from 2% (in electrical engineering) to 18% (in shipbuilding).

It should be noted that the estimates given above understate the true influence of unions. This is because they refer to the difference in wage that an individual could expect if that individual alone changed his or her union membership status; the estimates assume that overall union density is given. A more comprehensive picture of union impact may be obtained by comparing the wages of union members whose wages are determined by collective bargaining with those of non-members whose wages are not determined by union-firm agreements, simultaneously controlling for variation in other factors which determine earnings. Such an exercise has been conducted by Blackaby *et al.*,[29] who find a differential of 22% between the wages of covered unionists and those of uncovered non-unionists in 1983.

The extent of the union mark-up is likely to be determined by a number of factors. Beenstock and Whitbread[30] argue that the differential rises if union density and the real value of unemployment benefit increase. Moreover, they find that the mark-up is some five percentage points lower under a Labour government than under a Conservative government. This last observation implies that unions respond more to government calls for wage restraint

[27] M. B. Stewart, 'Union Wage Differentials in the Face of Changes in the Economic and Legal Environment', *Economica*, 58 (1991), 155–72.

[28] M. B. Stewart, 'Relative Earnings and Individual Union Membership in the UK', *Economica*, 50 (1983), 111–25.

[29] D. H. Blackaby, P. D. Murphy, and P. J. Sloane, 'Union Membership, Collective Bargaining Coverage and the Trade Union Mark-up for Britain', *Economics Letters*, 36 (1991), 203–8.

[30] M. Beenstock and C. Whitbread, 'Explaining Changes in the Union Mark-up for Male Manual Workers in Great Britain, 1953–83', *British Journal of Industrial Relations*, 26 (1988), 327–38.

when Labour is in office. There is, however, no evidence to suggest that incomes policies influence the extent of the mark-up.

Time-series estimates of the union mark-up have been used by Layard and Nickell[31] in an attempt to explain the growth in unemployment between the late 1970s and the early 1980s. Although unemployment rose by seven percentage points over this period, only 0.8 percentage points can be attributed to the growth of the union:non-union wage differential. Most of the rise in unemployment was found to be the result of a deficiency of demand.

Strikes

An important weapon in the armoury of trade unions is the ability to take industrial action. Of the forms which such action can take, strikes generate the most animated debate. Despite the publicity which they attract, strikes are quite rare. A time-series of the number of working days lost per thousand workers through strike action in Britain is shown in Fig. 10.19. There has, in recent years, been a considerable fall in strike activity. But even in 1979—the year of the 'winter of discontent'—the average worker lost little more than a single day through industrial stoppage over the whole year.

There are several useful empirical studies of strike incidence.[32] The first

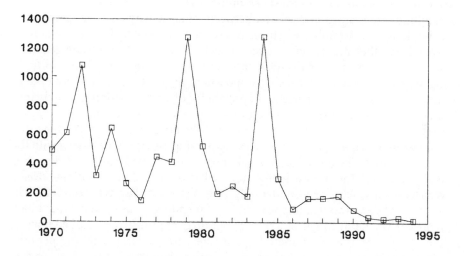

Figure 10.19. Working days lost through industrial stoppages, per thousand workers, 1970–1994.

Source: Employment Gazette; Labour Market Trends.

[31] P. R. G. Layard and S. J. Nickell, 'Unemployment in Britain', *Economica*, 53 (1986), S121–S129.

[32] D. G. Blanchflower and J. Cubbin, 'Strike Propensities at the British Workplace', *Oxford Bulletin of Economics and Statistics*, 48 (1986), 19–40.

significant determinant of strike activity is the size of the bargaining group. Strike incidence rises as the bargaining group increases in size. This suggests that strikes are more likely to occur in larger establishments than in smaller ones. Furthermore, strikes are more likely in multi-establishment firms than in single-plant firms.

Second, unionization affects strike-proneness in a number of ways. The coexistence of a number of unions at an establishment serves to raise the strike propensity, owing to inter-union competition; this takes the form of demarcation disputes between unions and a desire on the part of each union to convince workers of its own effectiveness. In addition, the presence of a large number of unions complicates negotiations with the employer and makes it difficult to resolve disputes peacefully. Manual bargaining groups are more strike-prone than non-manual or mixed groups, and the presence of manual shop stewards also raises the propensity to strike.

Third, the adoption of payments by results schemes raises the probability of a strike occurring. Such schemes lead to uncertainty concerning remuneration levels and this can cause frustration on the part of the workforce.

Fourth, there is a high degree of persistence in industrial action: the probability of a strike occurring this year is higher than elsewhere at an establishment where a dispute occurred last year, other things being equal. This persistence leads to a distinct pattern of strike activity across industries and regions—some are more strike-prone than others (see Table 10.15).

Fifth, there is a pro-cyclical link between strike activity and macroeconomic conditions. In particular, when unemployment is high strike activity is relatively low, other things being equal; at such times, firms' profits are generally squeezed so that there is relatively little surplus over which workers and firms can bargain. Further, strike activity appears to be greater during times of high inflation than in other periods. Expectations of high inflation are built into union wage bids, and this can lead to an impasse in negotiations.

It is instructive to study the pattern of strike duration. Fig. 10.20 shows the manner in which the probability of a strike ending on a given day varies with the length of the strike hitherto. This is known as the hazard rate for strikes. It is easily seen that the hazard is high for strikes of very short duration—over a quarter of all strikes are over after only a day. Once a strike has lasted more than a couple of days, though, the probability of it ending on any given day is much reduced. The hazard then slowly rises, but there are some very marked blips in the series. The timing of these blips is likely to be affected by the periodic meeting of negotiators; the hazard rate is higher than trend at 10 days, 2 weeks, and about 4 weeks, 6 weeks, and 7 weeks after the commencement of the strike.

Industrial Relations

The nature of British industrial relations has changed markedly over the last 15 years, largely as a consequence of changes in legislation. The Employment Acts

Table 10.15. Percentage of bargaining groups experiencing strikes, by region and by industry, 1979–89

Region or industry	% of groups experiencing strike	Mean strike duration in days
South-East	3.1	9.7
South-West	1.3	4.5
East Anglia	1.6	33.0
East Midlands	1.8	15.6
West Midlands	2.2	7.4
North-West	3.7	11.6
Yorkshire and Humberside	2.2	15.1
North	1.5	16.4
Wales	1.7	11.6
Scotland	3.4	32.3
Food, drink, and tobacco	2.4	11.2
Coal and petroleum products	2.0	52.0
Chemicals	1.5	15.1
Metal manufacture	1.9	36.6
Mechanical engineering	3.0	11.4
Instrument engineering	3.2	9.4
Electrical engineering	4.5	7.1
Shipbuilding	0.0	0.0
Vehicles	4.5	9.6
Miscellaneous metal goods	2.5	10.6
Textiles	1.2	11.2
Leather goods	1.9	2.0
Clothing and footwear	0.0	0.0
Refractories	1.9	11.6
Timber	3.7	4.4
Paper, printing, and publishing	1.7	10.8
Other manufacturing	2.3	1.5

Source: P. Ingram, D. Metcalf, and J. Wadsworth, 'Strike Incidence and Duration in British Manufacturing Industry in the 1980's', Centre for Economic Performance Discussion Paper no. 48 (London: LSE, 1991).

of 1980, 1982, 1988, and 1990, together with the Trade Union Act of 1984 and the Trade Union Reform and Employment Rights Act of 1993, have fundamentally altered the balance of power between employers and trade unions. This being so, it is important to consider the current state of the law as it affects employee relations in the UK.

Pay bargaining in Britain traditionally takes place at national level; although many employers have recently allowed special consideration for workers in the South-East, where labour is scarce and housing is expensive, the main sources of inter-regional variation in wage rates in Britain are small firms and differences in industry mix.[33]

It is usual for unions and employers to bargain over pay deals which are of twelve months in duration. There are exceptions to this rule, of course, and these exceptions have in recent years been getting more common, especially in

[33] J. Walsh and W. Brown, 'Regional Earnings and Pay Flexibility' in A. Bowen and K. Mayhew (eds.), *Reducing Regional Inequalities* (London: Kogan Page, 1991).

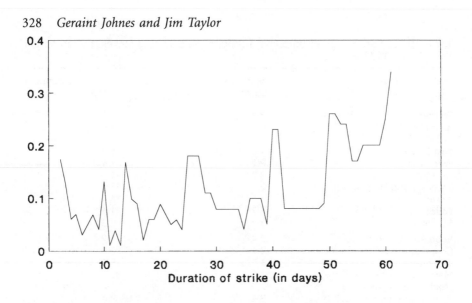

Figure 10.20. The hazard rate for strikes: probability of a strike ending.

Note: Vertical axis = probability of strike ending on day x, conditional on it having lasted $x-1$ days.

cases where bargains have been late in being struck. Moreover, many issues which do not (directly) concern pay (such as tea breaks, working hours, or overtime rates) are negotiated much less frequently than once a year.

Employers may, during a dispute, dismiss striking workers, and can employ alternative labour for the duration of the strike. Within a period of three months the employer may not selectively re-employ workers who have been dismissed in this way (unless the strike is unendorsed by the union). If the employer breaks this rule then unfair dismissal charges may be made. After the period of three months has expired, however, the employer may legally engage in the selective re-employment of dismissed workers.

The effective abolition of closed shops in 1990, where union membership was compulsory for all workers at an establishment, is an example of legal changes which have increased the voice of individual workers at the expense of the collective voice of the unions. Another example concerns the provision in the 1988 Act which ensures that a union cannot discipline individual members who choose not to participate in a strike or other dispute which has been legitimized by majority vote.

At the same time, the circumstances in which a union can call a strike have been changed by law. Since 1984, a secret ballot of members must be conducted before a strike can take place; any strike which occurs otherwise can be stopped by the employer concerned by appeal to the courts. Since 1988 individual union members have the right to restrain the union from striking prior to conducting a secret ballot. The most recent reform, enacted in 1993, requires postal ballots (rather than secret ballots at the workplace), and also requires a union to give a week's notice in advance of any strike action.

Before 1980 trade unions had no legal entity. That meant that the unions enjoyed immunity from civil law action. In 1982 these immunities were withdrawn, and it became possible for a union to be sued for damages when acting unlawfully. This inevitably put union funds at risk through court orders and sequestrations. The scope of union strike activity has also been reduced by recent changes. In 1980 a code of practice was introduced which aimed to limit the number of pickets operating at the premises of the firm directly involved in a dispute. In 1990, it became illegal to engage in any form of secondary action.

The changes listed above have contributed to a weakening of the unions' position in bargaining. They have been credited for the decline in union membership, the decrease in strike activity, and the increasingly positive perception of unions' contribution to the economy in the eyes of the public. Whether these are truly the effects of legislation remains to be seen. As we saw earlier, there are many reasons why the number of trade unionists has declined; the popularity of the strike as an industrial weapon declined partly as a result of the protracted miners' dispute of 1984–5; and the popular acclaim more recently enjoyed by the unions might simply be the consequence of a period of inactivity caused by factors other than legal changes.

11

THE BALANCE OF PAYMENTS

C. J. GREEN

11.1. Understanding the Balance of Payments and Net External Asset Position

Introduction

The importance to the UK of the balance of payments, foreign trade, and investment is probably too obvious to require emphasis. Although all countries are affected to some extent by external developments, the UK is a particularly open economy and is correspondingly dependent on its international trading and investment position. In 1994, for example, exports of goods and services were 25.6% of GNP (at market prices), and imports of goods and services were 26.6% of GNP. Meanwhile, the UK's gross external assets and its gross external liabilities were each more than twice the GNP. All these figures are substantially higher than in the 1960s,[1] although in the last decade, they have largely stabilized. This high degree of openness implies that the growth of the UK economy, the level and structure of production and employment, and the overall standard of living in the UK are all greatly influenced by external events, most of which impinge on the economy in the first instance through the balance of payments. The purpose of this chapter is to outline the main features of the UK's balance of payments and its associated net external asset position, and to discuss certain of the economic policies adopted to influence them in recent years. In Section 11.1, the main concepts which are relevant for understanding the balance of payments are introduced. Section 11.2 discusses the UK's overall balance of payments performance, emphasizing in particular the role of the exchange rate. Finally, in Sections 11.3 and 11.4, the UK's current and capital accounts, respectively, are examined in more detail.

---

[1] In 1965 the export-GNP ratio was 18.2% and the import-GNP ratio was 19.2%.

Basic Concepts

The balance-of-payments accounts. The concept of the balance of payments is central to a study of the external economic relationships of a country but, as with any unifying concept, it is not free from ambiguities. It is most straightforward to consider the concept first as a system of accounts. Thus we may define the balance of payments as a systematic record, over a given period of time, of all transactions between domestic residents and residents of foreign nations. In this context, residents are defined as those individuals living in the UK, and UK government agencies and military forces located abroad. Transactions are recorded as sterling money flows, and when transactions are invoiced in foreign currencies, their values are converted into sterling, at the appropriate exchange rate. Ideally, all transactions should be recorded at the time of the change of ownership of commodities and assets, or at the time specific services are performed. In practice, trade flows are recorded on a shipment basis, when the export documents are lodged with the Customs and Excise, and at the time when imports are cleared through Customs. As the time of shipment need bear no close or stable relationship to the time of payment for the goods concerned, this method gives rise to errors in the recording of the accounts.

Like all systems of income and expenditure accounts, the balance-of-payments accounts are an *ex-post* record, constructed on the principle of double-entry bookkeeping. Each external transaction is in principle entered twice, once to indicate the original transaction and again to indicate the manner in which the transaction was financed. The convention is that credit items which give rise to a flow of funds into the UK (e.g. exports of goods and services and foreign investment in the UK), are entered with a positive sign, and that debit items, which give rise to a flow of funds out of the UK (e.g. imports of goods and services and investments by UK residents overseas) are entered with a negative sign. It follows that, by definition, the balance-of-payments accounts always balance—the total of credit items must equal the total of debit items. Thus, the interpretation of the accounts depends on dividing them up in particular ways.

The structure of the balance of payments. The UK balance-of-payments accounts are itemized following the recommendations set out by international agreement through the International Monetary Fund (IMF). However, the grouping and aggregation of individual items in official UK balance-of-payments statistics have changed over the years, whereas the IMF recommends a useful standard presentation which has remained largely unchanged for many years. Therefore, the summary statement of the UK's balance of payments for

1980–94, contained in Table 11.1, follows with one exception the IMF's presentation rather than that in official UK sources.[2]

The first major feature of the IMF presentation is the distinction between current and capital accounts and, for many purposes, this is the most convenient summary division of the accounts. The current account records all trade in goods and services, including current transfers (Table 11.1: lines A1–A5); whereas the capital and financial account records all transactions in assets and liabilities (Table 11.1: lines A6–A13).[3]

First in the current account are the so-called 'visible' trade items, consisting of the exports (A1) and imports (A2) of commodities. These are shown separately in Table 11.1 whereas all subsequent items are shown on a net basis, i.e. receipts less payments. Full details of separate debit and credit items are given in the official sources. Exports are recorded 'free on board' (f.o.b.), that is at their value at the port of exit excluding the cost of international shipping and insurance. Import statistics are more usually collected c.i.f. (cost, insurance, freight), that is at their value inclusive of international shipping and insurance. As shipping and insurance are not part of the producer cost of a product, import data are adjusted to their f.o.b. basis for reporting in the balance of payments. The remaining items in the current account are the so-called 'invisibles'. Services (A3) include receipts and payments arising from charges for the insurance and shipping services associated with international trade. When imports are adjusted from a c.i.f. to an f.o.b. basis, much of the adjustment is imputed back into the accounts as services purchased. Other services arise independently, notably the expenditures of tourists when abroad, and consultancy services. Remittances on account of investment income (A4) arise when, for example, British firms pay dividends to foreign shareholders (a debit) or vice versa (a credit). Asset holders perform a service in lending capital funds to firms and governments, and the dividend or interest payments are their rewards for performing this service. Note that interest and dividend income from assets appear in the current account, but revenues from the purchase or sale of an asset appear in the capital account. Current transfers (A5) are so-called 'unrequited' in nature, as they do not directly arise from the sale of goods and services or of assets. Remittances home by immigrant workers, payments to and from the EC, and foreign aid payments are the main examples.

---

[2] It should be emphasized that the individual items in the accounts emanate directly from UK official statistics; it is their aggregation and grouping in Table 11.1 which follow the IMF presentation. The IMF presentation is summarized in the annual *Balance of Payments Statistics Yearbook*, IMF, Washington DC. The reference manual for IMF balance of payments statistics is *The Balance of Payments Manual*, fifth edition, IMF, Washington DC, 1993. UK balance of payments statistics are published annually in the CSO, *United Kingdom Balance of Payments*, HMSO: also known by its cover as 'the Pink Book'.

[3] The 'capital and financial account' replaces the old 'capital account' in the 5th edition of *The Balance of Payments Manual*. For brevity, in the rest of this chapter we will continue to use the old terminology 'capital account'.

Table 11.1 UK summary balance of payments 1980; 1990–1994 (£m: credits + /debits –)

	1980	1990	1991	1992	1993	1994
Current Account						
A1 Exports (f.o.b.)	47149	101718	103413	107343	121409	134465
A2 Imports (f.o.b.)	45792	120527	133697	120447	134787	145059
B1 Balance of visible trade = A1+A2	1357	–18809	–10284	–13104	–13378	–10594
A3 Services	3653	3689	3708	5051	5685	3790
A4 Investment incomes	–183	723	–574	3694	1890	10519
A5 Transfers	–1984	–4896	–1383	–5109	–5239	–5399
B2 Balance of invisible trade = A3+A4+A5	1486	–484	1751	3636	2336	8910
B3 Balance on current account = B1+B2	2843	–19293	–8533	–9468	–11042	–1684
Capital and Financial Account						
A6 Capital transfers	—	—	—	—	—	—
A7 Direct investment	–512	8024	1	–2332	–7510	–9735
A8 Portfolio investment	–2823	–4630	–13969	–3184	–39144	48382
A9 Other capital n.i.e. = A9.1+A9.2+A9.3	–1438	13025	26577	11239	56418	–41210
A.9.1 Government	(–419)	(–2284)	(565)	(2787)	(–6662)	(1877)
A.9.2 UK banks	(935)	(7191)	(9567)	(–5625)	(28310)	(–2293)
A.9.3 Other	(–1954)	(8118)	(16445)	(–14077)	(34770)	(–40794)
A10 Foreign authorities' sterling reserves	1262	1779	–1406	744	4447	53
B4 Balance on capital flows = A6+A7+A8+A9+A10	–3511	18198	11203	6476	14211	–2510
A11 Balancing item	917	1172	6	4409	–2470	5245
B5 Balance for official financing = B3+B4+A11	251	76	2679	–1407	698	1045
A12 Allocation of SDRs & IMF reserve tranche position	180	—	—	—	—	—
A13 Official financing = A13.1+A13.2 = –(B5+A12)	–431	–76	–2679	1407	–698	–1045
A13.1 Official reserves (increase–)	(–291)	(–76)	(–2679)	(1407)	(–698)	(–1045)
A13.2 Change in net IMF position	(–140)	(—)	(—)	(—)	(—)	(—)

Source: Pink Book and ET

Turning to the capital account, capital transfers (A6) are invariably difficult to distinguish from current transfers, and most transfers are, in practice, recorded in the current account. Direct investment (A7) consists of transactions undertaken to acquire or extend control over a foreign enterprise; portfolio investment (A8) consists of transactions aimed at securing investment income or capital gains. The distinction between these two groups is clearer in practice than it might appear. Direct investment abroad by the UK involves the construction and equipping of factories abroad or the acquisition or sale of foreign subsidiaries by British firms. Thus, direct investment has as its main purpose the production of goods or services in a foreign country. In contrast, agents undertaking portfolio investment act 'at arms length' and have no direct managerial interest in the activity in which the investment is made. Portfolio investment involves the purchase or sale of securities of overseas companies or governments. Such securities are typically held by financial institutions, such as pension funds, as part of their overall investment operations.

Other capital not included elsewhere (n.i.e.) is relatively heterogeneous. Government transactions recorded in this section (A9.1) include long-term intergovernmental transactions, subscriptions to the World Bank, and certain short-term lendings and borrowings. Two particular items are recorded elsewhere. First is the borrowing which is counted by overseas monetary authorities as part of their reserves (A10); second is loans from the IMF and government liquid asset transactions, both of which are shown in official financing (A13). Transactions by UK banks (A9.2) consist of the vast majority of their sterling and foreign-currency transactions with overseas residents, including all their loans and deposits but excluding their transactions in long-term bonds, which are recorded with portfolio investment in A8. Finally in this group, 'Other' (A9.3) consists of the identifiable transactions of other sectors. Items of note here include transactions with foreign banks by UK residents, and net trade credit which is the immediate counterpart of a high proportion of export and import payments. The amount of trade credit outstanding at any one time (mostly of one to six months maturity) is very large, although it has a rapid turnover and the net flows are usually relatively small.

Foreign Authorities' sterling reserves (A10) consists of movements of funds arising from transactions made by overseas monetary authorities (mainly central banks) who hold sterling assets as part of their own official reserves. These assets include deposits with UK banks and with the Bank of England, as well as holdings of government bonds and Treasury Bills. Foreign holdings of sterling for official reserves purposes amounted to £22.3 billion at the end of 1994, up from £4.6 billion at the end of 1980. The IMF recommends that transactions in these assets be recorded as part of official financing, so as to ensure that the sum of all countries' official financing surpluses worldwide is, in principle, equal to the sum of official financing deficits. This procedure is not followed by the UK and several other countries because movements in these funds are largely outside the control of the domestic monetary authority and they can therefore equally well be seen as generating a requirement for official financing as much as they can be seen as contributing to that financing. Here we take the view that movements in these funds are best thought of as generating a requirement for official financing and we therefore depart from the IMF presentation and show them contributing to the balance on capital flows. It should be emphasized, however, that this is just one of many occasions when the appropriate classification is a matter of judgement and no one view can be regarded as unambiguously 'right' or 'wrong'.

We come next to the balancing item (A11), which is the residual in the accounts, and which is required to compensate for the total of measurement errors and omissions. These can arise from a variety of sources. In general, the two sides of any given transaction cannot be recorded simultaneously. For example, the value of commodity exports is recorded mainly by the Customs and Excise Department but the proceeds from these exports are recorded only indirectly, using statistics provided by banks and other financial institutions. Although, in principle, the accounts should balance, in practice numerous discrepancies in recording procedures generally give rise to a positive or negative balancing item reflecting unrecorded receipts or payments respectively. The major source of errors and discrepancies in the accounts arises when data are collected mainly by sample surveys, especially if respondents have an incentive to under- or over-report. These circumstances occur particularly in the recording of trade in services and in capital-account items other than those reported by government or financial institutions. Particular problem areas include revenues and expenditures associated with tourism, trade credit, and other intra-private sector capital flows.

Line A12 relates to the UK's membership of the IMF. Allocations of Special Drawing Rights (SDRs) to the UK are treated as a credit item, even though they do not correspond to any actual transactions, because an allocation increases the UK's reserves (A13). Likewise, when the UK's quota in the IMF is increased, the UK is required to subscribe 25% of the increase to the IMF (the 'reserve tranche') in the form of SDRs or other 'convertible' foreign currencies,[4] and the official reserves fall by the corresponding amount.

The remaining lines of the balance of payments constitute official financing. Line A13 gives the amount by which the country's foreign-exchange reserves increased (−) or decreased over the year. Foreign-exchange reserves consist of the immediately liquid foreign currency assets of the central bank, together with its automatic drawing rights at the IMF. These play a specific role in balance-of-payments and exchange-rate policy. The transactions which make up the balance of payments involve a myriad individual decisions many of which involve a purchase or sale of foreign currency. There is no guarantee that, in aggregate, demands by domestic residents to purchase foreign currency

---

[4] A currency is said to be 'convertible' if it can be freely exchanged into other currencies by domestic and foreign residents.

in exchange for pounds will exactly match sales of foreign currency for pounds. Given the price of foreign currency, an excess demand or supply of foreign currency has to be met from some source. It is the central bank in a country (in the UK, the Bank of England) which acts as the last line of defence in supplying foreign currency if there is an excess demand for it, or in acquiring it if there is excess supply. Of course, excess demand or supply could lead to a change in price—of the foreign-exchange rate—but this is a large subject in its own right and is deferred to Section 11.2. In reckoning a country's official foreign-exchange reserves, only assets are included as these are immediately available. In a crisis, central banks can find it difficult to borrow without the attachment of conditions. Indeed, the inclusion of a country's automatic drawing rights in the IMF in this reckoning acknowledges that the only guaranteed source of foreign-currency borrowing for a central bank resides in these rights. An amount equal to 25% of a country's quota (the reserve tranche position) may be used automatically. Along with the IMF members, the UK has further access to four credit tranches, each of which corresponds to 25% of quota, but access is dependent on the adoption of economic policies which meet with the approval of the IMF, this being particularly so for drawings beyond the first credit tranche. Borrowing in the credit tranches is recorded separately under official financing in line A13.2.

Main balances in the balance of payments.   As we have seen, in an accounting sense it can be said that the balance of payments always balances. The interpretation of the accounts therefore depends on their being divided up in particular ways. It is customary to select a number of main 'balances' in the accounts which give a summary picture of different aspects of a country's overall balance of payments (Table 11.1, lines B1–B5). Two major balances are those on current account (B3) and on the capital account excluding the balancing item and official financing (B4). These two balances give, respectively, the net receipts or payments on account of all identified transactions in goods, services, and transfers (the current account), and in assets and liabilities other than official financing (the balance on capital flows). The balance for official financing (B5) is also regarded as important for the reasons given above—it shows the amount of 'last resort' activity undertaken by the central bank in buying or selling foreign-currency reserves. The balance for official financing is often called the 'overall balance'. Within the current account itself, a distinction is made between the balance of visible trade (B1) and the invisible balance (B2). To some extent, this is because statistics on the visible trade balance become available more rapidly than other items in the accounts apart from official financing, and therefore provide a leading indicator of possible trends in the accounts.

The balance of international indebtedness.   The balance of international indebtedness is a reckoning of the net external assets and liabilities of a country. It therefore gives the value of all assets held abroad and borrowing from abroad by UK residents, as well as all assets held in the UK and borrowing from the UK by overseas residents. Whereas the balance of payments gives a record of transactions and therefore of flows of funds during some particular time-period, the balance of international indebtedness gives the stocks of assets and liabilities outstanding at a particular point in time. Thus the total balance of international indebtedness on any given date is equivalent to the UK's total net overseas assets. As far as possible, the stocks of assets and liabilities in this balance are valued at current market prices.

Table 11.2 gives the balance of international indebtedness for the UK over the 1990–4 period. The classification of this account is similar to that of the capital account of the balance of payments, as the latter shows transactions in the same assets and liabilities whose outstanding stocks are given in the balance of international indebtedness. However, the capital account in any particular year is not simply equal to the change in the corresponding items in the balance of international indebtedness over that year. There are differences due in part to errors and omissions in the procedures for estimating the stocks of assets and liabilities and for recording the net transactions which make up the balance-of-payments account. However, differences also arise more particularly because the value of a nation's assets and liabilities can change for two reasons: first, new net lending or borrowing may take place, which is recorded in the capital account. Second, the price of an asset or liability may change, and this is not recorded in the capital account because it does not correspond to any transaction but to a valuation change.

A major cause of changes in international asset values is exchange-rate movements. Thus, when the price of sterling in terms of foreign currencies falls, the pound is said to depreciate.[5] Each unit of foreign currency will exchange for more pounds than before. Hence UK residents holding assets overseas whose values are denominated in foreign currencies will experience an increase in the sterling value of their assets—they will make capital gains. UK residents who have loans denominated in foreign currencies will experience an increase in the sterling value of their liabilities—they will make capital losses, as increased sterling amounts will be required to repay the loans. The reverse is true when the pound appreciates. However, it should be emphasized that not all overseas assets and liabilities are denominated in foreign currencies; many are denominated in sterling, as for example when the British Government sells sterling gilt-edged securities (bonds) to overseas residents. The sterling values of such assets and liabilities are not directly affected by movements in the exchange rate.

In general, therefore, the relation between the capital account of the balance of payments and the balance of international indebtedness is not a simple one. Moreover, when the exchange rate of sterling changes, overseas residents who hold sterling-denominated assets or liabilities will make capital gains or losses

---

[5] Thus a move from £1 = US$ 1.70 to £1 = US$ 1.60 represents a depreciation of the pound *vis-à-vis* the dollar, and a move in the other direction represents an appreciation.

Table 11.2 UK: net external assets and liabilities 1990–1994 (£bn. end of period)

		1990	1991	1992	1993	1994
1	Direct investment	6.5	5.0	25.0	38.1	43.6
2	Portfolio investment	69.4	95.2	110.4	167.2	128.8
3	Other capital n.i.e.	−86.3	−111.8	−137.4	−196.4	−163.2
	3.1 Government n.i.e.	(18.1)	(20.3)	(22.7)	(32.4)	(29.1)
	3.2 UK banks	(−85.9)	(−96.1)	(−105.8)	(−130.6)	(−134.3)
	3.3 Other	(−18.5)	(−36.0)	(−54.3)	(−98.2)	(−58.0)
4	Foreign authorities' sterling reserves	−17.9	−16.7	−18.6	−24.7	−22.3
5	Reserves	22.7	26.3	27.9	29.0	30.7
	5.1 Official reserves	(22.7)	(26.3)	(27.9)	(29.0)	(30.7)
	5.2 Net IMF positions	(—)	(—)	(—)	(—)	(—)
6	Net UK assets	−5.6	−2.0	7.3	13.2	17.7
7	Change from previous year	−59.3	3.6	10.9	5.5	4.5
8	Current account balance (calendar year)	−19.3	−8.5	−9.5	−11.0	−1.7
9	GNP at market prices (calendar year)	551.8	574.7	600.9	632.6	679.4
10	Net UK assets in per cent of GNP(%)	−1.0	−0.3	1.2	2.1	2.5

Note: Net Liabilities are shown with a negative sign
Source: Pink Book

in terms of their own currencies. Clearly, exchange-rate movements have complex effects on international asset and liability holdings and thus on individual decisions to adjust these holdings. These effects are considered in more detail in Section 11.2.

Equilibrium and Disequilibrium in the Balance of Payments

It is obviously important to have clear concepts of balance-of-payments equilibrium and disequilibrium. It would simplify matters if we could calculate easily the 'deficit' or 'surplus' in the balance of payments, and thus refer to the balance of payments as being 'out of equilibrium' or ' in equilibrium' if the deficit or surplus were thought to be sufficiently large or small in magnitude, respectively. However, the formulation of such concepts is not easy and depends on the purpose for which they are to be used. The time-span over which equilibrium is defined is obviously important, and it is generally accepted that a sufficient span of years should be allowed so that the effects of cyclical fluctuations in income will have no appreciable net impact on external transactions. The exchange-rate regime in force and the degree of intervention by the authorities are also important. If the authorities are intervening in the external accounts it becomes necessary to consider which interventions are intended either to restore or perturb an equilibrium and which are carried out for other purposes largely incidental to the balance of payments. Thus, sales of foreign-currency bonds to augment the official reserves on the one hand, and the granting of foreign aid on the other, both have an impact on the external accounts, but decisions about the latter would not normally be thought of primarily as constituting 'balance-of-payments policy'. In practice, equilibrium in the balance of payments is usually defined with reference to one of the various balances introduced in the previous section.

Balance for official financing (overall balance). This is the most commonly used concept of equilibrium, and the Balance for Official Financing (BOF) is often simply referred to as 'the balance of payments surplus' (or deficit). Its rationale arises from the role of the central bank in the foreign exchange market. If the exchange rate is allowed to float freely to equate the supply and demand for foreign exchange, including central government foreign transactions incidental to balance-of-payments policy, then equilibrium in the market is always attained automatically and this coincides with the fact that the BOF will, under these circumstances, always be identically zero.

Since 1972, successive UK governments have allowed sterling to float, but this float, like that of other countries, has never been completely free. The authorities have intervened in the foreign-exchange market and, as shown in Table 11.1, the BOF has never been identically zero but has often been quite large. When the exchange rate is managed by the authorities to any degree, a key role is assigned to the central bank as the last-resort provider of foreign currency, although this is by no means the only instrument which can be used to influence the exchange rate. If the BOF is positive (in surplus), the Bank of England has been able to increase its reserves at the prevailing sterling exchange rate, suggesting an excess supply of foreign currencies at this rate and consequent upward pressure on the exchange rate; whereas the existence of a deficit on the BOF suggests an excess demand for foreign currencies and consequent downward pressure on the exchange rate.

A further advantage of the BOF is that it shows the potential increase (decrease) in the UK money supply as a result of a surplus (deficit) in the balance of payments and hence gives an estimate of at least the general direction of expansionary (contractionary) forces in the economy emanating from the external accounts. The link between the BOF and the supply of money arises through the central-bank balance-sheet. As a matter of necessity, an increase (decrease) in central-bank foreign assets must be exactly balanced by an increase (decrease) in its liabilities. In general, the counterpart of a purchase (sale) of foreign exchange by the central bank is an increase (decrease) in its sterling deposit liabilities to the commercial bank from which it purchased the currency. Such deposits are included in a commercial bank's 'operational deposits', and an increase (decrease) in these deposits allows an expansion (contraction) in the commercial bank's loans and hence in its deposit liabilities, thus leading to an increase (decrease) in the money supply. The central bank can offset this effect by carrying out what is commonly called 'sterilization'. A sale (purchase) of Treasury Bills or bonds to the commercial bank in question will sterilize the monetary implications of the surplus of the BOF by drawing down (increasing) the commercial bank's operational deposits to their original level. Thus, while the link between the BOF and the potential change in the money supply is a direct one, the link between the BOF and the actual change in the money supply is a good deal more tenuous, depending as it does on the sterilization policy of the authorities and the exact responses of commercial banks to changes in the levels of their operational deposits.[6]

A final argument for focusing on the BOF is that most other definitions of surplus or deficit involve some element of arbitrariness in classifying the accounts. In particular, all other definitions fail to take into account the balancing item which, by its very nature, cannot be allocated among the identified items in the accounts. Such definitions are therefore inherently subject to some degree of mismeasurement and hence misinterpretation.

There are, however, arguments for not focusing exclusively on the BOF, the main one having to do with the role of the authorities. Acquisition or use of reserves is not the only nor even the most common method for the authorities to influence the balance of payments and the exchange rate. The level of interest rates in the economy has a direct influence on the exchange rate. More generally, the level of income affects most items in the balance of payments, and thus has a powerful, if indirect, influence on the exchange rate. Thus, the authorities may pursue policies which produce equilibrium in the BOF but which result in unacceptable levels of interest rates, unemployment, or inflation in the economy. This implies that the authorities have to keep in mind the other policy objectives as well as equilibrium in the BOF and, in designing policies, must recognize the interactions between the balance of payments and the rest of the economy.

The current account balance.   This is of interest because it marks the division between trade in goods and services and transactions in assets. Examination of the current account balance also brings out the relationship between the balance of payments and the national income and expenditure accounts. In discussing this relationship it is helpful to use some notation. Let: Y = GDP at Market Prices; C = Consumers' Expenditure; G = Government Expenditure; I = Private Investment; X = Export of Goods and Services; Z = Imports of Goods and Services; S = Private Savings; T = Tax Revenue; and F = Net Transfers Abroad. Using this notation, GDP calculated from the expenditure side can be written as:

$$Y = C + I + G + X - Z \tag{1}$$

In this identity, we see that the balance on goods and services ($X - Z$: equal to

[6] For useful accounts of the links between external transactions and the domestic money supply, see 'External Flows and Broad Money', *BEQB*, Dec. 1983; and 'Measures of Broad Money', *BEQB*, May 1987.

the current account balance exclusive of transfers) is arithmetically identical to the excess of domestic income (Y) over domestic expenditure ($C + I + G$). This fact often leads to a statement that a deficit in the goods and services balance is *caused* by an excess of domestic expenditure over domestic income. Since one is identical to the other, attribution of causation is incorrect; it is necessary to look more deeply for the causes of the excess of domestic expenditure over income. However, it is true that, if it were thought desirable to reduce a deficit on goods and services, this would of necessity involve a cut in domestic expenditures *relative* to domestic incomes. More generally, any policy which influences the balance between domestic incomes and expenditures will also necessarily affect the current account.

It is also illuminating to write the disposition of the GDP by income receipts as:

$$Y = C + S + T + F \tag{2}$$

Deducting (2) from (1) and rearranging the resultant identity gives the following:

$$(X - Z - F) = (T - G) + (S - I) \tag{3}$$

This states that the current account surplus (deficit) is arithmetically identical to the sum of the government budget surplus (deficit) and the private sector's surplus (deficit) of savings over investment. Since (3) is an identity, we still cannot describe either side of the identity as causing the other, but we can again state that policies which influence saving and investment must, unless they are exactly offsetting, of necessity affect the current account balance.

The current account balance is also related in an important way to the balance of international indebtedness. The private sector surplus (deficit) is equivalent to its net acquisition of financial assets (liabilities); likewise the government budget surplus (deficit) is equivalent to net government lending (borrowing). By analogy, the current account surplus (deficit), which is identical to the capital account deficit (surplus), is equivalent to the net acquisition (sales) of overseas assets by UK residents. As we have seen, the value of the UK's net external assets may change either because of net new lending or borrowing, or because of changes in the price of existing holdings of assets and liabilities. Net new lending or borrowing in total is equivalent to the current account surplus or deficit. In Table 11.2, the current account balance is shown together with the change in the UK net overseas assets, the difference between the two being attributable to valuation effects and net errors and omissions.

The concepts of equilibrium compared.   It should be emphasized that no single concept of equilibrium can be universally applicable. Different items in the balance of payments are interlinked. For example, an outflow of capital may produce a once-for-all deficit on the capital account, but the return flows of investment income in later periods will lead to a smaller but continuing inflow which improves the current account. Other less obvious linkages are too numerous to mention. Thus, whatever concept of equilibrium is used, it should be justified as being appropriate for the purpose to which it is applied.

With this in mind it should be clear that whereas the BOF focuses on the role of the authorities, the current account position draws attention to the interaction between the balance of payments and the economy as a whole. A reasonable summary of their relative uses would emphasize that the BOF is a relatively short-run equilibrium concept while the current account balance is of more interest in the longer run. Thus a substantial deficit on the BOF generally requires some immediate action on the part of the authorities if they are not to run out of reserves to finance the deficit. Indeed, in the era of relatively fixed exchange rates between 1945 and 1972, the IMF defined a 'fundamental disequilibrium' in the balance of payments as a deficit on the BOF which could not be financed or rectified by the authorities without a change in the exchange rate. On the other hand, a deficit on the current account can be financed for relatively long periods by capital inflows, but at a cost of steadily increasing international indebtedness.

The existence of a deficit in the balance of payments is usually thought to be a source of concern and to call for some policy actions to restore equilibrium. However, it can be argued that a balance of payments disequilibrium can only arise as a result of the activities of the public sector. If the private sectors in different countries freely enter into contracts which imply that one particular country (say the 'home' country) runs a persistent current account deficit, this cannot be a source of concern, otherwise foreign creditors would not have entered into these contracts. For example, suppose that foreign investors choose to reinvest in the home country all the profits they earn in that country. If all other items in the balance of payments have a net balance of zero, then the home country will have a current account deficit which is equal to the investment income outflows to foreign investors, but one which is exactly matched by an inflow of foreign portfolio and direct investment from the 'same' investors, giving an overall balance of zero. This current account 'imbalance' can persist without adverse effects for as long as foreigners choose to reinvest their profits in the home country. This argument would suggest that it is a public sector imbalance and not the balance of payments which is the problem.[7] However, the argument is by no means conclusive. Perhaps the most important counter-argument is that private markets do not

[7] In Britain, this view originated with the Cambridge group viz: W. A. H. Godley, T. F. Cripps, and M. Fetherston, 'Public Expenditure and the Management of the Economy', evidence submitted to the Select Committee on Public Expenditure (HC328 for 1974). More recently it has been espoused by a variety of authors; for example T. G. Congdon, 'Do Economists know How to Recognise a "Balance of Payments Problem"?', *Lombard Street Research Occasional Paper*, 2, Oct. 1989. Congdon cites the example of Singapore, which ran substantial and continuous current account deficits for 23 years without any apparent difficulty. For a recent appraisal of these arguments consult W. M. Corden, *Economic Policy, Exchange Rates, and the International System* (Oxford: Oxford University Press, 1994).

guarantee efficient investment and pricing decisions. In the context of the balance of payments, private sector decisions may produce deficits which are not sustainable but equally not correctable without government intervention. Governments may not necessarily make better decisions than the private sector, but judicious government intervention may improve private sector decisions. A particularly dramatic example is provided by the international debt crisis of the mid-1980s, when massive flows of bank-lending to third-world countries produced an unsustainable debt situation which was eventually resolved by a variety of *ad hoc* reschedulings and write-offs, largely under the spur of government and international agency intervention. Although banks lent mainly to third-world governments, the lending was on commercial terms and a substantial proportion of the business proved to be a major business error by the banks.[8] Nevertheless, there is an important core of truth in the argument that private sector deficits are 'unimportant'; and it is that the *magnitude* of a balance of payments deficit is likely to be a very unreliable indicator of the *severity* of the underlying problem involved, and of the consequent need for policy action. The latter depends on a deeper analysis of the contributions of the public and private sectors to the deficit. This point is particularly important when we turn to analyse the UK's recent balance of payments performance in Section 11.2.

11.2.   UK Balance of Payments Performance

The Role of the Exchange Rate

The foreign exchange market.   Before we consider in more detail the UK balance of payments, it will prove useful to outline the relationships between the balance of payments and the exchange rate.

Since nations maintain separate currencies for internal use, international transactions invariably proceed with the simultaneous exchange of national currencies. Exchange of currencies takes place in the foreign exchange market, and it is there that the relative prices of different currencies—exchange rates—are established. An important policy issue for the government of any country is the exchange rate regime which it wishes to adopt; that is, the set of rules which govern the exchange of its own currency with the currencies of other nations. Apart from sterling's brief (1990–2) period within the Exchange Rate Mechanism (ERM) of the European Monetary System (EMS), successive UK governments have, since 1972, pursued a policy of allowing sterling to take

---

[8] The best-known and most revealing anecdote from this era was the statement by the then chief executive of Citibank (one of the leading exponents of third-world lending), Walter Wriston, that 'governments cannot go bankrupt'.

whatever values the balance of demand and supply for foreign exchange might dictate, i.e. the sterling exchange rate is a floating rate.

Even though sterling is floating, the government must still decide whether to intervene in the exchange market by buying and selling foreign currency. The authorities also have considerable scope for influencing the exchange rate by less direct means, particularly involving interest rates and capital flows. The relationships among interest rates, capital flows, and the exchange rate are complex. The main determinants of capital flows are the relative rates of return on domestic and foreign assets, allowing for the effects of risk and taxation. These rates of return are affected by variations in domestic and foreign interest rates, and also by anticipated exchange rate changes which would result in capital gains or losses for holders of foreign currency assets. If sterling depreciation is anticipated, for example, this will provide an incentive for wealth-holders to switch any sterling-denominated assets they hold into foreign-currency-denominated assets in order to avoid the expected capital loss on holdings of sterling assets. Variations in the relative rates of return on domestic and foreign currency assets will affect capital flows and hence the demand and supply of sterling and therefore, the spot exchange rate.

However, in these calculations, a distinction must be drawn between short-term and long-term investments. For assets of up to three months maturity, it is usually possible to obtain forward cover. For example, suppose a foreign investor purchases £1 million of three month sterling bills paying an interest rate of say 2% per quarter (8% per annum). The investor must buy £1 million of spot sterling but she can simultaneously sell the proceeds of the bills (£1.02 million) in the three month forward exchange market and thus avoid any risk of loss or gain over the three months due to a possible depreciation or appreciation of sterling in that period.[9] The Covered Interest Parity Theorem states that, provided arbitrage funds are in perfectly elastic supply, the percentage difference between the spot and forward exchange rate in any pair of currencies will equal the interest differential between assets of the corresponding maturity denominated in these currencies. Evidence for the period since 1972 is that forward exchange rates up to three months have mostly approximated their interest parity values, implying that the limits between interest rates and the exchange rate for such short-term assets are particularly close.[10] However, for assets with a maturity in excess of three months, where forward cover is difficult or impossible to obtain, judgements

[9] The 'spot exchange rate' is the price of foreign currency for immediate delivery, that is, at the time transaction is agreed (or, strictly, within two working days). A 'forward exchange rate' is the price for foreign currency for delivery at a specified date in the future. The most widely traded forward contract in practice is that for delivery in three months. The arguments in the text also abstract from the transactions costs involved in buying and selling securities and foreign exchange.

[10] For a more detailed discussion of covered interest parity see, for example, R. MacDonald, *Floating Exchange Rates: Theories and Evidence* (London: Unwin Hyman, 1988). An interesting survey of empirical work is provided by D. L. Thornton, 'Tests of Covered Interest Rate Parity', *Federal Review Bank of St Louis Review*, 714 (July/Aug. 1989), 55–67.

about the expected future course of the exchange rate are a key ingredient in most foreign investment decisions.[11] In summary, therefore, any policy measure which affects interest rates or the market's expectations of the future spot exchange rate will, given foreign interest rates, influence the current spot exchange rate and the forward rate.

The exchange rate and the adjustment process. The discussion so far has focused on capital flows and the exchange rate. Before the current epoch of internationally mobile capital, great emphasis was placed on the role of the exchange rate in current account adjustments; and we turn next to the different approaches to this topic. The 'elasticities approach' emphasizes the effect of an exchange-rate change in altering the relative prices of domestic and foreign goods and services. Thus, a depreciation raises the domestic price of imported goods, depressing the demand for imports, and lowers the foreign price or increases the domestic profitability of export goods, thus tending to stimulate the export effort, and by these means improving the current account.[12] The 'absorption approach' lays stress on the fact, noted in Section 11.3 above, that a current account deficit is associated with an excess of domestic expenditure in relation to income. On this view, a depreciation improves the current account by stimulating incomes through the expansion in exports. Expenditures will typically rise by less than incomes as a part of the increase is saved, and so the current account improves. A depreciation may also depress expenditures by increasing domestic prices which may reduce demand directly, as well as indirectly through a rise in the rate of interest, if the quantity of money is being tightly controlled.

The 'dependent economy' (or 'Australian') model distinguishes between traded and non-traded goods. The former are freely traded on world markets at competitive prices. The latter never enter international trade, either because they are location-specific, or because international transport costs are such that the good is not competitive in international markets. The prices of non-traded goods are determined in each country by its own domestic supply and demand. Over time, goods and services may switch from being traded to non-traded or vice versa, depending on the evolution of international transport costs. In this approach, a current account deficit is associated with domestic excess demand for traded goods. A devaluation increases the domestic currency price of traded goods given the price of non-traded goods. This

[11] Reference may be made here to 'uncovered' interest parity which is said to hold if the interest differential between assets of a given maturity denominated in different currencies is equal to the 'expected' percentage change in the spot exchange rate between now and the maturity date of the asset. Uncovered interest parity holds when speculative funds are in infinitely elastic supply, but available evidence suggests that, in general, this is not the case.

[12] In the special case in which trade is initially balanced and supply elasticities of traded goods are infinite, then a depreciation improves the trade balance provided that the sum of foreign and domestic elasticities of demand for imported goods exceeds unity. For a discussion of the evidence on import and export elasticities, see J. Williamson, 'Is There an External Constraint?' *NIER* (Aug. 1984), 73–7.

stimulates production of traded goods for the export and switches demand from traded goods previously imported into non-traded goods, thus improving the current account. However, to the extent that demand for non-traded goods has increased and supply fallen, in order to prevent a rise in prices of non-traded goods, some deflation of domestic monetary demand is typically required to sustain the current account improvement. To this extent the dependent economy model synthesizes the elasticity and absorption approaches by providing a role both for changes in relative prices and for changes in domestic monetary demand.

Finally, the 'monetary approach' concentrates on the BOF, noting that an overall deficit implies that there is a net outflow of reserves and thus corresponds to excess supply of money in the domestic economy relative to demand, with the excess being 'worked-off' through the balance-of-payments deficit. In this approach, a depreciation works primarily through the money market by increasing the price level and thus reducing the real supply of money in the economy, with the central bank being required to maintain tight control over the nominal money supply. A reduction in the supply of money in its turn has a familiar deflationary impact on the economy as a whole.

It should be evident that these different approaches are interlinked.[13] Different aspects of the adjustment process are important at different times but, in practice, exchange-rate changes work, at least to some extent, through all the channels listed above. However, different circumstances will call for different supporting policies to accompany an exchange-rate change. For example, at full employment, a depreciation will only increase domestic money incomes rather than real incomes, and emphasis has to be placed on deflating the economy while also switching domestic expenditures away from import goods.

Arguments for floating exchange rates.   In its simplest form, the case for floating exchange rates rests upon the efficiency and automatic nature of the free-market mechanism in reallocating resources in response to changing circumstances. In a dynamic world in which comparative advantages change over time and national inflation rates differ, changes in exchange rates are necessary, if widespread misallocation of productive resources is to be avoided. The advantage of floating rates, it is argued, is that the amount and timing of the necessary changes can occur progressively at a pace dictated by the costs and profitability of resource allocation, and not, as in a fixed rate system, by periodic discrete jumps, often dictated by speculative pressures and political expediency.

The main difficulty in practice with floating exchange rates is that, in a

---

[13] For an entertaining account of these different approaches and their deficiencies, see A. P. Thirlwall, 'What is Wrong with Balance of Payments Adjustment Theory?', *RBSR* (Mar. 1988), 157. For an empirical study of the adjustment process in the UK, see D. A. Currie and S. Hall, 'The Exchange Rate and the Balance of Payments', *NIER* (Feb. 1986), 74–82.

relatively free international capital market, the exchange rate affects both the prices of internationally traded products and the prices of internationally traded assets. The exchange rate which is determined in a free market depends on the demand and supply of foreign currency emanating from trade both in products and in assets. There is no reason to expect any immediate relationship between day-to-day transactions in foreign currency generated by product markets and those generated by asset markets, and the equilibrium exchange rate implied by product market considerations may be very different from that implied by asset market considerations.

It is now generally recognized that, in the short run, the exchange rate of a currency which is freely floating is determined mainly by asset market considerations, particularly by relative international interest rates and expectations of future economic trends. Product market factors may reassert themselves in the longer term, but it is unclear just what 'longer term' means in calendar time. In the short term, if the markets for foreign exchange are to be cleared continuously without the intervention of the monetary authorities and without undue fluctuations in the exchange rate, it is important that speculators in the foreign exchange market operate in a stabilizing manner, selling sterling when the rate is temporarily 'too high' and buying sterling when the rate is temporarily 'too low'. One can argue that speculative activity will be stabilizing because destabilizing speculation (buying when the rate is 'high' and selling when it is 'low') is unprofitable.[14] However, this presumes that speculators can predict the 'true' equilibrium value of the exchange rate. The converse argument is that the exchange market will be dominated by too much uncertainty for speculators to recognize the equilibrium rate. Waves of optimism and pessimism will follow the frequent revision of expectations and will generate substantial movements in exchange rates, which are unrelated to 'fundamental' economic considerations. However, such destabilizing speculation can disrupt any exchange-rate framework. One of the major drawbacks of a fixed exchange rate system is that it invariably gives a one-way option to currency speculators, with weak currencies being under far more pressure to devalue than are strong currencies to revalue. Even if the authorities take drastic action to defend the value of a weak currency by a substantial rise in interest rates, the action is often interpreted as a signal that a devaluation is inevitable, which in turn encourages a large speculative movement of funds out of the currency and precipitates the devaluation predicted by speculators. The European Monetary System was designed to minimize these one-way pressures but, even so, the Exchange Rate Mechanism succumbed to speculative attacks on one or two occasions, most notably in September 1992, when Sterling and the Italian Lira suspended their participation in the system. An important advantage of floating exchange rates is that the problem of

---

[14] See M. Friedman, 'The Case for Flexible Exchange Rates', in *Essays in Positive Economics* (Chicago: University of Chicago Press, 1953).

recurrent one-way speculative options at the expense of the authorities is eliminated.

Floating rates may nevertheless be volatile; and it has been argued that such volatility increases the uncertainty faced by international traders and investors and may therefore deter trade. However, volatility will not be a serious problem insofar as speculation is able to stabilize floating exchange rates, and the balance of the evidence is that floating rates are not in fact a serious deterrent to trade.[15]

A more subtle argument is that the exchange rates 'overshoot': if a disturbance requires an appreciation of the pound, it will tend to over-appreciate in the short run and subsequently depreciate to its equilibrium value. This is explained by the flexibility of the exchange rate relative to other prices in the economy particularly money wage rates. If a general adjustment in wages and prices is required, this will take time; in the meanwhile, asset prices, particularly the exchange rate, must 'over-adjust' to compensate for the sluggishness of wages and product prices. In this connection, it is important to distinguish between the concept of 'volatility' and that of 'misalignment'. The exchange rate may be highly volatile on a day-to-day basis but nevertheless stay relatively close to its equilibrium value. However, when the exchange rate overshoots its equilibrium value for long periods, it can be said to be misaligned, and such misalignment may cause a systematic misallocation of resources in the economy. In this situation, a freely floating exchange rate may be detrimental rather than advantageous. Evidence on this issue is hard to find because of the difficulty of identifying the equilibrium exchange rate. However, as described below, the appreciation of sterling in 1979–81 appeared in part to correspond to an overshooting of the exchange rate.

Overall, the balance of argument and evidence is that some flexibility in exchange rates is desirable as a means of promoting efficient resource allocation and reducing the vulnerability of the economy to external disturbances. However, there is still considerable room for debate about the optimum balance between flexibility and management by the authorities. Thus, if undue volatility and overshooting of the exchange rate prove serious, the authorities can engage in exchange-market intervention. This implies that, even with a floating exchange rate, the authorities must maintain a stock of exchange reserves.

Trends in the UK Balance of Payments and the Exchange Rate

Historic position.   We turn now to consider more specifically the balance-of-payments performance of the UK. For this purpose, we examine first Table 11.3,

---

[15] For a review of the impact of exchange-rate volatility on international trade, see 'The Variability of Exchange Rates: Measurement and Effects', *BEQB* (Sept. 1984), 346–9. The managers of industrial firms frequently cite exchange-rate volatility as a deterrent to trade. See House of Lords, *Report from the Select Committee on Overseas Trade* (HMSO, 30 July 1985).

Table 11.3 Trends in the UK balance of payments, annual averages for selected periods (£m.)

		1952–62	1963–7	1968–72	1973–9	1980–5	1986–90	1991–4
1	Balance on visible trade	−158	−326	−303	−3182	−617	−17223	−11840
2	Balance on invisibles[a]	269	249	762	2360	4198	4454	4158
	Government	(−277)	(−589)	(−733)	(−1676)	(−3493)	(−6234)	(−7865)
	Private	(546)	(838)	(1495)	(4036)	(7691)	(10688)	(12023)
3	Current account balance	111	−77	459	−822	3582	−12768	−7682
4	Portfolio and direct investment	)−145	−136	−99	−154	−8627	−4389	−4763
5	Capital account n.i.e.	) na[b]	171	10	765	3013	17261	6009
6	Balancing item	58	15	−65	1039	1481	2336	7190
7	Balance for official financing	24	−27	305	828	−551	2440	754
	GNP at market prices (£bn.)	22.3	36.1	53.4	129.8	294.2	472.8	621.9
	Net external assets (£bn.; end of period[c])	1.5	2.3	6.4	12.4	71.0	−5.6	17.7

[a] The Government/Private split for 1952–62 is partly estimated
[b] Not separately available
[c] Amount outstanding at end-1962, end-1967 (etc.)

Source: Pink Book and ET

which contains average annual figures for the main items in the balance of payments covering selected periods since 1952, together with movements in the GNP and outstanding net external assets over the same periods. The averaging process hides substantial variations in the accounts from year to year but it also helps uncover any longer-term trends in the accounts.

A useful starting-point is with the characterization of the UK balance of payments given by Cooper in 1968.[16] This consists of four main propositions: (1) the UK normally has a deficit on visible trade which is more than offset by a surplus on invisibles, implying a surplus on current account; (2) the UK normally experiences net outflows of long-term capital; (3) the role of the UK as an international banking centre tends to produce volatile short-term capital flows which have an important influence on the overall balance of payments; (4) these activities are all carried out with a very inadequate underpinning of official exchange reserves.

By and large, this was the picture throughout the 1950s and 1960s, although in 1963–7 the visible trade balance worsened sufficiently to produce a deficit on current account. This precipitated a devaluation of the pound in 1967, followed by an improvement in the current account. Table 11.3 also confirms the picture of the UK as a net exporter of long-term capital. As far as reserves and short-term capital are concerned, Cooper's summary is again broadly accurate for the 1950s and 1960s. A convenient reckoning of the strength of a country's official international reserve position is in terms of the number of months' imports which could be financed by outstanding reserves. The UK's official reserves were broadly stable at about 3 months' imports over the period 1952–62, decreasing to 2.3 months' average over 1963–72. In comparison, industrial Europe as a whole (excluding the UK) maintained reserve levels averaging about 6 months' imports throughout the 1950s and 1960s. The UK's reserve position might have been more tenable were it not for the large swings in short-term capital to which Cooper refers. When the UK balance of payments deteriorated, short-term capital flowed out of London as its holders feared a possible devaluation of the currency. However, this very outflow often turned a manageable position into a crisis and such crises were a recurrent problem in the 1950s and 1960s. Essentially they were brought on by the combination of limited reserves and volatile short-term capital flows.

After 1972, the balance of payments underwent important changes, most of which can be traced back to three major factors. First, the floating of sterling in 1972 presaged a more general move towards floating exchange rates by the major industrial countries. This changed considerably the rules and constraints associated with balance-of-payments mangement. The second factor was the UK's accession to the EC in January 1973, which, it is estimated, resulted in the UK running a larger balance-of-payments deficit or smaller surplus than would

[16] Ch. 3 in R. E. Caves (ed.), *Britain's Economic Prospects* (London: Allen and Unwin, 1968).

otherwise have been the case.[17] Third was the discovery and subsequent exploitation of North Sea oil. Accompanying these developments were dramatic changes in the world price of oil: sharp increases in 1973 and 1979, followed by a precipitate slump in 1985–6. The period immediately following the floating of sterling (1973–9) saw a sustained worsening of the visible trade balance and a succession of current account deficits. The deficit on long-term capital also persisted over this period, despite a substantial inflow of private capital in connection with North Sea oil exploration. Successive governments chose to accommodate the current account deficit to some extent by a substantial programme of official short- and long-term borrowing, with repayments effectively guaranteed by a portion of future North Sea oil revenues. Thus the UK was able to absorb a sequence of large current account deficits without having to undertake such a major adjustment programme as would otherwise have been required in the absence of North Sea oil.

The balance of payments since 1979. The period 1980–5 saw a dramatic turnaround in the balance-of-payments position. The oil price rise of 1979 coincided with the coming on-stream of major North Sea oil-fields. Oil exports rose sharply, even as the non-oil visible balance deteriorated further. The net result was a shrinking of the visible trade deficit which, together with the continued strengthening of the invisibles balance, combined to produce a sequence of record current account surpluses. On the capital account, the abolition of exchange controls in 1979 followed by a sharp appreciation of the sterling exchange rate prompted record outflows of long-term capital. The result was a massive increase in the net external assets of the UK from £12.4 billion at the end of 1979 to £71.0 billion at the end of 1985. However, the existence of a deficit on average in the BOF during this period illustrates the hazards of placing too much emphasis on one particular measure of the balance-of-payments deficit or surplus. Despite the underlying strength of the balance of payments, official reserves fell, as the UK continued its programme of repayments of official foreign debt.

The most recent period has been marked by a further dramatic shift in the accounts. The fall in the price of oil in 1985–6 coincided with a levelling-off of output from the North Sea and resulted in a fall in the net oil contribution to the visible balance. The visible trade deficit reached record proportions, averaging 3.6% of GNP during 1986–90 compared to 2.4% during 1973–9.

In 1991 there was a sharp improvement in the current account, associated mainly with an improvement in the non-oil visible balance. Between 1991 and 1994 the current account remained in deficit but at a substantially lower level than in the preceding period. On the capital account, the averages mask substantial year-to-year variations in individual items. However, the position remained one of substantial net outflows of long-term capital more than offset

---

[17] See M. H. Miller 'Estimates of the Static Balance of Payments and Welfare Costs Compared', ch. 6 in J. Pinder (ed.), *The Economics of Europe* (London: Charles Knight, 1971).

by short-term capital inflows. Despite the weakness of the current account, the authorities have generally accumulated reserves, particularly in 1987 when sterling was sold as part of an active policy of exchange rate management aimed at preventing an excessive appreciation of the currency. Indeed 1992 was the only year in the last decade in which the overall balance of payments was in deficit. This was associated with the authorities' need to use reserves to defend an unrealistic sterling exchange rate within the ERM immediately prior to sterling's exit from the system in September 1992. Finally, even though the UK has run continuous current account deficits in the last decade, since 1990, net external assets have increased, from a low of −£5.6 billion to £17.7 billion in 1994. We return to this point below.

The evolution of the exchange rate since 1979.   With sterling only one of many currencies engaged in a simultaneous float, there is no simple index of movements in the international value of sterling. Sterling may appreciate in terms of some currencies while, at the same time, it depreciates in terms of others. Current practice is to rely upon the 'effective exchange rate' index, which is a weighted average of the bilateral exchange rates between sterling and sixteen other currencies, the weights being given by the relative importance of the countries concerned in the UK's trade in manufactured goods.[18]

   The broad trends in the movement of the effective exchange rate (EER) since 1979 can be divided into four phases. The first, to January 1981, was one of rapid appreciation from 103.9 in January 1979 (with 1985 = 100) to 133.4 in January 1981. From then, the EER depreciated, reaching a low of 86.4 in November 1986. The third phase, from December 1986 to September 1992, includes sterling's two-year participation in the ERM. In this period, the EER moved in a fairly narrow band between 86.9 and 99.4. Taking the average of these two values as a central reference rate, the EER fluctuated within a range of about 6.7% either side of this central reference rate. In September 1992 sterling exited from the ERM, and the EER entered a fourth phase, depreciating from 88.9 in August 1992 to a low of 75.6 in December 1995, a fall of about 15%. However, much of this depreciation took place immediately after sterling's exit from the ERM—by end-October 1992 the pound had already depreciated by 11% from its end-August level.

   In order to evaluate these movements in the EER, particularly in the context of the balance of payments, it is helpful to begin by relating the EER to its purchasing power parity (PPP). The theory of PPP suggests that the equilibrium exchange rate between the currencies of two countries is proportional to the ratio of the price levels in the respective countries. Providing this factor of proportionality remains constant, the proportionate rate of change of the exchange rate will be approximately equal to the difference between the

[18] For details, see 'Revisions to the Calculation of Effective Exchange Rates', *BEQB* (Nov. 1988), 528–9. Reference to earlier methods of calculating the effective rate may also be found in this article.

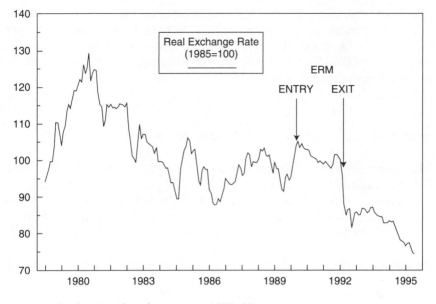

Fig. 11.1. Sterling's real exchange rate 1979–95

inflation rates in the two countries.[19] With the exchange rate in equilibrium, the current account would be in balance. To study movements in the exchange rate relative to its purchasing power value, it is helpful to calculate an index of the real exchange rate (REX).

Figure 11.1 shows the monthly movements from 1979 to 1995 in the sterling REX, measured as the ratio of the effective rate (EER) of sterling (in the computation of which the OECD countries have a weight of 100%), to the consumer price index (CPI) in the combined OECD countries realtive to that in the UK. In symbols:

$$REX = \frac{EER}{OECD\ CPI/UK\ CPI}$$

The larger the value of this index, the more appreciated is the sterling exchange rate relative to its PPP value. Thus, movements in REX correspond to deviations from PPP. However, it should be emphasized that the index only measures relative movements. It is normalized to 1985 = 100 for convenience, but we cannot infer that sterling was at its equilibrium purchasing power value in that year.

Movements in the REX since 1979 reflect quite closely those of the EER: sharp appreciation in 1979–80 followed by an almost equally rapid depreciation. From about 1985, relative stability in the EER was accompanied by

---

[19] Probably the clearest statement of the purchasing power parity theory is still contained in J. M. Keynes, *A Tract on Monetary Reform* (London: Macmillan, 1923), 70–93. A textbook treatment of exchange-rate theories can be found in MacDonald, *Floating Exchange Rates*.

continued faster inflation in the UK than in other OECD countries on average, implying a gradual appreciation in the REX. In 1992, from just before sterling's exit from the ERM, the REX depreciated sharply—by 20% over the last nine months of the year. Since then, the REX has continued to drift downwards, but at a much more gradual rate.

Evaluating UK Balance-of-Payments Performance since 1979

The balance of payments and the exchange rate.   It is evident that even though PPP may capture longer-term trends in the EER, in the short-term there have been substantial deviations from PPP.[20] In addition, movements in the REX do not by any means correspond to UK balance of payments 'deficits' or 'surpluses'. In part, this is because the UK economy has undergone major changes in the last fifteen years. A brief summary of these changes will help explain some of the broader movements in the balance of payments and the exchange rate.

The single most important factor in the UK economy in the 1980s was North Sea oil. The world market price of oil rose from US$14 per barrel in June 1979 to US$36 per barrel in December 1980, a level at which it was broadly maintained until December 1985, after which it fell precipitously, reaching just US$10 per barrel in April 1986. The oil price increase of 1979–80 coincided with the UK's move into oil self-sufficiency. This factor alone must have played a major role in the sharp appreciation of sterling in 1979–80. The direct oil effect on the current account balance was reinforced by indirect effects of confidence and capital flows. From 1979 there was, in effect, a favourable reassessment of the long-term prospects for sterling and the associated exchange risks of holding sterling-denominated assets. A further structural influence on the exchange rate was the depth of the UK recession. Between 1978 and 1981, UK industrial output fell by 6.8% and unemployment rose sharply. The depth of the recession was associated with a decline in domestic demand and therefore an improvement in the current account. This in turn would have contributed to the buoyancy of sterling. A final factor was the rise in UK nominal interest rates, particularly short-term interest rates, relative to those in other OECD countries. Throughout 1979 and much of 1980, UK short-term rates were between 2% and 4% higher than comparable rates in the United States. This would tend to induce a capital inflow into the UK and hence raise the value of sterling. However, the 1979 abolition of exchange controls should, by facilitating a capital outflow, have moderated the rise in sterling to some extent. In addition, the authorities sold sterling and accumulated reserves amounting to $9 billion in 1979–80 in

[20] There is fairly considerable evidence that the major currencies (including sterling) have deviated substantially from PPP. Cf. G. Hacche and J. Townsend, 'A Broad Look at Exchange Rate Movements for Eight Currencies 1972–80', *BEQB* (Dec. 1981).

intervention aimed directly at checking sterling's appreciation. Overall, there remains some disagreement both about the relative contribution of each factor to the appreciation of sterling and about whether, when put together, they provide a complete explanation of this appreciation.[21] It seems certain that increased confidence in sterling as a petro-currency must have contributed to some part of the appreciation, but this is to assert little more than that we cannot fully explain why the pound rose so strongly in 1979–80.

Between 1981 and 1982 the pound depreciated again almost as sharply as it had risen. A part of this depreciation simply reflected the appreciation of the US dollar over the same period, but the fact that the 1979–80 appreciation was so largely and rapidly reversed lends some support to the argument that sterling's overall movements in the 1979–82 period were consistent with the overshooting hypothesis. Sterling fell once more in 1985–6 as the world oil price tumbled, but the depreciation was less marked than the movements at the beginning of the decade.

From about 1985, the authorities made more active efforts to manage the exchange rate than had been the case in the earlier part of the decade. For example, in 1987 US\$ 21.5 billion of reserves were accumulated in an effort to curtail the appreciation of sterling against the Deutschmark. More generally, interest rate policy was used to manage the exchange rate instead of to control the money supply as had been the case during the Medium-Term Financial Strategy which was in place during the early 1980s. In October 1985, the authorities announced that policy would include adjustments to short-term interest rates required to help maintain the external value of the pound within a desired range. This policy culminated in sterling's entry into the ERM in October 1990, and it was undoubtedly the major factor in the relative stability of the REX from 1985 through late 1992. However, this policy paid insufficient regard to the balance of payments, the current account of which was in large and sustained deficit throughout the late 1980s. By October 1990, when sterling entered the ERM, at a REX which was more appreciated than at any time since mid-1985, it seems reasonably clear that sterling was overvalued, a hypothesis which is supported by calculations of the equilibrium exchange rate which suggested an over-valuation of about 10% at the time of ERM entry.[22] As we have seen, in attempting to defend this rate, the UK experienced its only overall balance of payments deficit in the last decade, and the pressures on the exchange rate proved impossible to resist, so that sterling exited from the ERM in September 1992.

Appraisal.　Cooper's characterization of the UK balance of payments position continues to be strikingly accurate, except perhaps in one particular. The UK

[21] For an appraisal of the causes of the rise in sterling, see W. H. Buiter and M. H. Miller, 'Changing the Rules: Economic Consequences of the Thatcher Regime', *Brookings Papers*, 1983: 2, 305–65.

[22] See for example J. Williamson, 'FEERs and the ERM', *NIER* (Aug. 1991), 45–50.

has now run a current account deficit for 14 of the last 22 years. During these 22 years, a period which included six years of exceptionally high North Sea oil revenues, the deficit averaged about 1% of GNP. Although the current account improved sharply in 1994, thanks mainly to a large swing in investment income, there is little sign of further improvement in the first 9 months of 1995. Overall, it seems reasonable to conclude that the UK now more generally runs a small current account deficit with the surplus on invisibles not being sufficient to offset the deficit on visible trade. The remaining aspects of Cooper's characterization still appear to be valid.

The causes of the UK's changing current account position are discussed in Section 11.3. Here we concentrate on the overall balance of payments position. As we have already emphasized, current account deficits are sustainable provided foreign residents are willing to increase their lending to the UK to finance these deficits. Provided British industry offers an internationally competitive rate of return, there is no reason why the necessary lending should not be forthcoming. Moreover, it is interesting to note that the current account deficits of the last four years have been accompanied by a steady increase in the UK's net external assets. The explanation for this apparent paradox is the UK's traditional position noted by Cooper as a 'banker' in international capital markets, engaging in net short-term borrowing and net long-term lending. Net short-term borrowings are mainly by banks and invariably in the form of claims which are 'capital-certain' i.e. their capital value does not change over time, apart from changes in foreign-currency-denominated liabilities due to exchange rate fluctuations. UK long-term lending, on the other hand, is typically in the form of portfolio and direct investment claims which are 'capital-uncertain', such as stocks and shares. The world-wide stock-market boom of the last decade has produced a steady increase in the market value of the UK's portfolio investment assets in particular, an increase which is not offset by any corresponding rise in the value of UK liabilities. Thus, the structure of the capital account itself provides a cushion for the UK's net external asset position and implies that, even with a persistent (small) current account deficit, the UK is unlikely to experience growing net foreign indebtedness. Overall, therefore, and barring unforeseen developments, the UK's balance of payments and net external asset position appear to be broadly sustainable for the foreseeable future.

In one respect, however, the structure of the balance of payments does pose a potential problem. The net flows of funds across the foreign exchanges which represent the various balances may be small, but the gross flows in either direction which underlie these balances are typically very large. For example, the five-fold increase in investment income between 1993 and 1994 reflected a mere 6.5% rise in gross credits and a 6.5% fall in gross debits! Small changes in the gross flows can produce large swings in the main balances. Furthermore, international capital flows are highly interest elastic, so that small changes in relative prices and interest rates often lead to very large flows of funds among countries. This means that the UK balance of payments, with its especially large capital flows, is likely to be particularly vulnerable to sudden speculative flows across the foreign exchanges. Indeed, this too is an issue which Cooper originally highlighted. However, these speculative flows can be accommodated if a mechanism exists to cushion their impact. The key to this is an adequate degree of exchange rate and interest rate flexibility. Over the last decade, the UK balance of payments experienced most pressures during the two years when sterling was a part of the ERM and consequently there was little or no scope for flexibility in exchange rate management in response to developments in the balance of payments. In summary, therefore, the structure of the UK's balance of payments is such that it is essential to retain a substantial degree of exchange rate flexibility. Arguably, this renders sterling's re-entry into the ERM both impracticable and undesirable, certainly in the medium term.

Table 11.4 Area composition of UK merchandise trade 1955–1994

	1955	1970	1985	1990	1994
Exports (f.o.b.: in percent of total)					
Western Europe	28.9	46.2	58.3	62.0	61.3
EC[a]	(15.0)	(29.4)	(46.3)	(53.1)	(57.0)
North America	12.0	15.2	17.0	14.4	14.4
USA	(7.1)	(11.6)	(14.7)	(12.5)	(12.4)
Other OECD[b]	15.3	11.8	3.5	5.6	4.0
Japan	(0.6)	(1.8)	(1.3)	(2.5)	(2.2)
Sub-Total	56.2	73.2	78.7	82.0	79.7
Industrial Asia[c]	3.4	3.4	3.1	4.1	5.9
Easter Europe[a]	2.1	3.8	2.0	1.7	2.1
Oil-exporting countries	5.1	5.8	7.6	5.4	4.2
Other	33.2	13.4	8.3	6.1	7.9
Total	100.0	100.0	100.0	100.0	100.0
Imports (cif: in percent of total)					
Western Europe	25.7	41.5	63.1	64.8	62.1
EC[a]	(12.6)	(27.1)	(46.0)	(52.2)	(55.7)
North America	19.5	20.5	13.8	13.2	13.3
USA	(10.9)	(12.9)	(11.7)	(11.4)	(11.8)
Other OECD[b]	12.1	9.5	6.3	7.4	7.1
Japan	(0.6)	(1.5)	(4.9)	(5.4)	(5.9)
Sub-Total	57.3	71.5	83.1	85.4	82.5
Industrial Asia[c]	1.7	2.5	3.8	5.1	6.5
Eastern Europe[a]	4.3	4.2	2.2	1.8	1.9
Oil-exporting countries	9.2	9.1	3.3	2.4	2.1
Other	27.5	12.5	7.4	4.6	6.8
Total	100.0	100.0	100.0	100.0	100.0

Note: There are minor changes in definition over time of some of the classifications. The components do not sum exactly to 100% as items valued at less than £50 (1955, 1970); £200 (1985); £600 (1990, 1994) are not classified by area.

[a] The former German Democratic Republic is included under 'centrally planned economies' through 1989 and under EC thereafter.
[b] Australia, Japan, New Zealand.
[c] Thailand, Malaysia, Singapore, Taiwan, Hong Kong, South Korea.

Source: AAS 1963, 1976, 1989, 1994; MDS Jan. 1996

11.3.   The Current Account

Long-Term Trends

The structure of trade.   In this section we shall examine the major structural developments in the current account of the UK since 1950, concentrating in particular on the performance of merchandise trade, services, and transfers. Investment incomes are considered with the capital account in Section 11.4.

There have been substantial changes in the pattern of the UK trade in the last 45 years. Turning first to the geographical composition of merchandise trade (Table 11.4), the single major factor is the shift towards increased trade with other Western European countries—particularly but not exclusively the EC—largely at the expense of trade with other Commonwealth countries. This shift began well before UK entry into the EC but continued for at least a decade after UK entry. In the last decade, however, the share of trade with Western Europe has stabilized at rather more than 60%. In the light of the popular conception of Japanese strengths, it is interesting to note that Japan still only supplies 5.9% of UK imports, although the importance of Japan as a UK export

Table 11.5 Commodity composition of UK merchandise trade and services 1955–1994

SITC Code	Description	1955	1970	1985	1990	1994
Exports (f.o.b.: in percent of total merchandise exports)						
	Merchandise					
0,1	Food, beverages, tobacco	5.8	6.4	6.3	6.8	7.5
3	Fuel and lubricants	4.8	2.6	21.4	7.5	6.6
2,4	Basic materials	3.9	3.4	2.7	2.2	1.9
5,6	Semi-manufactures	38.9	34.3	25.3	28.0	28.5
7,8	Manufactures	43.5	49.9	41.7	53.2	54.5
9	Unclassified	3.0	3.4	2.5	2.2	1.1
	Total merchandise	100.0	100.0	100.0	100.0	100.0
	Private services					
	Transport and travel	22.4	25.8	14.7	18.5	14.6
	Financial and related services	11.6	15.0	15.5	18.0	14.3
Imports (cif: in percent of total merchandise imports)						
	Merchandise					
0,1	Food, beverages, tobacco	36.2	22.6	10.9	9.8	9.8
3	Fuel and lubricants	10.4	10.4	12.4	6.2	4.1
2,4	Basic materials	28.7	15.1	6.3	4.8	4.1
5,6	Semi-manufactures	19.2	27.7	25.0	26.0	26.1
7,8	Manufactures	5.2	22.9	43.7	51.9	55.3
9	Unclassified	0.3	1.3	1.6	1.3	0.6
	Total merchandise	100.0	100.0	100.0	100.0	100.0
	Private services					
	Transport and travel	19.0	23.1	13.2	14.6	16.8
	Financial and related services	4.8	5.7	5.4	5.2	5.4

Source: AAS 1963, 1976, 1989, 1994; MDS Jan. 1996; Pink Book.

market is smaller still. Indeed the newly industrialized countries of Asia together enjoy a larger share of UK trade (both imports and exports) than does Japan. The decline in importance of the oil-exporting countries as a source of UK imports since 1980 is a direct result of the exploitation of the UK's North Sea oil resources.

The switch towards a greater trade dependence on the industrialized, high per capita income countries of Western Europe has been matched by significant changes in the commodity structure of UK trade (Table 11.5). Most important here is the increase in the proportion of imports of manufactures and the decline in the proportion accounted for by foodstuffs, beverages, and tobacco. Imports of manufactures (SITC Codes 5–8) now account for over 80% of total UK imports. This same trend has also been experienced by other EC countries, although it remains the case that the UK has a higher proportion of imports of non-manufactures than does, for example, France or Germany. On the export side changes in structure have been less marked. The influence of North Sea oil can be seen in the decline in the import share of fuels and lubricants, and a corresponding rise in the export share of these products (particularly in the early 1980s), reflecting, respectively, the import-substitution and export-generating aspects of North Sea oil.

For services, both debits and credits in proportion to total merchandise imports have declined somewhat since the 1950–70 era.[23] The positive balance on services in more recent years can be attributed largely to a rapid expansion in receipts from financial services (other than investment incomes) as net receipts from travel and transport have fluctuated with no clear trend.

The final element in the current account is transfers, the most important and certainly the most (politically) controversial item in this respect being those involving UK contributions to and receipts from the EC budget. In this connection, the structure of the UK economy is such that, despite various rebates agreed over the years, the UK will continue to make a substantial net positive contribution to the EC budget for the foreseeable future.

In summary, UK trade is increasingly dominated by an exchange of manufactured goods and services for other manufactured goods and services with the advanced industrialized nations. These structural changes imply that British industry has experienced and will continue to experience greater foreign competition in home and export markets.

Competitive performance. The trend towards increased non-oil visible trade deficits has often been interpreted as evidence of a general lack of competitive edge in British industry relative to foreign industry. Related evidence is provided by the progressive decline of the UK's share of the total exports of

---

[23] Some degree of stability in service credits and debits is to be expected because of the method of estimating certain invisibles, such as shipping and insurance, as a fixed percentage of the value of merchandise trade.

manufactured goods of the major industrial countries,[24] and by the increased import penetration of the UK market by foreign products. These trends have prompted fears of the 'de-industrialization' of the UK, with the manufacturing base so eroded by foreign competitors, that full employment and balance-of-payments equilibrium cannot, in the long run, be achieved simultaneously.[25]

The UK share of world exports of manufactures fell steadily from 20.4% in 1954 to 8.8% in 1974. Since 1974, however, the UK's share has fluctuated, falling further in the early 1980s at the height of the boom in North Sea oil exports, but recovering in the last decade to about 8%. Of itself, the decline in export share need not give rise to concern, since it may simply reflect a decline in the UK share of world manufacturing production, the natural result of her early industrial start. (In 1899, the UK accounted for 32.5% of world exports of manufactures and 20% of world manufacturing production). However, the decline in the UK's share in world manufacturing production may itself reflect the same factors which hinder UK trade performance. On the import side, there is also some evidence of a loss of competitive edge. Even though all the major industrialized nations, with the exception of Japan, have experienced a rising import share since 1955, the UK seems to be relatively more import-prone than her competitors and to have a relatively high income elasticity of demand for imports. A customary measure of import penetration is the ratio of imports to domestic consumption. For manufactured goods this ratio increased from 17% in 1968 to 26% in 1978 and again to 37% in 1989.[26] This trend appears widespread across manufacturing industry and is not confined to any one sub-sector. However, some care is required in interpreting these figures, since, in part, they reflect the increasing division of labour in the international economy which has occurred since 1958. Thus, similar calculations on the export side show a corresponding, albeit less marked, trend increase in the proportion of UK output which is exported, with the average ratio of UK manufacturing exports to manufacturing production rising from 18% in 1968 to 26% in 1978 and 30% in 1989.[27]

At the most general level, trade performance is concerned with 'competitiveness'. This is a concept which can be defined in a variety of ways but perhaps the most useful definition is one given by Corden (1994): competitiveness is 'the degree to which a country can, under free and fair market conditions, produce goods and services which meet the test of international markets, while simultaneously maintaining and expanding the real incomes of

[24] These consist of Germany, France, Italy, Netherlands, Belgium, Luxembourg, Canada, Japan, Sweden, Switzerland, USA, and UK.

[25] See F. Blackaby (ed.), *Deindustrialization* (London: Heinemann, 1979); and J. Williamson, 'Is There an External Constraint?', *NIER* (Aug. 1984), 73–7.

[26] The collection of these data was suspended for seven years and they have only become available again from 1993. While the new figures are not strictly comparable with the old, they do suggest a further upward drift in import penetration.

[27] As for imports, there is a seven-year break in the collection of these data. The new data suggest that the UK's export ratio in manufacturing has risen sharply since 1989.

its people over the long-term.' This definition focuses particularly on productivity growth. A country with low productivity growth may be price-competitive if its exchange rate is depreciated *vis-à-vis* other countries, but in the long term its living standards will fall behind those of countries with more rapid productivity growth. Relatively slow productivity growth is undoubtedly at the root of the relatively poor long-term UK trade performance, and this also explains the long-term downward trend in the sterling exchange rate which has been required to maintain price competitiveness. Productivity growth is at the heart of economic performance more generally, and the precise reasons for the UK's problems are not easy to quantify; several interrelated factors are involved and the relative weight to be attached to each is difficult to establish. However, it is interesting to note that similar problems with poor competitive performance are generally thought to have been an issue at the end of the nineteenth century.[28] Moreover, similar concerns have been expressed in almost all the major industrial countries in the last decade, particularly the United States, where 'national competitiveness' has almost become an obsession.[29] These concerns have been prompted particularly by Japanese trade performance and latterly by the extraordinary growth and trade performance of selected Asian economies, often referred to as the 'tigers'.

Explanations of Trade Performance

Intra-industry trade. Traditional trade theory explains patterns of international trade by reference to national differences in endowments of factors of production, a country exporting those commodities which use relatively intensively its abundant factors. The theory assumes homogeneous outputs of each industry, equal access to technical knowledge in all countries, and all factors of production of equal quality. Clearly, these assumptions do not reflect the reality of modern industrial competition, i.e. conditions of imperfect competition with non-price factors being dominant in competitive performance. It is not obvious that the theory can explain the dominant component of world trade: the exchange of manufactures between industrialized nations.

A powerful indication of the weakness of traditional theory is provided by the phenomenon of intra-industry trade, the simultaneous importing and exporting of products of the same industry, which is estimated to comprise

---

[28] R. Hoffman, *Great Britain and the German Trade Rivalry 1875–1914* (Pittsburgh: Pennsylvania University Press, 1973), 21–80.

[29] This debate was prompted in part by M. E. Porter, *The Competitive Advantage of Nations* (London: Macmillan 1990), which effectively linked national success with a concept of national competitiveness. For a trenchant comment on Porter's work see P. Krugman, 'Competitiveness: A Dangerous Obsession', *Foreign Affairs* (Mar./Apr. 1994). For a more general statement of what might constitute 'national competitiveness' consult Corden, *Economic Policy, Exchange Rates, and the International System* (Oxford: Oxford University Press, 1994).

some 60% of trade between developed countries.[30] In part, of course, this phenomenon is a statistical aberration, reflecting the lack of detail within even the finest classification of industrial statistics. For example, within the steel industry, there are many qualities of steel, each of which is a poor substitute for the other in many applications but which are treated statistically as if they were perfect substitutes. More fundamentally, it reflects the role of intra-industry product-differentiation as a key element in the competitive process.[31] It is no puzzle that the UK should simultaneously import and export whisky or automobiles of different brands, given the many grades of product which exist within these commodity groups, each defined by a unique set of characteristics. Design, technical sophistication, after-sales service, durability, and reliability are easily recognized as elements which successfully differentiate products in the minds of consumers. The major determinants of intra-industry trade relate to product differences as much as to cost differences, and may be outlined as follows. First, there must exist a diversity of preferences for commodities of many different kinds within countries. Second, the domestic market is important to the initial development of a new commodity, which implies that the types of commodities produced in an economy reflect the pattern of domestic preferences. The same industry within different countries will then produce different product designs. Third, the existence of economies of scale in industrial production induces firms to specialize within particular product niches. In general, specialization will be directed to those products in which home demand is greatest. Economies of scale and diversity of preferences then create the basis for intra-industry trade between industries organized in an imperfectly competitive fashion.

The conditions which generate intra-industry trade also make technological innovation an important element in trade performance. Economists have long recognized the connection between technical innovation, technology transfer, and changes in the structure of foreign trade. Three factors are recognized as being of importance here: time-lags in the inter-country transfer of technology; differences in the national rate of diffusion of innovations; and differences in the rates of growth of national production capacity to exploit innovations.[32] From this perspective, a country's trade performance is determined by the rate at which it acquires and exploits new technologies relative to its major competitors. Moreover, as technologies mature, the inputs which are required for effective exploitation change significantly. A new technology requires major scientific and technical manpower inputs to compete effectively. But as it

[30] D. Greenaway and C. Milner, 'On the Measurement of the Intra-Industry Trade', *EJ*, 93 (1983), 900–8.

[31] Inter-industry trade and other aspects of 'new' theories of trade patterns are discussed in D. Greenaway (ed.), *Current Issues in International Trade: Theory and Policy* (London: Macmillan, 1985).

[32] The classic reference is M. V. Posner, 'International Trade and Technological Change', *OEP*, 13 (1961), 323–41.

matures, production processes become standardized and the emphasis shifts to the exploitation of economies of scale and access to cheap labour.

These dynamic considerations can be reconciled with the factor endowment theory of trade, provided we interpret human capital skills and the state of technology as part of the endowment. However, unlike raw material endowments, human capital skills change over time, often rapidly as new knowledge is discovered and transmitted into the workforce by formal education and practical experience. Seen in this light, it is clear that long-term trade trends will be particularly influenced by the level of education and training of the labour force and its ability to innovate and adapt to new technologies. However, the exact ways in which they impinge on trade patterns are still not well understood.

In this perspective, the UK's disappointing trade performance is related to deep-rooted forces which can only be changed gradually over time. These include in particular inadequate investment in research and development by firms, lack of satisfactory training programmes in technical and management skills, and inflexible working practices, often but not always rooted in restrictive trade union agreements. It appears that British firms have been particularly weak at integrating R & D with manufacturing innovations. For example it is noteworthy that areas in which British firms have traditionally been successful in world markets are those, such as pharmaceuticals, which require particularly intensive R & D but where the final manufacturing process is essentially very simple.

Competitiveness.   Much of what we have said stresses the role of non-price factors in trade performance. Relative prices also play an important role in two major respects. First, if productivity growth is slow the exchange rate must depreciate to avoid erosion of price competitiveness. Second, the relation of prices to costs (i.e. the profit margin) determines the financial basis from which firms may engage in R & D investment, and marketing.[33] In addition, the export of modern industrial products typically involves a substantial initial investment: in market research, in the establishment of a shipping and distribution network, and in advertising the product in foreign markets. From a firm's point of view, these are fixed or 'sunk' costs. Once the firm is established in exporting to a foreign market it will not necessarily withdraw if an exchange-rate change renders its foreign sales unprofitable at existing foreign prices. First, in an era of floating exchange rates, the exchange rate change may be temporary and soon reversed. Second, once a firm withdraws from a foreign market, re-entering will be costly. Often therefore, a firm may decide to 'hang on' and wait for an improvement in market conditions such as an exchange-rate change could bring. The analogy is with the purchase of a financial option. The decision to enter or exit from

[33] For a discussion of these issues, see 'The Terms of Trade', *BEQB* (Aug. 1987), 371–9.

a foreign market involves not only the concrete costs of entry or exit, but also the costs of possibly reversing the decision at a later date. Staying in a foreign market, even if it is temporarily unprofitable, preserves the option to continue when the market becomes more profitable, without having to pay the fixed costs of (re-)entry. For these reasons, it may take very large changes in prices and profitability to induce firms to alter their exporting strategies. These arguments also give rise to the hypothesis of 'hysteresis': if an exchange-rate appreciation (say) is sufficiently large as to induce home firms to withdraw from foreign markets, merely reversing the appreciation will not necessarily return the trade balance to its original position as it will not be sufficient to pay the fixed costs of firms to re-establish themselves in foreign markets. This hypothesis is particularly relevant to the 1979–80 appreciation of sterling and the difficulty experienced in reversing the current account deficit of the late 1980s.[34]

In the last fifteen years, the British economy has undergone some major changes, many of which have been aimed at improving the competitiveness of British firms. In addition, there is little doubt that there have been substantial positive spill-overs from the high level of foreign (especially Japanese) investment in Britain by firms whose technology and working practices have offered a salutary example to their British counterparts.[35] More recently, there have been signs of improvement in Britain's trade performance, but it is far too early to claim that the problems of the past have been overcome. Recent studies suggest that Britain's rate of productivity growth has increased markedly, but that this has not (yet) translated directly into cost advantages over our immediate competitors because of continued higher wage inflation than in competitor countries.[36] In addition, the UK's overall rate of R & D investment is still appreciably below that of key competitors such as Germany, the USA, and Japan; and finally, it is far from clear that technological and management training has yet reached an adequate level.[37]

Overall, therefore, the determinants of competitiveness are complex, and include such factors as the structure of costs, the size and nature of different industries, and the existence of economies of scale, labour productivity, the

---

[34] The hypothesis of hysteresis and the role of sunk costs in foreign trade were first studied by A. V. Dixit, 'Hysteresis, Import Penetration and Exchange Rate Pass Through', *QJE*, 104 2 (May 1989), 205–27. A simplified account of Dixit's ideas, as well as a more general review of pricing factors in international trade under floating exchange rates, is given by P. Krugman, *Exchange Rate Instability* (Cambridge: MIT Press, 1989), ch. 2.

[35] For a broad review of these issues see W. Eltis and D. Higham, 'Closing the UK Competitiveness Gap', *NIER* (Nov. 1995), 71–84. A number of studies over the years have emphasized the link between productivity and training. See e.g. S. J. Prais, *Productivity and Industrial Structure* (Cambridge: Cambridge University Press, 1981).

[36] See N. Oulton, 'Labour Productivity and Unit Labour Costs in Manufacturing: The UK and Its Competitors', *NIER* (May 1994), 49–60, and M. O'Mahoney 'International Differences in Manufacturing Unit Labour Costs', *NIER* (Nov. 1995), 85–100.

[37] For a discussion and more optimistic conclusion, see W. A. Eltis and D. Higham, 'Closing the UK Competitiveness Gap', *NIER* (Nov. 1995), 71–84.

pricing policies of individual firms, and movements in wages and interest rates. The hysteresis argument suggests that the relationship between competitiveness *per se* and trade performance is also not a simple one. Moreover, it is likely that price competitiveness interacts with technological factors, with a deterioration in competitiveness resulting in a loss of markets, a slow rate of economic growth, and concomitant lack of resources to invest in new technologies. This, in turn, makes a country less competitive in other markets, thus exacerbating the problem further in a form of vicious circle. As technologies mature, the centre of comparative advantage moves to low-real-wage economies, so an advanced country such as the UK can only maintain its comparative advantage by continuously shifting resources into production at the frontiers of technologial change and close to 'world best practice'. Only thus can the UK expect to maintain its historically high living standards.

Trade Policy

Arguments for free trade and protection. Trade policy is concerned, in the first instance, with the effects of tariffs and subsidies aimed at influencing the prices of exports and imports and thus the performance of exporting and import-competing industries. However, virtually any form of government intervention in the economy has some impact on the trading position. In this section we concentrate on policies which have as their primary purpose the influencing of international trade flows. Even thus defined, trade policy is by no means confined to tariffs and subsidies on exports and imports but includes also a wide array of so-called 'non-tariff barriers to trade', such as import quotas, taxes, and subsidies on domestic production, and taxes and subsidies on the use of labour and capital in different industries. Over the years, government intervention in this area has become increasingly complex and ingenious. Subsidized export credit, differential treatment of foreign firms in bidding procedures for government contracts, the establishment of product quality standards which favour particular firms, and voluntary export restraints are all examples of differing forms of trade intervention aimed at securing a competitive advantage for particular groups of firms or industries. In general, most of these kinds of trade policy involve, to differing degrees, some element of protection for domestic industries.

The principles of comparative advantage suggest that interventions in the flow of trade are generally harmful both to the country imposing the intervention and, if several countries act or 'retaliate' in this way, to the world as a whole. The case for free trade is largely analogous to the case for *laissez-faire*. It enables each country to produce the goods in which it has a comparative cost advantage and thus to export products which it can produce relatively cheaply, and import products which can be produced relatively cheaply elsewhere. Each individual country, and thus the world as a whole, benefits from this international specialization.

Nevertheless, countries have intervened in trade over the years in a wide variety of ways, the most common being the imposition of tariffs on imports. Under certain assumptions, an import tariff can be expected to raise real wages in the tariff-imposing country, even though national income, and therefore overall welfare, in that country will fall as a result.[38] More recently, arguments have been devised to show that individual countries can benefit from certain forms of protection.[39] These arguments stem from a recognition that most industries do not correspond to the perfectly competitive paradigm of the theory of comparative advantage. There are numerous examples of 'natural' monopolies or industries where economies of scale are such as to keep the number of firms in the industry relatively few in number. In these cases, firms in the industry typically earn more than normal profit, i.e. they receive an economic rent. Intuition and theory suggest that it may pay an individual country to protect a firm in such an industry so as to help secure a share in the worldwide economic rents to be earned in the industry.

A related argument is that certain industries create external economies in their operations; that is, their activities help reduce the costs of other firms. Knowledge-based high-technology industries are generally cited as examples of this phenomenon. 'Silicon Valley' computer firms are usually thought to benefit from their proximity to one another. Here, too, there is an argument for the protection of certain 'strategic' aspects of the activities of such industries which may be regarded as central to the operation of the industry as a whole but in which firms in the industry no longer enjoy a comparative advantage. Thus, local production of microchips is often regarded as strategically important to American and European industry, even though other countries may well have a cost advantage in their production and thus, according to the theory of comparative advantage, should be the ones to specialize in their production.

Such strategic aspects of protection have been at the forefront of recent international discussions of trade policy. However, it should be emphasized that these strategic arguments rest on the idea that an individual country can gain from protection. It must be questioned whether such protection produces any worldwide benefits, or merely involves a transfer from one country to another.

Trade policy in the UK.   In considering the level of protection of an individual product, it must also be remembered that the actual tax or subsidy rate does not, on its own, measure the full extent of the protection which that product enjoys. In particular, import-competing goods which use imported inputs and

[38] This argument was originally set out by W. F. Stolper and P. A. Samuelson, 'Protection and Real Wages', *Review of Economic Studies*, 9 (1941), 58–73. For a detailed study of arguments relating to the pros and cons of tariff protection, see W. M. Corden, *Trade Policy and Economic Welfare* (Oxford: Oxford University Press, 1974).

[39] For a comprehensive study of these arguments, see P. R. Krugman (ed.), *Strategic Trade Policy and the New International Economics* (Cambridge, Mass: MIT Press, 1986).

raw materials can be protected in (at least) two ways: first, by the imposition of a tariff on imports of the product itself, but second, by a cut in the tariff or the imposition of a subsidy on imports of the inputs and raw materials used in its manufacture. Thus a logical tariff system needs to take account of the industrial structure of the economy. Protection of products which are widely used as intermediate inputs can easily result in negative protection (or 'disprotection') of the wide range of goods for which the intermediate inputs are required. The concept of 'effective protection' has been developed to measure the degree of protection afforded to an industry after allowing for tariffs and subsidies on intermediate inputs. Recognition of the industrial structure of an economy also gives rise to the principle of 'escalation'; that is, a rational tariff structure should involve increasing rates of tariff for goods which are relatively more highly processed, with the lowest tariff rates applying to commodities and raw materials.

It will probably come as no surprise to learn that few countries have a rational tariff structure and the UK is no exception in this respect. The most recent study[40] of the tariff structure of the UK (for 1979) found some evidence of escalation overall. However, in 99 industry groups only 44 had an effective tariff, while 53 had an effective tariff rate less than the nominal rate; the remaining two had equal nominal and effective rates. This means that for the 53 industries concerned, the nominal protection afforded by the tax on competing imports was partly or wholly offset by tariffs on intermediate inputs. The influence of agricultural protection was particularly marked. Thus agriculture itself enjoyed a nominal tariff of 16.3% but an effective tariff of 47.3%. However, food-processing industries such as milk and meat slaughtering, while nominally enjoying a tariff of 7.5% and 5.8% respectively, actually experienced substantial disprotection through the high cost of their agricultural raw materials with effective tariff rates of −22.4% and −14.6% respectively, amounting to a net import subsidy.

These figures highlight the underlying absurdity of a good deal of protection. In practice, protection is often granted to an industry on an *ad hoc* basis as the result of an industrial lobby aimed at protecting real wages in that industry. The overall effects of this protection, both direct and indirect, are rarely taken into account. The result is a system in which consumers pay higher prices than necessary for some products while industries, often only distantly connected to the original protective measures, are unable to compete in world markets because they too have to pay higher prices than necessary for their raw materials and other inputs.

---

[40] See D. Greenaway, 'Effective Tariff Protection in the United Kingdom', *BOUIES*, 503 (1988), 311–24. The concept of the effective rate of protection was devised by W. M. Corden and is discussed in detail in his *The Theory of Protection* (Oxford: Oxford University Press, 1971).

11.4.   The Capital Account

Portfolio and Direct Investment

Influences on overseas investment. In this section, we examine in more detail the main influences on portfolio and direct investment and consider some of the possible costs and benefits of such investments. As part of these analyses we also consider the relationships among the investment flows recorded in the capital account and the return flows of income from these investments ('investment incomes') which are shown in the current account.

From the viewpoint of individual investors the main forces governing overseas portfolio and direct investment are not likely to be qualitatively very different from those governing domestic investment, with the overriding factor in decisions to invest being the anticipated rate of return on the project or security relative to the cost of any funds which have to be borrowed to finance the investment, and relative to the perceived riskiness of the investment. In this calculation, investors will obviously be comparing the prospective risks and returns of overseas investments with those of alternative domestic investment opportunities.

In practice, the calculation for overseas investment is more complex than that for domestic investment. Beginning with portfolio investment, investors do not only have to evaluate the prospects of the company in which they are investing but also, to some extent, the overall prospects for the particular foreign economy in which the company operates, especially for interest rates, as these are likely to affect the performance of the stock market on which the shares of the company are quoted, and this in turn will have an impact on the share price of the individual company itself. Movements in the exchange rate also affect the return on overseas investment, with a depreciation of sterling increasing the sterling rate of return of a foreign currency investment, and vice versa.

For direct investment the calculations are more complex still, as foreign countries typically impose different rules and regulations on company investment activities covering matters as diverse as taxation, quality control, employment standards, and information disclosure requirements. All these factors involve both costs and benefits. Indeed, to a large extent, foreign direct investment is just one mechanism by which modern corporations seek to gain competitive advantages over their rivals by siting their production, administration, and marketing activities in a combination of locations designed to take maximum advantage of differential tariffs, investment incentives, wage levels, and demand conditions for their products. Direct investment must also be considered in relation to exporting and foreign licensing of its products as just one of several ways by which a firm can extract maximum advantage from its knowledge and human capital base.[41]

---

[41] Cf. R. E. Caves, 'International Corporations: The Industrial Economics of Foreign Investment', *Economica*, 38 (1971), 1–27.

Overseas investment may also be constrained by regulation, and UK overseas investment was strictly regulated by exchange controls until their abolition in 1979. Exchange-control abolition produced a clear and relatively unambiguous effect on portfolio investment. Outward portfolio investment, largely by financial institutions such as unit trusts and pension funds, rose steeply from £0.96 billion in 1979 to £3.3 billion in 1980, and it reached £22.3 billion in 1986. Many fund managers reported that their activities corresponded to a one-and-for-all portfolio adjustment to bring overseas assets to the desired proportion in their portfolio following which the outflow would level off.[42] This took place in 1987 when the gross outflow was dramatically reversed, with UK residents repatriating a net £16.9 billion of portfolio investment. Since then, outward portfolio investment has fluctuated without any clear trend. To the extent that there was a substantially increased outflow following exchange-control abolition, it can be concluded that this policy was successful in helping to limit the oil effect on the sterling exchange rate and widening the ambit of profitable investment opportunities for UK residents.

The impact of exchange-control abolition on outward direct investment is harder to quantify because the practical effect of the controls in this area was less severe. The main implication of abolition is that firms face a wider range of financing options than before—they can either borrow from abroad or within the UK; or they can use retained earnings from abroad or from the UK. It is probably reasonable to conclude that direct investment was stimulated by exchange-control abolition, but the exact magnitude of the stimulus remains a matter for debate.

Other structural factors influencing the portfolio and direct investment position include North Sea oil, and UK membership of the EC. As far as North Sea oil is concerned, it can be estimated that, during the main period of North Sea oil investment during 1976–83, about 10% of total inward investment into the UK (capital account) and 10% of the return investment income flows (current account) could be attributed directly to the North Sea.[43] The influence of EC membership on UK foreign investment is more difficult to quantify. From 1974 to 1983 only 8% of total outward direct investment flows went to other EC countries whereas in the following ten years (1984–93), 28% of the total went to the EC. There was also a marked increase in other EC countries' direct investment in the UK over the same period. Any explanation for these flows must be very tentative in nature. One possibility is that a major motive for outward investment is for large firms to avoid tariffs and other import restrictions imposed by the host country. On this interpretation, the dismantling of such barriers within the EC largely obviated the need for UK firms to invest in other EC countries, and provided incentives for them to concentrate their foreign investment activities instead in non-EC markets

---

[42] See 'The Effects of Exchange Control Abolition on Capital Flows', *BEQB* (Sept. 1981).
[43] See 'North Sea Oil and Gas' *BEQB* (Dec. 1986).

where barriers to imports may be more important. The more recent surge in investment in the EC, and by the EC in the UK could, in turn, be associated with the progressive dismantling of internal barriers in the EC with the formation of the Single European Market. However, these two explanations are not entirely consistent with each other; and the exact reasons must await more detailed analysis.

Costs and benefits of overseas investment.   Historically, foreign investment has been the subject of debate in the UK, one strand of thinking arguing that investment overseas has an adverse effect on the UK economy because it creates jobs in overseas countries rather than in the UK, while at the same time producing balance-of-payments pressures through the outflow of funds associated with the investment activity. While it is obviously correct that overseas investment helps create overseas jobs, it is far from being the case that this is the only effect of such investments or, as a result, that overseas investment harms the UK economy. In fact, to consider the full costs and benefits of overseas investment, it is necessary to take account of its overall effects both on the balance of payments and on the domestic economy as well as of the opportunities open to domestic investors.

    First, under a floating exchange rate, overseas investment by UK firms tends to depress the sterling exchange rate because of the outflow of funds which is implied. There are circumstances in which such a relative depreciation of the exchange rate is desirable and cannot easily be brought about by other means. This was exactly the situation in the early 1980s when North Sea oil production and high oil prices were placing strong upward pressure on the currency. At that time, the strong portfolio outflow of funds, stemming from the abolition of exchange controls, was desirable as a way of relieving the upward pressure on the exchange rate. Second, it is often argued that foreign direct investment leads directly to a fall in exports and a rise in imports because output which could have been produced in the UK is now produced overseas. This argument presumes that the output could have been produced profitably in the UK, and in many instances, the structure of costs, availability of raw materials, and other factors mean that this is not the case. If the project could not be carried out profitably in the UK, it is sensible for British firms to undertake the investment overseas because the profit will subsequently accrue to UK residents. Third, foreign investment may well be complementary to exports rather than competitive with them. An overseas investment project may generate UK exports in the form of the plant and equipment needed to set up the project or in the form of exports of semi-finished goods required to run the plant.

    Clearly these factors are complex, and quantifying them is not easy. Available evidence does indicate that on balance UK overseas investment does not

Table 11.6 Estimated rates of return on domestic and overseas assets 1990–1994

	Year average: % per annum				
	1990	1991	1992	1993	1994
Calculated rates of return[a]					
UK direct investment overseas	12.73	10.67	10.67	11.09	12.82
UK portfolio investment overseas	3.60	4.87	5.17	5.18	3.62
Overseas direct investment in the UK	7.04	4.03	4.38	8.49	7.15
Overseas portfolio investment in the UK	6.90	7.91	6.93	5.76	4.77
Depreciation of the pound[b]	−7.86	2.25	12.17	−3.17	2.09
Market rates of return					
UK equities: earnings yield	11.70	8.72	6.75	5.26	5.52
UK equities: dividend yield	5.29	4.98	4.68	4.10	4.07
UK government bonds: flat yield on consols	10.88	9.99	9.16	7.27	7.62

[a] Calculated as the ratio of the current year flow of earnings (Investment Income account) to the stock of assets outstanding at the end of the previous year (Net External Assets Account).
[b] Percentage change in the Bank of England sterling exchange rate index from year-end to year-end: depreciation (+); appreciation (−).
Source: Pink Book, EG, BEQB

adversely affect the UK economy.[44] More generally, the proposition that the UK should not invest overseas runs contrary to the principles of comparative advantage. If taken to extreme, the proposition could easily imply that the UK ought to attempt self-sufficiency in all areas of the economy—clearly an absurd and exceedingly wasteful proposal. Ultimately, foreign investment should satisfy many of the same criteria as domestic investment; that is, it should be profitable. If UK firms cannot find profitable investment opportunities in the UK then, *prima facie*, if they can find such opportunities abroad they should exploit them. Rough calculations of rates of return on domestic and overseas investment as well as on overseas investment in the UK are given in Table 11.6.[45] These data suggest that the return on UK direct investment in the 1990s has generally been substantially in excess of the domestic earnings yield on UK equities, the appropriate benchmark for comparison. In contrast, it appears that portfolio investment has earned a rate broadly comparable to that of the UK dividend yield. However, this latter comparison has to be particularly qualified, as the implied figure for UK portfolio investment includes a substantial proportion of assets which are taxed at source by the foreign government. Therefore the figure for portfolio investment is more nearly a post-tax return, whereas the UK dividend yield is expressed on a gross (pre-tax) basis. Thus, the comparable rate on portfolio investment overseas is probably rather more in excess of the UK dividend yield than it appears from Table 11.6. For overseas investment in the UK, it is no surprise that portfolio investment earns a rather higher return than the dividend yield on the equities, as a relatively high proportion (some 20% at the end of 1994) of such investment is in the form of UK government bonds, which do not offer investors any long-term capital appreciation. It is more surprising that overseas direct investment in the UK has earned a substantially lower rate of return than UK investment overseas, a fact which is the exact opposite of the situation in the 1980s.[46] It does, however, need to be emphasized that these figures give only a very approximate comparison. Exchange-rate changes also affect the return on overseas investment and the generally downward movement in sterling since 1990 has served to increase the realized sterling rate of return on overseas investments because the sterling value of investments denominated in foreign currencies rises as the exchange rate depreciates, producing sterling gains for UK investors.

[44] The seminal study is by W. B. Reddaway, *The Effects of UK Direct Investment Overseas* (interviews and final report) (Cambridge: Cambridge University Press, 1968). The study has been partially updated and the new results are summarized in D. Shepherd, 'Assessing the Consequences of Overseas Investment', *RBSR*, no. 152 (Dec. 1986). See also E. J. Pentecost, 'A Model of UK Non-Oil ICC's Direct Investment', *Bank of England Discussion Paper*, no. 30 (Nov. 1987).

[45] These estimates differ from those given in W. Amos, 'The External Balance Sheet of the United Kingdom—Recent Developments', *BEQB* (Nov. 1994), 353–60. This article calculates rates of return as the ratio of current year earnings to end-year assets, whereas in Table 11.6, they are calculated as ratios of current year earnings to assets outstanding at the end of the *preceding* year.

[46] See the figures given in the 13th edn. of this book.

Other Capital Transactions

The remaining items in the capital account consist chiefly of two components. First, those involving bank loans and deposits, representing either the business of UK residents with overseas banks or, more commonly, the business of overseas residents with UK banks, and second, transactions (some of which are included in banking transactions) which are related to the finance of foreign trade.

These short-term capital movements have traditionally played an important role in the overall UK balance-of-payments situation. Some short-term capital movements reflect changes in the sterling balances which foreign governments and individuals have acquired as matters of commercial and financial convenience (line A10 in Table 11.1). The remainder reflect the role of London as the major centre for the Eurocurrency, Eurobond, and other international financial markets, with banks in the UK lending and borrowing extensively in dollars and other currencies. The development of the Eurocurrency markets since 1958 has meant the increasing integration of European and American capital and money markets.[47] The volume of deposits and the ease with which they may be switched between currencies have important implications for the stability of exchange rates and the conduct of national monetary policies.

With floating exchange rates, the impact effect of a net capital flow falls directly upon the spot exchange rate: a capital outflow will tend to depreciate sterling, and an inflow to appreciate sterling. Moreover, any such change in the exchange rate acts upon the current account in the same way as a policy-induced parity change. Hence, a capital inflow which generates an appreciation also has the effect of discouraging exports, encouraging imports, and depressing the inflation rate. With a fixed exchange rate, a speculative outflow necessitates official intervention to maintain the exchange rate. This in turn leads to a loss of central bank reserves, and to the extent that sterilization is impossible, a reduction in the money supply, putting downward pressure on domestic prices and incomes.

It should be clear, therefore, that large, sudden capital flows can provide difficult policy problems for economies under both floating and fixed exchange rates. Until 1979 the UK attempted to exert some direct influence over capital flows by using exchange controls, but the history of the post-1945 era shows that these controls did not prevent periodic short-term speculative outflows from and inflows to sterling. Following exchange control abolition in October 1979, the capital and money markets of the UK became fully integrated with those of the rest of the world, and the main weapon for influencing capital flows is now the manipulation of domestic interest rates.

---

[47] Eurocurrency deposits are bank deposits in currencies other than that of the country in which the bank in question is located. For the working and development of the Eurocurrency markets, consult R. B. Johnston, *The Economics of the Euro-Market* (London: Macmillan, 1983). See also 'Eurobanks and the Inter-Bank Market', *BEQB* (Sept. 1981).

A longer-term effect of exchange control abolition is that it has substantially boosted the foreign (and mostly foreign currency) businesses of UK banks. The scale of this business is worth emphasizing. As of March 1995, the total of all countries' commercial bank foreign liabilities outstanding in all currencies reported to the IMF was US$ 8533 billion. UK-based banks' share of this total was US$ 1389 billion or 16% (including foreign banks operating in the UK), compared with the USA's share of 11% and Japan's share of 9%. The exact figures fluctuate from month to month as exchange rates change, but these are broadly representative. Borrowing and lending abroad by commercial banks do not in and of themselves affect the balance of payments and the exchange rate except to the extent that they generate bank profits and to the extent that total borrowing and lending are not equal to one another. UK banks have typically had an excess of foreign liabilities over foreign assets which is larger (particularly in proportion to the size of the home economy) than is that of banks operating in the USA or Japan, although US banks' net foreign liabilities have increased sharply in the last decade. Thus, in March 1995, British banks had net foreign liabilities of US$ 90 billion; US banks had net liabilities of US$ 282 billion; and Japanese banks had net foreign assets of US$ 376 billion. Changes in net foreign liabilities may help to finance a balance-of-payments deficit but a large imbalance between assets and liabilities also creates the potential for disruptive flows across the foreign exchanges, if foreign residents withdraw short-term deposits from home commercial banks, and this has periodically been a problem for the UK in the past.

Further Reading

Amos, W., 'The External Balance Sheet of the United Kingdom: Recent Developments', *BEQB* 35/4 (Nov. 1995), 353–60.

Corden, W. M., *The Theory of Protection* (Oxford: Oxford University Press, 1971).

———— *Economic Policy, Exchange Rates, and the International System* (Oxford: Oxford University Press, 1994).

CSO, *United Kingdom Balance of Payments*, 'The Pink Book' (London: HMSO, 1995).

Dumble, A., 'UK Trade: Long Term Trends and Recent Developments', *BEQB*, 34/3 (Aug. 1994), 223–31.

Ellis, W. A., and Higham, D., 'Closing the UK Competitive Gap', *NIER* (Nov. 1995), 71–84.

Greenaway, D. (ed.), *Current Issues in International Trade: Theory and Policy* (London: Macmillan, 1985).

Johnston, R. B., *The Economics of the Euro-Market* (London: Macmillan, 1983).

Krugman, P. R., *Exchange Rate Instability* (Cambridge, Mass.: MIT Press, 1989).

———— (ed.), *Strategic Trade Policy and the New International Economics* (Cambridge, Mass.: MIT Press, 1986).

MacDonald, R., *Floating Exchange Rates: Theories and Evidence* (London: Unwin Hyman, 1988).

McGiven, A., 'Trade with Newly Industrialized Economies', *BEQB*, 36/1 (Feb. 1996), 39–78.

Melliss, C., 'Tradable and Non-Tradable Prices in the United Kingdom and the European Community', *BEQB*, 33/1 (Feb. 1993), 80–91.

Winters, L. A., *International Economics*, 4th edn. (London: Harper Collins, 1991).

INDEX

Note: All references are to the UK unless specifically indicated otherwise